THE TARNISHED CROWN

THE
TARNISHED
CROWN

Princess Diana
and the House of Windsor

ANTHONY HOLDEN

Random House   New York

All rights reserved under International and Pan-American Copyright Conventions.
Published in the United States by Random House, Inc., New York.
Published in England by Bantam Press, a division of Transworld Publishers, London.

The Parliamentary Bill which appears on pages 341–353 is Parliamentary Copyright.

Appendix D is taken from the report of the Crown Estate Commissioners for the year
ending March 31, 1988.

Grateful acknowledgment is made to *The New Republic* for permission to reprint an excerpt from
"The Cult of Diana" by Camille Paglia. Copyright © 1993 by The New Republic, Inc.
Reprinted by permission of *The New Republic*.

Library of Congress Cataloging-in-Publication Data

Holden, Anthony
The tarnished crown : Princess Diana and the House of Windsor / Anthony Holden.
p.   cm.
ISBN 0-679-42426-1
1. Diana, Princess of Wales, 1961–   .   2. Great Britain—Princes
and princesses—Biography.   3. Monarchy—Great Britain—
History—20th century.   4. Windsor, House of.   I. Title.
DA591.A45D5319   1993
941.085′092—dc20
[B]   93-10402

Manufactured in the United States of America
2 4 6 8 9 7 5 3
First U.S. Edition

FOR
BENJAMIN AND SIENA COLEGRAVE

*'There can be no doubt that criticism is good
for people and institutions that are part of public life . . .
This sort of questioning can also act, and it should do so,
as an effective engine for change.'*

QUEEN ELIZABETH II
Guildhall, London, 24 November 1992

CONTENTS

LIST OF ILLUSTRATIONS

Between pages 48–9

Götterdämmerung: The Great Fire of Windsor symbolizes the Queen's 'annus horribilis' *(Nunn Syndication/Chris Finch).*

As Prince Charles continues to see Camilla Parker-Bowles (with him at Balmoral *(Nunn Syndication/Jim Bennett);* with her husband at Windsor *(Alpha/Dave Benett),* Diana sends lonely 'postcards' home from the Taj Mahal and the Pyramids *(both Alpha/Dave Chancellor).*

The decline and fall of Fergie, Duchess of York *(John Frost Historical Newspaper Service. Reproduced by kind permission of the editor of the* Daily Mirror./*Nunn Syndication/Robin Nunn)* eventually exiled from her £5 million Windsor mansion *(Nunn Syndication/Jim Bennett).*

June 1992: A bad month for the Queen as the Yorks wave from the crowd at Royal Ascot *(Nunn Syndication/Steve Ward),* and Charles and Diana cannot conceal their mutual antipathy before the family's 'Garter Day' summit *(Rex Features/*The Sun*).*

Diana rejects Charles's attempts at affection for the cameras *(Rex Features)* and soon breaks down in public tears *(Rex Features/*Today*),* but both put on brave faces for the Queen's fortieth anniversary gala at Earl's Court *(Alpha).*

November 1992 begins with the Wales marriage visibly collapsing in Korea, and ends with the Queen's 'annus horribilis' speech *(both Tim Graham)*.

For William and Harry, it's Christmas at Sandringham with their father *(Nunn Syndication/Bennett/Parker)* and New Year in the Caribbean with their mother *(Alpha/Dave Chancellor)*. For the Queen it's time to reflect on the monarchy's uncertain future *(Alpha/Jim Bennett)*.

Between pages 144–5

The tabloid papers, tribunes of the people, smell blood *(John Frost Historical Newspaper Service)*.

Four failed marriages: Princess Margaret and Lord Snowdon (1960) *(Popperfoto)*, Princess Anne and Captain Mark Phillips (1973) *(Popperfoto)*, Prince Charles and Lady Diana Spencer (1981) *(Tim Graham)*, and Prince Andrew and Sarah Ferguson (1986) *(Syndication International)*.

Princess Margaret with Peter Townsend, the royal equerry she was not allowed to marry *(Rex Features)*; and Princess Anne with Tim Laurence, the royal equerry she did marry – second time around *(Tim Graham)*.

A decade sees the Wales's 'fairy-tale' marriage slowly collapse *(left-hand page: top: Tim Graham; bottom left: Camera Press/Glenn Harvey; bottom right: Rex Features; right-hand page: top: Syndication International; bottom: Tim Graham)*.

How not *to be royal:* Prince Edward, the Yorks, Marina Ogilvy Mowatt (with her husband, Paul), and Charles, Earl Spencer, the Princess of Wales's brother *(all Rex Features)*.

In the Royal Enclosure at Ascot, the Queen and Prince Charles disapprove of the fun-loving ways of Diana and Fergie *(top: Camera Press; bottom: Alpha)*.

Queen Elizabeth II is not amused by the events of 1992–93 *(Rex Features)*.

Between pages 240–1

Matriarch: Queen Victoria with four of her great-grandchildren, including the future Kings Edward VIII and George VI *(Popperfoto)*.

As Head of the British Commonwealth, the Queen endures the touch of the Australian prime minister *(Rex Features)*, and enjoys a ritual African welcome *(Camera Press/Stewart Mark)*.

As Diana begins to steal his limelight *(Alpha/Dave Chancellor)*, Charles seeks consolation in plants *(Rex Features/Dave Hartley)* and architecture *(Alpha)*.

An increasingly powerful public speaker, Diana is determined to continue her work for such 'unroyal' causes as leprosy and AIDS *(all Alpha)*.

Royal Perks: The Queen's private yacht costs the British taxpayer £12.6 million a year, and her three private jets £2,000 an hour *(all Tim Graham)*.

Part of the royal car pool at Ascot. The Queen's jewels are valued in billions *(both Tim Graham)*.

The future King Mother will continue to play a vital role in the upbringing of King William V *(Alpha)*.

Text illustrations

p.40 Cartoon by Griffin *(Mirror Group Newspapers)*.

p.179 Instrument of abdication *(Popperfoto)*.

p.227 Cartoon by Tom Johnston *(Tom Johnston/*The Sun*)*.

p.301 Cartoon by Garland *(The Sunday Telegraph Ltd, London, 1992)*.

PART ONE
THE MONARCHY
IN CRISIS

CHAPTER 1

A HOUSE DIVIDED

'If a house be divided against itself, it cannot stand.'
ST MARK, 3:25

FOR A QUARTER OF THE EARTH'S POPULATION, THE SECOND of June 1953 symbolized the dawn of a post-war age of un-imagined promise. On the morning of Queen Elizabeth II's coronation, as if by some royal magic, her subjects awoke to the inspirational news that Mount Everest had been conquered by a British expedition. Six hundred and fifty million people around Britain and the Commonwealth were fired by the opti-mism of the prime minister, Winston Churchill, about this 'new Elizabethan era'. The editors of *Time* magazine, casting around for a figure to symbolize the hopeful spirit of the Fifties, nominated the twenty-six-year-old British monarch to 'repre-sent, express and affect the aspirations of the collective sub-conscious' of the entire free world.

Forty years on, in June 1993, most of those aspirations had been cheated. After the false boom of the Eighties, the United Kingdom languished beneath the worst recession since the 1930s. Amid record numbers of homeless and unemployed, bankrupt and redundant, the monarchy too slumped into a seemingly symbolic decline. The fortieth anniversary of the

Queen's accession to the throne was marked less by retrospective
rejoicing than a sudden and unexpected struggle for survival.

The crown, like the country, had its back to the wall.
Throughout the 1980s a festive succession of royal marriages
and births had rendered the institution of monarchy as popular as
at any time in its thousand-year history. Now all those marriages
had collapsed, and with them the royal ratings, Elizabeth II found
herself forced into a series of desperate remedies.

Barely twelve months after the House of Commons had
laughed out a private member's bill for the monarch to pay
taxes, she volunteered to do just that. Breaking with 200-year-old
precedent, she also agreed to dispense with direct public subsidy
for her daughter, two of her sons and all of her cousins. The
future of her private yacht, train and planes were all 'under
review'. She was even resigned to the removal of her head from
the postage stamps of the Royal Mail.

'You can tell a lot about a country which refers to the *Royal*
mint and the *national* debt,' wrote William Cobbett. Nearly two
centuries on, Cobbett's sentiments were not out of place in the
Britain of 1993. Republicanism had been a spent force since
the 1870s, when the widowed Queen Victoria's long self-exile
from society fed ammunition to rebellious spirits. Now a former
Labour cabinet minister introduced a parliamentary bill to establish a British republic, with an elected head of state; and for
the first time in living memory front-bench members of Her
Majesty's Opposition began to ask searching questions about
the constitutional monarchy. Elizabeth II found herself obliged
to offer the leader of the Opposition a monthly audience, as a
counter-balance to her weekly meeting with the prime minister.

Not to appear too supine, the Queen launched an angry and
almost unprecedented lawsuit against a tabloid newspaper –
source of many of her woes - although even her supporters
considered it a misjudgement. The same week the prime minister
also reached unexpectedly for his lawyer, to sue two minor
journals which had printed rumours about his private life. As
the writs of the mighty flew, even more eyebrows were raised
by the restraint of the Prince of Wales, who, by contrast, declined
to take action over the published transcript of a bugged telephone

call which persuaded most of the nation that the heir to the throne, the would-be Defender of the Faith, was a lavatory-minded adulterer.

'When sorrows come,' in Shakespeare's words, 'they come not single spies, but in battalions.' After forty unimpeachable years, Elizabeth II seemed suddenly to have been ambushed by woes, and the stability of the throne threatened as at no time since the abdication of her uncle, King Edward VIII, in 1936. The royal melodrama had indeed taken on Shakespearean proportions as civil war between the future king and queen divided the nation, more in sorrow than in anger, into fiercely feuding camps.

At centre-stage was and is the world's most popular princess, cruelly neglected by her husband, and schemed against by his coterie of cronies. A vandalized icon, a betrayed innocent, a manipulative hysteric: Diana, Princess of Wales is many things to many people. But for the editors of *Time*, as for the vast majority, there is no doubt who has now come to 'represent, express and affect the aspirations of the collective sub-conscious.' Diana, wrote *Time* at the end of 1992, is 'another Joan of Arc . . . a feminist heroine.'

In her eleven short years of membership, the Princess of Wales has proved both the making and the potential breaking of the House of Windsor. In the best traditions of flagging soap operas, this glamorous new female lead boosted the ratings beyond the producers' dreams – and, contrary to expectations, maintained them for more than a decade, until she precipitated the dramatic denouement now holding the watching world in thrall. Will Charles and Diana divorce? Will she ever be Queen? Can the House of Windsor survive without her? Don't miss next year's thrilling instalment.

In this role, the once 'shy Di' can lay claim to have become the most powerful image in popular world culture today, an ever-changing feminine archetype steeped in resonance to the modern cult of celebrity. She began life as a custom-built Cinderella, whose prince came to rescue her from an unhappy childhood, complete with two older sisters, a wicked stepmother and an over-indulgent, hard-up Baron of a father. There followed a period as a silent movie star, an entirely visual media icon, prevented by her contract with the royal studio system from shattering the illusion by opening her mouth. Then came the neo-Renaissance Madonna, a *mater dolorosa* hugging her orphan-like children, her loyalty spurned by an absentee husband, apparently the only man in the world not in love with her. Now she is Rapunzel, the princess in the tower, the damsel-in-distress awaiting rescue-by-white-knight. Around her in shadowy corners lurk clutches of hostile courtiers, whispering cruel plots against her; across the moat, ready to storm portcullis and drawbridge, stand the massed ranks of her devoted followers.

Her friend 'Fergie', the court jester – a royal duchess given to nuzzling her accountant, topless, in front of her children – has already been written brusquely out of the script. In its desperation to rehabilitate Prince Charles, and thus to secure the monarchy's future, the secret machinery of the British establishment is now at work to marginalize Diana. It is a scenario involving politicians and civil servants, the church and the armed forces, academics and the media, not to mention the secret service. Phones are bugged, houses burgled, documents stolen, false stories planted in newspapers – all the classic ingredients of a campaign of black propaganda, with just one aim: to minimize the influence of a thirty-year-old woman on a thousand-year-old institution which has survived wars, insurrections and violent overthrow.

The monarchy is the oldest institution of British government. The present Queen is a direct descendant of King Egbert, who united Britain under his rule in AD 829. Only once in the subsequent millennium, for a mere eleven years, has there been a brief republican interregnum: the Commonwealth initiated in 1649, after the execution of King Charles I, by the Lord Protector, Oliver Cromwell.

It is another son of Huntingdon, John Major, on whom the crown is relying to steer it through its present difficulties. But Major's interventionist approach to the monarchy, not unlike Cromwell's, has proved a mixed blessing. Those who paint Diana as the villain of the piece are missing two central strands of recent history: the present royal family's capacity for self-destruction, and Major's for helping it along.

★

On 28 November 1990, the day he succeeded Margaret Thatcher as prime minister, John Major stood on the steps of 10 Downing Street and vowed to make Britain a 'classless' society. Moments before, upon formally taking office, he had gone down on bended knee to kiss the hand of the nation's supreme symbol of hereditary wealth and privilege.

It was an irony apparently lost on Britain's new leader. In the ensuing two years, while he continued to talk of a nation 'at ease with itself', Major's government managed more to exacerbate than to narrow class distinctions. As recession turned to slump, the growing armies of the British unemployed, homeless and bankrupt were not alone in resenting the disproportionate wealth of a maladroit monarchy. The mood of the hard-pressed middle classes – their businesses failing, their homes repossessed in record numbers, their domestic budgets stretched to the limit – was to abandon their instinctive loyalty to most of the major institutions at the heart of British life.

From the Church of England to the Bank of England, the House of Commons to the Old Bailey, Fleet Street to the BBC, schools to local government, the law courts to the police: each pillar of British society faced both challenge and change as the average Briton's customary deference to authority gave way to a healthy, well-motivated scepticism. 'The gap between myth and reality is widening,' as one newspaper put it in late 1992. 'People are discovering . . . that judges are fallible and the police corruptible; that parliament is neither representative nor sovereign; that many of the most important decisions affecting their lives are no longer made in Westminster but in Brussels, Washington or Tokyo, the boardrooms of multinationals and the dealing rooms of banks.'

Also at stake were the fundamental verities upon which most British institutions rely: not just faith in the hereditary principle, but the self-regulation of the professions, the neutrality of the Civil Service, the integrity of the law, even the sovereignty of parliament. The growing influence of the European Community on every aspect of British life was forcing further reappraisal and self-doubt. Major's self-declared mission to carry the United Kingdom to 'the very heart of Europe' served as a final, overdue farewell to the splendours of Great Britain's imperial past. But it was a farewell many British institutions still seemed reluctant to take – none more so than the monarchy, inevitably caught napping through this sea-change in British society, clinging to its eternal assumption that it was somehow above the fray, that it had a divine right to fiddle while Britain burned.

The monarch to whom Major swore allegiance in November 1990 lived above the law administered in her name. She had statutory immunity, for instance, from all legislation promoting equal opportunity and banning racial or sexual discrimination in the workplace. Thus it came to pass that the head of the British Commonwealth, titular leader of millions more non-white than white subjects, chose with impunity not to employ one non-white person, male or female, in the Royal Household.

She lived at public expense, tax free, despite possessing one of the largest private fortunes in the world (shrouded in secrecy, but estimated at several billion pounds).* Her income from the Civil List, the annual subsidy voted by parliament, amounted to an inflation-proof £10.5 million, a sum which also supported ten of her close relatives. In addition, the Queen and her family enjoyed the use of the world's biggest private yacht, costing the taxpayer £12.5 million a year, a fleet of private jets costing £6.9 million, and a 14-coach, private train costing £2.6 million. In 1992 the yacht, HMY *Britannia*, was used by the royals for twenty-seven days (at £462,962 a day), the train for thirty-seven days (at £67,000 per trip) and the planes at an average cost to the taxpayer of £2,000 per hour. In March 1993, *en route* to deliver a speech in Florida which was not a royal engagement, Prince Philip had *Britannia* to himself for a ten-day Caribbean cruise, serviced by a crew of 277 at a total cost to the taxpayer of more than £5 million. He flew out to the West Indies, moreover, on one of the three £16 million British Aerospace jets owned by the Queen's Flight, at a cost to the public purse of £40,000, twelve times the first-class return fare aboard British Airways.

Besides the two private castles she had inherited from her father, purchased by their ancestors on surplus public money, the

---

*A full analysis of the royal finances can be found in Chapter 5.

Queen also enjoyed sole use of six other royal palaces maintained by the taxpayer to the tune of another £26.4 million a year, or £72,500 a day. Add civil air fares (£820,000), overseas visits (£620,000), the administration of the honours system (£210,000) and sundry other items – from publicity (£380,000), computers (£123,000) and stationery (£139,000) to equerries (£210,000) and the Yeomen of the Guard, or 'Beefeaters' (£40,000), and the cost of the monarchy to the British taxpayer in 1992 exceeded £75 million. This came to much the same, on a conservative estimate, as the Queen's tax-free income that year on her private investments. The monarchy, in other words, was costing the British public £192,000 per day – more than thirteen times the average national wage, before tax, per *year*.

The monarchy also enjoyed immunity from telephone bills and postage costs. Even the £75 million did not, however, include the expense – borne by the Home Office and estimated at £20 million a year – of royal security. At the heart of the operation lay round-the-clock protection by a team of armed, highly trained police protection officers – two of whom were photographed taking their ease beside a pool beneath the Mediterranean sun in August 1992, as Fergie frolicked with her financial adviser. The security services who controlled these officers were later to be held responsible for the emergence of a series of tape-recordings of bugged royal phone calls, which discomfited the Princess of Wales and humiliated her husband.

It took the conduct of the Queen's heirs and successors, to whom Major had also sworn his allegiance, to inflame public resentment beyond the prime minister's or the monarch's control. And so, two years after he took office, Major was obliged to interrupt his own fight for political survival with a series of radical announcements about the monarchy's financial and constitutional future.

Margaret Thatcher's legacy, compounded by Major's obsession with Europe, was a jealous, spiteful and debt-ridden Britain; as 1992 drew to a close, it was at last ready to abandon the deferential cringe which had so long crippled its national strength of character. The United Kingdom was faced with a stark end-of-century choice about its head of state: to cut down its over-lavish monarchy to a more appropriate scale, along the lines of the lounge-suited 'bicycle kings' of continental Europe, or to use the misconduct of a fickle royal generation to do away with the institution altogether.

The only other option – to cling to a tarnished crown still enjoying the trappings of a long-lost imperial past – was to consign twenty-first-century Britain to the realms of Ruritania.

In the last decade of the twentieth century, as the United Kingdom struggles to remain in the first division of a federally minded Europe, its Lord Chamberlain is still required to walk backwards in the presence of the head of state. Not merely has the Queen come to seem disproportionately wealthy; she is surrounded by figures beyond the wildest imaginings of Lewis Carroll.

It might be thought, for example, that the Queen's financial manager, officially known as the Keeper of the Privy Purse, was now quite busy enough negotiating on her behalf with the Inland Revenue, whose dread buff envelopes – ironically inscribed 'On Her Majesty's Service' – were due to arrive as of 5 April 1993. Even so, the Keeper's other duties still include the exercise of a power of veto over the naming of flowers after his employer. The Queen's head butler, alias the Master of the Royal Household, meanwhile doubles as Chairman of the Board of Green Cloth, in charge of the licensing of pubs within the vicinity of Buckingham Palace. The Household's senior female member is the Mistress of the Robes, who outranks the Ladies of the Bedchamber (not to be confused with the Women of the Bedchamber). Buried somewhere in the monarchy's £75 million budget are the meagre salaries of a team employed by the tax-payer to help the sixty-seven-year-old monarch and her heir, a forty-four-year-old father-of-two, get themselves dressed in the mornings.

The Royal Household consists of a complex, three-tiered hierarchy known to each other as Members, Officials and Staff, the most senior of whom are allowed to live free of charge in 135 'grace-and-favour' residences owned by the Queen, from

Mayfair to Hampton Court. Also dancing attendance, apart from the Pages of the Backstairs and the Pages of the Presence, are a dozen Gentlemen Ushers, among them the Gentleman Usher to the Sword of State and the Gentleman Usher of the Black Rod – the famous rod which he is required to beat three times on the door of the House of Commons at the State Opening of Parliament.

Always absent from this solemn occasion is the hapless member of parliament unfortunate enough to have been appointed Vice-Chamberlain of the Royal Household, who is required to remain at Buckingham Palace throughout the State Opening as a hostage against the sovereign's safe return. While parliament is sitting, this elected representative of the people must further neglect his constituency duties to pen a report of each day's proceedings for the monarch, who insists that it reach her before dinner.

The litany of royal retainers and their antique titles stretches almost to the crack of doom, from the Royal Bargemaster and the Keeper of the Queen's Swans to the Yeoman Bed Hanger, the Backstairs Sauce Chef and the Yeoman of the Glass and China Pantry. 'All are essential to the Queen's well-being,' in the words of one student of the genre. As if to help us suspend our disbelief, he adds: 'That *is* how she sees them.'

While walking gingerly backwards, the Lord Chamberlain is also required to carry a white staff, which he will break over the Queen's grave when she dies. Amid the profusion of wands, swords and rods guarding the British head of state is an ebony truncheon with a gold head, wielded as a security measure against assassins by another character called Gold Stick. His second line of defence is a deputy aptly named Silver Stick-in-Waiting, whose job since the Popish Plot of 1678 has been to hover nearby, ready to smite anyone who smites Gold Stick. Given the nature of these duties, it is not surprising that they traditionally go, *ex officio*, to soldiers. Gold Stick is always a Colonel of the Life Guards, while the Lieutenant-Colonel of the Household Cavalry lurks in the shadows as Silver Stick.

In recent years this happened to be Lieutenant-Colonel (now

Brigadier) Andrew Parker-Bowles, who has had to endure many
a boorish pun on his *alter ego* as Silver Stick-in-Waiting. Once
his wife Camilla became celebrated throughout the world as
the Prince of Wales's *innamorata*, Parker-Bowles's friends also
took to calling him 'Ernest', in affectionate memory of Mrs
Wallis Simpson's second husband. Early in 1993, when the
press printed extracts from an intimate, explicitly sexual, telephone conversation between two lovers widely identified as
the Prince of Wales and Mrs Parker-Bowles – the so-called
'Camillagate' tape – neither party issued any denial, demanded
a retraction, or pursued the Press Complaints Commission's
offer of a formal inquiry. That weekend's newspapers mocked
Silver Stick as a man 'prepared to lay down his wife for his
country'.

It was this unlikely conjunction of antique mumbo-jumbo and
contemporary sleaze which brought John Major to his feet in
the House of Commons at 3.30 p.m. on 9 December 1992, to
make his second dramatic announcement in a fortnight about
the changing face of the monarchy. For one historic moment,
a twentieth-century Queen's reliance on quaint seventeenth-
century methods of self-protection intertwined poignantly with
an equally time-honoured royal tradition: the apparent penchant
of Princes of Wales to exercise *droit de seigneur* over other men's
wives.

Though it was only three days before a summit meeting on
which he had staked his political future, the prime minister had
cancelled a meeting with Jacques Delors, the president of the
European Commission, to make his statement to the House.
Evidently, Major considered it of more importance to tell Members of Parliament in person that the heir to the throne and his
wife had decided – 'with regret' – to separate.

It was not a statement the Queen's first minister needed to
make. Major's words were a mere echo of an announcement
simultaneously made by the more obviously appropriate source,
Buckingham Palace. What Delors made of the British prime
minister's priorities that day went mercifully unrecorded amid
the ensuing furore. Britain was then in its last month as President of the European Community; that weekend's Edinburgh

summit was set to decide the fate of the embattled Treaty of Maastricht, itself billed as the key to the long-term political and economic future of Britain and Europe. The summit, of course, was wiped off the front pages by Major's news about the Waleses.

To a prime minister dedicated to a 'classless society', as to the tabloid press, the troubles of the monarchy seemed to come before those of the country. Nor was this the first time Major had given them precedence. The previous September, the weekend before 'Black Wednesday' had seen him at Balmoral Castle, gently urging Britain's richest non-taxpayer to trim her demands on the public purse. Three days later his government was forced to wipe billions off the national reserves in a vain attempt to defend sterling, which it wound up devaluing by 20 per cent (the very course which Major had dismissed the week before as 'a betrayal of Britain's future').

The events of 'Black Wednesday', 16 September 1992, were later described by *The Sunday Times* as 'the greatest act of economic mismanagement since Churchill returned to the gold standard in 1925'; for a while, even the royal fortunes had to take a back seat to Britain's (and the government's) immediate future. Doggedly, Major stood by his Chancellor of the Exchequer, Norman Lamont, turning away universal demands for his resignation. Two months later, on 26 November, the prime minister was still busy defending Lamont – this time through another political scandal, the Chancellor's use of public funds to settle a private legal bill – when he was again forced to break off from economic policy to make another announcement of more moment. It came less than a week after fire had devastated the Queen's beloved Windsor Castle and just three days after the National Heritage Secretary, Peter Brooke, had told the Queen that the taxpayer would naturally be footing the £60 million bill. So immediate and universal were the outraged protests from the taxpayer that both monarch and prime minister were panicked into premature announcement of a supposedly face-saving gesture. The Queen, Major told the House, had 'offered' – after forty years of avoidance – to pay some taxes. It was only three weeks since Chancellor Lamont had told the same House, in a written parliamentary answer, that the government had 'no plans' for the sovereign to do any such thing.

Major's pragmatic approach to the monarchy's problems was a welcome contrast to the deference of his predecessor, Margaret Thatcher, whose rampant iconoclasm had stopped well short of Buckingham Palace. 'Never in a hundred years,' said one of Thatcher's former government colleagues, 'would Maggie have asked the Queen to pay tax.' Elizabeth II had welcomed the arrival of an informal and affable new premier, the ninth in her forty-year reign, after eleven years of stifling deference from the Mayor of Grantham's daughter. In this as in so many other political causes, however, the sympathetic support of John Major could prove decidedly double-edged.

Two weeks after announcing the Queen's tax concession, he strove to secure the prospects of the heir to the throne by taking personal charge of the separation announcement – yet somehow managed to achieve the opposite. Not content with ending the tabloid 'fairy tale' of the Wales marriage, thus calling the immediate future of the crown into considerable doubt, Major contrived to talk his way into a deeper constitutional crisis. 'Their Royal Highnesses,' he continued, 'have no plans to divorce. Their constitutional positions are unaffected . . . The succession to the throne is unaffected.' Even MPs gasped when he added: 'There is no reason why the Princess of Wales should not be crowned Queen in due course . . . The Prince of Wales's succession as head of the Church of England is also unaffected.'

Unaffected? Major's addenda to the Palace's unadorned statement now opened yet another can of royal worms. The prime minister had chosen to make public, with the full authority of his office, remarks confined by the Palace press office to off-the-record, background 'Guidance Notes' distributed to newspapers and broadcasting organizations. Was he really suggesting, for instance, that the Supreme Governor of the Church of England, whose canon is firmly fixed against divorce, could be crowned alongside a queen long since estranged from her husband? Could the church, come to that, comfortably crown an adulterous king?

Already in a state of schism, since its recent vote in favour

of the ordination of women, the Church of England was made
to look more hypocritical, less relevant than ever. Thanks to
Major, it too was now enmeshed in the unenviable problems
of the crown. In questioning the future of two major national
institutions, the prime minister raised issues that elbowed aside
more humane expressions of sympathy for the royal couple.
What should have been a poignant moment, whose implications
could well have unfolded with a gradual dignity, turned instead into a constitutional spasm.

Antidisestablishmentarianism, every British schoolboy's favourite dictionary word, was ineluctably dragged on to the national
agenda. Major's remarks had been informed by the advice of
religious as well as legal and political advisers; he had gone so
far as to quote the Archbishop of Canterbury in the Prince of
Wales's defence. But the logic of the ensuing debate was to come
to quite the contrary conclusion: that until the established church
was safely separated from crown and state, no monarch or future
monarch could comfortably be divorced as well as being its
titular head. By clinging to the archaic convention propounded
by Major, argued *The Economist*, the future king would be pushed
into the 'absurdly avant-garde' notion that the princess could
one day become queen. 'Even in the let's-pretend world of
Hollywood, people recognize that a separation involves withdrawal, detachment, even sacrifice. To ordinary Britons, and
to millions more of the Queen's subjects around the Commonwealth, it would seem not just odd to have a separated couple
as king and queen; it would seem hypocritical nonsense.'

The royal family had got itself stuck 'with one foot in a
sixteenth-century morality and the other in a contemporary
amorality that makes no connection between rights and duties,
benefits and responsibilities'. It would have made more sense for
all involved to have been honest about the ways of the modern
world: to accept that a failed marriage, however lofty, invariably
results in divorce. Evidence was offered by the royal family
itself that very weekend, with the remarriage of Prince Charles's
divorced sister, the Princess Royal, albeit in a clandestine ceremony under the auspices of the Church of Scotland.

Princess Anne had been obliged to remarry at Crathie Kirk,

the parish church on the royal family's private estate at Balmoral, because the official policy of the Church of England (of
which the bride's mother is Supreme Governor) is to forbid the
remarriage in church of divorcees whose former spouse is still
living. The Church of Scotland prefers to leave the matter to
the individual consciences of its ministers. Even so, the royal
family was obliged to 'bend' Scottish law in an attempt to
keep the ceremony secret. With the knowledge of the Lord
Chancellor, Lord Mackay of Clashfern, no attempt was made
to meet the statutory requirement that intention to marry must
be notified to the relevant registrar at least fifteen days in advance
of the wedding. By hiding the event from the press behind a
strategically parked phalanx of Range-Rovers, the royals also
managed to hide it from the public.

The Church of England, ironically enough, was itself founded on
a divorce. Its sole *ratio vivendi* was to enable King Henry VIII, the
original Defender of the Faith, to divorce his first wife, Katharine
of Aragon – so as to marry his second, Anne Boleyn, whom he
subsequently beheaded. Even poor Katharine had lasted three
times as long as Sarah, Duchess of York, whose marriage to
the second son of Elizabeth II had failed after six years. The
Queen's only sister, Princess Margaret, and her only daughter,
Princess Anne, had each stuck out an unhappy marriage for
fifteen years; her son Charles had separated after eleven. For
all his infamy in the marital stakes, Henry VIII had managed
to stay married to the first of his six wives longer than any of
his late twentieth-century descendants.

    Henry was to divorce and kill again before he was through
trying to breed male heirs. But the ensuing four centuries saw
only two openly adulterous Supreme Governors of the Church:
Queen Victoria's notorious uncles, George IV and William IV.
Suddenly, during the present century, *laissez-faire* had become
the royal norm, with the private lives of Edward VII and Edward
VIII preceding those of Charles and Di, Andrew and Fergie as
the stuff of TV mini-series. In 1936 Edward VIII had abdicated
when both church and government decreed that a twice-divorced
American woman could not become his queen. How then, in

1992, could both church and government decree that a divorced prince could become king? It was a question neither church, government nor monarchy chose, as yet, to address.

Before the premature demise of all four royal marriages celebrated between 1960 and 1986, George V, George VI and Elizabeth II had all led blameless private lives. Each had been head of a church whose followers now, however, numbered a mere 2 per cent of the population. Disestablishment, *The Economist* was not alone in concluding, was long overdue. 'In many countries down the years, the separation of church and state has been a cornerstone of an open and tolerant society . . . The Church of England's special status has not been particularly intrusive or oppressive, but that is by luck rather than by design.' For several reasons, primarily the changing cultural and ethnic mix of Britain, the time had come for the ties between church, crown and state to be severed.

It was for similar reasons, in the wake of the Camillagate scandal, that the Archbishops of both Canterbury and York envisaged the need for amendments to the Coronation oath before either of them could crown the putative King Charles III. Britain was now a multiracial society, with Sikhs and Muslims, Catholics and Jews vastly outnumbering Anglican communicants. On the weekend of the Wales separation, one newspaper asked: 'Why should a British prince not marry a Catholic Spanish princess?' One of its readers wanted to go further. 'Why not have a Head of State who could marry a Muslim, a Jew, an agnostic or an atheist? Let us get rid of all restrictions, not just the Catholic one, and go for a change fit for the next century. Disestablish the Church of England and make Britain a republic with an elected president. The head of the House of Windsor could stand and, if elected, could *truly* represent and encapsulate the whole nation.'

Disestablishment of the church need do no damage to the constitutional monarchy, which might well be strengthened by adjusting to the contemporary realities of a secular state. The specific problem for the Royal House of Windsor, however, is that it occupies the throne precisely *because* it is Protestant. By the 1701 Act of Settlement, the British crown passed to the Hanoverian Electress Sophia and her heirs, 'being Protestant'.

On its Protestant faith alone, and thus on its links with the
established Anglican Church, rests the legal status of the present
royal dynasty. Disestablish the church, thus removing its link
with the crown, and hundreds of Catholic descendants of King
Charles I would emerge from obscurity to mount superior legal
claims. The present royal family, in the view of one authority, would immediately be cast as 'usurpers', with their supporters 'guilty of high treason'.

The royal family's marital policy – a breach of all anti-
discrimination measures signed into law by the Queen – was not
the only spur for the unwonted display of republican sentiment
which followed the separation of the Prince and Princess of
Wales. In readers' letters to newspapers the *vox populi* was turning against the crown for a number of reasons. 'I feel betrayed,'
wrote one Lancastrian. 'I had begun to think that I must be the
only one who feels that the royal couple have opted out of
their royal responsibilities. However hypocritical, a united front
should have been presented to us, their future subjects, for the
sake of the institution of monarchy as a lifelong commitment.'
At least she was in favour of preserving the succession. An Essex
man doubted the feasibility – then under wide discussion – of
Charles's stepping aside so that the crown might pass to his
son, William. 'What cannot be achieved by monarchists is to
skip the generations of commoners necessary to support him.
I find it impossible to believe that children of Prince William's
age, who even now are accepting that there must be equality of
race, religion and so on, will continue to support a system that
is based on inequality of class.'

A *sine qua non* of the abolition of monarchy was the simul-
taneous abolition of the hereditary upper chamber of parliament,
the House of Lords. 'Is not this the time to complete the hierarchical change by abolishing the second chamber?' asked a Suffolk
reformist. 'It is indefensible that we should be in part governed
by a huge unelected body of men and women of whom the
great majority [800] inherit a right of governance over us. Let
us now have a properly elected upper house.' It was another
sign of the country's changing mood that *The Times* printed the
kind of letter it would not have considered for publication only

months before. 'Is it beyond our wit,' wrote an overt republican, Professor Stephen Haseler, 'to bring this whole national embarrassment to an end, and resolve that when the present Queen goes we should dispense with this medieval institution altogether, join the modern world and become a republic?'

As they reluctantly became fully fledged Europeans, the people of Britain were still subjects rather than citizens, with no written constitution, no Bill of Rights, no Supreme Court, no Freedom of Information Act. These were among the blessings on offer over the horizon as a potential Republic of Britain became a more realistic (and widely discussed) prospect than at any time this century. Among its vocal champions was the far from revolutionary figure of Ludovic Kennedy, the writer and broadcaster, who argued with some eloquence that the United Kingdom would face a better future with an elected head of state. Earlier in 1992, in the right-wing journal *The Spectator*, Kennedy had suggested that Britain 'could rejuvenate itself as a republic, encouraging us to look outward as we once used to instead of gazing at our navels'. Recent events had persuaded him even more forcibly that the institution of monarchy, though 'durable' throughout British history, had now outlived its usefulness. 'The trappings of monarchy, the Irish state coach, the cap of maintenance* and the paraphernalia of palaces, castles, jewels and pictures beyond price belong more to the glories of an imperial past than to the shrunken and utilitarian world we live in today.'

A distinct change of climate had been perceptible since the Great Fire of Windsor in November and Major's precipitous announcement about the Queen's financial arrangements. It was not just the maverick Labour MP Dennis Skinner who seized the moment to suggest that parliament gratify the monarchy's apparent wish to 'press the self-destruct button'. Rather less radical figures such as Robert Maclennan, home affairs spokesman of the Liberal Democratic Party, argued that the Queen's decision raised wider questions: 'The Civil List cannot be considered apart from the purposes to which it is put. What

---

*Made of crimson velvet trimmed with ermine, the cap of maintenance is one of the insignia of royalty, carried before the sovereign on ceremonial occasions, atop a white wand, by the Hereditary Bearer, the Marquess of Winchester.

Britain needs is a modern monarchy with a modern constitution.'
On 14 December 1992, Tony Benn MP reintroduced his Bill
for a Commonwealth of Britain, specifically calling for the
abolition of the monarchy (and the House of Lords) and the
establishment of an elected presidency. Benn was at pains to
stress that his objections to the monarchy were a matter of
principle, not of personalities; he pointed out, to some surprise,
that his proposals would even permit the ex-Queen to continue
living in Buckingham Palace.

Like it or not, however, the personal issues involved in the
debate had become inextricably linked with the constitutional
arguments. Political objections to the hereditary principle were
fundamentally buttressed by a more human question: was it
possible for *any* family, in this age of the rampant mass media,
to sustain the hopes and expectations imposed on British royalty,
not least by themselves? The underlying lesson of 1992 was
that the royal family had failed in the primary role expected
of it: not so much, that is to say, in the execution of its ill-
defined duties as in the provision of a group of archetypal
figures for its followers to idealize and emulate. In a secular
age, the royal family had become objects of quasi-religious
worship, hitherto capable of inducing the suspension of normal
critical faculties. Now the succession of royal *faux pas* which
marked the Queen's 'annus horribilis' seemed to be leading them
towards a wholly avoidable demise.

To err is human, to gossip divine. Though the British royal
family hates being likened to a television soap opera, all its
members have established roles deep in the national psyche –
thanks in part to their very ubiquity, their own decisions to
appear in, present, even produce television programmes. In the
age of Oprah Winfrey and Phil Donahue, *Neighbours* and *Dallas*,
humankind likes to live its life by electronic proxy, anaesthetizing
its own problems by relishing those of others. Each figure
in each saga becomes the spectator's private possession, seen
through the prism of their own lives, causing heated debate
when they step out of character. The House of Windsor, to
one observer, is not just another soap opera: 'It is *our* soap

opera. Its characters may be rich and arrogant, live in palaces and treat us with contempt. But we pay them. They are our creatures . . . ' The televised, or fictionalized, royal family thus takes on more reality than the real one.

'Saint and sinner; madonna and whore; golden angel and flame-haired sorceress. Are these the archetypes encapsulating Diana and Fergie? Or is it simply that sexism and medieval attitudes to women still linger beneath the surface in twentieth-century thinking?' When it comes to the royal soap opera, one critic's loyal indignation is another's feminist fury. 'Why, after all, haven't male members of the royal family, or male consorts married into the royals, attracted the same level of invective levelled at Fergie? On the other hand, why does no male member of the royals, however worthy and hard-working on behalf of the disadvantaged, attract the same adulation as Diana? It does seem that women are still stereotyped as in the nursery rhyme about the little girl who had a little curl right in the middle of her forehead: when they are good, they can do no wrong, and when they are bad, they are seen as outrageously horrid.'

Somewhere beneath all these dinner-table arguments about the royals lurks a dark and immutable truth: that those passing public figures who gratify humankind's need for larger-than-life superheroes must live and die by a pattern as timeless as the Aristotelian conventions of Greek tragedy. The media cycle has long been familiar. First, take a figure capable of capturing the public imagination by means of their looks, their personality, occasionally their achievements; mould and build them to suit the public's obsessive need for contemporary icons; immortalize them in television and magazine images, on posters and T-shirts, record sleeves and dustjackets; then destroy them.

'While a star might think he has the public in his hand,' in the words of an analytical psychologist, specifically apropos of the British royals, 'we, the public, have set him up. He is our stooge.' Whatever the rewards of success on this scale, 'sooner or later, archetypal figures flip over into their opposites.' Hubris, in other words, will always meet with its inevitable nemesis. 'Those who try to live up to what is collectively believed of them restrict themselves miserably . . . It is a psychological law that while our adulation is manifesting itself on the surface, an equivalent envy is generating unknowingly underneath. Thus we wait patiently to bring down those we venerate.'

The parallels are clear: since 1969, and the television documentary *Royal Family*, the monarchy and its advisers have consistently used television and the print media to build carefully shaped images for both major and minor royals; in their case, moreover, the iconography extends beyond posters and T-shirts to tea towels and chocolate boxes, commemorative china and postage stamps, lodging them even deeper in the national consciousness. There was bound to come a point when some members of the family would prove unequal to the demands made on archetypal figures and fall victim to the cycle of resentment and self-destruction. As one of the Queen's more intelligent biographers, Robert Lacey, put it on the occasion of Princess Anne's separation from Mark Phillips: 'The trouble is that [the] mysterious presumption of specialness is extended beyond the exterior, social function of royal people, and into their personal characters as well. Members of the royal family come to be endowed in the popular imagination with almost superhuman qualities – charm, wit, consideration, and more native intelligence than any ordinary mortal could possibly possess. So when they inevitably show themselves, in reality, to be as normal and fallible as anyone else, the disillusion can prove quite shattering.'

The monarchy's mistake was to descend to such inappropriate public-relations ploys in the first place. Behind them lies hidden a crucial psychological question to which the royal family has offered, at best, an inconsistent response: does the Queen expect her subjects to think of herself and her family as ordinary people, with the same mundane problems as themselves? Or are we required to look up to them as distant, symbolic objects of worship, to be bowed and scraped to, addressed as 'Sir' and 'Ma'am'? As Ludovic Kennedy perceived, 'It is the wholly unusual, indeed almost schizophrenic lifestyle of the royal family, half the time highnesses a cut above us, half the time as frail and vulnerable as the rest of us, that has attracted the press like a magnet to the real-life soap opera.'

From the Queen's point of view, there were pros and cons

to either approach. Most ordinary families go through all those domestic strains, often leading to divorce and remarriage, which excite unusual, perhaps unfair interest when they befall royalty. At such moments ordinary, decent people lean towards sympathetic fellow feeling. But ordinary, decent people also pay all taxes imposed by law. It was the Queen's misfortune that her home burnt down at a time when the average British taxpayer could not afford his own house insurance, let alone compensate the world's richest woman for failing to take out hers. Suddenly, the island was full of strange noises: seditious mutterings from traditional royalists as much as from the rising generation whose parents had not fought in the Second World War, that great bonding process between crown and people.

More last-ditch loyalists haemorrhaged when the Prince and Princess of Wales announced their separation, thus failing those who believed it the couple's duty to soldier on through all adversity for the sake of the institution they were due to inherit. The publication of the prince's vulgar intimacies with Mrs Parker-Bowles then sank his reputation – and that of the monarchy – to an all-time low. The would-be head of the church appeared to have been caught breaking at least two of the Ten Commandments.

In a desperate attempt to shore up the crumbling institution which was his birthright, Prince Charles maintained a low profile in the wake of Camillagate, while the British establishment rounded on the Princess of Wales in a concerted attempt to discredit her (*see* Chapter 9). The Queen meanwhile ordered senior courtiers to chart a new course for the monarchy, to 'conduct far-reaching soundings about the relationship between Palace and people'. It seemed a sign of lost confidence in her private secretary, Sir Robert Fellowes, that his assistant, Sir Kenneth Scott, joined the Lord Chamberlain, Lord Airlie, and the royal press secretary, Charles Anson, in a series of meetings with leading figures from all the major British institutions. Even Conservative MPs began to talk about the need for a parliamentary debate on the monarchy. Said one, Philip Oppenheim: 'There is less confidence in the monarchy and less respect for it than there used to be. It is time we had a national debate on its future.'

Again, there is just one constitutional problem. Parliament is not allowed to debate the monarchy without the Queen's permission.

As the Prince and Princess of Wales embarked on separate lives, with separate staffs planning rival schedules, the already embattled House of Windsor began to look like a house fatally divided. With Diana beginning to challenge her husband's standing on the world stage, it was increasingly doubted that Charles could ever become king. It seemed unlikely, moreover, that a little gentle taxpaying would avert the eyes of the Queen's subjects from her exorbitant inherited fortune, amassed by her ancestors at the expense of theirs. Should the monarch subject herself to the indignities of public transport, encouraging her children to trade in their designer ermine for Armani suits, and mount the symbolic bicycles favoured by the second-league monarchies of the Low Countries? These were the issues on the royal agenda as the Queen's 'annus horribilis' turned into an even uglier-looking 1993.

Throughout the world the early 1990s had already proved a period of unimagined change. Since the dismantling of the Berlin Wall, and the collapse of state communism, the face of Eastern Europe had been ineradicably altered. At much the same time the fall of Margaret Thatcher saw Britain in a state unrecognizable when she came to power eleven years before. It was an age in which anything seemed possible, and the monarchy was an issue on which the forces of left and right were for once united. The identity of Britain was in any case merging into the rest of Europe. Was this the moment to think the unthinkable?

As one royal divorce followed another, it was as if the British people's own long love affair with its royal family had begun to turn sour. As in so many marriages, the demise of romance unleashed bitter arguments about mutual regard, about personalities, about money. For the first time in generations, the lawyers could lick their lips at a realistic prospect of the ultimate, constitutional divorce.

CHAPTER 2

'ANNUS HORRIBILIS'

<hr>

'1992 is not a year on which I shall look back with undiluted
pleasure.'
QUEEN ELIZABETH II, 24 NOVEMBER 1992

THE COURT CIRCULAR FOR 17 JULY 1992 RECORDS THAT Queen
Elizabeth II spent a busy day in the North-West of England,
visiting Manchester, Bury, Rochdale and Oldham. The Prince
of Wales was in Wiltshire, attending an employment conference,
leaving his wife on her own for the first night of the Promenade
concerts at the Royal Albert Hall. The Queen Mother visited deaf
children in Margate, while the Dukes of Kent and Gloucester
handed out graduation degrees at the University of Surrey and
anti-smoking awards in Park Lane.

No-one, not even the royal family themselves, noticed that
the date marked a milestone in the history of the House of
Windsor – the seventy-fifth anniversary of the day on which
King George V, with great reluctance, abandoned his dynasty's
German name for an English one at the height of the First
World War. Three-quarters of a century later the royal headlines
belonged instead to an unemployed, homeless young man from
Peterborough, a fairly typical product of contemporary Britain,
who climbed over the wall of Buckingham Palace, wandered

in through some wide-open French windows and was finally apprehended in an upstairs corridor, twenty yards from the Queen's private apartments. 'I am not a fan of the royal family, but I didn't want to hurt anyone,' explained Darryl Marcus. 'I did it as a protest.' Ominously for the Queen, many of her rank-and-file subjects knew exactly what he meant.

Ten years after another unemployed youth named Michael Fagan had found his way into the Queen's bedroom, apparently to ask her for a cigarette, Marcus's adventures naturally prompted renewed concern about the amateurish security in operation at the home of Britain's head of state, one of the world's prime terrorist targets. There being no apparent law under which to charge him, Marcus was chauffeur-driven by police back to his hostel for the homeless in Peterborough. Far from causing much embarrassment to the Windsors, the next day's anxious headlines came as a welcome diversion from what was already proving a long, hot summer.

The last decade of the twentieth century had opened inauspiciously for the House of Windsor, with the disintegration of the marriage of the Queen's only daughter, open hostility between the Prince and Princess of Wales, and widespread criticism of the unseemly antics of the younger royals. Nineteen ninety-two was supposed to change all that. The month of February, which marked the fortieth anniversary of the Queen's accession to the throne, was seen by the Palace as a springboard for year-long celebrations, echoing the national euphoria which had greeted her silver jubilee fifteen years earlier.

But February passed with little sign of the usual emotional tributes, no vestige of the hoped-for national *rapprochement*. The Queen's fortieth anniversary was instead shouldered out of the headlines by a typically British sex scandal surrounding Paddy Ashdown, the leader of the Liberal Democrats. This was scarcely surprising, given the way the royal year had started. Though barely a month old, 1992 had already seen the discovery in a London flat of photographs of the Queen's daughter-in-law, the Duchess of York, in apparently compromising poses with a Texan oil millionaire. Three weeks later, Elizabeth II's fortieth birthday on the throne was marked less by dutiful eulogies than by protests about the high public cost of subsidizing the world's wealthiest woman, who also happened to be the nation's only non-taxpayer. The Queen herself registered the scale of the ill feeling just in time to veto her son Charles's plans – woefully misjudged in the depths of a recession – to launch a national subscription to fund a neo-classical fountain in her honour in Parliament Square. It was just as well. There was worse, much worse to come.

By the end of February the marriage of the Prince and Princess of Wales was visibly crumbling during a disastrous visit to India, where the princess posed poignantly alone at the Taj Mahal. Despite a widely publicized, long-standing promise to take his bride there, the prince opted to remain behind in Delhi for a meeting with trainee journalists. Elsewhere in the Commonwealth, the brash new Australian prime minister, Paul Keating, was treating the Queen with a brand of cavalier familiarity to which she was quite unaccustomed – putting his arm around her waist, and dropping broad hints that upon her death Australia would abandon the monarchy. A year later, Keating would win re-election on a promise of Australia becoming a republic by the year 2000.

March saw the Palace itself breaching political tradition. With the sudden announcement that the Duke and Duchess of York were to separate, the monarchy managed to *bouleverse* the democratic process by sweeping the first week of a British general election campaign off the front pages. Far from making a sensibly bald statement, and leaving the politicians to get back to their hustings, the Queen's press secretary proceeded to prolong the furore into the election's second week by roundly denouncing the duchess. Charles Anson was eventually obliged to offer Fergie a public apology for telling journalists that she was 'unsuitable for royal and public life'; but the Queen declined to accept his offer of resignation.

The politicians had barely managed to complete their general election before the next royal scandal, when the Prince of Wales offered minimal public support to his wife through her father's funeral, arriving late and leaving early. But the

Fergie saga was far from over. On the day that the Duchess of York left Britain for a five-week Far East holiday with her financial adviser, another Texan millionaire – taking her children out of school for the duration – the Palace was obliged to announce that Princess Anne's divorce from Captain Mark Phillips had finally become absolute.

A week later Anne was seen in public for the first time with her new beau, Captain Tim Laurence. Amid rumours that the royals were negotiating the Duchess of York's silence – newspapers having offered seven-figure sums for her story – the Princess of Wales was photographed forlornly alone again, this time at the Pyramids. Although they had flown out on the same aircraft, the princess disembarked in Egypt for an official visit while her husband proceeded to Turkey to see the Sufi whirling dervishes at Konya.

May should have restored some measure of the Queen's dignity, with her first visit to the European Parliament in Strasbourg. But a clumsy advance leak of her speech conspired to embroil the monarch in the ruling Conservative Party's long-running civil war over Europe. As the first rumours surfaced about an imminent book on the Princess of Wales, supposedly chronicling her misery over her husband's infidelity, new confusion arose over the Yorks. The morning after the duke and duchess had been seen 'celebrating' together at a fashionable London restaurant, prompting suggestions of the reconciliation sought by Prince Andrew, his wife moved out of her marital home and into a new residence beside Wentworth golf club – all, still, at public expense.

Could the royal fortunes sink any lower? Even the venerable Queen Mother now came under attack for unveiling a statue of Sir Arthur 'Bomber' Harris, wartime commander of the RAF's Bomber Command, whose order for the blanket destruction of Dresden in February 1945 had resulted in 130,000 civilian deaths. There followed five torrid weeks in which the Wales marriage was publicly undone by newspaper extracts from a book by Andrew Morton, *Diana: Her True Story*, which revealed that the future queen's marital miseries were acute enough to have driven her over the years to five forlorn attempts at suicide. To Diana,

Princess of Wales, Camilla Parker-Bowles was 'the Rottweiler'.

Even her senior courtiers doubted the Queen's wisdom in publicly taking her son's part, going out of her way to welcome the Parker-Bowleses to the royal enclosure at a Windsor horse show. After Royal Ascot had got off to an unconventional start, with the Yorks and their daughters among the crowd waving to a surprised-looking royal procession, Elizabeth II rubbed salt in Diana's wounds by inviting Camilla's husband, Andrew Parker-Bowles, a sometime escort of Princess Anne, to join them both in the royal box. For the benefit of the cameras Charles and Diana left Ascot together that day – only for the royal limousine to stop a mile down the road so that the couple, in full view of the astonished royal press corps, could go their separate ways.

Public sympathy was entirely with the princess. In Lancashire she wept openly when the crowd shouted messages of support. Amid tabloid uproar, it was reported that Charles had told his parents that he doubted he would ever become king; he had also discussed with them the constitutional consequences of divorcing his wife. This was the moment chosen by the Princess Royal's ex-husband, Captain Mark Phillips, for a first public appearance on the arm of his new companion, Jane Thornton, a thirty-two-year-old Lancashire travel agent, daughter of the Mayor of Wigan's chauffeur.

'We must not let in daylight on magic.' It was 125 years since the journalist Walter Bagehot, in his classic work *The English Constitution*, had warned of the dangers for the mystical institution of monarchy in becoming too familiar to its people. In recent years, as that daylight grew into a hole in royal ozone layer, Bagehot's famous phrase had itself become overfamiliar, repeatedly reached for by newspaper leader writers in moments of royal crisis, trotted out *ad nauseam* on radio and television by latter-day Bagehots such as Lord St John of Fawsley, sitting at the same desk in the same chair in the same Cambridge study, saying the same thing over and over again.

Yet still Buckingham Palace did not seem to listen. Had Elizabeth II, loyalists could be forgiven for wondering, ever read her Bagehot? How could she have allowed matters to reach the point where one daughter-in-law was revealed to have made five apparent suicide attempts while the other paraded topless on front pages the world over? By the summer of 1992 Britons were living in an age when cabinet ministers were apparently to be forgiven a taste for adulterous foot fetishism; but could the same really apply to the immediate family of the Supreme Governor of the Church of England? With her only sister and her only daughter divorced, two sons *en route* and the third conspicuously unmarried, the Queen was presiding over a domestic shambles fast curdling to a constitutional crisis. 'If this were an ordinary family visited by the local social services,' wrote Bernard Levin in *The Times*, 'the lot of them would by now have been taken into care.' Perhaps, he suggested, it was time to institute a formal ceremony called 'The Severing of the Ties'. A reader's letter to *The Times* wondered whether the royal family would be repaying the public money lavished on all those weddings.

On the surface, the House of Windsor's woes had been brought about by the inability of its younger male members to marry the right sort of women – or, depending on your point of view, to treat them as the equal partners generally assumed to share most modern middle-class marriages. Buckingham Palace maintained its traditional, supposedly dignified silence on the subject, adopting its familiar if increasingly desperate optimism that this was just another storm which would blow over. The crown's more vocal supporters meanwhile downplayed the crisis by invoking British history: many a reign had seen more scandalous royal conduct, the monarchy had survived far worse than this. Both camps, however, were overlooking fundamental shifts in British society during the present Queen's reign. If not yet a more genuinely democratic, egalitarian society, post-war Britain at least nourished such aspirations.

By 1992 a three-year recession declining into slump had sharpened class distinctions, bringing with it resentment against the royal family's apparently oblivious pursuit of pleasure; and as Britain hesitantly progressed towards the heart of a federalist Europe, the crown's constitutional role was by definition in danger of erosion, if not extinction. Suddenly, the pomp and circumstance of monarchy, in which Britons had traditionally taken such pride, looked like an incongruous symbol of Britain's imperial past – currently the perquisite of a pampered, un-deserving élite heedless to the hard times being endured by their fellow-countrymen. The generation advancing towards the seats of power no longer shared the unthinking, tribal loyalty to the crown engendered in its parents.

'Above all things,' Bagehot also wrote, 'our royalty needs to be reverenced . . . We have come to regard the Crown as the head of our *morality*.' With the ancient institution of monarchy visibly buckling beneath the strain, July was now to prove the cruellest month. It began and ended with the Prince and Princess of Wales conspicuously apart on her thirty-first birth-day and their eleventh wedding anniversary. In the wake of the Morton book, meanwhile, a concerted campaign of leaks from a group of unnamed 'friends of Prince Charles' set out to blacken the princess's name. A series of articles in *Today* by Penny Junor painted Diana as a hysterical neurotic, primar-ily responsible for the breakdown of the marriage, subverting the children against their father. Junor later revealed on televi-sion news that she had been prompted to write the articles by 'sources close to Prince Charles'.

To counter the public perception that he was an absentee parent, the prince unwontedly took his younger son to school – an event considered momentous enough to lead the front page of the London *Evening Standard*. The most celebrated marital feud since Samson and Delilah was being conducted almost entirely in public – through the columns of the very tabloid press which the protagonists affected to despise. But the media blitz of Charles's friends did him no good at all. A *Daily Express* poll showed that the public squarely blamed the prince for his marital problems, still favouring Diana as far and away the most popular royal on 34 per cent (with Princess Anne 22 points behind in second place, the Queen herself in third place on a mere 11 per cent and Charles a distant fifth on just 9 per cent).

The British press had no need for a 'silly season' in the summer of 1992. This August would see the Duchess of York's topless French frolics earn her final banishment from Balmoral, a senior Conservative politician despairing of the whole royal spectacle as 'vulgar and brutish', and the House of Windsor in a turmoil widely seen as terminal. Could it have inherited the curse on the House of Atreus? Comparing the Duchess of York with Woody Allen, whose marital troubles surfaced the same week, even the super-sober *Sunday Telegraph* felt moved to conclude: 'There is no such thing as a free bonk.'

With exquisitely unfortunate timing, *Forbes* magazine chose this moment to promote the Queen from seventh to sixth in its annual survey of the world's richest individuals. With the revelation that she had applied for a grant of £300,000 of public money to build a fence on her Scottish estate, resentment over the royal finances returned to fan the flames. Under the auspices of *The Sun*, more than 60,000 Britons were at the time paying some £100,000 in telephone bills to listen to an affectionate conversation purportedly between the Princess of Wales and her friend James Gilbey, illicitly and illegally tape-recorded nearly three years before. Few believed the tabloid tale that this was the work of a seventy-year-old retired bank manager, who sat all day in his garden shed idly taping other people's phone calls. Technical experts on both sides of the Atlantic testified that a recording so sophisticated – Gilbey was speaking from a carphone – could only have been an inside job. But who was trying to discredit Diana, and why?

By the end of August even the Queen's preferred morning reading, the unflinchingly loyal *Daily Telegraph*, was gently suggesting her retirement to Sandringham, sadly describing the royal family as 'a sentimental Victorian concept with progressively little basis in reality'. When the sovereign loses the *Telegraph*, she has lost her oldest and strongest constituency. The monarchy's popularity now reached an all-time low – with a majority of its subjects, for the first time in living memory, believing that it would not outlast the present reign.

Still the attempts continued to blacken the name of the Princess of Wales. The beginning of September saw widespread publication of a document purporting to be an internal Palace memo criticizing Diana, which was quickly exposed as a fake. *The Sun* meanwhile claimed that the princess had enjoyed a 'physical' relationship with Major James Hewitt, who had taught Prince William and Prince Harry to ride; the major promptly lodged a suit for libel. Other newspapers reported that Diana had enjoyed six secret rendezvous with James Gilbey at a 'safe house' in Norfolk, persuading her police protection officers to take the night off. When Scotland Yard denied the story, apparently at the behest of Buckingham Palace, events had reached the point where Britons were surprised to find the Palace defending the princess.

The Duchess of York's mother, Mrs Susan Barrantes, further muddied the waters by claiming that there had been a concerted campaign to discredit her daughter, implying secret service involvement in the topless French photos. But the decline of Fergie's fortunes continued. In advance of the prime minister's annual visit to Balmoral, a Downing Street briefing suggested that she would be stripped of the rank of HRH, as part of a reappraisal of the monarchy's immediate future. Three days later, thanks to the events of 'Black Wednesday', the royals found their troubles spared the front pages for the first time in six months.

For all the assaults on her reputation, this chaotic chain of events appeared to have done nothing to diminish the Princess of Wales's public popularity. When she gave up her £72,000 Mercedes sports car that September, at the height of anti-German feeling over the sterling crisis, a caller to a London phone-in programme suggested that she should have 'kept the car and traded in the husband'.

Speculation over the Waleses' marital future continued unchecked through October, completely overshadowing a showbiz gala at Earl's Court designed to celebrate the Queen's forty years on the throne. The following evening, when Charles and Diana went to the Royal Opera House to hear Placido Domingo sing Otello, it was the first time in three years that they had attended the same function together on two consecutive nights. Knighted newspaper editors who should have known better were persuaded by the Palace to use this remarkable statistic to run suddenly optimistic articles about the couple's future. You only had to look at the princess's smile, ran the captions; all the negative publicity had been wrong. It took just three days for these fantasies to return to haunt the Palace strategists, not to mention the editors. Early November saw the royal press corps off with the Waleses to South Korea, where the death throes of their marriage were finally enacted before a world which watched slack-jawed.

Nineteen ninety-two had already become the most traumatic year of Elizabeth II's reign, precipitating the House of Windsor's darkest hour since the abdication crisis of 1936. When Windsor Castle was ravaged by fire in November, it was widely seen as some sort of divine judgement.

For a few days it looked as if the resonant name of Miss Viola Pemberton-Pigott might ring for ever through British history. As Conservator of the Queen's Pictures, she was the only restorer at work in the Queen's private chapel at Windsor Castle when flames were first spotted there on the morning of 20 November 1992 (which also happened to be the Queen's forty-fifth wedding anniversary). Whoever was responsible for starting the Great Fire of Windsor, the embers of which sparked the symbolic crisis for the royal house of that name, might well find fame with posterity as the author of the *Götterdämmerung* which finally reduced the tarnished British crown to molten metal.

Within a week, Miss Pemberton-Pigott had been absolved of all personal responsibility for the blaze. At first, it had been thought that the highly inflammable white spirit and acetone used by the royal picture restorers might somehow have ignited the flames. But the official report two weeks after the fire – which ran to all of one-and-a-half double-spaced pages – blamed a spotlight trained upon a curtain. Who had leant a picture-frame against the curtain, pushing it dangerously close to the spotlight? And who had turned on the light? The report deliberately frustrated the instinctive human quest for one hapless individual on whom to pin the rap. By then, there were larger questions to answer – above all, whose castle was it, anyway?

For three years before the fire, Windsor Castle had been undergoing extensive renovation. On several occasions during that period the conservation body English Heritage had applied to Buckingham Palace for access to those areas currently open to workmen; the building works represented a rare opportunity to make a 'long overdue' survey of the artistic and architectural treasures housed in the Castle, and supposedly belonging to the nation. On each occasion, the Queen's representatives had turned English Heritage down.

'Why should they think they have access?' the Palace was reported to have said. The building's fabric and contents were 'the responsibility of the royal household' . In the wake of the fire, when few could believe that this had really been its attitude, the Palace confirmed that it had been accurately quoted. Such high-handedness now seemed typical of the monarchy's attitude to its subjects – and to the national possessions it held, supposedly on their behalf.

Similar evidence came from Dr Robert Wilkins, a historian who had applied in 1988 for permission to use the Windsor library for research on a project on the Tudors and Stuarts. The royal reply read, in part: 'Unfortunately our records at Windsor do not go back beyond George III. However, were you tempted to research the Hanoverians or later, I regret that I would be unable to grant you admittance.' Dr Wilkins' response to November's developments was understandable: 'The idea that the nation should meet the expense of the damage caused by the fire at Windsor Castle has left me ambivalent. If the contents of the library are private and unavailable for research, then to regard them as part of the nation's heritage, and there-fore the nation's financial responsibility, would seem to be like having your cake and eating it.'

One man allowed to use the library, though not noted for his interest in matters historical, was Prince Andrew, Duke of York, who was apparently 'conducting research' there at the time the fire broke out. What on earth, wondered millions, could 'Randy Andy' have been researching? The Queen's second son proceeded to help out the fire services, and was duly hailed in the press as some kind of national hero for behaving perfectly normally. Perhaps the old magic of monarchy had not rubbed off, after all. Suspended critical faculties were soon restored to healthy 1990s cynicism when his brother Edward, the Queen's youngest son, that night described estimates of his mother's wealth as 'absolute crap'. If she was worth £6 billion, said the prince, 'I'd like to know where it is.'

There was suddenly no greater symbol of the gulf between monarchy and people than the fire at Windsor, and there was no figure more representative of bygone Britain than the Rt Hon. Peter Brooke MP, the courtly, plummy-voiced Secretary of State for National Heritage, who stood in front of the smoking ruins next day to express his deep sympathy for the Queen and tell her, in effect, not to worry about the bill. Without having consulted parliament, Brooke immediately and unequivocally pledged that the taxpayer would of course cough up the £60 million then estimated as the cost of repairing the damage. It did not seem to have crossed his mind that anyone might seriously think otherwise. But the minister's political largesse was to prove, in the words of one political columnist, 'spectacularly out of touch with the people who are supposed to underwrite it'.

Like the monarch and her advisers all year, Brooke had gravely misread the public mood. This was the same politician who had recently been criticized for agreeing to sing *My Darling Clementine* on Irish television on the night of a terrorist atrocity in Ulster; his offer of resignation as Secretary of State for Northern Ireland, amid the public outcry, had been defiantly declined by John Major. The same week as the fire, however, Brooke quite competently engineered the launch of a controversial govern-ment policy document on the future of another totem-like British institution, the BBC. When it came to the monarchy, as to the victims of terrorism, his patrician instincts betrayed his ageing political antennae.

Windsor Castle, it transpired to universal astonishment, had not been insured against fire. In the ensuing furore over the cost of repairs, it was pointed out that whereas Balmoral and Sandringham were the Queen's personal property, Windsor Castle was but one among six of her eight residences which belonged to the state. Yes, it was the Queen's favourite place of weekend sojourn, which she regarded as her real home; and yes, technically, it was a state museum; but no, in fact, only some of it was open to the public for some of the year. In other words, as the *Times* columnist Janet Daley succinctly summed up: 'While the castle stands, it is theirs, but when it burns down, it is ours.'

The intensity of the backlash outblazed the fire itself. In a front-page editorial headlined WHY THE QUEEN MUST LISTEN, the mid-market, middle-class *Daily Mail* roundly denounced Brooke's pledge: 'Why should the populace, many of whom have had to make huge sacrifices during this bitter recession, have to pay the total bill for Windsor Castle when the Queen, who pays no taxes, contributes next to nothing?' The House of Windsor, said the *Daily Mirror*, had sown 'the seeds of its own destruction . . . Meanness, greed and blinkered disregard for the feelings of the people are the mark of a dying, not a lasting, dynasty.' *Today* accused the Royal Household of being to public relations 'what Laurel and Hardy were to the removals business'.

The Windsor fire was to prove a double disaster for the monarchy. Not merely did it expose the myth of the government's view of royalty, and indeed royalty's view of itself, as standing at the apex of a blindly loyal society which would rush without question to its aid. It also proved an urgent and irresistible catalyst for change – change of the kind the Queen had resisted far too long.

As he stood his ground in the House of Commons, repeating that he had 'no hesitation' in pledging £60 million of public money to restore 'a precious and well-loved part of our national heritage', Brooke was accused by angry MPs of 'writing a blank cheque' to the royal family. The cost of restoring Windsor would mean cuts in a government spending programme already pared to the bone. The £60 million was equated, for instance, with the cost of keeping open two of the five hospitals which the government was then scheduling for closure in London alone. Labour's Shadow Secretary for National Heritage, Ann Clwyd, put it to Brooke that his pledge might just have been over-hasty. 'Have you,' she asked him, 'ruled out contributions from the royal family? And would you welcome such a contribution if it were offered?' Brooke stonewalled. There was 'a great deal of legitimate public concern,' Clwyd countered, that the total cost should not be borne by the taxpayer.

She was not short of evidence. Ninety-five per cent of the 30,282 people who phoned ITV's *This Morning* programme thought it wrong that the taxpayer should foot the Windsor bill. A Harris poll for Independent Television News went further, suggesting that only one in five of those questioned thought the monarchy and royal family represented good value for money. Seventy-six per cent agreed with the proposition that 'some way should be found to cut costs'. No fewer than 59,553 readers of *The Sun* took the trouble to call the paper's 'You The Jury' telephone line to say that the Queen herself should 'pick up the tab' for the Windsor repairs. Only 3,843 – or 6 per cent – thought the taxpayer should pay.

Amid much talk of hospital closures and other public spending cuts, one *Sun* reader from Leicestershire asked: 'If I stop paying my home insurance, and my flat burns down, will the Queen pay?' The same day, it was revealed that the Duchy of Cornwall had recently doubled the rent of numerous tenants of the Prince of Wales. Among them was Bill Jones of Newton St Loe, near Bath, whose cottage was so riddled with damp that it cost more than his state pension to heat. The proposed increase, said Mr Jones, would force him out – perhaps to Cardboard City, the refuge of the homeless on the South Bank of the Thames, whose huddled masses living in cardboard boxes had become one of the most notorious symbols of Thatcher's (and now Major's) Britain.

The Leader of the House of Commons, Tony Newton, had no alternative but to repeat Brooke's pledge, moving one Labour MP, Bill Michie, to call for similar state aid for housing repairs in his constituency. 'Everyone's home,' he declared, 'is their castle.' Even backbench Conservatives found it hard to support the government line. One of them, John Carlisle, suggested that the way to resolve the argument was to leave the castle as a ruin.

It was the next day, four days after the fire, that the Queen volunteered her candid confession that 1992 had been an 'annus horribilis', a year on which she would not be able to look back with 'undiluted pleasure'. At what was supposed to be a celebratory lunch in her honour in the City of London's Guildhall, the grim-faced monarch made no specific mention of her children's marital troubles, or the public ill-feeling about her tax-exempt status; nor did she make any offer (as had been widely predicted) to contribute from her huge private wealth to the cost of rebuilding Windsor Castle. Her extraordinary speech was nevertheless the most candid and personal the monarch had ever delivered – a heartfelt confessional made all the more poignant by the throaty weakness of her voice, due to laryngitis inflamed by smoke inhalation at Windsor. Sadly, she croaked:

> I sometimes wonder how future generations will judge the events of this tumultuous year. I dare say that history will take a slightly more moderate view than that of some con-temporary commentators. Distance is well known to lend enchantment, even to the less attractive views. After all, it has the inestimable advantage of hindsight. But it can also lend an extra dimension of judgement, giving it a leavening of moderation and compassion – even of wisdom – that is sometimes lacking in the reactions of those whose task it is in life to offer instant opinions on all things great and small.

For all its barbs against the media, especially the tabloid press, the Queen's speech was clearly intended as an olive-branch of sorts. And it was taken as such in a standing ovation from her distinguished City of London audience – every one of whom, apart from the prime minister and the leader of the Opposition, bore a title she had bestowed.

But the editors of the tabloid newspapers, latter-day tribunes of the people, were distinctly underwhelmed. As the Queen appealed for 'gentler' criticism, expressed with 'good humour and understanding', their instinctive reaction was to scent blood and close in for the kill, as ruthlessly as a royal on a fox hunt. Having the previous day proclaimed its contents 'Hotter Than A Night In Windsor', *The Sun*'s front-page coverage of the Queen's speech was now irreverently headlined: ONE'S BUM YEAR. A

GRIFFIN'S EYE

"May I say on behalf of everyone here, how sorry we all are about your horrible year."

cartoon in the *Daily Mirror* showed a spokesman for huge crowds of the homeless, the unemployed and the bankrupt approaching the throne to tell a stern but comfortable-looking Queen: 'May I say on behalf of everyone here, how sorry we all are about your horrible year.' (The rest of the page was filled with predictions from the paper's astrologer that 1993 would prove another 'annus terrificus' for the royals.) *The Star* printed a spoof letter from the Queen: 'After a disastrous fire at my gaff in Windsor, I am down to my last three homes, not counting my royal yacht, my personal railway train and of course my airline.'

Even by the standards of Hogarth and Rowlandson, this was strong, seditious stuff. Next day saw *The Sun* having scatological fun with the Queen's rare venture into Latin, printing its price in roman numerals ('To Pay More Would Be Horribilis') and denouncing its rivals with the slogan 'Other Papers are a Pain in the Annus'. Hitherto the Queen's only catch-phrase in forty years had been her familiar way of beginning too many speeches, 'My husband and I . . . ' Now her doleful version of Dryden's 'Annus Mirabilis' passed swiftly into the language. Rather than winning the sympathy she sought, however, it rebounded upon her. Why had the monarch, not noted for the breadth of her education, chosen to unburden herself in Latin? Was the Queen's English not good enough for the Queen? A pun in a dead language seemed all too apt a summary of the monarchy's current plight. It could scarcely sound more alien – and thus counter-productive – to the ears of those very rank-and-file subjects to whom she was trying to appeal. 'If the Queen wants the sympathy of her people,' sniped the London *Evening Standard*, 'she should stick to English.'

Even the sympathy of the 'quality', broadsheet newspapers, most of them resolutely right-wing and royalist, was muted. 'What matters,' said *The Times*, 'is the national sense that something is wrong with the state of the royal family, that, while the monarch remains high in her subjects' esteem, the rest of "the firm" is variously at fault and failing to live and work as it should.' *The Independent* considered the speech 'self-abasing', while *The Daily Telegraph* sniffed that the royal family had contributed to 'an unusually low point in national self-esteem'.

The House of Commons proved equally unsympathetic. The day after the Queen's speech, as MPs pointedly denied themselves a pay rise, the all-party public accounts committee ordered the National Audit Office to conduct an immediate inquiry into the 'value-for-money' given by the £26.4 million paid annually by the taxpayer for the maintenance of the six royal residences owned by the state: Buckingham Palace, Windsor Castle, Kensington Palace, St James's Palace and Clarence House in London, and Holyrood House, Edinburgh. The committee rejected a Labour member's demand that the inquiry should be broadened to include all payments of public money to the Queen and her family, but the move was a clear indication that the monarch's attempt to clear the air had failed. Both financially and constitutionally, on the personal front as much as the public, the Queen looked set to remain under a degree of hostile pressure unprecedented during her forty years on the throne.

How had it come to this? Until the 1990s, Britain's tribal
loyalty to its monarchy could perennially be relied on to disarm
criticism and marginalize dissent. Now the spate of scandals
which saw the collapse of the 'family' monarchy had created a
mutinous climate in which the royal finances could also come
under sustained scrutiny. As recently as the late 1980s it would
have been 'unthinkable', as one senior courtier put it, for parliament to debate a bill calling for the Queen to pay income tax,
with national newspapers reflecting the popular disenchantment
evident from regular opinion polls. In the wake of a series
of political scandals, even a spate of debates about personal
privacy – plus the threat of legislation to curb the excesses of a
tabloid press prone to feeding frenzies – looked like diversionary
tactics by politicians as anxious to save their own scalps as
to gratify hurt royal feelings. It was anyway too late to lock
the door of the royal stables; the thoroughbred was already
galloping across the horizon.

As the private lives of the younger royals fell apart, depriving
the monarchy of its role as a paradigm of Christian family life;
as the government still declined, despite the wishes of 80 per cent
of the electorate, to require the monarch to pay tax on her vast
private income; as the breach between the Prince and Princess
of Wales called the entire future of the institution into doubt, the
Windsor crisis of 1992 became much worse than that of 1936,
whose intense drama had at least been played out in a matter of
months, after the Prince of Wales had become king. The decay
in the fabric of the House of Windsor now looked set for open-
ended erosion as the heir to the throne and his wife – as yet
unofficially – embarked on separate lives, both private and public.
Could Elizabeth II's 'annus horribilis' amount to the most serious
threat to the crown's survival since 1649, the beginning of that
one brief interregnum in more than a thousand years of British
monarchy? Fanciful overstatement, shrugged most observers.
But this was certainly the first time in more than a century that
Britons could detect a distinct whiff of republicanism in the air.

At the end of the Queen's 'annus horribilis' speech, Prime Minister John Major leant conspicuously across their host, the Lord

Mayor of London, to offer his sovereign what appeared to be a few words of reassurance. Forty-eight hours later, he was on his feet in the House of Commons announcing that the Queen had indicated her willingness to pay some taxes, and to reduce the burden of her family on the taxpayer. In response to a question craftily pre-arranged with John Smith, leader of Her Majesty's Opposition – an unusual deal which itself roused Labour ire and caught his own backbenchers unawares – Major declared: 'The Queen has asked me to consider the basis on which she might voluntarily pay tax, and further suggested she might take responsibility for certain payments under the current Civil List arrangements. The Prince of Wales has made a similar request.'

Though he convinced no-one, the prime minister went to some pains to stress that the Queen's 'request' had been made 'some months ago, before the summer recess', and that the timing of his announcement had nothing to do with recent events. Buckingham Palace, describing the move as 'an appropriate step to take in the 1990s', said it had been mooted by the Queen as early as the previous July.

It was quite clear that Major had been rushed into the statement by the angry public reaction, via the press, to meeting the cost of the Windsor fire, and that the Palace team then negotiating with the Treasury and Inland Revenue had hoped to finalize a package before announcing a *fait accompli* in the New Year. If the Queen had asked Major to look into this as long ago as July, why had he not told the nation at the time? The only begetter of the Citizen's Charter, self-declared champion of open government, seemed to have contracted the British disease of secrecy. Had the Queen's first minister chosen to announce the plan earlier, he could have spared her the whole demeaning row about the costs of the fire damage, and much else that was to flow from it. As it was, the monarchy was immediately cheapened by appearing to make a somewhat desperate response to a surprising outburst of public resentment. Responding to public opinion is the lot of mere politicians; it is supposedly part of the magic of monarchy to rise above the fray.

Major's tax announcement, moreover, raised more questions than it answered. Would this new ploy, like the National Audit

Office review of the royal palaces, take at least a year to emerge in detail? Was it just another political manoeuvre to neutralize a problem by buying it time? No, the prime minister pledged that the Queen would start paying tax at the beginning of the next financial year in April 1993. She would also be slimming down the Civil List by taking financial responsibility for all members of the royal family except herself, her husband and her mother; in other words, she would be returning to the Treasury the £879,000 of public money granted annually to the Duke of York, Prince Edward, Princess Anne, Princess Margaret and her aunt, Princess Alice, Duchess of Gloucester.

There was, it appeared, much complex detail still to be worked out. As well as income tax on her earnings as both landlord and investor, for instance, would the Queen join her subjects in the struggle to cope with capital gains, inheritance and other taxes? Death duties notoriously tended to wipe out the wealth of old British families in a couple of generations. Would Her Majesty's accountants employ the latest tax avoidance ploys to reduce her liability to almost zero? Might the head of state consider the perfectly legal but less than patriotic option of offshore investment? The Prime Minister ducked all such questions, undertaking to report back to the House with full details 'early in the New Year'.

The taxing of the Queen's private income would be a voluntary arrangement, not enshrined in legislation. But a crucial principle, both cosmetic and constitutional, had been conceded. Only twelve months before, the Liberal Democrat MP Simon Hughes had been showered with obloquy for even suggesting the idea of taxing the sovereign – which was smartly dismissed, despite the support of 80 per cent of their electorate, by a House of Commons still tugging its collective forelock to the last. Thanks more to the mob than to its elected representatives, a desperate-looking monarchy had now been forced into signalling its readiness to contemplate change, if not quite to adapt to the times. From the people's point of view, it was a start. But was it, from the crown's, too little too late?

The prime minister's announcement was a watershed in the modern history of the monarchy's relations with its subjects. In a twentieth-century version of the Peasants' Revolt, the Queen's concession was a clear victory for what *The Sun* proudly called 'people power'. Now the *Daily Mail* could claim to have succeeded in its efforts to make the monarch listen. Just a few months before, during the press campaign against his friend and colleague David Mellor over his affair with an actress, John Major had indignantly asked: 'Who chooses the members of the Cabinet? The prime minister or the editor of the *Daily Mail*?' The question had proved a rash hostage to fortune; by accepting Mellor's resignation the following week, Major had given himself the most humiliating of answers. His capacity for political misjudgement was sucking the monarchy into the web of ineptitude and disarray surrounding his government.

His announcement of the formal separation of the Prince and Princess of Wales followed in barely a month. Two days after the prime minister had stunned the Commons with the news, the Queen hosted a formal dinner aboard *Britannia* for European leaders attending the Edinburgh summit. It was a measure of Diana's continuing importance to the monarchy's future that the seating plan placed her with the Queen at the top table, between President Mitterrand of France, and the British foreign secretary, Douglas Hurd. Prince Charles was relegated, along with Prime Minister Major, to Table Three.

It was a rare moment of sharp public relations on the Palace's part, reluctantly reflecting the continuing public support for Diana as the aggrieved party in the marital breakdown. The previous week had seen the Royal Household in more typical mode, refusing to allow the unsighted Dr Julia Schofield to take her guide-dog into Buckingham Palace while receiving an MBE from the Queen. That the Palace was famously infested with corgis made no difference to the Lord Chamberlain's office; rules were rules, and the public was not permitted to introduce animals into the royal presence. To a nation of notorious dog-lovers, none more so than the head of state on whose behalf this diktat was issued, it was a piece of Palace pomposity defying belief.

Princess Anne's remarriage on 12 December, three days after the announcement of the Waleses' separation, was the only bright moment in the Queen's 1992 calendar – though even that was marred by the Queen Mother's apparent reluctance to attend, and the need for a clandestine, almost conspiratorial ceremony. Although the traditional family gathering at Sandringham that Christmas would welcome a new family member in the shape of Tim Laurence, accustomed to eating downstairs with the equerries, more familiar royal faces were conspicuous by their absence. While the Princesses Beatrice and Eugenie joined their father, Prince Andrew, at the Queen's Christmas lunch table, their mother was exiled two miles away to Wood House Farm, a small cottage on the Sandringham estate where once King George V had pored over the royal stamp collection.

For the first time in more than a decade, the Princess of Wales was also absent. Though invited to lunch by the Queen, she opted for the more congenial company of her brother and his family at Althorp, her childhood home. Diana's Christmas was marred not merely by the unwonted absence of her father, who had died in February, but of her children, who were at Sandringham at their grandmother's bidding. Every chance was seized for the Prince of Wales to be photographed out walking with his sons, teaching them to stalk, even (at their tender age) to shoot – making up for lost time in the paternal department. Diana's absence was used by her foes to criticize her hitherto unimpeachable qualities as a mother; like it or not, the argument went, she should have put up with an uncomfortable Yuletide amid the royals for the sake of her sons. The consensus, however, was that the Queen had again miscalculated. So brutal a demonstration that the young princes were regarded as the monarch's grandchildren first, and Diana's sons second, smacked of all that was wrong with the House of Windsor. To *The Times*, it was 'the unacceptable face of monarchy'.

After lunch on Christmas Day, like many another family around the land, the Windsors make a habit of sitting down to watch the Queen's annual television broadcast to Britain and the Commonwealth. Although the monarch's Christmas message has long since atrophied into a string of pious platitudes, read from an autocue with a curious absence of warmth or commitment, it remains a central part of Christmas Day in most traditional British households. At the end of the Queen's 'annus horribilis', there was unusually eager anticipation of this perennially anodyne fifteen minutes. Would she seize this chance to turn public opinion around? A rare display of emotion, for once quite understandable, could provoke a sudden rush of sympathy. During the preceding few days, loyal politicians and journalists alike were generous with their advice to the monarch on how to cap her confessional Guildhall speech – which had, of course, predated her agreement to pay taxes, her daughter's second wedding, and the final breakdown of her heir's marriage.

'The monarchy is at a watershed, and its future – in the widest sense – must be addressed,' counselled the renegade figure of Alan Clark MP, son of the art historian Lord (Kenneth) Clark, and recently responsible for miring Major's government in the damaging Matrix Churchill scandal. 'Now is the time for an exposition of [the monarchy's] duties and responsibilities, both what they include and what (as in the immunity from taxation) are no longer appropriate.' For too long the Queen had been advised to confine her Christmas text to secondary topics: the ozone layer, the disabled, the plight of minorities, the Commonwealth and other worthy subjects indistinguishable from upmarket charitable appeals. 'The Palace's terror of controversy has had the effect of pushing royalty further and further out into the margins of triviality. But the monarch must now address *real* topics.'

Clark warned the Queen against discussing her domestic problems with her subjects. 'The small change of family scandal is utterly irrelevant,' he declared, rashly predicting that 'such mischief as it has done' was now 'finished'. But Sir John Junor, one of Britain's most widely read Sunday columnists, disagreed. 'It has indeed been a terrible year for the Queen and her family. But why not speak openly and frankly about it, and of her especial sadness at the break-up of the marriage of Prince Charles and the Princess of Wales? And of her concern for the future of their children?' Stressful though the effort might prove, it would be 'infinitely less damaging for the monarchy than if she were to sidestep the whole issue altogether'.

Despite all that had come to pass in 1992, Junor and his ilk still felt the need to preface such presumptuous counsel to their monarch with a deferential by-your-leave, Ma'am: in Sir John's case, 'I mean no disrespect. Quite the reverse . . . ' Not so the columnist Alexander Chancellor, who had wisely taken up exile in America before labelling the Queen a 'villain' in the magazine he used to edit, the Saturday supplement of *The Independent*.

To Chancellor (now the editor of *The New Yorker*'s 'Talk of the Town' column), the Queen's Christmas broadcast was 'a modest sermon about the moral values on which our society is, or should be, built – high among them the values of the traditional Christian family'. In the past, 'with a fair degree of plausibility', she would have offered her own family as a model. 'But is there any aspect of the Windsor family, with its broken marriages and its burning palaces,' he asked, 'that can still be held up to Britain as an example of how things ought to be?' As the monarchy plunged deeper into crisis, it had become impossible to believe that the monarch herself was without blame. 'To use an expression popular in American political journalism, all the royal disasters have taken place "on her watch". She has been head of the firm while it has been lurching towards disaster. Must she not assume some responsibility for what has gone wrong?' Unless the Queen made better preparations for the continuing royal troubles ahead, she could 'go down in history as the monarch who blithely presided over a series of avoidable disasters which, cumulatively, were sufficient in due course to deprive Britain of its most ancient and revered institution.'

The Queen did not appear to be listening. Just to add to her woes, the text of her Christmas message was leaked by *The Sun* three days before it was due to be broadcast (in reprisal for which the paper's photographer was banned from the traditional Christmas morning photo-call at Sandringham parish church, and the Queen eventually brought an action for breach of copyright). Otherwise, it was as if nothing much untoward had happened to the monarchy in 1992. As she clung rigidly to her usual soporific formula, the monarch's only gesture towards populism was a mournful reprise of her 'annus horribilis' sentiments:

Like many other families, we have lived through some
difficult days this year . . . It has touched me deeply that
so much [support] has come from those of you who have
troubles of your own. If we can sometimes lift our eyes from
our own problems and focus on those of others, it will be at
least a step in the right direction.

A week later, on New Year's Day, Queen Elizabeth II was seen
out riding in a hard hat. Throughout the forty years of her reign,
riding without a safety hat on her scarf-clad head – despite annual
protests about the bad example she was setting to children – had
been one of the monarch's few puzzling blind spots. She had once
told James Tye, director-general of the British Safety Council,
that she was 'too old to change'. Perhaps her 'annus horribilis'
had, after all, persuaded the custodian of the institution of British
monarchy that a few changes might be called for?

By then her grandchildren were back where the nation had
decided that they belonged – at their mother's side. After an
unprecedented six days apart from her sons, Diana promptly
swept them off for a New Year vacation with friends on the
Caribbean island of Nevis. On the nine-hour journey on a
scheduled British Airways flight, the princess chose to join her
travelling companions in an economy seat, while observing due
protocol by seating her royal sons up front in first class. It was a
shrewd piece of public relations – as was the deal she made with
the paparazzi who besieged her holiday hotel: in exchange for a
relaxed, thirty-minute photo-session each morning, they would
leave her in peace for the rest of the day.

In the resulting deluge of public postcards home, the future
King William and his brother looked much happier at play
beneath the West Indian sun than they had amid the freezing
formality of Royal Norfolk.

Shortly afterwards, in mid-January 1993, the government suffered yet more embarrassment with the leaking of Sir David
Calcutt's report on proposed legislation to curb press excesses.
Major and his senior colleagues were revealed to have been
officially informed that the Prince and Princess of Wales had both

been feeding information to the press throughout the very period when both Palace and government were blaming it for invading their privacy. The previous summer, stealing a phrase from Virginia Woolf, the chairman of the Press Complaints Commission, Lord McGregor of Durris, had luridly accused journalists of an 'odious exhibition' of 'dabbling their fingers in the stuff of other people's souls'. Now he revealed that he had been disabused the very next day, by evidence from newspaper executives that the royals were orchestrating the dabbling themselves. He had even received an apology from the Queen's private secretary, Sir Robert Fellowes, for misleading him 'in good faith'. In the ensuing six months, however, McGregor had never withdrawn his celebrated, 'deliberately emotive' accusation.

Had one part of the report not been leaked, the British people would never have known of the exchanges between the Queen's private secretary, the chairman of the Press Complaints Commission and senior newspaper executives which now appeared to vindicate Fleet Street's recent coverage of the Waleses' marital problems. One of Calcutt's informants, Lord Rothermere, proprietor of the *Daily Mail* and *The Mail on Sunday*, had specifically requested that his charges against the royal couple remain confidential. A leak to *The Guardian* dutifully defied his wishes, again foiling the prime minister's growing penchant for secrecy. Publication of the Calcutt Report was hurriedly brought forward by two weeks, to prevent the shower of dissident leaks from revealing its entire contents in advance.

Thanks as much to Major as to her children, the Queen's Happy New Year was turning into an 'annus horribilior', even worse than 1992. The day after Lord McGregor's revelations, publication of the transcript of the Camillagate tape dragged the crown as deep into the mud as at any time in the five hundred years since Henry VII found it there at Bosworth Field. The Prince of Wales who that same day put a brave face on his visit to the scene of the Shetlands oil disaster, escorted by his worried-looking father, knew all too well that his chances of becoming king had been severely – perhaps terminally – damaged.

As Prince Charles continues to see Camilla Parker-Bowles (with him at Balmoral, above; with her husband at Windsor, left), Diana sends lonely 'postcards' home from the Taj Mahal and the Pyramids.

Previous page: *Götterdämmerung*: The Great Fire of Windsor symbolizes the Queen's 'annus horribilis'.

FERGIE.. IN CONFERENCE WITH HER FINANCIAL ADVISER

LIGHTING-UP TIME: A break in negotiations and a shared cigarette

COOLING-OFF PERIOD: A welcome splash in the pool

By JAMES WHITAKER

HE was acting by royal command, lending a professional ear to the Duchess of York's marriage troubles.

Their relationship, he said, was approved by the Queen and was "business only." But observers who saw Fergie in conference with her financial adviser found that kissing and cuddling was high on the agenda for the poolside sessions.

These were days of wine and laughter in the shimmering heat of St Tropez.

Johnny Bryan and topless Fergie exchanged tender glances and whispered confidences like lovers do.

They shared the same cigarette and frolicked in the pool. He massaged her legs and kissed her left foot. SHE rubbed sun cream on his balding head. Twice in recent weeks I have asked John Bryan if he is having an affair with Fergie.

Absurd

Each time he laughed easily and said No.

He has told me: "It is completely absurd to suggest there is anything unprofessional in my friendship with the duchess. I am acting in a purely professional manner.

"I really don't care if people think I am having an affair with her. We know what is what."

This was a typical day at the

'secluded hideout. 11am. Fergie appears at the pool. If daughters Beatrice, four, and two-year-old Eugenie are there she does not go topless. If they are absent, she does.

NOON or 12.15pm. Bryan joins Fergie. He kisses her and slips an arm around her waist.

2pm. As the children rest after lunch, Fergie and Bryan return to the pool.

4pm. The girls join them for a final splash in the pool.

PRESSING ENGAGEMENT: Bryan joins Fergie. Her arms encircle him . . . and she holds him close

THERE'S THE RUB: A quick dab of sun cream by the duchess . . . and Bryan's baldness is protected from sunburn

SOLE MATES: Bryan plants a tender kiss on Fergie's feet after massaging her legs. A giant inflatable cockerel perches between the couple, ready for the next session in the magnificent pool

MAN AT THE TOP: Now the agenda calls for some intense discussion

POOLSIDE PARTNERS: Bryan snuggles up to Fergie to share a whispered confidence. A friend snoozes on her lounger in the blazing heat of the French Riviera

THE TENDER TOUCH: Fergie leans over to kiss Bryan. When the children were taken off to play, the couple smooched the happy hours away

‘It's completely absurd to suggest that there is anything unprofessional in my friendship with the Duchess. I am acting in a proper professional manner’

The decline and fall of Fergie, Duchess of York, eventually exiled from her £5 million Windsor mansion (nicknamed 'SouthYork').

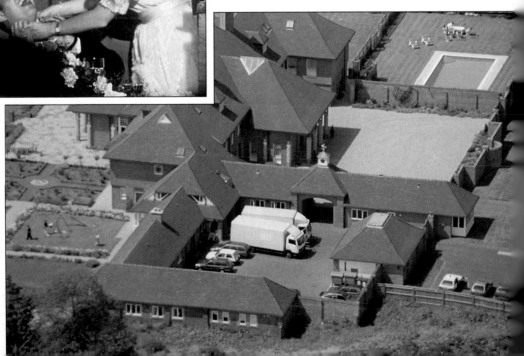

ne 1992: A bad month for the Queen as the Yorks wave from the crowd at Royal Ascot,
d Charles and Diana cannot conceal their mutual antipathy before the family's 'Garter
y' summit.

Diana rejects Charles's attempts at affection for the cameras and soon breaks down in public tears, but both put on brave faces for the Queen's fortieth anniversary gala at Earl's Court.

ovember 1992 begins with the Wales marriage visibly collapsing in Korea, and
ds with the Queen's 'annus horribilis' speech.

For William and Harry, it's Christmas at Sandringham with their father and New Year in the Caribbean with their mother. For the Queen it's time to reflect on the monarch's uncertain future.

CHAPTER 3

FOUR FAILED MARRIAGES

*'Marriages in the royal family are of the highest importance
to the state.'*
ROYAL MARRIAGES ACT, 1772

'LEARNED SCHOLARS,' IN THE WORDS OF PRINCE CHARLES,
were quite wrong to describe him as 'a manic depressive, who
suffered from sexual frustration, a difficult wife, and hideous
family problems – all acting upon an inherently unstable character which finally gave way under the strain.'

Charles was writing not about himself, but his great hero
among his Hanoverian ancestors, King George III. To most of
posterity, George was the 'mad monarch' best known for throwing away Britain's American colonies (as recently portrayed at
the Royal National Theatre in Alan Bennett's highly successful
play, *The Madness of George III*). To Charles, however, George
has always been a 'much maligned' monarch who was 'almost
over-dedicated to duty . . . the father of his people'.

How ironic, therefore, that George's waywardness was responsible for the single piece of legislation which has perhaps
caused Charles more grief than any other: the Royal Marriages
Act of 1772. The King's brothers, the Dukes of Cumberland
and Gloucester, had married commoners; so, even worse, had

his son, the Prince of Wales, who compounded the felony by marrying a Catholic, Mrs Fitzherbert. George himself drafted the Act, which did not specifically rule out non-royal spouses, but prevented members of the royal family from marrying without the consent of the sovereign and parliament, in an attempt to forestall any more such aberrations and protect the succession from undesirable interlopers. 'Never was an act passed,' said Walpole, 'against which so much was said, and for which so little.' It nevertheless remains law to this day.

Too late to redeem his brothers, George's new rules also failed to instil any sense of responsibility in his own children. Of his twelve living descendants in 1818, not one could produce a legitimate child to inherit the throne. Queen Victoria's 'disreputable' uncles, in the view of the Duke of Wellington, were 'the damnedest millstone around the neck of any government'.

George III believed that royalty should marry royalty – as does his descendant, Queen Elizabeth II. It was not just as custodian of the royal blood line that the Queen tried to steer her son and heir towards a royal match. Presciently, as it turned out, she suspected that it would take a fellow-royal to understand and to tolerate the unique demands of marriage to a future king. Not merely would Charles's bride be expected to put duty before pleasure, submerging her own personality in his. She would be required to turn a blind eye, as royal tradition dictates, to any roving by his.

Though as much their monarch as their mother, the Queen has always proved an extremely indulgent parent to all her children. This is the only facet of her character occasionally sanctioned by Buckingham Palace as an 'official fault', conceded to add a touch of colour to otherwise sycophantic profiles. 'In the Queen's eyes,' in the words of one despairing courtier, 'her children can do no wrong.'

When it came to the plighting of their troths, it was of course only human of the Queen to suppress her own lineal instincts in the simple hope that her children would be happy. In the year in which she celebrated her own forty-fifth wedding anniversary, however, she was to see her only daughter divorced and both her married sons separated within nine traumatic months. Her husband and both her daughters-in-law had been the product of broken homes; now the same would be true of all six of her grandchildren.

'A princely marriage,' in one of Walter Bagehot's most celebrated *pensées*, 'is the brilliant edition of a universal fact, and as such it rivets mankind.' Less familiar, perhaps, is the cynical sentiment which led Bagehot to reach this conclusion: 'No feeling could seem more childish than the enthusiasm of the English at the marriage of the Prince of Wales. They treated as a great political event, what, looked at as a matter of pure business, was very small indeed.'

Had Elizabeth II studied her Bagehot, she might have discerned the danger in relying so much on her children's marriages to generate such a degree of goodwill for a monarchy otherwise clinging to tradition, bereft of new ideas. When all three of those marriages foundered – two of them amid sexual scandal of the most demeaning order – there was a mighty whirlwind to be reaped.

Throughout the 1980s, a succession of royal weddings and births held the nation in thrall, melting the hearts of housewives, reducing strong men to tears and moving poets laureate to laughably schmaltzy verse.* 'Great weddings; shame about the marriages,' as the *Times* columnist Valerie Grove put it after they had all collapsed. None was a more potent advertisement for the modern monarchy than that of the heir to the throne – the biggest media event in history, watched by some 700 million people throughout the world. Britain was *en fête* for a week, spoon-fed a fairy-tale it was only too eager to swallow.

But behind the scenes of the fairy-tale, we now know, the Wales marriage was already doomed. Indeed, the danger signs were there on the very day the couple announced their engagement, when a television interviewer asked if they were in love. 'Yes – whatever love means,' replied Charles with painful candour. 'Of course,' added his bride-to-be, shooting him a rather anxious glance. Throughout that period, Charles gave

---

*'Millions of leaves on the pavement', for Anne and Mark, by Sir John Betjeman; 'Out of the sun there swoops a song', for Andrew and Sarah, by Ted Hughes.

the impression of a busy public man to whom an obligation to marry was an unnecessary irritant, another straw for his already overloaded back.

Cherchez la femme. In the shadows, then as now, lurked the proverbial Other Woman. The Prince of Wales and Mrs Camilla Parker-Bowles had a long-standing relationship which neither had the slightest intention of giving up. Even Diana could not realize quite how apt was her fear, confessed to friends in the week before her wedding, that she would go to St Paul's 'like a lamb to the slaughter'.

The 'fairy-tale' wedding was just that: a sugar-coated, gift-wrapped fiction, whose manufacture by fervently loyal imaginations served to disguise a marriage of convenience. It was happily swallowed by a well-meaning British public in dire need of some romance in their lives. Mid-1981 also saw the country riven by a series of alarming civil disruptions; rioting and street violence, arson and looting marked a long, hot summer from South London to Liverpool, Bristol, Birmingham and Manchester. It was part of the magical role of royalty to blot out such home truths with romantic dreams-come-true.

Then still in love with its monarchy, Britain had yet to discover the extent to which it had misunderstood Prince Charles. Persuaded (with some justice) to accept him as a caring, compassionate young man, his mother's loyal subjects were now prepared to believe that these were the qualities he would bring to his marriage – that Charles, as the fairy-tale continued, would prove a model middle-class husband, changing his share of the nappies and treating his wife as a respected equal partner.

When the opposite proved true, it was as if the last, innocent scales had been lifted from the eyes of the vast majority of the British people, who had idealized this family and offered it their unqualified loyalty for so long. The Prince of Wales had been their shining hope for the future; now, even for many of the staunchest royalists around the land, his treatment of his wife was more than they could accept. The subsequent evidence of his apparent infidelity – despite the unworthy means by which it was obtained – dispelled the doubts of those not prepared to believe him capable of such conduct.

The truth, of course, was that Charles could never have escaped his family conditioning. The very concept of an equal relationship with anyone, especially a 'commoner', was quite alien to him. As Antony Armstrong-Jones, Mark Phillips, Sarah Ferguson and now Diana Spencer can testify, to marry into the British royal family is to be treated as a second-class citizen, someone who will never quite be 'one of us'. Not merely do the 'born' royals believe they have the same right as their ancestors to betray their spouses with impunity. They look on them as *arrivistes* lucky to be given the price of admission. Only towards the end of the twentieth century has anyone dared give the Windsors their due by heading, with predictable drama, for the exit.

The House of Windsor has always expected its princesses to put up and shut up. The most notorious example this century – before Diana – was that of Queen Alexandra, the dignified Danish princess who stood loyally by her husband, both as Prince of Wales and as King Edward VII, while he enjoyed the favours of a lifelong string of mistresses. It is an essential part of Diana's elemental appeal that she was not prepared to tolerate such a sham of a marriage. By publicly stamping her glass slipper, with a crash which echoed around the world, this unlikely Cinderella-turned-Boadicea has moved previously unimpressed feminists to hail her for striking 'a great blow for womankind'.

Camilla Parker-Bowles, an equally unlikely *femme fatale*, may have been the running sore in the long, slow collapse of the Wales marriage – strenuously denied, of course, throughout the years it was so visibly happening. But there were other ways in which Charles and Diana were a mismatch from the start. The innocent nineteen-year-old, naturally flattered by the attentions of the heir to the throne, had genuinely high hopes of a marriage which the prince saw merely as a matter of necessity.

No royal choice of spouse had been more difficult than Charles's. As heir to the throne, and prospective head of the church, he was supposedly selecting not merely a partner for life – his commitment to her sanctified by the most publicly taken vows in history – but, of course, a future

queen. He had to get it right. The restrictions on his choice
were, however, formidable. Under the 1689 Bill of Rights
– enshrined in the 1701 Act of Settlement, by which his
family's legal claim to the throne is established – the Prince
of Wales was forbidden to marry a Catholic. Under George
III's Royal Marriages Act, he was barred from marrying before
the age of twenty-five without the consent of his mother
– or, after that age, the consent of both Houses of Parliament and the parliaments of all the dominions.* As the
future Supreme Governor of the Church of England he could
not marry a divorcee. Royal protocol, furthermore, discreetly
required that his bride be *intacta*.

It was thus far from easy for Charles to gratify his mother's
expressed preference that he marry a royal princess. Given the
collapse of so many European monarchies this century, eligible
non-Catholic virgin princesses were in somewhat short supply.

The prince was dating Diana's older sister Sarah, cheering
her through a bout of *anorexia nervosa*, when he first noticed
the shy, gamine teenager in 1977. His quest for a bride had
come to haunt him; at thirty-two, he was the oldest unmarried
Prince of Wales in British history. A late developer sexually,
as in other ways, Charles had spent his late twenties making
up for lost time – 'falling in love,' by his own confession,
'on countless occasions', and enjoying romances with numerous women from blue-blooded English roses to less obviously
suitable actresses and models. By his thirtieth birthday, when
many potentially complaisant brides had given up on him and
married others, his duty to wed had become an uncomfortable,
almost pathological obsession.

'Married, aren't you?' he would ask even casual acquaint-
ances. 'Fun, is it?' The seemingly perennial bachelor forlornly
told friends: 'Whenever I invite people to a dinner party these
days, they all seem to have got married.' To his small circle of
intimates, he talked of little else. At twenty-seven he had made
the serious mistake of telling an interviewer that he thought thirty

*At present: Australia, Canada and New Zealand; Antigua and Barbuda, the Bahamas,
Barbados, Belize, Grenada, Jamaica, Papua New Guinea, St Kitts and Nevis, St Lucia,
St Vincent and the Grenadines, the Solomon Islands and Tuvalu.

was 'about the right age to marry'. Now the remark returned, with a vengeance, to haunt him.

It took two more years of heartache, speculation and intrigue before Charles chanced upon the apparently perfect candidate in the girl (for once, literally) next door, born on the royal estate at Sandringham. The sight of blushful young Diana Spencer among the muddied hunting pinks at Althorp, her father's ancestral home, bore all the unlikeliness of a Midlands mirage. She was strikingly beautiful, poised for her age, and seemed to possess a quality close to his heart: a sense of humour.

Charles had known Sarah Spencer's baby sister since she was a baby. Their parents were lifelong friends. But his younger brothers' childhood playmate had never crossed his mind as a potential bride until that memorable moment in a ploughed field, in a corner of the Althorp estate known as Nobottle Wood, in November 1977. At sixteen she still seemed childlike; it took two more years of casual acquaintance, until Diana blossomed into young womanhood, before he began overtly to woo her. But the autumn of 1980 saw him confirmed in his original view that this sprightly if somewhat chubby siren was 'really rather stunning'. Once a journalist spied them embracing beside the River Dee at Balmoral, the world had a chance to think so too.

Diana, not unnaturally, thought her prince had come; and she set out with the proverbial determination of a Canadian 'Mountie' to get her man. The thirty-one-year-old prince was soon putty in her nineteen-year-old hands. Diana's manipulative instincts might have warned a more worldly man of trouble ahead; but the pair of them anyway had entirely different expectations of marriage. That they were never discussed at this stage sowed the seeds of relatively short-term disaster. As the product of a broken marriage, Diana was seeking the security of a genuinely loving, stable relationship, with plenty of children to bless a relationship of equals. Charles was looking for a broad pair of hips to breed him heirs – a decorative, acquiescent appendage to adorn his public life while leaving him free to maintain his settled bachelor ways.

None of the parties involved has chosen to deny the evidence in Andrew Morton's book *Diana: Her True Story*, which has

Charles's fiancée intercepting a gold bracelet, a few days before
their wedding, from her prince to his old flame. It was inscribed
with the initials 'F&G', in honour of the illicit lovers' mutual (and
uniquely awful) nicknames for each other, Fred and Gladys. On
the royal honeymoon, pictures of Camilla fluttered out of the
prince's diary. When President Sadat of Egypt came to dinner,
Charles was wearing a new pair of cuff-links in the shape of two
intertwined golden Cs. Confronted by his bride, he shrugged
them off as 'a gesture of friendship' from Camilla. A year
later, soon after the birth of their first son, Diana overheard
her husband telling Mrs Parker-Bowles – from his bathtub, on
a mobile phone – that he would always love her.

Camilla Parker-Bowles was always going to be trouble. Née
Shand, daughter of a decorated war hero, she is the great-
granddaughter of Mrs Alice Keppell, the favourite mistress
of Charles's great-great-grandfather, Edward VII – so close to
the King that Queen Alexandra graciously invited her to visit
him on his deathbed. On first meeting Charles in 1972, Camilla
is said to have told him of this unusual connection, adding a
jaunty, 'So how about it, then?' He was serving in the Navy
at the time, she dating his polo friend Andrew Parker-Bowles.
Camilla was Charles's kind of girl – bright, jaunty, fond of polo
and hunting. The bachelor prince was immediately smitten.

He was soon deeply in love with Camilla, and she with him.
According to one of Charles's biographers, Camilla would have
married him 'at the drop of a hat'. Alas, he never asked her.
Charles was in his dithering phase, easily prone to the charms
of other women. So Camilla gave up on him and married his
friend Parker-Bowles. It was only when she was 'irretrievably
gone' that the prince realized what he had lost.

But Camilla remained a major force in Charles's life. He
became godfather to her first child, who was named after him.
In an uncanny reprise of the bachelorhood of the last Prince of
Wales, the future Duke of Windsor, the unmarried Charles was
well known to be close to two married women: Camilla and
Dale, Lady Tryon, who now sells designer fashions under the
label of 'Kanga', the nickname Charles gave her. The two chaired
an informal committee to vet virgins fit to marry their prince and

put Diana's name top of the list. It was no coincidence that it was in the Parker-Bowleses' back garden, beside the cabbage patch, that Charles finally proposed to Diana.

Camilla's committee had in fact nominated their youngest and most innocent rival – the one they thought would cause them least trouble. Diana was too naive, they believed, to see off Charles's existing female friends. For a while the theory looked to have backfired, and the opposition to have underestimated the new princess, as she set about a thorough cleansing of the royal stables, purging both staff and friends who predated her arrival on the scene. In rapid succession, Diana meanwhile presented her husband with the proverbial 'heir and spare' to ensure the succession, relieving him of another of the monstrous duties imposed by his birth. To the public, the fairy-tale continued.

Behind the scenes, however, Diana was already deeply un-happy. The *bulimia nervosa* to which she now succumbed was a disease caused by a sour marriage – not, as Charles's friends were to suggest, a disease that made a marriage go sour. 'Diana became ill because of the anger and hurt of finding out she wasn't loved,' testifies her former nanny, Mary Clarke. After their formal sep-aration was announced, Mrs Clarke wrote a 'Dear Sir' letter to the Queen's private secretary, Sir Robert Fellowes – whose wife Jane, Diana's older sister, had also been her charge. Lamenting the 'diabolical mess' into which the monarchy had got itself, Mrs Clarke described Charles as 'a spoilt little boy wallowing in self-pity', arguing that Mrs Parker-Bowles 'must share equal blame for the damage done to the monarchy. She should have told Charles to grow up, and sent him packing, back to his wife.'

In her letter to Sir Robert (which received a courteous, if non-committal reply), Mrs Clarke wondered whether it was still too late, even after prime ministerial announcements, to try professional counselling. The truth is that it had already been too late for several years, for the reason she herself suggests: 'Instead of questioning why [Diana] behaved the way she did, instead of trying to help, instead of wondering if it could possibly have anything to do with him, Charles wallows in self-pity and being misunderstood and thus becomes increasingly irritated. So he runs to Camilla Parker-Bowles.' The story of the next few years is one of polar opposites, their twelve-year age gap widening, accentuated by different interests and friends, different enthusiasms and priorities. Punctuated by Diana's five forlorn gestures towards suicide – cries for help in a royal world which was not listening – matters declined, as of 1987, into the end of any pretence of normal marital relations.

Irritated by the public adoration accorded his wife, while he himself had become little more than a figure of fun, Charles became increasingly dismissive of, and patronizing towards, Diana. After the huge boost she had single-handedly given the royal ratings, he should have known better than to go out of his way to demean her, both privately and publicly. When she began, tentatively, to make public speeches, he insisted that they were submitted to him in advance for approval. He would refuse her permission to venture into areas he regarded as his own, such as education and the environment. He told joint staff that their prior loyalty was to him, not to her.

All the time he grew ever closer to Camilla, whose brooding presence in Gloucestershire increasingly kept Diana away from Highgrove, the Waleses' country home just a few miles from hers. Charles soon had Camilla acting as weekend hostess there, discussing meals with the chef and *placements* with the butler, while Diana stayed in London with the children. On Diana's rare visits – usually when her sons had the weekend off from their nearby school, Ludgrove – she would press the redial button on Charles's phone and invariably hear Camilla's voice.

In Gloucestershire's 'royal triangle', where other neighbours include the Princess Royal and the Michaels of Kent, Camilla had long been accepted as the prince's partner at the dinner tables of close friends. They were among their own class, people they knew they could trust. Camilla was soon confident enough, when asked for her expert advice on rose-growing, to invite people to 'come and see how mine are doing at Highgrove'.

When the Camillagate tape was finally published, Diana was 'shocked and appalled' by what she read. She had known all too long, of course, of the liaison. But she was astonished by the apparent intensity of the relationship, and hurt to hear mention of friends who had offered the couple their homes for secret trysts.

Above all, she was stunned to hear such affection, however crudely couched, from a man who had offered her none.

By then, however, she was free.

Charles, ironically enough, was the author of his own undoing. The beginning of the end can be traced back to Diana's thirtieth birthday in July 1991. After five years and more of remorselessly bad press, the Prince of Wales was in a mood to counter the constant charge that he was an absentee husband and father. Enraged by press innuendo as to why he would not be with Diana on her birthday, 'close friends of Prince Charles' told Nigel Dempster of the *Daily Mail* that he had offered to throw his wife a party, but she had turned him down.

Suddenly, to universal astonishment, the Waleses were washing their dirty marital linen in public, via the tabloid newspapers long a royal anathema. It was a process which would continue for more than a year, eventually earning the public rebuke from Lord MacGregor, chairman of the Press Complaints Commission, that both had been manipulating the very press coverage he had publicly denounced on their behalf.

It was soon after the leak to Dempster, by no coincidence, that Diana's own separate circle of friends began to talk to a journalist they felt they could trust, Andrew Morton. Although supposedly bound by the same code of silence as Charles's, Diana's friends could no longer endure to watch her decline. They broke the rules unilaterally, out of concern for her physical and mental health. Even she was surprised by the degree of detail which eventually surfaced in Morton's book.

Not that she was dismayed by its impact. Charles's public humiliation was some compensation for her sufferings at his hands. To the prince, however, Morton's book was the ultimate betrayal. He found it impossible to believe that Diana's friends had talked so freely without her encouragement. Like his brother Andrew, he had been publicly humiliated by his wife.

His parents openly took his side, going out of their way to be seen with the Parker-Bowleses. Now Charles discussed with

them the feasibility of divorce; together they mulled the damage
done to his prospects of inheriting the throne. But their main
problem was Diana. So popular did she remain – infuriatingly
so, to the prince – that she would have to be handled with care.
She would certainly have to be treated better than the Duchess
of York, whose parting gift from Buckingham Palace had been
that highly counter-productive trashing from the Queen's press
secretary.

On 15 June 1992, while the drip-drip of Camilla gossip was
causing more damage every day, the Queen summoned the
couple to a family 'summit' after the annual Garter ceremony at
Windsor. Asked what she wanted, Diana told her parents-in-law
she wanted out. Out of the marriage, out of the royal family
– out of the royal roadshow which denied her the slightest
chance to rebuild herself some sort of life while still in her
early thirties. So strong was her loathing for Charles that she
could not bear to be in the same room with him. She would
certainly not be going through with their official visit to South
Korea scheduled for early November.

To Elizabeth and Philip, bemused by such forthrightness,
this amounted to an unthinkable breach of royal protocol. The
Waleses' joint visit to Korea had already been announced. But
such tedious royal nuances no longer mattered to Diana. She
was quite prepared, she told her astonished parents-in-law, to
flout royal protocol – even to renounce the prospect of becoming
queen.

Now the royals were stymied. Diana was by far the family's
most popular member, more so than ever as Charles's treatment
of her unfolded in daily newspaper stories eagerly devoured –
and believed – by millions. As the wife and mother of future
kings, she would have to be accommodated in a royal residence;
given a handsome financial allowance; allowed to retain her royal
rank and titles – and, of course, to remain the mainstay of her
children's lives. No royal princess had ever posed quite such a
problem.

But could she continue her public work? As the senior royals
hesitated, Diana called in lawyers to reinforce her insistence
on this. Her growing commitment to a number of causes had

helped compensate for the emptiness of her marriage. She was genuinely passionate, for instance, in her support for cancer hospices and, above all, AIDS research (a cause Charles considered 'inappropriate' for royal involvement, even though his childhood friend Guy Nevill, a godson of the Queen, was dying of the disease). Diana's public work, as the royals were all too aware, was one of the main sources of her huge popularity. The Queen's advisers remained dubious about her being allowed to continue it as an independent agent. A visibly active Princess of Wales, working outside the royal family, would further undermine Charles's credibility as monarch-in-waiting.

And then, of course, there was the delicate matter of future relationships. In an age of rampant mass media, whose invasions of princely privacy were the main source of their proprietors' profits, royal adultery could no longer (as throughout history) command deferential discretion. The thought of the future king's wife pictured in gossip columns, dancing in night-clubs with other men, caused the Palace walls to tremble. Remarriage was now fine for lesser royals, such as Princess Anne; but a 'King Stepfather' would be an unnerving adjunct to the next King Mother.

After the Windsor summit, the negotiations continued mainly via a bizarre form of internal royal memo. Throughout an exchange of plain-spoken letters with her father-in-law, Diana retained the upper hand. Lawyers and staff helped her draft polite but firm responses to his pointed reminders of her duty. The bulimic butterfly, supposedly broken on the royal wheel, was defiantly standing her ground.

But Buckingham Palace still had one crucial hold over Diana. At this stage it was made clear that any attempt to remarry, or conduct public relationships with other men, would involve exile abroad – and the loss of her children. It was unthinkable that the future king and his brother should not grow up in Britain. Were she to opt for exile, and some kind of *vita nuova*, the princes would remain in Britain as 'wards of the Queen' (not, intriguingly, as their father's sons).

For now, as a result, Diana played the game the Palace's way – even agreeing to take a Mediterranean cruise with Charles

aboard a yacht on offer from the Greek tycoon, John Latsis.
Optimistically billed as a second honeymoon, it turned into
another disaster – not least when Diana picked up the ship-to-
shore phone to hear Charles talking to Camilla.

Back ashore, her upper hand in the negotiations was temporarily shaken by the sudden appearance of the so-called
'Squidgygate' tape: the transcript of a forty-minute telephone
conversation, dating back to New Year's Eve 1989, between
the princess and an affectionate male later identified as her
friend James Gilbey. Printed in full in *The Sun,* apart from ten
minutes deemed too risqué for publication, it was also available
for eavesdropping on the paper's telephone 'hotline'.

For a breathless moment, as the nation listened in on her
most private moments, Diana's popularity wobbled. Had she
been shamming innocence in the face of Charles's duplicity?
The very naivety of the rambling, teenage duologue seemed
in itself to clear the pair of anything untoward; and Diana won
over most listeners with a candid remark early on in the tape,
after confessing that she 'nearly started blubbing' at lunch that
day: 'I felt really sad and empty. I thought, "Bloody hell, after
all I've done for this fucking family".'

There followed some sarcastic talk of 'the redhead' (alias
Fergie) and her attempts to cling to Diana's coat-tails. The
princess also mentioned receiving some 'weird' looks from
the Queen Mother. Most of the time, however, Gilbey was
to be heard waxing sloshily sympathetic, calling her by the pet
name of 'Squidgy', professing his undying love and asking for
kisses (which were duly blown down the phone three times).
Amid much clack about mutual friends, he said with a sigh:
'I get so possessive when I see all those pictures of you. I
get so possessive . . . I just see them and think "Oh God, if
only. . ."

'I just want to see you and be with you,' he goes on. 'It's going
to be such bliss, back in London . . . You don't mind it, darling,
when I talk to you so much?'

'Oh no, I love it,' replies Diana. 'Never had it before. I've
never had it before.'

'Darling, it's so nice being able to help you.'

'You do. You'll never know how much. You'll never know how much.'

In all, Gilbey calls Diana 'Darling' more than fifty times during the conversation, and 'Squidgy' (or 'Squidge') fifteen. 'Oh Squidgy,' he cries at one point, 'I love you, love you, love you.'

Replies Diana: 'You are the nicest person in the whole wide world.'

A letter on Buckingham Palace notepaper, purporting to be an internal memo about the 'damage' she was doing the monarchy, soon proved to be a forgery; but it had been a cruelly stressful summer, and an exhausted Diana was in the mood for compromise. Worried about her health, her friends persuaded her to agree to the Queen's (now habitual) request for a three-month 'cooling off' period, during which Charles would base himself at Highgrove and she at Kensington Palace. It amounted to a *de facto* separation, during which the couple would occasionally meet for joint public appearances. Her long-term interests, she had decided, would be best served by going along with the royals for now. If she tried not to put a foot wrong, she would be better placed to win out in the end. So she climbed down on her refusal to go with Charles to South Korea.

Buckingham Palace was delighted. All summer it had been trying in vain to persuade the princess to issue a statement dissociating herself from Morton's book. Now the press office saw the chance to generate some positive publicity. The couple's joint trip to Korea that week had been foolishly billed by the Palace as a 'goodwill' tour. Private advance briefings to compliant newspaper editors had duly resulted in curious, out-of-nowhere special features about a sudden new happiness in the marriage. It was 'official': all was well with the Waleses.

After five years of negative press, the Palace press office really believed that Korea could be the start of a new era in public perceptions of the marriage. Upon the couple's presumably triumphant return, it stood ready to announce two more joint tours in the New Year, to the United States and New Zealand.

It was the bureaucrats' way of attempting to give the lie to yet another wave of corrosive publicity, sparked by the paperback version of Morton's book, complete with a new gloom-and-doom chapter.

Yet again, however, the Palace had gravely miscalculated. Even as Charles and Diana descended the aircraft steps in Korea, their body language alone spelt out the truth. Yards apart, they were able to smile at their reception committee but not at each other. If they were still hiding the fact that they couldn't bear to be in the same room together, it was quite clear they couldn't bear to be in the same country.

For four days, the newspaper coverage continued in the same vein – Diana grim-faced when with Charles, radiantly happy when off on her own, conducting those distaff engagements always arranged on such tours. In vain did the Palace plead that they were attending a memorial service, laying wreaths on a tomb to the British war dead, and that radiant smiles would scarcely have been appropriate. If the caption-writers had cheated on that one, there were plenty more tense close-ups from which to choose.

Only the Buckingham Palace press office could set itself up for a fall of such monumental proportions. It did not take Confucius to see that the trip to Korea stood every chance of proving – as indeed it did – the final undoing of the Wales marriage. November 3 saw history made in the United States, with the election of the first Democratic president for sixteen years. It was also the day on which an unpopular British government stood poised to fall, on a European debate which it wound up winning by just three votes. Neither of these events made much impact on the front pages of Britain's tabloid press, all of whom were more interested in events in South Korea.

On Friday 6 November, within hours of the princess's return from a miserable five days in the Far East, a fifty-three-word statement was issued from Kensington Palace:

> The Princess of Wales would like to single out from the recent waves of misleading reports about the Royal Family assertions in some newspapers this week directed specifically

against the Queen and the Duke of Edinburgh. The suggestion that they have been anything other than sympathetic and supportive is untrue and particularly hurtful.

From Hong Kong, whither he had proceeded from Korea without her, the Prince of Wales 'warmly endorsed' his wife's sentiments. Although the statement had been issued in her name, the princess had in fact had nothing to do with it. She was far from displeased, however, with its impact – the precise opposite, as usual, of that intended by its Palace authors.

Not unnaturally, royal code-breakers wondered just what it was that the Queen and her husband had had to be 'sympathetic and supportive' *about*? For the first time in almost a decade of rumour, it sounded remarkably as though someone involved had at last issued official confirmation, if only by implication, that all was not well with the Wales marriage.

A week later, on the day before Charles's forty-fourth birthday, the *Daily Mirror* revealed the existence (if not yet the precise contents) of the Camillagate tape. A formal statement announcing the couple's legal separation became inevitable.

The Wales marriage had suffered many unique pressures, among them the forgotten fact that it had begun as well as ended with bugged phone calls. As they pored over the transcripts of the Squidgygate and Camillagate tapes, searching for dirt to dish on the royals, the world's electronic voyeurs overlooked the fact that the royal phone had first been tapped way back in 1981, when the wide-eyed Lady Diana Spencer kept telephonic tabs on her fiancé around Australia. The text, published at the time in the German magazine *Die Aktuelle*, and reproduced in the original English by *Newsweek*, now made for cruelly ironic reading:

Diana: 'Won't it be nice when we can go out together again?'
Charles: 'Perhaps we won't know what to talk about.'
Diana: 'Well, you can start by telling me about all those blondes who chase you and I can laugh because you belong to me.'
Charles: 'Yes . . . ' [Cut to the end of the call] 'I'm glad to be out of New Zealand. Now I know everything I need to

know about the paper industry in New Zealand. But I
ask myself all the time about what you were up to.'

Diana: 'I really miss you, darling. I'm not really alone, but it
bothers me that thousands of people can be with you
and I can't. I'm really jealous.'

Charles: 'Yes, I know. It's too bad, but in a couple of years you
might be glad to get rid of me for a while.'

Diana: 'Never.'

Charles: 'I'll remind you of that in ten years' time.'

The announcement of the Duke and Duchess of York's formal
separation in March 1992 coincided with the first rumours of the
forthcoming book which was to hasten the demise of the Wales
marriage. The following month Princess Anne's divorce came
through – leaving her free to remarry, as she duly did within the
year. It was thus an extraordinary six-week period which saw the
public collapse of all three marriages of the Queen's offspring,
before the eyes of an astonished and disenchanted public. Her
fourth child, Prince Edward, remained single – although publicly
denying, perhaps ill-advisedly, that he was homosexual.

It was the breakdown of the Wales marriage which clearly
carried the gravest constitutional implications. But it was the
Princess Royal's remarriage which signalled even more starkly
the dramatic changes in domestic British lifestyles during the
forty years of her mother's reign. Four decades earlier, the
new young Queen had been instrumental in persuading her
own sister, Princess Margaret, to abandon her hopes of marrying a divorced man, Group Captain Peter Townsend, who
also happened to be a royal equerry. Twenty-five years later,
Margaret was permitted to divorce the man she married instead, the photographer Antony Armstrong-Jones, ennobled as
the Earl of Snowdon. Snowdon remarried, but Margaret did
not.

Now, in 1992, the Queen's only daughter was permitted not
merely to divorce, but to get remarried – to an equerry. The
Queen Mother was not the only royal with mixed feelings
about this new family trend. Of the tiny band who gathered
at Crathie Kirk on the Balmoral estate on 12 December 1992,

for the ceremony which joined Anne in matrimony to Commander Tim Laurence, none can have felt more wistful than the bride's aunt, Princess Margaret.

Marriage to Townsend might have offered the princess a happier private life than she was subsequently able to enjoy. But the story of the three-year ordeal through which the young princess was put by Palace, church and government – to erode a love they considered unsuitable – also foreshadows the institutional heartlessness shown towards two other young and inexperienced princesses forty years later.

On 2 June 1953, while leaving Westminster Abbey after her sister's coronation, Princess Margaret Rose was seen to brush a piece of fluff from the jacket of a dashing young air force officer, a celebrated hero of the Battle of Britain, then on secondment to the Royal Household. This simple but intimate gesture was to haunt the next several years of the young queen's reign, and to underline all the cruel contradictions inherent in her family's attempt to live a twentieth-century life by eighteenth-century rules.

It was less than twenty years since King Edward VIII had been obliged to renounce his throne in order to marry a divorced woman. The public issue in the early 1950s was whether the sister of the monarch, also Supreme Governor of the Church of England, was herself free to marry a man only recently divorced. In both cases, the Church of England took a very different position than it has in the early 1990s over the possibility of a divorced Prince of Wales advancing towards the throne.

Twenty-one when her sister became Queen, Margaret had known Group Captain Peter Townsend since she was a schoolgirl. As a tactful and loyal member of George VI's entourage, Townsend had become so close to the King that Margaret's father was said to look on him as the son he had always wanted. But it was not until the year after the King's death – which coincided with Townsend's divorce from his wartime bride, on the grounds of her adultery – that they had pooled their troubles and discovered a mutual attraction. 'Our love, for such it was,' Townsend later recalled, 'took no heed of wealth and rank and all the other worldly, conventional barriers which separated us.'

Domestically, there was also the brutal question of whether a member of the royal family should marry a mere equerry, a member of the staff. There were strong feelings about this around the Queen, especially from her mother and her private secretary, Sir Alan ('Tommy') Lascelles. When first informed, although they must have foreseen trouble, the Queen, Prince Philip and the Queen Mother all responded sympathetically. Not so Lascelles, who told Townsend: 'You must be either mad or bad.' Amid the romantic and religious controversy, this 'backstairs' aspect of the Townsend affair went underplayed during subsequent decades, until the divorced Princess Anne's remarriage to an equerry reopened forty-year-old royal wounds.

But this had been an age in which divorced persons were not allowed into the Royal Enclosure at Ascot (which today would exclude most of the Queen's immediate family). Under George III's Royal Marriages Act, Margaret would need her sister's consent to her marriage – until her twenty-fifth birthday, when the sovereign's veto could be overruled by a vote of the British parliament, plus the parliaments of all the dominions (then Canada, Australia, New Zealand, South Africa, India, Pakistan and Ceylon). Winston Churchill's advice was that it would be disastrous, especially in Coronation Year, for the Queen to consent to her sister's marriage to a divorcee.

It was a far cry from Churchill's attitude to the constitutional crisis of 1936, when he had asked Noel Coward, 'Why shouldn't the King be allowed to marry his cutie?'

'Because,' replied Coward, 'England doesn't want a Queen Cutie.' The more sombre reason was that Canon 107 of the Church of England, dating from 1603, sets the Anglican face against divorce; and the monarch, *ex officio*, is the Supreme Governor of the Church.

Unknown to the embattled young couple – even, it seems, to the Queen's press secretary, Commander Richard Colville – rumours about the Margaret–Townsend romance had already surfaced in the American and continental press. As if in a reprise of the last controversial royal romance, between Edward and Mrs Simpson in 1936, Americans knew all the steamy details long before the British. Margaret's attentions to Townsend were the main element in American coverage of Elizabeth II's coronation. Twelve days later, a British Sunday newspaper took the plunge: 'It is high time for the British public to be made aware of the fact that newspapers in Europe and America are openly asserting that the princess is in love with a divorced man and that she wishes to marry him . . . Every newspaper names the man as Group Captain Townsend.' The paper emphasized that the continental reports had not, as yet, met with any official denial.

To Townsend it was 'unbelievable' that Colville, the experienced former naval officer, had not yet taken what in his previous career he would have called 'avoiding action'. But this was only the beginning of 'a series of incomprehensible blunders'. The next day, after consultations between Queen and Prime Minister, it was decreed that Townsend must leave his post – and the country – at once. He was offered a choice of Brussels, Johannesburg or Singapore in which to take up the role of air attaché to the British Embassy.

For Townsend, as the father of two young sons of whom he had legal custody, it was 'Hobson's choice'. The closest to home, by several thousand miles, was Brussels. Thanks to the Queen (who, according to Townsend, showed him 'every possible consideration' throughout) his departure was delayed until Margaret returned from a tour of Rhodesia with her mother on 17 July. As they had said their farewells at Clarence House on 29 June, tactfully left alone by the Queen Mother, the couple had thought they would be meeting again in three weeks. In fact, they would not see each other for over a year.

The following day, 30 June, the Queen thoughtfully invited Townsend to escort her and Prince Philip, as equerry-in-waiting, on a day trip to Belfast. All went well until his posting to Brussels was announced right in the middle of the royal lunch, with the result that all attention was suddenly diverted from the monarch to her aide. On their return to London at the end of the day, to Townsend's astonishment, the Queen paused to chat to him on the tarmac. 'I never admired her more, above all for publicly defying the cries of scandal which were resounding about her sister and me. She was truly Elizabethan.'

Lascelles promptly informed him that his departure for Brussels had been brought forward to 15 July, two days *before* Margaret's return. Feeling, he said, like a political deportee, Townsend took his leave of the Royal Household, who were apparently counting on his exile to break up the relationship. 'It did not. It led, on the other hand, to a lamentable crisis in which crown, government and church were all embarrassed.'

> Could Princess Margaret and I have been left in peace, privately to live with our problem, time would have worked its soothing, helpful influence. We should have been able to discuss the immense and possibly insurmountable problems that marriage would involve. But now that our story had hit the world's headlines it was no longer our private affair, one that we could reason out among family and intimate friends. It had been tossed into the forum of worldwide debate, bandied about from continent to continent.

Then as now, there was a central paradox. The state, of which the Queen was head, condoned divorce; the church, of which she was also head, did not. Then as now, there was a considerable degree of characteristically English hypocrisy in the attitudes of many leading players in the drama. Thanks to division within the church on the question of remarriage of divorced persons whose former spouses were still living, a first cousin of the Queen's had recently been remarried in church.* The cabinet, who were against Margaret's marriage for political reasons, set no better moral example. Winston Churchill's own son, Randolph, was divorced and remarried; Sir Anthony Eden, soon to replace Churchill as prime minister, had recently divorced and remarried. Four members of the government had recently been through the divorce courts; three had remarried.

'Why shouldn't they marry if they want to?' – the popular cry about Margaret and Townsend – was sadly premature.

---

*Lady Anne Anson (née Bowes-Lyon), daughter of the Queen Mother's brother, had married Prince George of Denmark after divorcing Viscount Anson, father of the present Earl of Lichfield (alias the photographer Patrick Lichfield).

The constitution demanded a wait of another two years, until Margaret's twenty-fifth birthday in August 1955, before they could even contemplate it. During 1954 they enjoyed their first reunion for a year during a brief secret meeting in London. 'Our joy at being together again was indescribable,' recalled Townsend. 'The long year of waiting, of penance and solitude, seemed to have passed in a twinkling. We were together for a couple of hours and talked as if we had left off only yesterday. We did not discuss the future; all we knew was that for the present our feelings for one another had not changed.'

The following March, when Margaret returned from a Caribbean tour, the press decided it was time to take up the story again. In Brussels, Townsend found himself facing a barrage of intimate questions without any help or support from the Palace. His dilemma directly pre-echoed that of the Duchess of York and the Princess of Wales forty years later. 'I badly needed professional advice,' says Townsend. 'Since I was so closely bound up with Princess Margaret's future, it might have been better if Richard Colville, instead of leaving me to cope alone, had co-operated with me. But not once, during the whole affair, right up to its bitter end, did he contact me or attempt to evolve a joint front with me towards the press.'

Colville and the Queen's advisers (including her new private secretary, Sir Michael Adeane) apparently believed that the feverish speculation could be stilled by their own silence. Silence, Townsend agreed, could indeed be a powerful weapon – 'but it was not, in this case, effective'. A quarter of a century later, the only bitter memory that still lingered with him was that, as a result of the Palace's silence, 'the clamour increased to a deafening crescendo while the Margaret–Townsend affair sank deeper and deeper into a morass of frantic, popular sensationalism'.

Although he felt abandoned by the Palace, and worried about the strain on his long-distance relationship with Margaret, Townsend stuck remorselessly to an oft repeated 'No comment'. He was not prepared to deny the truth, or to tell lies. That, it seemed, was the prerogative of the Archbishop of Canterbury, Dr Geoffrey Fisher, who was asked his opinion on arrival in South Africa. 'The whole thing – and you can quote me,'

Fisher told a reporter, 'was a stunt.' So there was no truth in the rumours about a romance between Margaret and Townsend? 'None whatsoever.'

The Archbishop of Canterbury was brazenly denying a truth known both to him and to the Head of his Church, sister of the woman involved. To Townsend, Fisher was 'typically, fundamentally and – it might even be said – wonderfully British'. The Archbishop had 'brushed Christ aside in order to take sides with the Establishment'.

One of the fascinations of Townsend's eloquent testimony is that he himself, a devout Christian, still felt an objective respect for Archbishop Fisher's hard-line Christian orthodoxy against divorce. But in 1955, as Townsend points out, the Church of England's teaching on divorce was on uncertain ground. If Fisher's orthodoxy were to be taken to its logical conclusion, Henry VIII's marriage to Anne Boleyn would not be recognized by the 1955 church – leaving their daughter, the first Queen Elizabeth, illegitimate. It was a time when many leading churchmen were contesting the validity of the laws on divorce and remarriage, and many more consenting to remarry the 'wronged' or 'innocent' party to a divorce. The church, in short, preached the principle of the indissolubility of marriage, but did not practise it.

After 'deep and lengthy heart-searchings, in the light of the scriptures, of various learned texts and talks with Roman and Anglican priests,' Townsend found himself 'unable to feel that I would be doing wrong to marry again.' In this conclusion he believed he had the ecclesiastical support of the Archbishop of Canterbury, who had stated publicly: 'I do not feel able to forbid good people who come to me for advice to embark on a second marriage.' Townsend had never had the chutzpah to ask the Archbishop's advice. 'Perhaps I should have done.'

August 21st 1955 was Princess Margaret's twenty-fifth birthday – the date on which, should she choose, the law entitled her to ignore her sister's veto on her marriage and appeal for the consent of the British and dominion parliaments. But it was not until 1 October, at a Balmoral 'summit' joined by the prime minister, the recently remarried Eden, that the matter was again formally discussed. He advised the princess that marriage to Townsend would oblige her to renounce her place as third in line to the throne, not to mention her royal rights, privileges and indeed income.

On 13 October, at Clarence House, the couple met again. Although it was the first time they had seen each other for over a year, they had exchanged letters almost daily throughout Townsend's two-year exile, and were relieved to find that nothing had changed: 'Time had not staled our accustomed, sweet familiarity.' As press fever remounted, Colville defiantly declared on behalf of the Palace that 'No announcement concerning Princess Margaret's future is at present contemplated.'

If not 'at present', demanded the *Daily Mirror*, then when? 'Never has the crown been given such appalling advice.' Muttered the *News Chronicle*: 'The continuing mystery and efforts of the court, two years after the Group Captain's demotion and banishment, to make it appear that no question of marriage exists, intensifies speculation and creates annoyance.'

In retrospect, once the affair had reached what Townsend feelingly called its 'bitter end', *The Economist* felt moved to remark that 'the Queen's advisers were quite correct in making Her Royal Highness struggle past every obstacle before she made her decision.' Other press verdicts were not so favourable. As Townsend himself put it, 'If it were necessary to apply such a necessary exercise in mental cruelty – in public – to a girl hesitating on the verge of marriage, was it necessary to prolong it for over two years?'

On Tuesday 18 October the marriage was discussed by the cabinet, and the prime minister's audience with the Queen lasted ninety minutes instead of the usual thirty. The following day, Margaret dined with the Archbishop at Lambeth Palace. On Thursday the 20th the cabinet discussed the draft of a Bill of Renunciation, and the Labour Party (whose leader, Hugh Gaitskell, happened to be Townsend's cousin) declared its support. To override her sister's veto, however, Margaret had not merely to renounce her royal status, but to declare her intentions to the Privy Council, who would wield crucial influence with the MPs voting on her fate.

If they voted against her, she was still free to marry – but it would have to be abroad, it would be illegal, and any offspring would be illegitimate. 'There would be nothing left,' as Townsend put it, 'except me, and I hardly compensated for the loss of her privy purse and prestige. It was too much to ask of her, too much for her to give. We should be left with nothing but our devotion to face the world.'

Privately, over the following week, the couple made the decision into which they felt they had been cornered by both church and parliament. At 6 p.m. on 31 October, Margaret and Townsend said their farewells in the princess's sitting room at Clarence House. 'We did not feel unhappy,' he remembered. 'Without dishonour, we had played out our destiny. . . The story was ended, the book was closed. There remained only the glow, once shared, of tenderness, constancy and singleness of heart.'

An hour later, a statement (which Townsend had helped to draft) was issued on behalf of Princess Margaret:

> I would like it to be known that I have decided not to marry Group Captain Peter Townsend. I have been aware that, subject to my renouncing my rights of succession, it might have been possible for me to contract a civil marriage. But mindful of the Church's teaching that Christian marriage is indissoluble, and conscious of my duty to the Commonwealth, I have resolved to put these considerations before others.

Five years later, in 1960, Princess Margaret married Lord Snowdon, himself the son of divorced parents. Snowdon was a new breed of reluctant royal, who wanted to continue his successful career as a photographer rather than watch his wife unveil plaques, plant trees and launch ships. Prince Philip was not alone in thinking his new brother-in-law 'entirely the wrong kind of chap' to have joined the inner royal circle. Relations between the two brothers-in-law were never less than strained.

Margaret's fierce possessiveness meanwhile clashed with Snowdon's strong streak of independence. Staff at Kensington Palace reported turbulence early on; soon, via the tabloids, the rows had become semi-public. The couple separated in 1976 and were divorced two years later. Despite an immense furore at the time – it was the closest divorce had come to the throne since King Henry VIII – both parties behaved with a taciturn dignity which the next generation would have done well to emulate. 'I am naturally desperately sad in every way that this had to come,' said Snowdon at the time. He went on to 'pray for the understanding of our two children' and to 'wish Princess Margaret every happiness for her future'.

Tony Snowdon has ever since retained a special place in the royal affections, not least because of the utterly discreet way in which he has conducted himself. Unlike the next generation, male or female, he neither sought nor accepted any financial settlement. While returning full-time to his highly successful career, as both the leading portrait photographer of his day and the director of award-winning television documentaries, he remarried almost at once – another divorcée, Lucy Lindsay-Hogg, with whom he soon had a daughter.

But Margaret has since remained alone. Despite a handful of close friendships in which the press have revelled – notably that with a 'toyboy' gardener, Roddy Llewellyn – she has consigned herself to living the rest of her life a spinster. Every so often the press takes leave from the monarchy's current troubles to reflect how different life might have been for the Queen's sister, 'the tragic princess', had she been allowed to marry the dashing Group Captain Townsend. Among Margaret's few consolations has been a penchant for whisky and cigarettes, which have caused recurrent concern about her health; as recently as January 1993 she was hospitalized for a week with acute pneumonia. Small wonder that on the sofa of her sitting room at Kensington Palace there is a cushion inscribed with the hand-stitched motto: 'It's not easy being a princess'.

Elsewhere in the 'royal ghetto' of Kensington Palace, there is an identical cushion on a similar sofa: in the apartment once shared by the Prince and Princess of Wales, now occupied by the princess alone. By the time this marriage too finally foundered in

December 1992, the family of Queen Elizabeth II was exhibiting marital stability worthy of Henry VIII. At four failed marriages out of five, the family of the head of the church was certainly doing little to improve the national divorce statistics, then running at something over one marriage in three.

Like much else in the matriarchal society that the Windsors have long been, the trend was set by the female side of the family before the men followed suit. Although twenty months younger than her brother Charles, Princess Anne married eight years before him, on his twenty-fifth birthday, 14 November 1973. Anne was twenty-three. Her groom, Captain Mark Phillips, was a twenty-five-year-old cavalry officer and fellow equestrian whom she had met at a dinner party five years earlier. After romances with other Olympic horsemen, Anne had finally settled on the decidedly middle-class Phillips, son of a director of the Walls food company. He thus became the first commoner to marry a royal since Lady Elizabeth Bowes-Lyon, now the Queen Mother, fifty years before. Though Mark was the superior rider, an Olympic gold medallist and four-time winner of the Badminton Horse Trials, Anne reached the high-point of her own equestrian career that same year, when she became the European three-day event champion. In 1976, when the Queen bought them Gatcombe Park, in Gloucestershire, Mark eased out of the Army in favour of full-time farming and estate management.

As a young woman Anne had been, by her own confession, 'a huge disappointment to everyone concerned'. For many years she relieved her Aunt Margaret of the role of statutory royal 'black sheep'. Her undisguised distaste for the press, whom she famously told to 'naff off', earned headlines about 'Her Royal Haughtiness'. After a visit to the USA the *Washington Post* dubbed her 'Princess Sourpuss', and American journalists voted her the person they would least like to interview. Anne herself admitted that she had 'never been what some people think a princess should be'.

By the mid-eighties, however, thanks to her work as president of the Save the Children Fund, the headlines changed to 'The Caring Princess'. Anne enjoyed a public renaissance, becoming one of the most consistently popular royals, as she embarked on a series of visits to the deprived children of Third World countries. She was created Princess Royal by her mother in 1987, partly in recognition of her work for Save the Children, but also to distinguish her from the two *parvenues* princesses who had by then arrived to steal her thunder. The natural rebel of the family, Anne was always her father's favourite child – 'tougher', in his view, than any of his sons. For the last several years, visitors to Prince Philip's office in Buckingham Palace have noticed that Anne is the only one of his children whose photograph is on display.

Mark Phillips never appeared to fit comfortably into the royal photo-frame. His brother-in-law Charles gave him the nick-name of 'Fog' – supposedly because he was 'thick and wet' – and the rest of the family never warmed to him. A shy man, somewhat lacking in self-confidence, he always looked uneasy beside the princess on formal occasions, and escorted her on her engagements as rarely as possible. Alas, Mark did not have a Snowdon-like career to sustain him. He spent most of his time struggling to make Gatcombe into a profitable farm, earning hollow public laughter with his complaints about the trouble he had making ends meet, finally persuading the Queen to depart with tradition by allowing him to accept commercial sponsorship for the annual Gatcombe Horse Trials. Though the couple had two children, Peter (born 1977) and Zara (born 1981), Phillips began to spend more and more time away from home, pleading that he had to earn money running riding schools as far afield as Australia. The growing cracks in the marriage first became public as early as 1983, when the couple spent all of six months apart.

Anne's relationship with Tim Laurence became public in 1989, long before she was divorced, when he was named (by the Buckingham Palace press office, at its most inept) as the author of 'intimate' love letters stolen from her briefcase. Such was the degree of embarrassment at the Palace that Laurence offered his resignation as military equerry to the Queen. The incident could well have spelt the end of his naval career, and of any future for his relationship with Princess Anne. In an uncanny replay of Townsend and Lascelles, it earned him a stern rebuke from the Queen's then private secretary, Sir William Heseltine; but

Laurence had found a formidable ally in the Queen, who refused to let him be banished. When Phillips was accused of fathering a 'love child' in New Zealand – a charge he has always denied – Anne seized the moment to demand a formal separation. At the same time the Queen saw her daughter's chance for salvation in Laurence, and invited him to join Anne and the rest of the royal family on holiday at Sandringham. On the day he finally did leave her employ, to take command of the frigate HMS *Boxer*, she made Laurence a Lieutenant of the Royal Victorian Order. Anne's mother also made it possible for the couple to meet secretly during his shore leaves, by placing inconspicuous houses on the royal estates at their disposal.

The son of a naval engineer who also reached the rank of Commander, Tim Laurence is one of those rare people who won a place in the Royal Household on merit rather than background. He was educated not at Eton, Harrow, Winchester or any of the schools usually to be found on the curricula vitae of Elizabeth II's courtiers, but at Sevenoaks School in his native Kent. Contemporaries described him as 'a strait-laced plodder' and 'a bit of a swot', who made it to house captain. With A-levels in geography, maths and physics, he won a place at the Royal Naval College, Dartmouth, going on to read geography at Durham University. He captained his college cricket team and became editor of the university magazine, where he earned the nickname of 'Tiger Tim' for the vigour with which he chased fellow students for contributions. He left Durham with a second-class degree.

In 1979 Laurence served aboard the royal yacht *Britannia*, as household liaison officer, whose duties include responsibility for the royal luggage. Three years later he was given his first naval command, of the Ulster patrol boat *Cygnet*, policing IRA supply routes. Mentioned in dispatches, he had been rapidly promoted by the time he joined the Palace staff in 1986. He so charmed the Queen that she personally chose him for promotion as her military equerry.

Laurence's arrival in the royal circle coincided with the increasingly rapid decline of Anne's marriage to Phillips. Five years younger than the princess, the thoughtful young naval

officer offered solace for her sorrows. By the time of her formal separation in 1989, the couple were already conducting
the most discreet of romances. So rarely were they seen in
public together that the stolen love letters were the first indication of anything between them. Laurence was even smart
enough to lay a false trail for the press by taking the Princess of
Wales out to lunch. In 1992, two weeks after the four-minute
ceremony in which Anne's divorce became final, she openly
paraded her love for the first time by dancing with Laurence
at the Royal Caledonian Ball in London.

Symbolically, perhaps, Anne took delivery of an £80,000
yacht, the 36-foot cruiser *Blue Doublet*, on the day her divorce
from Phillips became final. Where she had shared a love of horses
with her first husband, it was a love of sailing she shared with her
second. Much of their courting had been conducted out at sea, far
from the prying eyes of the press. Months before the wedding,
Anne's yacht had been moved north to Scotland, and the couple
had enjoyed long cruises together to the Outer Hebrides, and
around the islands of Jura and Mull.

They were unofficially engaged for six months before their
wedding was finally announced, just a week in advance. It
was during this period that Laurence passed his final test with
the Queen as a potential royal. The engagement was to have
been made public much sooner, but the waves of bad publicity then washing over the other two royal marriages discouraged the Palace from announcing another so soon. However
dismayed he may have been, Laurence proved himself a true
courtier − and a fit candidate for family membership − by assuring his former boss, now his future mother-in-law, that he
would wait as long as she saw fit.

'As with the best members of the royal entourage,' in the
words of one student of the genre, 'he has made a study of being
unassuming and anonymous.' Laurence also knew the ropes. As
a royal familiar for some years, he had proved himself up to the
task − difficult in any walk of life − of marrying the boss's daughter. At a time of such crisis, it was reassuring for the Windsors
to be joined by an insider. It seems doubtful that they were in
the mood to take on any new arrival of whose character they

could not be sure. Even so, Laurence's background contained an unusual surprise. When news of the match was at last made public, the Laurence family tree moved the *Jewish Chronicle* to the joyful cry, 'At last, a real Jewish princess?' Laurence's paternal great-grandfather, the Revd Percival Laurence, was a Church of England clergyman, but his great-great-grandfather had been born Joseph Levy, son of Zaccaria Levy, a merchant of Venice. Joseph had changed his surname to Laurence in 1826. (Though rare in the royal genealogy, this was not the first Jewish branch to spring from the extended family tree; Lord Snowdon's mother was a Messel, descended from Aaron Messel, a banker of Darmstadt.)

Anne's divorce aroused less public indignation than those of her siblings because it was conducted without public rancour or misconduct. Her secret meetings with Laurence remained secret, and there were no indiscretions, no inappropriate liaisons, no public rows with her former husband. The princess continued to maintain her newfound popularity as one of the few royals deemed to work hard for her public money. Despite the shoddy treatment handed out to Mark Phillips, exiled at first to a flat over the stable block, Anne also seems to have handled the human consequences of separation and possible remarriage with more thought than either Charles or Andrew. Although their mother has publicly confessed to an unusual lack of maternal instincts – children, she once said, were 'an occupational hazard of marriage' – Peter and Zara have always been carefully protected from the public gaze. Now Anne prepared them to accept Laurence as their stepfather by taking them for regular visits to his small terraced home in Winchester. It was also a measure of her formidable character that she took on the might of the church and the privy council to negotiate a rare royal remarriage.

One new test of Laurence's diplomatic skills would be learning to live with the fact that his predecessor, Mark Phillips, would now be a near neighbour, living only two miles away at Aston Farm, an eighteenth-century cottage on the Gatcombe estate. As Phillips enjoyed equal access to his children, how would the princess's two husbands cope with bumping into each other every day? And as Laurence continued his naval career, now desk-bound at the Ministry of Defence in Whitehall, would the new Master of Gatcombe allow the old one to continue running the estate? In this, as in all things, Anne would presumably be making the decisions.

There were worries that Anne had married another weak, compliant man – this time five years her junior, only too eager to do her bidding. There seemed little doubt, for instance, that any urge on Laurence's part to have children would be subject to his wife's own choice in the matter. Did the haughtiness endemic in the young royals make members of the royal staff uncomfortably appropriate spouses? Would Charles and Andrew have fared better if they had married women of less character?

There were rumours of rifts in the Wales marriage even before 'Randy Andy' married his flame-haired Fergie at Westminster Abbey on 23 July 1986. Like so many other royal spouses this century – notably Prince Philip, Lord Snowdon and Lady Diana Spencer – Sarah Ferguson was the child of a broken marriage, in need of the security and affection which British royalty appears incapable of providing.

Sarah was fourteen when her mother, Susan, left Major Ronald Ferguson, Prince Charles's long-term polo manager, for the Argentinian polo star Hector Barrantes. She was also the first royal bride known to have had what the British like to euphemize as 'a past'. Unlike 'shy Di', Fergie was no publicly certified virgin. She married Andrew on the rebound from a three-year relationship with Paddy McNally, a motor racing fanatic twenty-two years her senior, a widower not yet ready to remarry. Also able to boast something of a past, Andrew too was on the rebound, from the starlet-turned-photographer Koo Stark. This sprightly combination may have led to a welcome update in the royal mores – before their wedding, to the dismay of staff, they openly slept together in Buckingham Palace – but it was otherwise less than promising. Sarah's reputation among the smart skiing set was for 'playfulness' in all departments. And it was her capacity to play, without knowing when to stop, that would eventually prove her undoing.

At Gordonstoun, where he followed his brother Charles as

Head Boy, Andrew had been known as 'The Great I Am'.
The expensive boarding school of which his bride had been
head girl, Hurst Lodge, had a reputation for turning out 'jolly
chalet girls with lots of bounce but not much upstairs'. Sarah was
typical of the budding career girl who answered the upmarket,
low-paid small ads in the posh papers, winning herself a job as
secretary/PA to a fine art dealer. At first her brash, extrovert
approach to royal life was seen as a breath of fresh air in a
world hermetically sealed to preserve its traditional values. In
retrospect, it was inevitable that she would soon be on a col-
lision course with the Palace establishment, where she made few
friends.

From the moment of her ritual TV engagement interview –
'It's going to be the best day of my life, and that's all there is
to it' – Fergie was going to be different. Her natural ebullience
was initially as popular as her Titianesque mane of red hair. The
new Duchess of York hit the royal ground running – donning air
ace-style leathers to win herself a pilot's licence, taking carriage-
driving lessons to endear herself to her father-in-law, learning to
fish, riding the Grand National winner in a charity race. If not
over-endowed with grey cells, Fergie was 'a sport'.

As her husband said at a wedding banquet in the City of
London: 'Sarah has a unique combination of qualities. She is
vivacious, cheerful, outgoing, vibrant. She sparkles, radiating
warmth and a sense of fun.' Accustomed to the free-wheeling,
unfettered life of top-drawer Eighties 'Sloane Rangers', Sarah
Ferguson never really attempted to come to terms with the
obvious strictures of her new position. Headstrong, wilful, flam-
boyant, she was determined to enjoy her royal lifestyle without
considering that there was a quid pro quo, the maintenance of
a certain decorum. Her first gaffe came in 1987, on a tour of
Canada, when she compounded some generally crude behaviour by accepting the gift of a fur coat, thus incurring the
wrath of the 'animal rights' lobby.

Gifts were to come to haunt Sarah. Not content with accepting
the offerings made to all royals, she soon developed a reputation
for soliciting them – especially in the travel department, earning herself the tabloid nickname of 'Freebie Fergie'. When this

was combined with her none-too-demanding workload, she was soon dubbed 'Princess Dolittle'. An increasing amount of time was spent abroad, on unofficial visits to the ski slopes and sun-drenched beaches, all at the taxpayers' expense. Once she was seen as greedy, her 'boisterous' high spirits became 'boorish'.

Rarely has the British public – via its intermediaries, the tabloid press – rounded on a new royal princess as quickly as it turned against Sarah Ferguson. Having initially been credited with the one quality the born royals lacked, the 'common touch', she was soon just plain 'common'. No word can be more damaging in royal ears. Her natural spontaneity also went against the royal grain. 'I just trust too many people,' she herself admitted to Independent Television News. 'I'm too spontaneous, and I act before I think.'

The Duchess of York's natural character belied the dignity supposedly attached to her rank as the fourth most senior royal female, outranking even the Queen's own daughter. Her galumphing, jolly-hockey-sticks approach to public appearances evoked enormously snobbish criticism; but the plain fact is that Sarah was never the average Briton's idea of a princess. Her friend Diana was at first seduced by the charms of some natural high spirits amid the suffocating stiffness of the royal goldfish bowl. Famously, they both dressed as policewomen to gatecrash Andrew's stag party. But Diana soon learnt from Fergie's mistakes, distancing herself from the high jinks and becoming ever more conspicuously elegant. Fergie's less than sylph-like contours, by contrast, often incongruously swathed in *haute couture*, again earned her the particular contempt of women, who somehow felt she was letting down their sex. Typically bitchy was the verdict of the women's editor of the *Daily Mirror,* Mary Riddell, to whom the Duchess of York's stomach and hips 'had acquired that unfortunate texture halfway between a satsuma and a helping of lumpy school custard'. Her thighs, meanwhile, 'appeared to be modelled from soft plasticine'.

One of the first signs that Fergie might be in difficulty came when she reneged on countless vows to remain herself by going on a crash diet. She cut her mane of hair and became a distinctly more subdued public figure, whose natural smile suddenly seemed forced. At regular intervals, however, the bread rolls still flew. Fergie just couldn't resist it, couldn't change. Sunninghill Park, the £5 million home custom-built for them near Windsor, became a much mocked and resented symbol of the sheer bad taste which characterized the Yorks. Paid for by the Queen, it was designed by the Edinburgh architectural partnership of Dunbar-Naismith very much to its clients' instructions. Not only did its Dallas-style ranchhouse design and tacky interiors earn it the derisory nickname of 'SouthYork'; but while Andrew's older brother lectured Britain about the need for conservation, it was built slap in the middle of a strictly protected section of the Green Belt.

Although her husband shared Sarah Ferguson's very basic sense of humour — at a formal British Embassy dinner in Washington, Andrew thought it appropriate to tell a crude joke about the recently drowned Robert Maxwell and an Irish tart — he was inevitably cursed with a characteristically split royal personality, which shies away from spontaneity and needs regular withdrawal into self-regard. Whatever the marital strains or misconduct on either side, it was a mistake to think that any son of Elizabeth II could successfully marry one so 'flighty'. That was how Sarah was always seen by her royal in-laws — and she was not helped by her father, who was foolish enough to be caught leaving a Soho 'massage' parlour, the Wigmore Club, in May 1988. Five years later it appeared that he had also been having an affair with a business woman named Lesley Player, who also doubled as the lover of one of Sarah's close Texan friends. While still unaware of this, according to Player, the Duchess had acted as her father's Pandarus, lending the couple Sunninghill Park for a secret tryst.

Sarah, Duchess of York, lost most of her public as early as 1988, when she left her infant daughter Beatrice behind in Britain to join her husband in Australia. At the time, the obvious and very physical affection between the couple was often cited as a welcome contrast to the increasingly cold body language of the Waleses. In a marriage which was eventually to break down, at least in part, because of Andrew's long naval absences, it might have been thought warm and wise of his wife to fly to his distant side. Given the political correctness of maternal 'bonding', however, British motherhood never wholly forgave her this abandonment of the infant princess.

Before the 'annus horribilis' of 1992, there was no lower point in the post-war royal fortunes than the television programme *It's a Royal Knockout*, in which Sarah and her pals dressed up in medieval costumes – themselves a mockery of the monarchy – to make upper-class twits of themselves at the behest of third-rate television comedians. The flying bread roll had become Fergie's emblem, the guffaw her mating-call. Then she turned venal.

It was breaking every royal rule to negotiate a six-figure fee for an interview with the *Daily Express*, which understandably demanded half its money back when she failed to disclose that she was pregnant. *Hello!* magazine was an altogether more sickly sweet symbol of the age – a glossy grown fat on sycophancy, only too happy to cough up £250,000 for forty-eight pages of pictures of the Yorks at home with their daughters. When the duchess turned to writing children's stories about Budgie, a playful helicopter, it was not so much the accusations of plagiarism which did the damage, but the donation to charity of only 10 per cent of earnings in excess of £100,000. Royals living off large public subsidies cannot expect to get away with exploiting their position for financial gain – especially if the proceeds are spent on an eternal cycle of expensive holidays, often subsidized by craven hosts, at the expense of any gesture towards public duties.

But Fergie was telling friends, to their astonishment, that she needed the money, as she had run up a six-figure overdraft. Having married into one of the world's wealthiest families, she was astonished to find that she could not keep up with her 'seriously rich' friends in the international jet set. To her, this was part of the royal prerogative; but her husband had turned out to be as parsimonious as his mother. The dashing, roguish figure with whom she had fallen in love was at heart an idle homebody. The only place to which Andrew could be tempted out was the golf course. Otherwise, on his rare shore leaves, he preferred the life of a couch potato, watching his favourite video, *Terminator*, and reluctant to hit the town. Sarah's old friends hung back, not wishing to seem pushy. The public had turned against her; and her mother-in-law's courtiers, supposedly at her service, were aloof and dismissive. Bored and depressed, in her loneliness, this highly-strung young woman turned a touch paranoid. When she heard the staff laughing in the Sunninghill kitchen, she stormed in and accused them of laughing at her.

By now Sarah seemed close to a nervous breakdown. When most under pressure, she received no support from the Palace machinery, which if anything aggravated her woes. Soon she became convinced (as later did her mother) of a conspiracy against her. 'The only advice I've been given in six years,' she told a friend, 'is to wave more slowly.' So frequent were the dressings-down from the Queen's private secretary, Sir Robert Fellowes (who also happened to be her second cousin), that she nicknamed him 'Bellows'. In one of the last interviews she gave before her separation – censored at the time by Sarah herself – she compared herself with Queen Victoria, who liked to escape from Buckingham Palace to her private residences as often as possible. 'Victoria and I just wanted to get away. To get away from the system, and people saying no you can't, no you can't, no you can't. That is what the system is . . . I am owned.' Asked to elaborate, she gestured around the rococo chamber of Buckingham Palace where the conversation was taking place: 'Modern life isn't, you know. . .' and rolled her eyes. 'I cannot stick to the guidelines because . . . well, we're not being real.'

The effervescent Fergie might have fared better if Her Royal Highness The Duchess of York had been a private individual, unreliant on state subsidy. Thanks largely to her, this has now become the case. But the fate of Sarah Ferguson – never given anything more by the Palace machine than enough rope to hang herself – cannot be blamed entirely on her vulgar high spirits. The royal system is equally at fault. That such a lightweight should by virtue of marriage become patron of more than a dozen charities, not to mention the Chancellor of Salford University, is a mark of the absurd self-expectations of monarchy.

As an example of what happens when the monarchy attempts to adopt a 'fresh and youthful approach' to its duties, the Duchess of York was a potentially terminal failure. To one appalled commentator she became 'the embodiment of the modern monarchy,' who 'might almost have "Do as I say, not do as I do" stencilled in gold on the back of her bomber jacket.' It was not her romantic escapades that troubled him, argued *The Sunday Times*'s Robert Harris, nor even her estimated fifteen holidays over the previous two years; these, after all, were the timeless prerogatives of the idle rich. 'It is her insistence on being called "Your Royal Highness" while exemplifying money-grubbing, unroyal lowness. . . Being asked to call Fergie "Your Royal Highness" is like being asked by a remote tribe to join in its worship of a gnarled tree-stump. You may go through the motions, but you secretly snigger at such primitive customs.'

The Yorks' marriage was slowly collapsing throughout 1991, when the ever more erratic Fergie grew increasingly isolated. Although the growing volume of their rows unnerved the royal staff, their marital problems were not so apparent to the public, who were completely taken by surprise when the end came. Royal observers, however, noted that the Yorks made only nine public appearances together that year; the duchess herself carried out only 170 official engagements, compared with 455 by the Queen, 258 by the Princess of Wales and 504 by the workaholic Princess Anne.

During the previous year, 1990, the peripatetic Andrew had spent only forty-two nights with his fun-loving wife, leaving her too much time on her hands for the dizzy round of parties, balls and holidays which were her natural bent. Stubbornly unwilling to adapt to the royal norm, Fergie committed the cardinal royal sin of allowing other men to squire her through her husband's absences. The beginning of the end came early in 1992, when a cleaner was reported to have found a cache of photographs in a Mayfair flat recently vacated by Steve Wyatt, a debonair Texan oilman of her acquaintance. They showed Wyatt and the duchess on holiday together in Morocco, apparently having a better time than was appropriate in her husband's absence. Although the pictures were handed to the police without being published, the tabloids' descriptions left little to the public imagination.

Through a loyal Palace source, Andrew had already seen his

wife's own snaps of the trip – among them, to his rage, a shot
of Wyatt hugging Princess Beatrice. The royal Christmas of
1991 was thus spent discussing the uncomfortable prospect of
the first male royal divorce since that of Henry VIII. Once
the New Year had dawned without any sign of reconciliation,
and with the duchess virtually withdrawn from public life, a
formal end to the marriage began to look inevitable. Advised
(which means ordered) by the Queen to cancel a scheduled
skiing trip, Fergie went anyway – without Andrew, but with
the children, despite the fact that they were not fully recovered
from chicken-pox. She then made matters worse by heading off
on yet another sunshine 'freebie' – this time to Palm Beach,
Florida, escorted by her father to a polo-club bash at which
she hoped to see Wyatt (who sensibly stayed away). In typical
Fergie fashion, she managed to grace with her royal presence a
club which excluded Jewish members. She also took along her
father's lover, Lesley Player, as an 'Extra Lady-in-Waiting', part
of the royal entourage. Even by her own standards, this was
Fergie at her most outrageous: apparently facilitating her father's
fornication at the taxpayers' expense.

Before boarding the flight home, Sarah disappeared into a
small room off the airport's VIP lounge to make a private
telephone call. Those nearby could not help but overhear her
increasingly anguished end of the conversation, which seemed
to end abruptly. They then watched the duchess re-emerge in
tears. Only later did they learn that she had been speaking to
her husband, who had hung up on her.

On the return flight her behaviour astonished even battle-
hardened royal reporters who thought they had seen everything.
As things stood, the red carpet was not exactly being shampooed
in readiness for the Duchess of York's arrival back in Britain.
Yet she chose this moment, in the first-class cabin of a scheduled
flight, to drink several glasses of champagne, smoke a few
cigarettes, put a paper bag over her head and wander around
throwing food at other passengers.

Although a sign of the desperate strain she was under, it was
to prove Fergie's last hurrah before the inevitable summons to
see her parents-in-law. The Queen, about to leave for Australia,

persuaded the couple to agree to the usual three-month 'cooling-off' period. This time, however, it was barely six weeks before Sarah's lawyer, Charles Doughty of Withers, was meeting the Queen's solicitor, Sir Matthew Farrer, to begin negotiating the terms of a formal separation. When news of the discussions leaked to the *Daily Mail*, Buckingham Palace was forced into a premature announcement on 19 March, the sixth anniversary of the day on which it had announced the couple's engagement.

> Last week, lawyers acting for the Duchess of York initiated discussions about a formal separation for the Duke and Duchess. These discussions are not yet complete and nothing more will be said until they are. The Queen hopes that the media will spare the Duke and Duchess of York and their children any intrusion.

Behind the bald fifty-four-word statement, from which the usual expressions of regret were markedly absent, there lurked a background briefing of unprecedented ferocity. The Queen's press secretary, Charles Anson, stressed to royal reporters that it was the duchess who had initiated the separation proceedings. All her forthcoming public engagements were cancelled as of that moment. She was accused of assisting the *Mail* in breaking the story – a charge roundly denied by its editor, Sir David English.

After the briefing, Anson talked further with the BBC's court correspondent, Paul Reynolds. Moments later, the results were relayed somewhat breathlessly to listeners to BBC Radio 4's lunchtime news programme, *The World at One*. 'The knives are out for Fergie at the Palace,' said Reynolds, himself sounding stunned by what he had just heard. 'I have never known such anger here.' Blaming the duchess for the leaks to the *Daily Mail*, Anson was now 'retaliating' by talking about her 'unsuitability for public life'. The detail which had apparently 'most stung' the Queen was the revelation in the *Mail* that she had granted Sarah a private lunch to discuss her problems. To the Palace, only the duchess herself could have been the source of this: 'It is highly unusual for this kind of lunch to pitch up in the papers.' The Queen was said to be 'very, very sad at the whole thing'.

She also thought the timing forced upon the Palace, in the first week of a general election campaign, 'highly undesirable'. If Reynolds wished to add that Her Majesty was 'pretty angry', he was advised, he 'would not be far wrong'.

Anson was subsequently obliged to offer a public apology to the duchess, and his resignation to the Queen (which she declined). The shoddy treatment meted out to Fergie then created a new and unlikely alliance between the errant Sarah and her press tormentors. 'Nothing in her life as a royal,' observed one reporter, 'has become her like the leaving of it.'

Over the next few months there followed a series of re-unions, joint appearances and apparent reconciliations between the Yorks, which thoroughly confused the watching world. Andrew appeared keen to salvage the marriage, while his wife still wanted out. Slowly it became clear that, in terms of their private differences, it was not so much Fergie's errant behaviour which had precipitated the split as Andrew's failure to support her through a long period of public and private difficulty.

Although she was on her best (that is, her least visible) pub-lic behaviour, even giving an interview to ITN to say that she was maintaining a 'low profile', Sarah ignored his pleas for a reconciliation and continued the negotiations towards a financial settlement. Taking her daughters out of school for a thirty-six-day wander around the fleshpots of the Far East was not the way to endear her to a nation which might otherwise have felt sympathy. When the 'family friend' who escorted her on that trip, an American financial adviser named Johnny Bryan, subsequently reappeared in the public prints, sucking her toes beside a swimming-pool on the French Riviera, Fergie's days as a royal were over. At the time, ironically enough, she was at Balmoral with the Queen, on her best behaviour while her financial settlement was being finalized. Banished from the castle the next day, she returned to London by public transport, and took her daughters home to face a less than regal future.

Little has since been seen of Sarah, Duchess of York. With the same brutal haste with which the abdicating King Edward VIII was hustled overnight into his overseas exile, the once popular Fergie had been declared, in royal terms, a non-person. And a non-person she must remain, as long as she wishes to accept financial support from the royal family. Although she eventually won £85,000 in damages from the French magazine which had first invaded her privacy, penalty clauses inserted into Sarah's settlement threaten withdrawal of funds, even the potential loss of her children, if she were to sell her story, write a book or otherwise compromise her former in-laws. Even so, they had reportedly scaled her down to a mere £500,000 lump sum, with an additional £1.4 million trust fund for her daughters, who would also own the £600,000 house in which she would be allowed to live.

'At the end of the day,' as Fergie put it before writing herself out of the royal soap opera, 'you die alone.'

CHAPTER 4

THE OVER-EXTENDED FAMILY

*'The royal scene is simply a presentation of ourselves
behaving well.'*

DAME REBECCA WEST

HAD RECENT BRITISH HISTORY TAKEN AN ONLY SLIGHTLY different course, Queen Elizabeth II's most obscure cousin, the Duke of Gloucester, would now be King Richard IV, and the Queen herself a 'fringe' royal: Princess Elizabeth, Mrs Philip Mountbatten. An older version, perhaps, of her cousin Princess Alexandra, suddenly deprived of the state subsidy on which she has relied all her life, the little-known Mrs Mountbatten would now find herself a member of a distinctly endangered species.

The sometime King Edward VIII and Mrs Simpson (later the Duke and Duchess of Windsor) died childless. Even if he had not been forced to abdicate – if he had been permitted to marry his American divorcee, morganatically or otherwise – it seems quite probable that Edward would have felt under no pressure to breed heirs. As king he would have had three younger brothers to ensure the succession or, if necessary, to succeed him themselves. The oldest of these, the Duke of York, had no sons – and, as it turned out, predeceased his older brother by twenty years. He would never have become King George VI, nor his daughter Elizabeth II.

On King Edward's death in 1972, he would have been succeeded by his second brother Henry, Duke of Gloucester – whose older son, Prince William, was killed in a flying accident that year. Already gravely ill, Henry himself died only two years later, in 1974. For nearly twenty years now, the British King would thus have been Henry's younger son, Prince Richard – whose ninety-one-year-old widowed mother, Princess Alice, Dowager Duchess of Gloucester, would now be the Queen Mother.

A practising architect who inherited his dukedom reluctantly, Richard would probably have made an even more reluctant king. So discreetly has he gone about his royal role with his Danish-born wife, Brigitte, and so clear has he made it that he would rather have remained a private citizen, that he is less widely known to the British public than some rather less royal figures: the Princess of Wales's brother, for instance, until recently Charles, Viscount Althorp, now the 9th Earl Spencer, a budding television star and leader of the sub-royal bratpack known as 'the nearly royals'. Along with Fergie, Princess Michael of Kent and the Queen's youngest son, Prince Edward, the 'junior royals' and the 'nearly royals' have between them done more to discredit the modern monarchy than a thousand obscure Prince Richards. Thanks to them, the dignity of the 'family monarchy' had been compromised long before the whole house of cards collapsed with all three marriages of the Queen's children in 1992.

In the National Portrait Gallery in London hangs a celebrated portrait by Sir James Gunn entitled 'Conversation Piece', depicting the royal family taking tea at the Royal Lodge, Windsor, in 1950. The inevitable corgi lurks bottom left while King George VI takes his ease, the Queen pours the tea in motherly fashion, and the two princesses hang upon their father's words. It is an idealized version of a scene which could be repeated in millions of less opulent households around the land. The portrait became an icon for the post-war House of Windsor: the first family of the land, leading a life of unimpeachable respectability, a family like any other enjoying a cosy domesticity.

A 1990 version would have included the Princess of Wales, the Duchess of York and Captain Mark Phillips – all of whom would now have to be 'whited out' in the manner of communist Chinese propaganda photographs. As mother, the Queen would be pouring tea for an immediate family whose private lives have been far from flawless. Sensibly, no such portrait has been commissioned.

The contemporary equivalent has been a long series of group photographs, usually taken by Lords Snowdon or Lichfield, showing a vast panoramic family gathering around the Queen at weddings, anniversaries and christenings. The family image has extended to include an ever-growing list of cousins, in-laws and other minor royals increasingly seen by the British public, their paymasters, as 'hangers on'. It was inevitable that some of them would let the side down.

Just as the monarchy, to survive, must rise above party politics, so it must practise the fiction of being 'beyond' class – unaligned, that is, with any specific stratum of Britain's entrenched class distinctions. Although self-evidently members of the landed gentry, with country seats scattered around the south of England and Scotland, most members of the royal family manage to some extent to pull off this difficult deception. Some, like Princess Michael, may go hunting; others, like her brother-in-law the Duke of Kent, may retain strong military connections. But the British aristocracy is, even by its own standards, remarkably snobbish. To most of Britain's oldest families, repositories of inherited wealth and privilege, the Windsors are a bunch of continental *parvenus*, much less inherently grand than themselves. As for those who marry into them, especially foreigners such as Princess Michael: they are the worst form of *arrivistes*.

In the mid-1980s, thanks to the arrival on the scene of Sarah Ferguson, Duchess of York, the hearty philistinism of her hus-band, the lack of direction of Prince Edward, and to some extent the mischievous high spirits of mid-period Diana, the junior court was branded with an all too distinct class label. To the consternation of the nation, at a time of national austerity, the younger royals firmly allied themselves with the nation's gilded youth, the upper-class Hooray Henrys who constituted an idle rich more loathed than at any time in the twentieth century. If this unseemly spectacle was symbolized by one specific moment, it would be that captured on camera at Royal Ascot when Sarah and Diana, bedecked in four-figure frocks and hats, playfully poked their umbrellas up the backside of the courtier clearing their path to the royal enclosure. Their victim, as fate would have it, was Major Hugh Lindsay, who would the following year lose his life in the skiing accident which nearly killed the Prince of Wales, and gave the young royals momentary pause.

Fergie, of course, was the worst offender, constantly on holiday, openly money-grubbing, eventually caught in the arms of another man; even before the revelations of 1992–93, the Duchess of York had passed beyond the pale. Her husband, Prince Andrew, showed little more sign of public service to justify the £249,000 a year of public money which supplemented his salary as a career naval officer. How much more public money did it cost, for instance, to maintain, let alone guard their vulgar £5 million mansion, which anyway stood empty for most of the year, at a time when record numbers of homeowners were being dispossessed and thousands slept rough on the streets?

Prince Edward's pursuit of a career in the commercial arm of the theatre, while doing little else to justify a public subsidy of £96,000 a year, also caused growing public offence. It was his 1986 television spectacular, *It's a Royal Knockout*, that reduced most of the 'junior' royals – Anne reluctantly included – to grotesque parodies of themselves. Marina Ogilvy, daughter of the Queen's cousin, Princess Alexandra, tarnished the family escutcheon by going public over her troubled relations with her parents. The £250,000 Charles Althorp had spare to lavish on his much-publicized twenty-first birthday party in 1985 (though he was, of course, nowhere near the Civil List) tarred them all with the same brush. From their trademark traffic offences to sundry tabloid excesses, the young royals were riding for a fall of dramatic proportions. As a catalyst, it required only a sharp focus of the kind which emerged early in 1991, when the nation had an unexpected, sombre measure against which to find the young royals wanting.

★

'This country is at war, though you would never believe it from the shenanigans of some members of Her Majesty's clan,' raged *The Sunday Times*, Britain's highest-selling 'quality' Sunday newspaper, in February 1991. 'It is the exploits and public demeanour of the minor royals and nearly royals which causes most offence.'

There were two ways of looking at the Gulf War, then three weeks old. One, held by a substantial and voluble minority, was that Britain had agreed to become a minor component of the largest military machine ever assembled, with a view to bombing into submission a desert state of sixteen million people whose only crime was to be led by a dangerous maniac. The other was that voiced by *The Sunday Times*: 'Britain's armed forces are waging war against the fourth-largest military machine in the world. They stand on the brink of the biggest land battle since the Second World War, a battle in which some of the nation's finest young men and women are expected to risk their lives.' The paper then warmed to its theme. On the home front, 'too many of the young royals and their entourages carry on regardless with their peacetime lifestyles, parading a mixture of upper-class decadence and insensitivity which disgusts the public and demeans the monarchy. The Queen should put a stop to it.'

The previous Thursday morning the editor of *The Sunday Times*, Andrew Neil, had been reviewing the daily newspapers on BBC Television's *Breakfast News* programme. At the height of the Gulf War, he was struck by the profusion of royal excess chronicled on the tabloid front pages. 'I once described some members of the royal family as behaving as if they were in a soap opera,' Neil concluded. 'Now I would like to apologize. I have been unfair to soap operas.' The programme's presenter, Nicholas Witchell, laughingly warned Neil that he might be run down by a Rolls-Royce as he left the studios.

Back at his office, Neil himself began to compose the leading article which was to prove so influential. 'It is unfortunate,' he wrote, 'that no member of the royal family is on active service in this war. The Duke of York served bravely in the Falklands but there are no royals, or nearly royals, in the Gulf.' On the contrary, the conduct of the younger royals 'at a time of national crisis' was 'helping to undermine the very role of the royal family'.

The Duchess of York, as usual, bore the brunt of the attack. On the ski slopes yet again the previous month, returning only after the war had broken out, she had that week been spotted 'playing with her gang, very publicly, at a high-spirited dinner in a London restaurant'. Her husband, still a serving officer in the Royal Navy, had meanwhile been enjoying a couple of days' golf on a 'sunny Spanish links'. The Duke of Edinburgh and the Prince of Wales *had* taken up arms, but only against innocent birds: 'Not even war, it seems, can stop the last shoot of the season at Sandringham.'

Prince Edward, then still working for a West End production company, was traduced for failing to lay on entertainment for the troops. The Princess of Wales's brother, Viscount Althorp, had recently confessed to an adulterous weekend in Paris with a journalist named Sally Anne Lasson. The Queen's nephew, Viscount Linley, twelfth in line to the throne, had 'graced the front page of Thursday's *Sun* in fancy dress, wearing red lipstick and holding on to various males in drag'. Linley had since absented himself to the Caribbean island of Mustique – whither his mother, Princess Margaret, had also been bound until the Queen had 'grounded' her sister in Blighty for the duration.

Neil failed to say that both these incidents had taken place long before the outbreak of war. Althorp's night of shame with Miss Lasson dated from a year before, but had resurfaced only recently when her account of the affair appeared in *The News of the World*. The Linley photographs dated from a birthday party on 29 November the previous year, six weeks before the outbreak of hostilities; but *The Sunday Times*'s sister paper, *The Sun*, chose not to point this out when printing the photographs that week. Neil also omitted to mention the fact that *all* the newspapers involved – *The News of the World, The Sun* and indeed *The Sunday Times* – belonged to the same man, Rupert Murdoch.

The following morning yet another Murdoch newspaper, *Today*, devoted its front page to the results of a television poll conducted by Murdoch's satellite television station, Sky News. Beneath the headline QUEEN IN CRISIS, *Today* reported that

83 per cent of Sky viewers who phoned in were 'disgusted' with the royals' behaviour. Why, asked *The Guardian* the next day, was the Murdoch press 'after' the royals? 'Unlikely as it is that he actually *orders* his editors to chastise or pillory the royal family, they must know that this is the way to his heart.'

Murdoch's other upmarket paper, *The Times*, dissented from the tirades of its siblings, loftily dismissing them as 'po-faced puritans'. *The Sun* also deemed it too early (as yet) to risk offending its readers' instinctive loyalty to the crown, indulging instead in some highly personalized internal warfare: 'With few exceptions, the royal family works a damn sight harder than their self-appointed critics. They have as much right to relax as the newspaper editors who criticize them.' In a self-important review of the episode the following Sunday (which began, ironically enough, with Neil and his 'senior editors' enjoying a night out at a fashionable London restaurant), *The Sunday Times* hit back at *The Sun* as 'the paper which has done most to debase the coinage of the monarchy'.

The petty editorial bickering did little to diminish the impact of the original article. *The Sunday Times* leader was to prove remarkably influential, starting the downward slide in the royal fortunes which would continue during 1992–93 – when the same paper would again be playing a major role in destabilizing the monarchy. Harangued in mid-1992 for serializing Morton's book about the Wales marriage, Neil essentially pleaded justification: that the story had been proved to be true, that the marriage of the future king and queen was a legitimate matter of public interest, and that the protests from the Palace and elsewhere were merely blaming the messenger for the message. Subsequent events entirely vindicated his decision.

At the time, however, both editor and proprietor inevitably stood accused of being republicans out to destroy the monarchy. They were not helped by their chief executive, Andrew Knight, who loyally defended his boss against charges of sedition in mid-1992, but later regretted the decision to serialize Morton. All three were to be key players in a long-running debate about the press's role in the monarchy's problems.

Rupert Murdoch, although well-known as an iconoclast on an

international scale, likes to be thought of as a monarchist. As an Australian by birth, if no longer by citizenship, he is in favour of abolishing the monarchy in his native land;* as the owner of vast British newspaper and satellite broadcasting companies, it is not in his interests to be perceived as anti-royal in the United Kingdom. In the words of Knight, overseer of his British operations, Murdoch 'may have been a republican in his youth' but he is now a convert: 'For all his explicit horror of English upper-class snobbery, [and] his suspicion of the British establishment, he believes strongly in the institution of monarchy here.'

Neil, too, has established a reputation as an anti-establishment figure, not least in a celebrated libel case in which he extolled the virtues of Tramp's discotheque over the Garrick Club as symbols of the 'new' and the 'old' Britain. Though he has never publicly expressed a personal view on the institution of monarchy, *The Sunday Times* under his editorship has been as vigorous in its assaults on this as on many another British institution. It took the Queen's 'annus horribilis', and the misbehaviour of the younger royals at public expense, for the rest of the press to pluck up the courage to echo his views. At the time of Neil's rage about the 'junior' royals in early 1991, however, *The Sunday Times* was left to fight its own battle. The profits of other newspaper proprietors, let alone their personal interests in the pursuit of power and titles, dictated that their editors still continue to toe the royal line.

Of those newspapers not owned by Murdoch, only the *Daily Mirror* supported *The Sunday Times*'s attack on the younger royals the following morning. Apart from Murdoch's *Today*, Britain's other four daily tabloids all devoted their front pages to the Palace rejoinder, under such belligerently loyal headlines as ROYALS SHOOT DOWN CRITICS (*Daily Mail*), even QUEEN FIRES A PATRIOT (*The Sun*). On the Tuesday, as the Prince and Princess of Wales visited naval personnel in Devon – an engagement which the Palace naturally claimed was

*The author speaks from personal experience. In April 1981, on becoming an executive of Murdoch's *The Times*, he was warmly praised by his new boss for an article in the previous week's *Observer* arguing that Prince Charles should not become Governor-General of Australia – where the monarchy was 'an irrelevance'.

pre-arranged – it began to look as if Neil might be losing his own private side-show to the real war in the Gulf.

As always, however, the editorial decisions of newspapers are adjudicated by their readers. By midweek, it became clear that Neil had struck a public nerve. The country was in need of some light relief from war coverage (especially when more Britons were being killed by their allies than by the enemy). Placed alongside the continuing unease over the royal finances, the junior royal cavortings aroused widespread indignation, at times high passion. Hosting a television discussion of the issue on the Wednesday morning, 13 February, the television talk-show host Robert Kilroy-Silk came to blows with a royalist member of his studio audience. Reporting the incident next day, the *Daily Star* advised the Queen to 'pull the handstitched royal bedclothes back over her pin-curled royal head' and try to forget all the fuss.

Then came the turn of the two rival columnists who took it upon themselves to speak for the long-suffering housewives of Middle England. In the *Daily Express* Jean Rook, the self-styled 'First Lady of Fleet Street' – and usually the first to leap indignantly to the monarchy's defence – seemed to have sniffed a changing public mood. Suddenly, she wrote in her weekly column, everything seemed to be slipping away from the Queen. Why was she allowing her more witless relatives to unpick her life's work? How could these unreal people rule a depressed, war-stricken, terrorist-torn country in which, apart from sensible Anne and genuinely caring Diana, they didn't appear to live on a day-to-day basis? 'She must sort them out. Because she alone is worth the whole Buck House balcony-full of the feeble lot of them.'

Alas for Rook, the editor of the *Daily Express*, Nicholas Lloyd, was due to receive the accolade of knighthood from the Queen the following Tuesday. He removed Rook's column after the first edition, replacing it with a feature on double-glazing, later explaining that he had thought her remarks 'unfair'.

But the editor of the *Daily Mail*, having already received his own knighthood, had no such inhibitions. Sir David English allowed free rein to his own First Lady of Fleet Street, Lynda Lee-Potter, who berated the young royals for 'louche, obtuse insensitivity'. The Queen, wrote Lee-Potter, 'is going through some of the most traumatic and dangerous days of her reign. She needs to look at the facts with clear realism. It's no use listening to deferential royal advisers, flunkeys, or even her husband, whose blinkered arrogance, self-satisfaction and irritability have multiplied over the years.'

After this intriguing, *en passant* side-swipe at Prince Philip, the editor shrewdly steered his columnist back to the financial argument which was invisibly sanctioning all this tabloid licence. After a prophetic call for belt-tightening – 'The Queen could start by asking the government to ensure that she paid tax on her income and investments' – Lee-Potter finally spoke up, on behalf of those Britons currently feeling most beleagured, as is the secret of such column's success. 'It is obscene to read of this unearned, soaring, exempted wealth when the elderly are dying of hypothermia, when homes are being repossessed because hard-working young couples can't keep up their mortgages, and when four hundred small businesses a week are going into receivership through high interest rates.'

Now it was open season on the royals. On TV-AM, Independent Television's rival to the BBC's *Breakfast News*, the cockney soccer star-turned-television pundit Jimmy Greaves accused the Queen of being 'lazy', and 82 per cent of 6,000 *Daily Star* readers phoned the paper's 'hotline' to agree. On *The Sun*'s even hotter line, more than 8,000 of its readers then overturned the paper's editorial stance by voting by a majority of 6-1 that the royals were 'slacking'. By the Friday, 15 February, the pollsters MORI had produced for the *Daily Mail* the results of a much more scientific survey conducted on the two days following *The Sunday Times*'s original assault. Billed on the front page as 'a shock for the Queen', it showed that only 35 per cent of Britons thought the Duchess of York was 'doing enough to support Britain's role in the Gulf'. Her husband, Prince Andrew, fared little better on 50 per cent, and her brother-in-law, Prince Edward, even worse on only 27 per cent.

Still careful in its editorial columns not to offend its largely royalist readership, the *Mail* scrupulously added that 69 per cent *were* satisfied with the Queen, 68 per cent with the Princess of

Wales and 63 per cent with Prince Charles and Princess Anne. Audibly astonished to find itself endorsing *The Sunday Times*'s Andrew Neil, the *Mail*'s editorial, like its columnist two days before, cautiously linked its support for the wave of criticism to pre-established public indignation about the royal finances. 'It is such thoughtless behaviour which gratuitously fans wider criticism of the royal family, such as the fact that the Queen does not pay tax on her income of £1.8 million a day.'* Only, indeed, because the *Mail* so fervently shared the British public's high esteem for the monarchy was it presenting the findings of the poll 'so that the royal family's advisers can digest their implications for the future'. Uriah Heep could not have phrased it better.

The week of 10–17 February 1991 had indeed given Buckingham Palace plenty to think about. As it had begun, even the Palace press office had realized that this was not just another of those storms which would, in its perennially over-optimistic phrase, 'blow over'. The Queen's senior staff had taken the onslaught seriously enough to issue a defensive statement, listing all recent royal engagements connected with the Gulf crisis, within hours of receiving the first edition of *The Sunday Times* that Saturday evening – even as Neil was arriving in Covent Garden for his celebratory dinner with colleagues. Later that night, before the final edition, Neil decided to print the royal rebuttal on the front page – secure in the knowledge that it would draw even more attention to his inflammatory editorial, and that his rivals would all be printing it anyway.

The following Sunday *The Sunday Times* concluded an eight-page pat on its own back by claiming that within a week 'one editorial in one Sunday newspaper, written during a war, had been backed by the editors of four papers, three of which support the Tory Party, read by 11 million readers every day.' Although the article again failed to specify the respective ownership of the relevant newspapers, its findings made undeniably grim reading for the Palace.

Already the *Mail*'s MORI poll had broadened the argument with some equally striking statistics. Only 38 per cent of the

---

*An inaccurate figure of which the *Mail* could not yet disabuse itself. *See* Chapter 5.

British people believed that Britain would still have a monarchy in a hundred years' time. One in five believed it would have gone within fifty years. In the previous few months, public esteem for the royal family had fallen among 14 per cent of voters; 38 per cent considered the royal family 'an expensive luxury the country cannot afford' (as opposed to 24 per cent a year before). On the financial front, 73 per cent said the Queen should pay income tax; 65 per cent said the royals 'should not receive as much money as they do'.

For all its opportunism, *The Sunday Times*'s Gulf War outburst had contrived to strip off another layer of the anti-royal feeling which had been steadily growing around Britain. This was still 1991; while condemning the younger royals with a vengeance, the paper had taken care to mollify its older readers by stressing that the Queen herself had 'of course' behaved 'impeccably'. It was a motif which was to recur constantly in press coverage of subsequent royal scandals. At the time, it took a lone reader's letter from Surrey to dissent from this judgement, suggesting that the Queen had 'refused to send the royal yacht *Britannia* to the Gulf, despite a refit which cost the taxpayer £7 million' and so was 'obviously not prepared to make personal sacrifices'.

Evidently unconcerned about his knighthood, Andrew Neil was to continue to haunt the royal family via the might of the organ at his disposal throughout the increasingly troubled days ahead. The controversial role of Murdoch, Knight and Neil in the demise of the Wales marriage will be further discussed later in these pages. But there are two important conclusions to be drawn from this early episode of the 'junior' royals and the Gulf War: that one newspaper's responses to another's story (royal or otherwise) is invariably conditioned by their own permanent circulation war, and that those newspapers boldly criticizing the monarchy – then as now – can justifiably claim to have the facts on their side.

Since the early 1980s the younger royal princelings and their wives had come to see themselves as media celebrities, posing for the covers of glossy magazines and selling snaps of their children to the women's weeklies. Every member of the royal family has now taken part in, often hosted, television programmes – from the Prince of Wales's long-faced documentaries on architecture and the environment to the demeaning antics of Prince Edward's *It's a Royal Knockout*. Even the Queen Mother (who hates the sound of her own voice, and thus rarely broadcasts) has taken part in a film on her racehorses. The Queen herself has escorted Huw (soon Sir Huw) Weldon on a tour of the royal treasures, and starred at the rest of her family's expense in an official BBC documentary about her forty years on the throne, *Elizabeth R*. If she resents the perception that the British monarchy has become an overgrown television soap opera peopled by would-be media stars, Elizabeth II knows all too well that she has only herself to blame.

It was in 1969 that the Queen was reluctantly persuaded by her imaginative young Australian press secretary, William Heseltine – more recently, as Sir William, her private secretary – to sanction a television film about her family's life, both on and off stage. *Royal Family*, screened throughout Britain and the Commonwealth on the night before Charles's investiture as Prince of Wales at Caernarvon, was an enormous popular success. The royal ratings had dipped during the 1960s; now, thanks entirely to this film, the monarchy began to bask in an affection and respect that remained undimmed until the mid-1980s. It was based on strong personal feelings about the individual players in the royal drama, which were awakened entirely by this film in the summer of 1969. For the first time in their history, the British public were able to peep into the private lives of their royals, to glimpse them at play as well as at work – to see them no longer as semi-divine, symbolic archetypes, but as mere human beings.

The next day's pomp and ceremony at Caernarvon was viewed in an entirely new context: Prince Philip, solemnly looking on in his Field Marshal's uniform, had last been seen rowing his son Andrew into a Scottish sunset; the Prince of Wales, now declaring himself his mother's 'liege man of life and limb', had reduced his brother Edward to tears by snapping a cello string in his face; and the majestic hands placing a coronet on her eldest son's head had last been seen wielding a Balmoral barbecue fork. The royals may not quite have been a family like any other; but for the first time they were very powerfully demonstrated to be a family, who did relatively normal things in relatively normal ways.

The era of the cosy domestic monarchy had been given a wholly fresh impetus. In the subsequent twenty years, its popularity has been consistently shored up by this dramatic new approach – anathema, no doubt, to previous generations (and, of course, to Walter Bagehot, who would have been rushing to draw the blinds). But its success has been double-edged. The voyeuristic fascination engendered by that film has not merely created an insatiable appetite around the world for the flimsiest titbits of royal gossip. It has given every Briton, even those indifferent to the institution of monarchy, views on the changing cast of royal characters as strong as those on their favourite television and movie stars.

It has also promoted the public perception that the royals are just another branch of show business, famous merely for being famous, and dutifully using that fame to raise money for charities of their choice. Since Princess Michael of Kent officially opened a motorway café, all the royals have been regarded as fair game for exploitation in board-rooms throughout the land. And beyond: Americans are now regularly charged thousands of dollars a plate to attend dinners graced by visiting royals, as if they were mere politicians running for office.

Royalty has thus begun to move increasingly closer to a commercial arena of which it had previously been rightly wary. Tradition dictates that no central member of the royal family can ever be seen to endorse a commercial product – although the curious system of royal warrants, by which shopkeepers and manufacturers can advertise that they supply goods to royalty, would seem to come perilously close. Early in his marriage, however, Mark Phillips was permitted by the Queen to accept commercial sponsorship, some discreet services to Daks clothes or Range-Rover cars further helping to pay off the expense of farming Gatcombe. From the Land-Rover Gatcombe Horse Trials it is but a short step to the sponsorship of monarchy as if it were a sporting event: today the BBC might televise the Courvoisier Princely Polo Challenge, tomorrow the Pimms Opening of Parliament.

Beyond the money-grubbing, showbiz dimension, a subtler consequence of the 1969 film was the subliminal impression that the entire royal family, the Queen included, were now card-carrying members of Equity, ready and willing to put on an act for the cameras. Did they really have barbecues at which Mum spread the tablecloth and Dad cooked the sausages? Or were they just laying one on for the telly? As the Sunday columnist Sir Peregrine Worsthorne perceived: 'Offstage Laurence Olivier did not have to go on being a king; no more, it was suggested, did the Queen have to go on being a queen. She, too, once her day's work is over, takes off her crown, lays down the orb and puts up her feet. Thus was the monarchy made to seem just another job – a very important, glamorous and well-paid job, to be sure, but not fundamentally different from that of the stars of stage and screen.'

One of the most eloquent royal apologists of recent years, Worsthorne was writing in 1991, early in the monarchy's present crisis. At the time of the film, in 1969, he was also among the first to perceive the dangers. Sounding uncannily like Walter Bagehot, he wrote:

> Mystery is essential to monarchy, and becomes more impor-
> tant as the real power drains away. When kings could chop off
> your head at whim they could afford to be friendly, accessible
> and human because nobody dared to take liberties for fear
> of losing their life. A constitutional monarchy, having no
> capacity to frighten, must needs overawe. That is why it is
> so much more important for a constitutional monarchy to
> keep up the barriers, to be hedged about with protocol, to
> be surrounded by chilling formality than for an absolute
> monarchy. Initially the public will love seeing the royal
> family as not essentially different from anybody else and
> in the short term letting the cameras in will enhance the
> monarchy's popularity. But in the not-so-long run familiarity
> will breed, if not contempt, well, familiarity.

The *Times* columnist Bernard Levin agreed that it had been 'a colossal mistake' for the royal family to 'come down off their thrones and thronelets, and show themselves to be human beings just like their subjects . . . Once the figures had stepped down out of the golden coach, they became fair game: until then, they were made of china, gingerbread, gold and silver, clouds, regal smiles, sceptres, glitter, understanding and history.' But the genie could not be put back in the bottle. 'If the royal family tried to get back to its remoteness, it would only make things worse; they would be charged with knowing nothing about the lives of ordinary people, and accused of selfishness, indifference and even stirring their tea anti-clockwise.'

This new perspective on royalty has come to engender confusion in the public mind between the monarchy and the royal family itself. Nothing could be more damaging to the House of Windsor, or indeed further from the constitutional truth, than the contemporary perception that the royal family *is* the monarchy. During the Queen's recent travails, it is royalists more than republicans who have been at pains to hammer this point home. No amount of salacious photographs, in the words of the politician and constitutionalist Enoch Powell, could undermine the authority, 'under God's providence', of the sovereign – because the United Kingdom is 'not governed by something called the royal family. It is governed by the single person of the sovereign.'

Under this heading, too, Worsthorne waxed cruel to be kind: 'Such disproportionate importance has been allotted to the royal family, as against the monarch herself, that even serious commentators seem to suppose that if the one falls into disrepute, so must the other. It is this assumption that needs to be most urgently challenged . . . It is not a family that is crowned. It is an individual.' *The Sunday Telegraph* subsequently took the views of its columnist (and former editor) further: 'We have been encouraged to confuse the whole entourage of princes, princesses, etc with the institution itself. But the divinity that doth hedge a king is no impediment to telephoto lenses: the fewer objects they are given to focus on, the less likely that the hedge will be uprooted altogether.'

In 1872, when church services were held to celebrate the Prince of Wales's recovery from a bout of typhoid, Benjamin Disraeli

was moved to declare that the influence of the crown was
not confined merely to political affairs. 'England is a domestic
country. Here the home is revered and the hearth sacred. The
nation is represented by a family – the Royal Family; and if that
family is educated with a sense of responsibility and a sentiment
of public duty, it is difficult to exaggerate the salutary influence
they may exercise over a nation.'

'It's a big if, ain't it, Dizzy?' asked *The Daily Telegraph*'s
Hugh Massingberd in August 1992, watching with dismay as
the Queen's daughter-in-law frolicked beside that French pool.
The more the junior royals let the side down, the more British
monarchists felt obliged to quote the exact wording of the Oath
of Allegiance taken by judges and soldiers, MPs and members
of the Privy Council – to the monarch herself and 'her heirs and
successors according to law'. The rest of the royal family, in the
words of Michael Ancram MP, chairman of the Conservative
Party's backbench constitutional committee, 'are not part of the
constitutional monarchy, and what they do should not raise
questions about it'. The purpose of any trimming of the Civil
List was 'to make the vital separation in the public mind between
the monarchy and the royal family, between the constitutionally
essential and the non-essential'.

The non-essential, to the British public who subsidize them,
have for years included those royals who do not give 'value
for money' – who do not, in other words, appear to perform sufficient public duties to account for their annual public
subsidy. In a somewhat crude but effective exercise, the 'value-
for-money' quotient is calculated by taking the amount of the
Civil List allowance paid to a particular royal and dividing
it by the number of official duties he or she undertakes.

In 1992, for instance, the fifteen 'senior' members of the
royal family carried out a total of 3,084 official engagements
in the UK, averaging 206 per person. Though this marked a
slight decrease on the 1991 figure of 3,100, an additional 378
days were spent on official duties abroad. Prince Philip had
the biggest individual drop in his UK workload, down by
nearly one-sixth on 1991, although he spent ten extra working
days abroad (*see* table on p.112).

In 1992, as frequently in previous years, the best 'value for money' was given by Princess Anne, whose Civil List allowance subsidized 471 public engagements in the UK at a rate per engagement of £484.08. Her brother Edward was only 78p more expensive, but with barely 40 per cent of her workload. Compare this with, for instance, £1,634.33 per public engagement for Princess Margaret, or £1,436 for Prince Philip. The worst value was given by the Duke of York, at £2,490 per engagement, many of which just happened to take place at golf clubs; in an already testing year for the duke, however, the number of his official engagements was (in the Palace's wording) 'necessarily reduced, due to his duties as a serving officer in the Royal Navy'.

The Civil List allowances of 1992 had been established under the so-called 'Thatcher deal' of July 1990 – a financial settlement negotiated for the royal family by the prime minister and her Chancellor of the Exchequer, John Major. Implemented without any public debate, it was immune to scrutiny, review or even discussion by parliament. The Queen's personal Civil List was fixed for the next ten years at an inflation-proof average of £9.15 million. At a time when much lower pay claims were being rejected in both the public and private sectors, the secret deal guaranteed the monarch and ten other members of the royal family annual increases of 7.5 per cent – more than double the then rate of inflation.

The full details of the £98 million package were, first, that the Queen herself would receive £7.9 million in 1991, rising over ten years to £10.4 million in the year 2000. Other members of the royal family would then share a further £2.5 million, also rising by 7.5 per cent a year, the Queen Mother receiving £643,000 in 1991–92, Prince Philip £359,000, the Duke of York £249,000, the Princess Royal £228,000, Princess Margaret £219,000, Prince Edward £96,000 and Princess Alice, Dowager Duchess of Gloucester £87,000, with the Dukes of Kent and Gloucester and Princess Alexandra on £212,000 each.

As part of the emergency measures announced by John Major in November 1992, the Queen Mother and Prince Philip will remain on the Civil List; but the Queen will henceforth 'return' her

ROYAL ENGAGEMENTS IN 1992 *(1991 IN BRACKETS)*

	★A	★B	★C	Total	Abroad (Days) ★D
The Queen	127	51	269	447 *(455)*	26 *(26)*
The Duke of Edinburgh	125	96	29	250 *(298)*	81 *(71)*
The Queen Mother	55	25	11	91 *(100)*	1 *(2)*
The Prince of Wales	151	65	99	315 *(301)*	38 *(54)*
The Princess of Wales	188	28	19	235 *(258)*	24 *(25)*
The Duke of York	65	31	4	100 *(83)*	5 *(9)*
Prince Edward	104	65	30	199 *(195)*	53 *(16)*
The Princess Royal	299	94	78	471 *(504)*	59 *(54)*
Princess Margaret	92	30	12	134 *(103)*	8 *(0)*
The Duke of Gloucester	131	25	17	173 *(144)*	17 *(25)*
The Duchess of Gloucester	113	26	15	154 *(97)*	10 *(7)*
The Duke of Kent	116	42	34	192 *(190)*	22 *(35)*
The Duchess of Kent	122	21	7	150 *(173)*	19 *(20)*
Princess Alexandra	119	15	10	144 *(148)*	17 *(7)*
Princess Alice	15	3	13	31 *(51)*	0 *(0)*

★A: Official engagements: opening ceremonies, and other engagements

★B: Receptions, lunches, dinners and banquets

★C: Other engagements: incl. investitures, meetings attended and audiences given.

★D: On official tours abroad the Queen carried out 141 engagements, the Duke of Edinburgh 384, the Queen Mother 2, the Prince of Wales 145, the Princess of Wales 107, the Duke of York 33, Prince Edward 218, the Princess Royal 215 and Princess Margaret 5.

other relatives' allowances, totalling £879,000, to the Treasury. She will continue to support them out of the £7.9 million she herself receives – on the same basis as she already supported the Dukes of Kent and Gloucester and Princess Alexandra. In other words, the 'fringe' royals, from Prince Andrew down, are not really 'axed' from the Civil List at all. They will continue to be subsidized to the same extent, merely lopping the odd £0.9 million off the Queen's £7.9 million – a reduction in her tax-free subsidy of just 11.1 per cent.

This may prove a serious mistake on the part of the House of Windsor, fuelling public resentment of the Queen's wealth by perpetuating the confusion in the public mind between the royal family and the monarchy. As the figures are examined, more-over, it will not go unnoticed that any normal employee would face a tax liability on perks such as free accommodation and a company car, not to mention lavish 'expenses', while the Queen and her family remain exempt. It might have proved wiser to opt for the plan under discussion in October 1992, whereby a central fund would be established to remunerate lower-ranking royals pro rata for undertaking public appearances. A central, computerized clearing system at the Palace would also be able to provide such back-up as transport and accommodation, rather in the manner of a theatrical agency handling its clients' bookings. With more than a thousand charitable organizations currently enjoying the patronage of a member of the royal family, some such system would streamline the business of the 'family firm' as well as making it less vulnerable to financial criticism. There would be no change, however, in the quid pro quo for mem-bership of the lucrative royal team: certain standards of decorous behaviour, both public and private.

Anyone coming from a much smaller lifestyle into the royal family is in for 'a major change', as the Duchess of York herself put it to BBC Radio 4's *Woman's Hour* in 1991. 'Suddenly you're thrown into the public eye and [you must] change totally to suit the outside media and the environment.' Sir Angus Ogilvy, Princess Alexandra's husband, has also privately remarked that no-one can quite imagine what it is like to marry into *that* family. But it does have its compensations.

Despite his own successful career in the City, Sir Angus's wife still receives her tax-free allowance from public funds of £212,000 a year, and the couple live in a royal residence, Thatched House Lodge in Richmond Park. The younger brother of the Queen's Lord Chamberlain, the Earl of Airlie, Sir Angus has at least managed to stay married to a royal princess for thirty years with the minimum of fuss. The Ogilvys' least savoury headlines were brought upon them by their daughter Marina, when she became pregnant in 1990 by her live-in boy friend, Paul Mowatt, and accepted money from one of the Murdoch papers, *Today*, for noising it abroad that her parents had disowned her, even that her mother had recommended an abortion. 'My parents have been horrible to us,' declared Marina, who posed for photographs wearing a fake crown above a mini-dress. 'This is the dark side of the royal family we are experiencing.'

Marina Ogilvy (now Mowatt), twenty-seventh in line to the throne, has since continued to play a distinctly rebellious role on the edge of the royal family, cheerfully posing for more outlandish photographs, this time as winner of the 'Rear of the Year' award, and writing an outspoken column in the *Sunday Express* in which she has not hesitated to comment on family matters. Welcoming the Queen's decision to pay tax, for instance, Marina asked: 'Anyone know of a good accountant who can make dog-food for corgis tax deductible?'

Marina's parents themselves narrowly avoided adding further to the Queen's troubles early in 1993, after the writer Quentin Crewe recalled that while on the staff of the *Sunday Mirror* thirty years before he had seen 'photographs taken with a long lens of a [recently married royal couple] making love in some bushes'. The lovers were subsequently identified in the London *Evening Standard* as the newlywed Angus and Alexandra, who had been pursued by paparazzi to the shores of Loch Muick in Scotland. Had the pictures been published, the modern-minded Marina might well have used her column to approve of this touching tale of her parents' youthful high spirits. Mercifully for all concerned, however, they remained locked in the vault where they have lain since 1974.

Marina Mowatt may be setting the right royal example by going out to earn her living, but the view from the Palace may well be that she is not going about it in quite the right way. That is certainly the view from Thatched House Lodge, where Marina's long-standing rift with her parents has made her unwelcome, although she has since married her child's father, and they live (in a modest semi-detached home) only ten minutes away. The unfortunate truth, for all her endearing *joie de vivre*, is that Marina is exploiting her royal connections for commercial gain. The same cannot quite be said of David, Viscount Linley, son of Princess Margaret and Lord Snowdon, who has built himself a highly successful career designing, making and marketing high-class woodwork and furniture. Although his name has obviously been no handicap, Linley can be taken as a model of how the younger royals should, perhaps, be shaping their lives in the twenty-first century. He and his sensibly low-profile sister, Sarah, owe a great deal to their parents for protecting them from the usual royal upbringing; unlike all their cousins, neither has ever planted a tree, launched a ship or unveiled a single plaque. Like his father, moreover, David Linley has worked hard to develop his own artistic talents and put them to considerable advantage. When *Today* reported that he had been involved in a pub brawl in Chelsea, it was to protect his reputation as a businessman, more than as a royal, that he sued (successfully) for libel.

Marina's own mother has set a more familiar example by living off the public purse in return for the traditional life of an occasional royal patron and guest. But she is in distinguished company. Like Alexandra, the royal dukes will continue to look to their cousin to provide them with financial support from her own state subsidy. Prince Richard, Duke of Gloucester, who pays tax on his income as an architect, inherited a substantial amount from his father, but will still receive his tax-free allowance from the Queen of £212,000 per annum (and rising). He lives between his inherited family home, Barnwell in Northamptonshire, and a grace-and-favour apartment in Kensington Palace. Prince Richard is president of the Cancer Research Campaign, the National Association of Boys' Clubs and the British Association of Dairy Farmers. The £87,000 received by his mother, Princess Alice, help her maintain a private secretary and two ladies-in-waiting. Especially active among war veterans, she is patron or president of some 100 groups, although her age now prevents her undertaking many engagements on their behalf.

The Duke of Kent, now in his late fifties, has never needed to take a job. Both he and his wife have handsome private incomes by inheritance; indeed, the duchess, the former Katharine Worsley, was once a member of seventeen insurance syndicates at Lloyd's of London. The couple live in York House, St James's Palace, and at Crocker End House, near Henley, Oxfordshire. The duke will still, however, accept a handout of £212,000 per annum from the Queen. He is Colonel-in-Chief of a number of regiments, and president of the Royal National Lifeboat Institute, the Commonwealth War Graves Commission and the Royal United Services Institute for Defence Studies.

Princess Anne and her new husband, Tim Laurence, have set a healthy new trend by renting a London apartment (in Dolphin Square, at the rate of £1,000 per month) rather than continuing to occupy a free suite in Buckingham Palace. The idea, apparently, is that Commander Laurence wishes to be seen to be supporting his wife, despite a meagre naval salary in the region of £40,000 per annum. While reluctant to begrudge the commander so worthy an aspiration, it is hard to overlook the fact that this will merely be the couple's London *pied-à-terre*; their main home will continue to be Gatcombe Park, bought by the Queen for her daughter, to whom she will also continue to provide her tax-free allowance of £228,000 per annum, rising by 7.5 per cent a year, out of public funds. This is designed to cover the cost of a private secretary and assistant, plus some allowances for clothes and travel for her seven ladies-in-waiting. Princess Anne is patron of the Save the Children Fund, the International Equestrian Federation, the British Olympic Association, a member of the International Olympic Committee – and, by public consensus, the one 'junior' royal who works hard enough to justify her hand-out.

Unlike most separated or divorced husbands, the Duke of York will not have to worry about maintenance payments to his former wife. Whether stripped of her HRH or not, Fergie will be looked after by a lump-sum settlement paid by the Queen. In his new bachelor life, based at the £5 million home bought by his mother, the duke will not be reverting to his pre-marital public subsidy of £50,000 a year, but continuing also to look to his mother for an annual allowance of £249,000 to supplement his naval salary of £38,000 as the new commander of the minesweeper HMS *Cottesmore*. The quarter of a million is designed to cover the cost of a private secretary plus one other full-time staff member. The £5 million trust fund established for Andrew at birth by his parents is now estimated to be worth some £40 million.

Still a bachelor at twenty-nine, and cruelly described as 'one prince too many', Prince Edward will continue to live rent-free in Buckingham Palace while the Queen pays out his former Civil List allowance of £96,000. He has a private secretary, Lt.-Col. Sean O'Dwyer, plus an assistant. Prince Edward is patron of the National Youth Theatre and the Duke of Edinburgh's Awards Scheme. He too has a trust fund, set up at birth, now worth almost as much as his brother Andrew's; but he has yet to make a significant contribution to the work of 'the family firm'.

The Queen is now also responsible for the £219,000 per annum state allowance to her sister, Princess Margaret, who lives rent-free in Kensington Palace, employing a private secretary and a lady-in-waiting. Apart from the Queen herself, Margaret is believed to be one of the richest members of the royal family, having received a handsome legacy from her father, King George VI, and inherited money from other friends and relatives. She is patron of the National Society for the Prevention of Cruelty to Children, the St John Ambulance Brigade and the Girl Guides.

The Queen Mother's £643,000 per annum will further deplete her daughter's Civil List funds, although she too has substantial means of her own from the bulk of the estate of her late husband, on which she was not required to pay death duties. She maintains staff at three houses, two of which are maintained at state expense: Clarence House in London and her weekend home, Royal Lodge in Windsor Great Park. As well as the Castle of Mey, her private Scottish residence purchased after her husband's death, the Queen Mother has use of Birkhall on the Balmoral estate. Her horses have won more than four hundred races over jumps; but she has recently cut down her string, currently keeping four in training with Tim Thompson Jones, three with Ian Balding and two with Nicky Henderson. Top stables like these charge as much as £200 a week per horse;

nine would cost as much as £100,000 a year. The Queen Mother's Household is headed by her own Lord Chamberlain, the Earl of Crawford and Balcarres, and her long-standing private secretary, Sir Martin Gilliatt. She is also supported by a posse of equerries on secondment from the armed forces.

Lesser royals who were not funded out of the Civil List, contrary to popular belief, include Prince and Princess Michael of Kent, who understandably resented public criticism after accepting financial or other recompense for carrying out the public duties or appearances expected even of minor royalty. Younger brother of the Duke of Kent, Prince Michael does, however, live rent-free in Kensington Palace as well as maintaining a home in Gloucestershire's 'royal triangle', Nether Lypiatt Manor, near Stroud.

As long as the over-extended royal family continues to pick up speeding tickets along the M4, as long as its members and friends continue to be caught out in scandalous liaisons and venal exploitation of their positions, they will continue to discredit a monarchy already facing a fight for survival. The Queen's difficulty throughout the past decade has been the sheer growth of the dramatis personae, many of them living off their royal connections as a substitute for public subsidy. This has helped swell the royal pageant into the soap opera which has, of late, turned all too steamy.

By the end of 1992, even Conservative MPs were concerned about the corrosive effect of the spectacle of young royals misbehaving at public expense. 'That some of the young members of the royal family have failed to live up to what the country expected of them is obvious,' in the words of one former back-bencher, Sir Kenneth Lewis. The custom of giving the highest honours available to young members of the royal family before they have earned them should, he argued, be stopped. 'Dukes beget Duchesses when they marry. We must have an end to the creation of young dukes just because of who they are. We also do not want spare duchesses staying in the headlines making money from the titles they have not justified.'

When and if Prince Edward marries, will the Queen heed Sir Kenneth and let the happy couple earn their spurs before handing out whatever royal dukedom is to hand? For all her own personal dignity, the Queen must bear some responsibility for relying so heavily on the popular appeal of the 'family monarchy' pioneered by Victoria, and reinforced by her father, King George VI, in the wake of the abdication crisis. Even by the standards of 1990s morality, it seems in retrospect to have been a supreme risk to shore up the stability and integrity of the throne by portraying the royal family as the embodiment of middle-class respectability.

As Janet Daley has argued in *The Times*, there is an inherent contradiction 'that one ordinary, congenial family' just happens to have 'inherited the consecrated spirit of the nation'. If the members of that family then fail to maintain the stable, respectable lifestyle expected of them, they would seem automatically to compromise their hereditary right to reign over others, be they blameless or not. Constitutional experts may argue, as they have throughout the present crisis, that the monarchy's legal functions are not compromised by private irresponsibility or scandal. To do so is to ignore that the subjects of the crown have long been persuaded otherwise, that they have been virtually brainwashed into believing that the family life of their royals is central to their position at the apex of society, embodying British values and aspirations at home and overseas. The modern monarchy has enjoyed a great deal of mileage out of this syndrome. Can it be allowed to pretend otherwise when things go so badly wrong?

'It would be futile to expect any philosophical or intellectual lead from these people,' in the words of Valerie Grove, 'when they are happiest on the polo field, their friendships are with money, old or new, and their pretensions to education are non-existent.' In a modern democracy, agreed Daley, it is unacceptable to be ruled by people whose personal expectations are wildly unlike those of most of us. If they fail to stand for all that we wish to idealize in our own domesticity, they come into disrepute and the throne itself into question. 'Marital peace and sexual purity are not optional extras. They are of the essence . . . Even a purely symbolic institution must symbolize something other than the need for such an institution. Stripped of the happy family image, the monarchy becomes an expedience to which we cling for fear of something worse.'

However sinful those casting these stones, they felt entitled to do so as long as the extended royal family was misbehaving at public expense. By the cosmetic gesture of volunteering to pay some taxes, the Queen had hoped to make her wayward relatives less publicly accountable. But the debate about the royal finances was not over yet.

CHAPTER 5

THE ROYAL FINANCES

'Thy choicest gifts in store
On her be pleased to pour . . .'
'GOD SAVE THE QUEEN,' VERSE TWO

IN MID-SEPTEMBER 1992, ON THE VERGE OF THE WORST
sterling crisis for sixty years, Prime Minister John Major chose
to spend the weekend at Balmoral Castle, discussing with the
world's richest woman the political advantages of a token cut
in her tax-free public subsidy.

If it seemed a strange priority for the prime minister, it was an
even stranger response to growing public unrest over the state
of the marriages of two of the Queen's sons. Throughout her
family's debilitating year of domestic woes, however, Elizabeth
II was also under fire on the financial front. Some sort of fiscal
gesture had become Whitehall's favoured option to staunch a
potential landslide of more generalized public disenchantment.
If the 'fringe' royals were those bringing the monarchy into
disrepute, the obvious (and easy) public rebuke was to cut them
off without a penny; and if the gesture also gave the appearance
of public-spirited self-sacrifice on the part of the Queen, so much
the better. The underlying cause of public unrest was the general state of the royal finances. Britons living through very

hard times were quite understandably questioning the logic of huge public subsidies to the one family least in need of them, by far the richest in the land, whose senior member paid no tax.

Few, as yet, were publicly questioning how that wealth had been amassed. There were more obvious and more urgent issues. The previous year, while Fergie's frolics were merely a familiar feature of the rich royal tapestry, almost 80 per cent of the British people had declared themselves in favour of a parliamentary bill requiring the monarch to pay income tax. When a Palace leak sought to elicit sympathy by suggesting that she might have to sell Balmoral, the national response was a collective shrug.*

It was an unequivocal comment on the stunning statistic which had sparked the debate: that the Queen, whose private wealth had for years been deemed immeasurable, in fact enjoyed a private, tax-free income of some £1.8 million a *day* from an investment portfolio worth more than £6 billion. Suddenly, to those Britons whose taxes support it, the monarchy seemed to be living it up in some financial twilight zone way beyond the £10 million Civil List. Swiftly sensing trouble, Buckingham Palace naturally dismissed the figures as 'absurd'. But *The Sunday Times*'s annual survey of Britain's 'Top 200' was not alone that year in estimating the Queen's fortune at £7 billion; *Fortune*, the respected American financial magazine, put her hereditary assets at $9.87 billion (£5.9 billion) and her personal wealth at $10.73 million (£6.5 million). In the absence of any specific figures from the Palace, which has long shrouded the monarch's finances in the utmost secrecy, enshrined in law, the British taxpayer had no option but to gasp in disbelief. They were soon joined by a large number of MPs, not least backbench Conservatives, who were only now waking up to the remarkably generous terms of the financial settlement awarded the royal family by Thatcher and Major in 1990.

The Civil List is neither, of course, a salary, nor is it royal 'pocket money'. It is more of a tax-free allowance designed to

---

*Damaging as this story was at the time, it was in truth less than reliable. The newspaper headline was based upon a careless chance remark, in a light-hearted moment in Edinburgh, from the Queen's private secretary, Sir Robert Fellowes. It had not been intended as any kind of policy statement.

assist with the costs of royal staff, living expenses and public duties, and to protect them from having to earn money from business or other activities which might compromise their ability to carry out those duties. Some 70 per cent of it goes on staff salaries, with the remaining 30 per cent covering 'working expenses' from maintenance of cars, kitchens, cellars and the horses and carriages of the Royal Mews to laundry, flowers, garden parties and presents for other heads of state. (Only the Prince and Princess of Wales have always been spared the embarrassment of Civil List subsidy, living off the £3.5 million or so the prince receives each year from his hereditary landholdings as Duke of Cornwall.)

Even when increased to £10 million per annum, however, the Civil List figures which now came under searching scrutiny took no account of the huge 'hidden' costs of the monarchy borne by government departments : the public money, to recap, required to maintain the royal yacht *Britannia* (£12.5 million in 1992, or £463,000 for each of the twenty-seven days the royals spent abroad), the Queen's Flight (£6.9 million, or some £2,000 per hour), the royal train (£2.6 million, or £67,000 per average single journey), the royal palaces (£26.4 million), not to mention civil air fares (£820,000), overseas visits (£620,000), the administration of the honours system (£210,000) and sundry other items from equerries (£210,000) to Yeomen of the Guard, or 'Beefeaters' (£40,000) – raising the global cost of the crown to the taxpayer in 1990–91 by a further £60.36 million. On top of that came a further sum estimated at £20 million a year, borne by the Home Office, for residential security and round-the-clock protection by a rotating squad of Special Branch police officers.

When these figures were juxtaposed with the Queen's tax-free private income, a striking series of polls showed just how much Britons resented them at a time when they themselves were experiencing the worst financial hardship since the 1930s. 'The evidence is obvious from my postbag,' said Simon Hughes, the Liberal Democrat MP who had initiated the unsuccessful parliamentary attempt in 1991 to end the monarch's tax exemption. 'When so many people are scraping along and asked to contribute tax on very low incomes, it seems grossly unfair that the person with the highest income escapes.'

With the timely publication of a distinctly rebellious book on the royal finances,* it emerged that the monarchy's exemption from tax was a much more recent development than generally assumed. Queen Victoria and her heirs, Edward VII and George V, *had* paid tax, however reluctantly, on their private income and investments; complete exemption had been negotiated only as recently as 1936–37 by the present Queen's father, George VI, in the wake of the abdication crisis. The final link between the monarchy and taxation had not in fact been completely severed until 1989, when the Queen was granted exemption from the successor to 'the rates' – the hated (and soon to be abolished) community charge, or 'poll tax' – on the principle that payment would set an undesirable precedent. Hitherto, she had paid rates of £17,000 a year on Buckingham Palace; now she declined to join her subjects in paying even the artificially low figure of £36 at which Westminster Council, thanks to central government assistance in the run-up to an election, had set its 'poll tax' that year.

Would the Queen be paying the 'council tax' soon to be introduced by the Major government in place of the 'poll tax'? Both monarch and prime minister were well aware, as they wandered the Balmoral estate in deep conversation that weekend, that this was another storm gathering not far over the horizon.

Before leaving for Scotland on the afternoon of Friday, 11 September, Major had gone out of his way to describe the monarchy as 'an entrenched, enduring and valuable part of our way of life'. In his pocket, however, was a letter from a senior Conservative MP, hand-delivered only hours before, summing up growing backbench disquiet about the royals. 'Revolutionary changes' were needed, warned Michael Colvin, Conservative MP for Romsey and Waterside, and chairman of the backbench

---

Royal Fortune: Tax, Money and the Monarchy, by Philip Hall, played an even more significant role than Andrew Morton's *Diana: Her True Story* in forcing change upon the monarchy in 1992. 'A masterly piece of investigative reporting, showing how, through secret deals connived at by sycophantic politicians, the royal family's wealth has swollen out of all proportion to that of the country it supposedly serves. A shameful story,' wrote Robert Harris in *The Independent on Sunday*.

foreign affairs committee, in full knowledge of the weekend's unofficial agenda. The events of that summer, wrote Colvin, had 'degraded' the royal family.

As each awoke amid Balmoral's tartan wallpaper that Sunday morning, neither monarch nor prime minister found much for their comfort in the newspapers. An even more significant Tory critic had entered the fray in the shape of a Marquess-in-waiting: Michael, Earl of Ancram, who, as well as being Conservative MP for Devizes and chairman of the Party's backbench constitutional committee, is heir to the 12th Marquess of Lothian and son-in-law of the Duke of Norfolk, Hereditary Marshal and Chief Butler of England. Stressing his staunch loyalty to the monarchy, Ancram argued that the time had come to slim down the Civil List. As to those 'lesser' family members who would no longer be passengers on the royal gravy train: 'There is a strong case for the public purse to recompense members of the royal family according to the specific duties they perform on what amounts to a pro rata basis.' If the public was not financing the royals, argued Ancram, the press would have less right to treat them as public property. But he was firmly against suggestions that the Queen should pay tax : 'Because the monarch at present pays no taxes, there can be no suggestion of a personal interest in the outcome of a general election.'

Subsequent political briefings suggested that Queen and prime minister had also spent the weekend discussing potential plans for privacy laws to prevent the kind of publicity which had dogged his government quite as much as her family throughout that summer. Though public opinion would not swallow legislation to protect the likes of David Mellor – as National Heritage Secretary, ironically, the minister with potential responsibility for steering it through the Commons – there was still the possibility of a privacy bill specifically to protect the royals, as opposed to politicians or other public figures. But the real issue was the financial one. As other Tory backbenchers joined in the chorus for reform, Paddy Ashdown, leader of the Liberal Democrats, also confided his private conviction that a slimmed-down royal family would be 'more in tune with the times'. On his return from Balmoral, Major discreetly let it be known that a reduction of £1.4 million a year in the Queen's Civil List – the axing, in effect, of most of the 'fringe' royals – had been discussed.

But where had this figure of £1.4 million come from? Could the surrender of £1.4 million a year by a woman who earned more every *day* in unearned, untaxed income really be portrayed as self-denial? Try selling that, went up the Labour cry, to the tens of thousands of families whose homes had been re-possessed that year, or the employees of the businesses going bankrupt at the rate of seventy-two a day. As fate would have it, the debate about the royal finances was promptly drowned, twenty-four hours after Major's return from Scotland, by the British economy's most extraordinary and agonizing day in living memory. With interest rates raised and lowered four times in twenty-four hours, £10 billion of the national reserves poured away in a vain attempt to shore up sterling, and the pound effectively devalued by 20 per cent thanks to its suspension from the European exchange rate mechanism, the royal finances were promptly restored to their accustomed and cosy obscurity. Their apparently open-ended relief from pressure would, how-ever, last barely two months, until cruelly interrupted by the Windsor fire and its aftermath.

Unexpectedly, at the time, the royal family's advisers were granted some breathing-space to reflect on the lukewarm recep-tion given their £1.4 million scheme, and the growing public demand for an end to the Queen's tax exemption. To keep them on their toes, the British press proceeded to indulge in lurid speculation as to the true scale of the monarch's private fortune. If the Palace felt obliged to dismiss some of their findings as 'gross exaggeration', its courtiers really had only themselves to blame. There were many other aspects of British society which fell far short of John Major's aspirations for 'open government', but few less open or more shrouded in layer upon layer of secrecy than the sovereign's personal and *ex-officio* wealth. It was a Pandora's box long overdue for opening.

Over the years, thanks to the legal protections afforded uniquely to the monarchy, Fleet Street's attempts to estimate the Queen's wealth had proved about as successful as its hunt for the Loch

Ness Monster. There was no doubt that many such efforts, especially those emanating from the United States, all too often confused the crown's public and private assets. Buckingham Palace and Windsor Castle, for instance, do not 'belong' to the Queen any more than do the crown jewels or the fabulous royal collection of paintings (7,000 paintings and 20,000 drawings including works by Michelangelo, Leonardo, Rembrandt, Rubens and Canaletto, as well as 500,000 prints, books and sculpture, valued as 'incalculable, but clearly running into several billion pounds'). Nor does the bulk of the royal collection of furniture (the catalogue of which extends to seventy-five volumes), jewellery (appraised in 1989 by the New York jeweller Harry Winston at £36–42 million), the royal stamp collection (started by George V, and now running to more than 350 albums) or sundry other treasures.

All these are assets deemed legally 'inalienable'; that is, they are the property of the monarchy, not of the person who happens to be monarch, who is not free to dispose of them and will be obliged to leave them to his or her successor. Other substantial assets in this category include Buckingham Palace, Kensington Palace, St James's Palace, Clarence House and Hampton Court in London, and Holyrood Palace in Edinburgh, not to mention the vast and valuable collection of gifts received from other monarchs and visiting heads of state. (In the 1980s, one royal tour of the Gulf States alone netted precious gifts worth more than £1 million.)

But the Queen *does* personally own the royal estates of 21,000-acre, 275-room Sandringham House in Norfolk and 50,000-acre Balmoral Castle in Scotland, between them estimated even during the 1991–92 property slump to be worth some £100–150 million. (Her father, King George VI, bought them in 1936 from his abdicating brother for £300,000, the equivalent of about £10 million today.) Both houses these days sport gift and souvenir shops, and are open to the public several months a year, not unlike the stately homes of the hard-pressed English aristocracy; the running costs of Balmoral are further offset to a considerable extent by forestry, a flourishing sawmill, commercialized pony trekking, shooting and fishing (when the family is not in residence), and the renting-out of 12,000 rich agricultural acres.

The Queen also owns forestry valued at £11 million. In July 1992, at the height of her family's other woes, she incurred an unusual dose of personal abuse when it was revealed that she had applied to the Forestry Commission for a £300,000 grant to build a fence on the Balmoral estate (from which, that very day, the embattled Duchess of York was being all too publicly banished). Such grants are available to woodland owners to keep out a particular species of red deer, which apparently nibble young trees to extinction. But was not *this* fence in fact designed to keep out another equally dangerous but rather more human species of unwelcome intruder? More important, should it really be financed by a grant of public money to the nation's richest non-taxpayer for one of her private estates – itself purchased on a Civil List surplus, or public money paid to the then monarch, Queen Victoria, in excess of her needs?

The Polhampton Lodge Stud in Hampshire (bought by the Queen in 1972) and the nearby Kingsclere and West Ilsley stables are also the Queen's private property, as are some thirty thoroughbred racehorses valued at £3.5 million. Despite huge stud fees, and a recent annual average of some £75,000 in prize money, the managers of the royal racing business insist that it runs at a loss. Newspaper estimates in 1992, by contrast, quoted industry experts as suggesting that the Queen made a profit of some £5 million a year from her wholly owned equine subsidiary – all of it, to the chagrin of her rival owners and trainers, blissfully tax-free for reinvestment.

Intriguingly, it is the 'convention' to regard as national property only those royal possessions purchased before 1936. As a 1992 survey for *The Times* pointed out, this would leave the Queen free to sell 'the many fine pictures, by Sidney Nolan, Graham Sutherland, L. S. Lowry et al., acquired since'. The position over some of the royal jewellery is also ambiguous: 'She may not wish to sell some, such as the Romanov jewels bought by Queen Mary from the Tsar's relatives in their English exile, which were valued at £10 million in modern prices –

but she is legally free to do so.' The privately owned jewellery has been valued at £40 million, although even that is a highly imprecise figure. 'As soon as the Queen wears any item of jewellery,' says Suzy Menkes, author of *The Royal Jewels,* 'that in itself increases its value.'

As hereditary Duke of Lancaster, the Queen also enjoys the income from the Duchy's 1,000-plus holdings of land and property spread across 36,500 acres, mainly agricultural, in Northamptonshire, Lincolnshire, Staffordshire, Cheshire, Yorkshire and Lancashire, as well as 15,000 acres of moorland in North Yorkshire and South Wales and the jewel in the Duchy's crown, freeholdings throughout London, including the Savoy area between Embankment and the Strand. The Duchy's assets, valued at some £55 million, produced a tax-free revenue of £3.1 million in 1991. At least a third of this was produced by the team of lawyers retained to pursue one of the monarch's most ancient privileges: to claim the estates of any Duchy resident who dies intestate. This brings in another £1.5 million in an average year, much of it at the expense of 'common law' husbands or wives deprived by their monarch of their worldly goods when their partners die without making a will.

Despite her fabulous personal wealth, the Queen has always exhibited the parsimony characteristic of 'old money'. She is renowned, for instance, for going around Buckingham Palace last thing at night, switching off lights. In 1990 she brought in Michael Peat, a partner in the City accountancy firm of Peat, Marwick, McLintock to the new post of director of finance and property services. His brief was to achieve costs savings of £5 million over the ten-year period of the 'Thatcher deal', and 'to establish a new framework for the family firm and to update the valuation of assets'. At the same time responsibility for the occupied royal palaces was transferred from the Department of the Environment to the royal household, with a separate budget of more than £26 million a year.

Overall supervision of the royal finances, and the extent of the government's contribution, rests with the three Royal Trustees: the prime minister, the Chancellor of the Exchequer and the Keeper of the Privy Purse (at present Sir Shane

Blewett, effectively the Queen's treasurer). In September 1992 *The Daily Telegraph* speculated that Major's £1.4 million saving 'may simply be the results of trimming by a prudent chief executive'. Even the *Telegraph*, however, felt constrained to add: 'If this is how Her Majesty explained it to the Prime Minister, he must have nodded his head warmly. He must also have wondered if it would be enough.'

Just how rich *was* the monarch? Even her opponents agreed that in the earlier years of her reign, before she had developed the neo-Victorian self-confidence she now exuded, the Queen had been obliged to dip into her private fortune in order to keep the monarchy afloat in the style to which it was accustomed. Andrew Morton's 1990 book, *Theirs is the Kingdom,* arrived at an estimated figure of £1.2 billion for the jewellery, bloodstock, investments and land. In 1992 Philip Hall reduced this figure to £900 million, whittled away by funding family members. Amid all the confusion, the Conservative MP Julian Critchley spoke for Middle Britain when he blithely declared: 'The Queen is stinking rich . . . She has more houses than the National Trust, more jewels than Ali Baba and more pictures than the National Gallery.'

By far the most controversial and jealously guarded area of the Queen's private finances is her personal investment portfolio. In 1971 the then Lord Chamberlain, Lord Cobbold, a former Governor of the Bank of England, described estimates placing its value at £50 million as 'wildly exaggerated'. In 1991, Granada Television's *World In Action* programme took the late Lord Cobbold at his word, and asked a City of London stockbroker to take a 1971 starting fortune of £30 million and project its 1991 value if 'sensibly invested in UK shares'. He came up with the figure of £496 million – an uncannily accurate echo of a similar exercise the previous year by Morton, this time from a starting figure of £35 million, which produced a 1990 estimate of £600 million.

On an investment portfolio of £600 million, the Queen would enjoy a private income of about £42 million a year, according to a 1992 assessment by Victor Levy, a Fellow of the Institute of Taxation, and a senior partner in the City of London accountancy practice of Arthur Andersen. At the standard 40 per cent rate

for tax on unearned income, her tax liability would be some
£25 million a year.

If he were advising the Queen along the same lines as his
other wealthier clients, Mr Levy continued, he would suggest
the investment of her private fortune in an offshore fund –
with the net result that she would pay no tax at all. Now he
was venturing into territory regarded by the Palace as No Man's
Land: the suggestion that the monarch should naturally reflect
her subjects' penchant for tax avoidance, if not tax evasion. Sheer
patriotism might preclude overseas or offshore investment, but
there were other tax shelters readily available closer to home;
by purchasing property, for instance, under the government's
building enterprise scheme. If implemented before April 1993
(when the scheme expired) this would have provided a 100 per
cent tax write-off spread over several years.

As a self-employed businesswoman, moreover, the Queen
could claim as tax-deductible the allowances she paid to relations not on the Civil List, such as her cousins of Kent and
Gloucester, provided she could prove that their assistance with
public duties was essential to the running of the royal firm. Part
of the maintenance and running costs of her private properties,
Balmoral and Sandringham, could also be offset. 'With careful
management,' Levy concluded, 'the Queen, like so many other
rich people, could end up paying practically no tax at all.'

Philip Hall started from the modest assumption that the
Queen had £20 million invested in 1971, less than half the
figure dismissed by the Lord Chamberlain. 'If that £20 million
had increased at the same rate as the UK stock market as a
whole, and if the dividends have been ploughed back, then
today [June 1991], it would be worth £341 million.' One political
commentator took Hall's figures further. 'The average dividend
on the top 100 companies is 5.4 per cent, suggesting an annual
income of £18.4 million. By not paying tax on this (which
would have been levied at 40 per cent), the Queen was saving
£7.3 million a year, or £20,000 *a day*.'

In January 1992 *The Economist* leapt loyally to her aid with a
curt dismissal of 'misleading' Sunday newspaper stories putting
the Queen's wealth at around £7 billion. Citing its sources (in the

best traditions of royal reporting) simply as 'those in a position to know', the magazine concluded that her private investments were now worth under £50 million. Six months on, *The Times* set the figure even lower, at 'something around' £30 million. Both articles reeked heavily of Palace briefings to stem the tide of demands for the monarch to pay tax. 'Allow an annual income of 10 per cent,' continued *The Times*'s court correspondent, 'and you arrive at a yield to the Inland Revenue of £1.2 million' – which he humbly dismissed as 'small beer'. The previous year, also in *The Times,* the Queen's loyal friend Lord (Woodrow) Wyatt produced the even lower estimate of £20 million, the same figure that Philip Hall estimated for 1971.

During 1992, as *The Financial Times* summed up, estimates of the Queen's investment portfolio (managed by the stockbrokers Rowe and Pitman) had varied from under £50 million to almost £600 million – all based on a portfolio said in 1971 to be worth about £30 million. Income from the portfolio had been put at anywhere between £1 million and £42 million. The higher estimates assumed all dividends to have been reinvested, which was unlikely. Spending had recently been high on her properties – as much as £1 million per annum on Balmoral alone – and she has always been generous to her children (for example, setting up £5 million trust funds for each of them at birth). She had bought two of them houses as wedding presents: Gatcombe Park for Princess Anne in the mid-70s and Sunninghill Park for the Yorks in the mid-80s. Now she would be dealing with her offspring's three divorce settlements, and enlarging the trust funds settled upon her six grandchildren to cover their education and upbringing after their parents' divorces.

As the experts' figures flew, Her Majesty's financially hard-pressed subjects were in danger of drowning by numbers. All they knew was that a topless Fergie was having her toes sucked beside a French swimming-pool, at their expense, while they themselves had been obliged to cancel their vacations. Whatever the arguments about her private and public assets, the Queen was clearly rich enough to finance her own family's ill-judged junketings, and to pay for her own garden fences. Post-Thatcher Britain was in a mean-minded, resentful frame of mind, leaving her successor in uncertain charge of an every-man-for-himself society. The national mood called for the Queen to pay her due in taxes, like twenty-five million of her subjects. Not merely should she 'cough up,' said the Labour MP Ken Livingstone, an avowed republican, but the crown should pay back-taxes 'avoided for the last sixty years'. As for the public subsidy to the crown, the so-called Civil List: it was time not merely to trim it, but to scrap it altogether.

The term 'Civil List' dates from 1698, when it was coined specifically to distinguish between civil and military expenditure by a parliament anxious to curb the crown's financial control over the Army. By voting William of Orange £700,000 a year for life - to cover the civil side of his government expenses, plus the costs of maintaining his Household – the Commons was in effect depriving the monarchy of its ancient and dangerous power to finance a standing army or raise a new one.

Various modifications ensued, largely reflecting the decline of the monarchy's political role, before the Civil List as we now understand it finally took shape in 1830. In 1702, for instance, a clause in Queen Anne's Civil List Act forbade the monarch to sell off remaining crown lands; in 1727 Walpole persuaded the Commons to permit King George II to keep any surplus from Civil List revenues (which in turn, of course, persuaded George II to retain Walpole as his prime minister). The Civil List was reviewed as a matter of course at the beginning of each new reign, and fixed at an agreed sum for the duration of that reign.

In 1760 came the reform still quoted today as an argument against the principle of taxing the monarch. George III, upon his accession, agreed to surrender certain hereditary revenues including that from the Crown Estate, excluding the Duchies of Lancaster and Cornwall, in return for a fixed annual subsidy. Parliament, in other words, was clawing back the Civil List surplus by diverting tax and crown lands into a government-controlled 'Aggregate Fund', from which the monarch would be paid his fixed sum. In the case of George III, it was set at a vast £800,000 a year, more than enough for him to continue distributing enough patronage and largesse to maintain sizeable support in parliament and beyond.

At this stage in the development of the monarchy and its finances, the king was still responsible for paying the salaries of the civil government – the civil service, diplomatic corps, judges etc. – as well as his own Household. In ensuing years, as the growth of Britain's world role increased these expenses, parliament gradually took them upon itself rather than grant more money to the crown for possible misuse to other ends. This process inevitably precipitated the decline of the monarchy's political powers, as ministers and other high officials were freed of financial dependence upon the sovereign.

In 1830, with the accession of William IV, came the final break between the crown and government expenditure, and thus the emergence of the Civil List as we understand it today. The annual amount voted to the monarchy at the beginning of each new reign was deemed henceforth to cater purely for 'the dignity and state of the Crown, and the personal comfort of Their Majesties'.

At the same time, on the initiative of the king himself, parliament agreed that for the first time the monarch might enjoy private financial status for his personal landholdings and other wealth, with the result that he could own property and other assets in his own right. For the first time in British history, the sovereign could henceforth make a will, disposing of such private assets as he chose. Hitherto the monarch had been deemed to exist only as the monarch, an entirely public figure, so that all his assets automatically passed, regardless of his wishes, to his successor. All land or property purchases had similarly been deemed to be crown acquisitions, the sale of which was forbidden by the 1702 Act. Now, unprecedentedly, the monarch could buy and sell land, property or other assets as he saw fit. The new law deemed it only natural, as did the monarch himself, that he should pay tax on any revenue from such dealings just as if it had been 'the property of any subject of this realm'.

Income tax, at the time, did not exist. Introduced in 1799 to finance the Napoleonic Wars, it had ended with them in 1816.

Although the principle of the monarch's liability to taxation was enshrined in the 1830 reforms, there was thus no income tax requirement of him at the time, nor indeed of Queen Victoria on her accession in 1837. On Peel's reintroduction of the tax five years later, however, the Queen quite naturally agreed to pay tax on all her income *including* her annual £385,000 from the Civil List. Although the supposedly temporary tax applied only to those earning in excess of £150 a year, at the minimal rate of 7d in the pound (a mere 3 per cent), Peel naturally used the Queen's co-operation as a shameless palliative to help sell an unpopular new tax to the electorate.

In 1849–50, when Prince Albert asked for a huge Civil List increase on the Queen's behalf, he avoided suggesting tax exemption. The size of the increase he was after anyway made the matter academic; Philip Hall's calculations suggest that, at present-day rates, Albert was requesting an increase from an already huge £1.5 million per annum to an astonishing £4 million (at a time, as Hall points out, when Britain was 'an incomparably poorer society', so that such sums were 'far greater in value than [they] would be today').

Albert was on extremely thin ice. Victoria was already making a handsome profit on the Civil List – enabling her, for instance, to purchase and develop Osborne, her substantial estate on the Isle of Wight, for a sum equivalent today to some £10 million. So what was the extra money for? Albert himself, he argued to the prime minister, Lord John Russell, needed more money for 'the *ordinary* establishment and pursuits of an English gentleman'.* Despite being turned down by Russell, much to Albert's annoyance, the royal couple were soon able to add to their private assets the Scottish estate of Balmoral (abutting 6,000 acres Albert already owned). Two months later their 'problems' were solved in the unexpected shape of a vast legacy from a loyal subject – almost half a million pounds, in the will of an eccentric Chelsea landlord named John Camden Neild. It enabled them to build Balmoral Castle, thus creating a

---

*My italics, in view of what Albert considered ordinary: 'a hunting establishment, a pack of hounds, a breeding stud, shooting establishment, a moor or forest in the Highlands of Scotland, a farm etc. etc.'

hugely valuable property which required several subsequent acts of parliament to protect its status as a private rather than a public asset.

After Albert's death, when Victoria retreated into widowed seclusion, the rebellious spirit of the day found a rallying-point in the royal finances. *What does she do with it?* was the title of a pamphlet circulated in the 1860s, rousing widespread public support for republican resentment that Victoria received a large annual grant of public money without performing any public duties to justify it. By hoarding her Civil List surplus in the Privy Purse, to which the government was then contributing £60,000 a year, Victoria built up a personal fortune worth well over £20 million at today's prices – thus laying the foundations for the vast personal wealth now enjoyed by her great-great-granddaughter. The private royal fortune of 1992, shrouded in secrecy even during the monarchy's agonized negotiations with the Inland Revenue, was built on excess *public* money dating back, in investment terms, to Victoria's day. Elizabeth II's principal private assets, Balmoral and Sandringham, as well as her huge (and still secret) investment portfolio, are the results of shameless profiteering by her immediate ancestors.

All this time, despite her non-existent public profile, Victoria was demanding considerable sums of the Treasury for the support of her numerous children and their growing broods. In January 1871 Sir Charles Dilke led a Commons revolt against the provision of a huge dowry for the Queen's daughter, Princess Louise. By July, public opposition had grown vehement enough for fifty-four MPs to vote for a reduction in the annuity proposed for Prince Arthur on his coming of age. Later that year Dilke was using the financial issue as a central plank of a wholesale republican platform. 'Have we not republican virtues and republican spirit?' he asked in a speech in Newcastle, at one of many meetings marked by noisy, often violent Tory dissent. 'Have we not the fact of self-government? Are we not gaining general education? Well, if you can show me a fair chance that a republic here would be free from the political corruption that hangs about the monarchy, I say for my part – and I believe the middle-class in general would say – let it come!'

Then Dilke made a fatal mistake. While accusing the Queen of 'a diversion of public monies amounting almost to a malversation,' he asserted that she paid no income tax. Gladstone was easily able to provide evidence to the contrary, and Dilke was forced to apologize – an unforced error from which the British republican movement never really recovered.

The twentieth century was to see the system undergo a rapid succession of amendments in the monarchy's favour. On Victoria's death in 1901, her son, Edward VII, tried to negotiate himself immunity from income tax but was persuaded by Lord Salisbury's Conservative government, at the height of the Boer War, to pay up. In 1910, on the succession of King George V, Lloyd George was persuaded to exempt the Civil List from taxation, helping to lay the foundations of today's vast investment portfolio. In 1932 the Treasury agreed to lift tax on income from the Duchy of Lancaster rents, but the monarch continued to pay tax until George VI finally negotiated complete exemption in 1936–37, in the wake of his brother's abdication. The details of the deal remain obscure, as the relevant papers have mysteriously vanished from the Public Records Office. But it was basically a quid pro quo from the crown to relieve the government of financial responsibility for the Duke of Windsor in exile. The new King, who had inherited some £750,000 from his father (about £25 million at today's values), was also allowed to reclaim previously paid tax on private investment income.

In 1952, upon Elizabeth II's accession to the throne, parliament went through the ancient ritual of reviewing the Civil List at the beginning of a new reign. There was a formal renewal of the agreement dating back to 1760 that revenues from the Crown Estate would be surrendered in return for a fixed annual subsidy. With a new monarch only twenty-five years of age, however, all thoughts of an arrangement to last her lifetime were bound to prove over-optimistic. After twenty years, the Queen was increasingly drawing on her private resources to supplement a fixed sum which Britain's economic difficulties had shrunk beyond recognition. The rate of inflation of mid-twentieth-century Britain was beyond the worst imaginings of the parliamentary draughtsmen of the late eighteenth century.

By 1969 Prince Philip felt obliged to tell American television interviewers on NBC's *Meet the Press* that the royal family was likely to go 'into the red' the following year. 'If nothing happens,' he continued in jocular vein, 'we may have to move into smaller premises, who knows? We had a small yacht which we've had to sell, and I shall probably have to give up polo fairly soon, things like that.'

Philip omitted to mention that he and the Queen still possessed a rather larger yacht – the largest in private hands in the world – which they had not been obliged to sell, as it was maintained at public expense outside the Civil List. (He in fact gave up polo two years later, on his fiftieth birthday, which he had long marked down as 'a suitable age for retirement', and because a polo injury had begun to turn his right wrist arthritic.) Philip's comments nevertheless sent shock waves through a loyal British public, hitherto unaware of the supposed strain on the royal finances. It was apparently an unpremeditated outburst – the Palace even made vain attempts to have it edited out of the broadcast tape – but it certainly proved effective.

There is a hallowed British tradition of royalty going crown-in-hand to its governments – not always successfully, as in Albert's case – but this was the first time that it had ever done so in public. Philip was obliged to turn down a good-natured offer from a group of Bermondsey dockers, to organize a whip-round in their local pub to buy him a polo pony. But he at least succeeded in having the matter discussed in cabinet. Harold Wilson, normally the most deferential of prime ministers, was now obliged to reflect the less instinctively loyalist views of such cabinet members as Barbara Castle ('His wife's one of the richest women in the world'). According to Richard Crossman's account of the meeting, Wilson compared the royal family's parsimony with the *noblesse oblige* of other wealthy aristocrats, who spent 'a good part' of their income on charitable and other public works: 'It takes royalty to assume that all their private income is to be kept to themselves and that they are not obliged to spend any of it on seeing them through their public life.'

The prime minister and the leader of the Opposition, Edward

Heath, were for once agreed in a Commons exchange that this was the most 'delicate' of matters to bring before the House. To put the whole subject off until after the next general election, Wilson proposed a Select Committee on the Civil List (not, as Castle and others wanted, on the Queen's private fortune). It was a commitment which Heath honoured after winning the 1970 election.

'When there is a Select Committee on the Queen,' wrote Walter Bagehot, 'the charm of royalty will be gone.' Yet this is exactly what Elizabeth II faced, thanks to her husband's habitual outspokenness, as she approached the twentieth anniversary of her accession. The monarch was obliged to convey to parliament a 'Gracious Message' – the traditional euphemism for a royal request for money – and to look on uncomfortably as her financial linen was then publicly washed and aired. As it happened, the instinctive deference of British politicians towards their monarch would ensure her immunity from financial embarrassment for another twenty years.

There was to be public discomfort, however, on an increasingly irksome annual basis. Legislation in 1972 arranged for an annual review of the Civil List as part of the Chancellor of the Exchequer's Budget statement each spring, which would give maverick republicans like Willie Hamilton MP a regular chance to ask such questions as 'What is Princess Margaret *for*?'. Only three years later, in 1975, the incoming Labour government instigated a further system of financial supplements to be agreed by the Royal Trustees. Fifteen years on, in 1990, the Palace managed to persuade the government that even this was proving inadequate. And so it was that prime minister Thatcher and Chancellor Major quietly introduced yet another arrangement, whereby the Queen herself received an inflation-proof sum for the decade, during which subventions to the other Civil List recipients would remain fixed. The 'Thatcher deal' was done.

By 1991, the first full year of the new arrangement, it became clear just how poor a deal the 1760 arrangement had become for the contemporary monarchy. The Queen's 1991 Civil List totalled £7.9 million – while the Crown Estate despite the slump in land and property values, poured more than £70 million into the Treasury. No wonder Prince Charles had told a journalist in 1987 that he was in favour of doing away with the Civil List and financing the monarchy from the Crown Estate (now 250,000 acres in England, Scotland and Wales, and property primarily in London, valued in 1992 at no less than £1.86 billion; *see* Appendix D). Amid a paean of praise for such progressive thinking from the monarch-in waiting, not one commentator noticed that he was in fact proposing a *tenfold* increase in the monarchy's income, without any mention of paying tax.

Even if this figure were to be subjected to normal taxation, at the top rate of 40 per cent, the Crown Estate's 1991 income of £70 million would still have yielded the monarch £43 million (as opposed to the Civil List's £7.9 million). It was a tantalizing but remote prospect. Royalists themselves raised the constitutional objection that to return the estates to the crown would in effect be to privatize the monarchy and turn the Queen into merely a super-rich landholder, just another 'old money' aristocrat. What would happen if the royal estates underwent a financial crisis? Would the monarch again have to approach his or her government for a handout? The nation, went their case, had an *obligation* to finance the monarchy in the style to which it was accustomed. It was a natural expression of patrotic pride.

In the autumn of 1992, when prime minister Major returned from Balmoral with news of the Queen's readiness to trim the Civil List, there were immediate fears that it might prove a cunning ploy to avoid the dread prospect of tax. 'For the Duke of York and Prince Edward to be freed of the necessity of maintaining Ruritanian retinues, and to have to earn a living for themselves, would boost their self-respect and ours,' commented the London *Evening Standard*. But the Palace should not be allowed to get away with some crafty double game. 'Parliament must not be manoeuvred into dropping the idea as a quid pro quo for a slimmed-down Civil List.' Amid all the speculation, it was generally believed that no Conservative government was likely to ask the Queen to pay income tax. Any such suggestion would have to come in the form of an offer from the Queen herself.

'There is no indication,' wrote *The Times* in September 1992, 'that any such offer is imminent.'

On 3 November 1992, in a written reply to a parliamentary question, the Chancellor of the Exchequer, Norman Lamont, confirmed that the government had 'no plans' to alter the Queen's tax-exempt status. The statement was carefully timed to get lost (as indeed it did) amid the US presidential election and the knife-edge Maastricht vote that same day, not to mention the public collapse of the Wales marriage in South Korea. Labour members of parliament were incensed that the government was still continuing to ignore the evidence of opinion polls that more than 80 per cent of Britons wanted the Queen to pay tax. Alan Williams, Labour MP for Swansea West, asked why a billionaire should pay no tax 'when her subjects on minuscule incomes' did. 'The Palace and the government make a serious error of judgement if they think people will tolerate this unquantified privilege.'

That same day the world's wealthiest constitutional monarch, her assets by now valued by *Fortune* at £7.3 billion, met the world's richest absolute ruler at Victoria Station as the Sultan of Brunei, worth some £20 billion, arrived for a state visit. It took Britain's only Labour-supporting newspaper, the *Daily Mirror*, to calculate that the Sultan became richer by £42,000 during the ten-minute greeting ceremony at Victoria Station – a sum which it would take a British Rail ticket collector several years to earn, 'even with maximum overtime'.

There followed in *staccato* succession the Great Fire of Windsor, on Friday 20 November; the Queen's 'annus horribilis' speech on Tuesday the 24th; and two days later, on Thursday the 26th, the prime minister's historic announcement that Elizabeth II had offered to pay some taxes *and* trim the Civil List. He would be announcing fuller details 'early in the New Year'.

The monarch's immunity from taxation was 'a serious issue, which should have been tackled long ago,' said John Grigg, the former Lord Altrincham. To Grigg, successive governments were 'culpably servile' not to have faced the implications, and the Queen herself was 'unwise to assume that their servility would guarantee the *status quo* (established by stealth within the present century) for the indefinite future'. Her prime ministers, in particular, had 'served her ill in this matter'.

Amid another hail of speculation that the Queen was worth billions – helpfully dismissed by her youngest son, Prince Edward, as 'absolute crap' – both Downing Street and Buckingham Palace took the chance to confirm 'unofficially' that an estimate of £50 million was 'not far out'. This, it was calculated, would produce between £1 million and £2 million for the Inland Revenue in the tax year beginning in April. But the Queen's income would be reduced immediately, because the dividends on her investments would now be taxed at source. Like all other taxpayers she would be allowed to make gains of up to £5,500 a year free of tax. But would the Queen aim to reduce her liability by instructing her brokers to 'bed-and-breakfast' her whole share portfolio – the practice of selling shares at the end of a financial year and buying them back to give them a new value for tax purposes? What other methods of tax avoidance might she practise? With the right advice, it was argued, the monarch could reduce her actual payment almost to zero.

It took Major two months to come up with the promised 'details', which turned out to be predictably few. On 11 February 1993 (pausing only to deal with the suggestion of Teresa Gorman MP that courts should punish rapists by 'cutting off their goolies') the prime minister told the Commons that the monarch would start paying full rates of income tax and capital gains tax on her private income as of April. The Queen would also pay the new 'council tax'. Thanks to the 'unique circumstances in a hereditary monarchy', however, the monarch would be exempted from inheritance tax on everything she passes on to her successor. There was 'no question', Major continued, of taxing such assets as the royal palaces, the crown jewels and the royal art collection, which the Queen owned 'as sovereign and not in a private capacity'. The royal art treasures – defined as 'a national treasure of which the Queen is custodian' – would now be administered by a charity, the Royal Collection Trust.

Nor would the Queen pay tax on income intended for her official duties, such as the Civil List and the revenues from the Duchy of Lancaster. The prime minister emphasized that this was a voluntary arrangement, which would not be enshrined in law, but that the Queen had 'every intention' that it should continue indefinitely. The precise amount of the Queen's eventual payment would naturally remain secret.

John Smith, the Opposition leader, immediately questioned the exemption from inheritance tax: 'Why should all private assets passing from one sovereign to the next be exempt?' There was a danger, replied Major, of the monarchy's assets being 'salami-sliced away' by capital taxation. All gifts and bequests from the Queen to the Prince of Wales, including the private estates of Sandringham and Balmoral, would be immune to taxation laws. Bequests to the next monarch, suggested Labour MP Alan Williams, were 'a greasy pole' down which assets could be passed tax-free. 'There's one tax regime for her and another for the ordinary punter,' complained Dennis Skinner from Labour's back benches. A Conservative member, Richard Page, leapt to the Queen's defence, deploring the idea of a 'cut-price bargain basement' monarchy. 'There are people in Britain who would like to be allowed to elect their Head of State, as America does,' replied Tony Benn, seizing the moment to call for a full inquiry into the constitution 'instead of all the creepy-crawly bowing and scraping we have had from so many MPs.'

Under the new arrangements, the Queen would even be able to claim tax against the £1 million paid by parliament to her husband and mother. She would also receive tax allowances for the running of her two private residences at Balmoral and Sandringham, and for the running costs of the Duchy of Lancaster. The Queen would be exempt from any of the normal taxation on 'company perks' such as her cars, yacht, train, planes and residences. All her payments to other members of the royal family could be claimed against tax. She could also claim the cost of royal uniforms, private medical and insurance costs connected with her royal duties, as well as 'donations, cups, prizes, flowers and presents given in an official capacity'. Parliament would remain debarred from any detailed examination of the royal accounts.

Paragraph 33 of the memorandum setting out the new arrangements was an 'opt-out' clause, by which the Queen could revert immediately to her tax-free status if a future government raised taxes. The head of state also had one other enviable advantage over Britain's twenty-five million regular taxpayers. As hers was a 'voluntary' arrangement, she would not be required to fill out the annual income tax form. A statement of income to be taxed would instead be 'prepared and delivered on her behalf' to the Inland Revenue each autumn.

Other senior members of the royal family fared even better under the new deal. It appeared that the Prince of Wales, who had hitherto voluntarily surrendered 25 per cent of his £3.5 million annual revenue from the Duchy of Cornwall, might actually end up with *more* money in his pocket. Though taxed at the top rate of 40 per cent, Charles would now be allowed to make various claims against tax: the expenses of running Highgrove, for instance, although he would now have to pay the Duchy a market rent for its use. The prince was exempted from capital gains tax on the Duchy's property dealings, but he could now claim as tax-deductible all expenses for his and the Princess of Wales's official duties, uniforms and other essentials.

The 'voluntary' repayment made to the Treasury by the Prince of Wales had been instituted not by Charles (who reduced it from 50 to 25 per cent on his marriage), but by his great-uncle, the Duke of Windsor, when heir to the throne in the 1930s. The annual saving to Charles during the tax years before 1993 was estimated at £500,000 per annum. In 1991, for instance, he 'returned' £725,599 of the Duchy's £2,902,397 profits; at the rate of 40 per cent, however, he would have paid almost £1.2 million.

The Duchy, started in 1337 by Edward III to support his son, the Black Prince, now owns some 130,000 acres across twenty-two counties, more than half of it in Devon, including 70,000 acres of Dartmoor. The prince is hereditary landlord of Dartmoor prison and the Oval cricket ground in Kennington, London, not to mention sundry golf courses and oyster beds, hundreds of farms and thousands of acres of woodland. In 1992, as part of its 'modernization' programme, the Duchy sold three hundred properties in South London, realizing £4.9 million. Rents total around £6 million per annum, offset by the costs of repairs, maintenance and wages to the Prince of Wales's household and other staff, who number more than a hundred.

As parsimonious as his mother, Charles has been known to negotiate 'trade' terms with fashion houses supplying clothes to his wife – who is, after all, the world's best mobile advertisement. Nor, like his less exalted ex-brother-in-law, Mark Phillips, is he above accepting brand-name sponsorship. Guests at a Buckingham Palace party in October 1992, hosted by the prince in honour of the eightieth birthday of Sir Georg Solti, noticed that the programme thanked by name the firm who had 'laid on' the champagne. All Charles's recent polo teams have also accepted commercial sponsorship; for the 1993 season he had joined Alcatel, funded by the Canadian-born communications millionaire John Manconi, before suddenly deciding to drop out of high-goal polo. After switching out the lights at night, however, the prince thinks nothing of spending some £30,000 to kit himself out for a day on the grouse-moors.

Under the Major dispensation Charles's father, Prince Philip, would continue to receive his £359,000-a-year allowance tax free, with no claim made by the Revenue against his rent-free residency of Buckingham Palace and six other royal palaces. The Queen Mother, who would also continue to receive her £643,000 annual allowance, untaxed, would not be charged for use of Clarence House, her London residence; upon her death, her estate would pass tax-free to the Queen. The Duke of York would still maintain a tax-free apartment in Buckingham Palace, as would Prince Edward. Princess Margaret would keep her royal and state pensions and her tax-free apartment in Kensington Palace.

Soon after Major's announcement in the Commons, the first press conference ever given about the royal finances was held in St James's Palace by the Lord Chamberlain, the Earl of Airlie. A past chairman of General Accident Insurance and the merchant banking firm of Schroder, this was one hereditary peer who knew his bottom line from his fishing-line. Under the watchful eyes of the royal ancestors, immortalized by sundry old masters, Airlie made the world's press wait forty minutes before arriving to read his statement:

It has been increasingly apparent over the last few years that a growing emphasis on royal wealth, tax and the Civil List, particularly during a period of recession, was tending to obscure and distort the contribution made by the Queen to our national life. Perhaps we tend to forget, except in times of grave crisis or celebration, the importance of the sovereign as a focus for national unity, as a source of stability and continuity, and as someone to encourage and reward excellence and achievement and to bring people together.

The new arrangements, said Lord Airlie, would place 'a considerable additional burden' on the royal finances.

For the first time since his predecessor, Lord Cobbold, in 1971, Lord Airlie proceeded to tackle rumours about the Queen's private wealth. 'This emphasis on the financial side derives, to some extent at least, from estimates of the Queen's private funds, often ranging from one hundred million to billions of pounds. Her Majesty has authorized me to say that even the lowest of these estimates is grossly overstated.' Defending the Queen's immunity from inheritance tax, her Lord Chamberlain went on: 'In order to be constitutionally impartial, the sovereign must have, and be seen to have, an appropriate degree of financial independence.' Asked by a television reporter if he accepted the argument that 'she is not like me', His Lordship replied merely with a disdainful 'Yes'.

That evening Michael Peat, the Royal Household's director of finance and property services, gave unprecedented television interviews to explain the new arrangements. 'The Queen is a very pragmatic person,' he said. 'She appreciates that there is a general feeling that she should pay taxes.' Savings would have to be made as a result. 'I have to say that the Queen's expenditure is not extravagant at the moment.'

The consensus over the next few days was that the Queen would wind up paying around £1 million in tax each year, which would have minimal impact on either the royal finances or the national debt. Even *The Daily Telegraph* felt that the government had only just succeeded in treading 'that narrow line between public acceptability and royal approval . . . The Queen's advisers must feel pleased that they have enabled her to

The tabloid papers, tribunes of the people, smell blood.

Four failed marriages: Princess Margaret and Lord Snowdon (1960), Princess Anne and Captain Mark Phillips (1973), Prince Charles and Lady Diana Spencer (1981), and Prince Andrew and Sarah Ferguson (1986).

Princess Margaret with
Peter Townsend, the royal
equerry she was not allowed
to marry; and Princess Anne
with Tim Laurence, the
royal equerry she did marry
– second time around.

decade sees the Wales's 'fairy-tale' marriage slowly collapse.

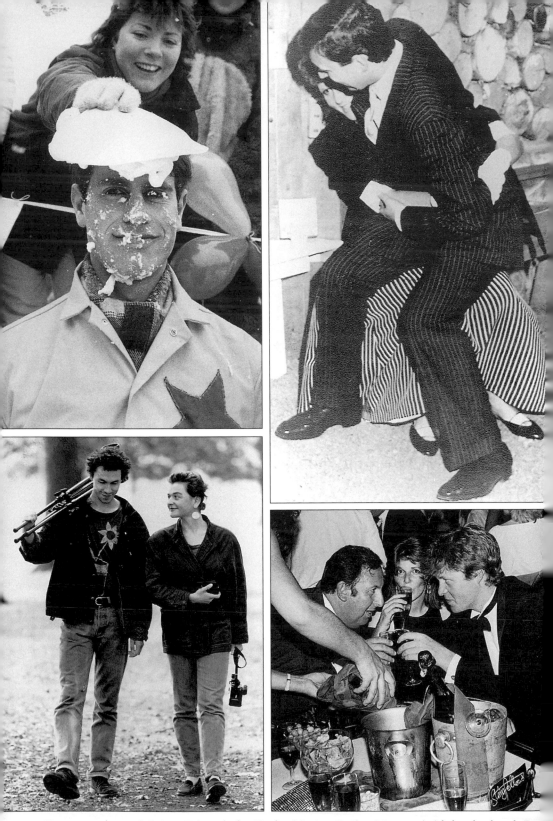

How not *to be royal*: Prince Edward, the Yorks, Marina Ogilvy Mowatt (with her husband, Pau
and Charles, Earl Spencer, the Princess of Wales's brother.

the Royal Enclosure at Ascot, the Queen and Prince Charles disapprove of the fun-loving
ys of Diana and Fergie.

Queen Elizabeth II is not amused by the events of 1992–93.

make this important gesture without denting her wealth to any real extent.' Estimating the royal share portfolio at £45 million, *The Times* praised the Queen's wisdom in subjecting herself 'as far as possible, to the same regime as everyone else . . . The concession should satisfy all but the most unreconstructed republicans. Now is the time for the sniping at the privileges of the royal family to stop.'

It didn't, of course. The *Daily Mirror* branded the Queen 'HM The Tax Dodger', complaining that 'so many royal perks will escape tax'. *The Independent* noted sourly that 'the employee or director who drives a company car, or is chauffeured in one, is taxed dearly if there is any suspicion that the vehicle has been used for even the shortest journey, even to and from work.' *The Guardian* wondered if Major had not allowed the Queen 'a tax-free palace too far'. Were *both* Sandringham and Balmoral really so vital to the Queen's public duties that they each deserve to be exempted from inheritance tax? 'Surely she goes there on holidays, not for official duties. Most monarchs manage to make do with just one country palace these days.'

'The Queen,' in the imperious reply of her director of finance, 'never goes on holiday . . . Every day of the year she has to read and respond to state papers.' This was a concept, felt one columnist, which could be usefully extended to many other taxpayers. 'How about newspaper columnists? Most columnists spend the entire week thinking about our columns. Waking and sleeping, eating and drinking, at home and at work, not a second goes by in which our column is not in our thoughts. Ergo, every single thing we do is tax-deductible.'

As to the newly redefined royal art collection: if, for tax purposes, it was deemed to belong to the nation, then why couldn't the nation go and look at it? Buckingham Palace, where many of the pictures were hung, was never open to the public, even though the public financed it for the Queen's tax-free use. The collection included, for example, the only extant Vermeer not on public display, *Lady at the Virginals*, valued at £50 million. As part-owners, Britons might perhaps feel entitled to take a look at it. The Queen's Gallery, risen from the ashes of the bombed Buckingham Palace chapel, could place on public view but a fraction of the 7,000 paintings in the royal collection – only a quarter of which were, at any given moment, on loan to exhibitions around the country. By far the largest selection was hung, in rotation, on the walls of Buckingham Palace, for the private enjoyment of the Queen and her family. Why not, therefore, open the palace's public rooms to the private gaze, and allow British taxpayers to inspect their property? An estimated million visitors a year at a charge of £10 a head, as Simon Jenkins argued in *The Times*, would bring in £10 million a year for the new Royal Collection Trust (to be chaired by the Prince of Wales). 'It would be one of the great visitor attractions of Europe, yielding a sense of royal accessibility without any royal inconvenience.'

Jenkins had started something. One of the declared aims of the Trust, after all, was 'to educate and inform the public about such collections and archives by exhibition'. Several papers echoed his call for the opening of the Palace: 'There needs to be greater openness in dealings between the sovereign and her people, a greater readiness to lower the barriers that separate them. Why, for example, can parts of Buckingham Palace not be opened to public inspection?' On 29 April 1993 it was announced that the Queen *would* be opening Buckingham Palace to visitors – but only for the two months per year she was well out of the way at Balmoral, only for an experimental five-year period, and only to raise money towards the £40 million required to repair Windsor. To avoid digging in her own pocket, she was proposing to charge Britons £8 a head to enter a building they owned and maintained, to inspect their own paintings and other state treasures. The point of principle had not been conceded. Again the monarchy had reacted hastily to public pressure; and again it had missed the point.

Sir Roy Strong, former director of the Victoria and Albert Museum, also favoured wider exhibition of the royal collection, but wondered about the terms of reference of the new Trust. 'We haven't really been told anything,' he complained. 'Does this mean there is a body of works of art separate from the Queen's tiara and other treasures that actually belong to her? If there is a discrimination between the two, what is it? It sounds like the old bottle with a new label.'

The tax exemption on assets passed from sovereign to sovereign was widely questioned. For the rest of the population, only wealth passed to a spouse is free of inheritance tax, which begins at 40 per cent on sums above £150,000. The Labour Party, already re-examining the monarch's powers to dissolve parliament and choose a prime minister, denied reports that it would revoke the Queen's immunity; but party leaders remained openly critical, among them the Shadow Chancellor, Gordon Brown. 'The challenge to the government,' he said, 'is to explain why it has exempted the monarchy from inheritance tax but done nothing to honour its election promise to cut the tax for millions of ordinary home-owning families.' Most contentious of all, however, was the continued use – entirely free of the taxes normally levied on such business 'perks' – of royal transport costing the taxpayer £22 million a year.

Where, for instance, had Prince Philip been on his forty-fifth wedding aniversary, the day Windsor Castle burned down? When Philip had married the Queen in November 1947, he had been a penniless immigrant, with only two suits to his name. Forty-five years later, on a tax-free annual income of £359,000 a year, he had spent the third week of November 1992 in Argentina for a meeting of the World Wide Fund for Nature, of which he is president. Although this was not a royal engagement, he had flown there in a British Aerospace 146 jet of the Queen's Flight, at a cost to the taxpayer of some £2,000 an hour (or £400,000 for the week away). The same week also saw Princess Anne use one of the royal jets to fly to Florence for a meeting of the International Equestrian Federation, of which she is president – another non-royal excursion at the taxpayer's expense.

Where was Prince Charles on the night his son William under-went emergency surgery for a fractured skull? After an evening at the opera, Charles took the Royal Train to York overnight, to spend the next day showing European Commissioners around the East Riding 'wetlands'. He then flew home by Royal Flight. The train thus spent the night in a siding, before travelling back empty while an empty aircraft flew up to collect him. Charles's Yorkshire 'awayday', while his wife kept vigil at their son's hospital bedside, cost the British taxpayer in excess of £70,000.

Even as Major and Airlie were making their announcements, HMY *Britannia* was steaming towards Cozumel, Mexico, to pick up the Prince of Wales for a Caribbean cruise. After one day in the United States and five in Mexico, his first overseas tour since his separation from the Princess of Wales, Charles wanted to relax in the sun for a few days, his every whim catered for by *Britannia*'s 277-strong crew. The royal yacht then sailed on to Dominica, to pick up his father for ten more days' royal relaxation before a non-royal speech in Florida.

As his wife's subjects buckled beneath Norman Lamont's latest budget, Prince Philip spent ten days on *Britannia* cruising the Caribbean at a cost to the taxpayer exceeding £5 million. 'Outrageous' and 'insensitive' were the words on the lips of MPs of all parties. 'Philip must need his head examining,' said a Conservative, David Evans, while Charles Kennedy, for the Liberal Democrats, thought it 'inept' of the Queen's husband to head for the sun 'when clouds are still gathering for the royals at home'. Labour's Tony Banks called the royal yacht 'a luxury the nation simply cannot afford'.

Banks had a point. At 412 feet and 5,769 tons, the six-deck *Britannia* is the world's biggest private yacht, manned by a complement of 21 officers and 256 men. Commissioned by Clement Attlee's outgoing Labour government in 1951, at a cost of £2.1 million, it was launched on the Clyde in 1953. Even Attlee felt obliged to justify the expense by arguing that it could rapidly be converted into a hospital ship in time of war.

Forty years on, in December 1992, *Britannia* was growing so aged that maintenance and refurbishment costs were not reflected in its annual public subsidy, which had risen from £11.4 million in 1991 to £12.5 million in 1992. The Armed Forces minister, Archie Hamilton, told the Commons it could not now be used as a hospital ship. The truth was that it never had been. Once, while sailing past Aden, the yacht picked up civil war refugees and dropped them at Mogadishu; but that is the only 'action' it has ever seen. It was a popular misconception that the royal yacht had taken part in the Falklands conflict; *Britannia* would not have been able to keep up with the rest of the fleet, which ran on diesel, because the royal yacht then burned heavy fuel oil

– so that its slow-revving engines would avoid disturbing the royal sleep. The Ministry of Defence spent £6 million converting it to diesel in 1984; but the yacht was not used in the Gulf War, either, as defence chiefs decided that it would be too expensive to bring it back from South America, where it was awaiting a royal visit, and to install helicopter decks for landing the wounded. According to the Labour MP John McWilliam, a member of the Commons Defence Committee, the royal yacht 'cannot be sent into action because there is no nuclear, biological or chemical protection on board. It is an elderly and labour-intensive vessel. It is a bit of a nuisance.'

In 1989 *Britannia* was used by the royal family on 55 days – the highest figure throughout the 1980s. This declined to 42 in 1990, 31 in 1991, and 27 in 1992. At £32,000 a day, the yacht thus cost the taxpayer £10.48 million for the time it sat idle. Other costs, meanwhile, were rising inexorably. Beside the £6 million on diesel conversion in 1984, a further £17.5 million was spent three years later on full-scale refurbishment, including £3 million on new royal apartments alone. The ship had another £7 million refit in 1992. The Ministry of Defence confirms that *Britannia* will need even more expensive repairs within the next five years to remain seaworthy. 'In view of her age, it is obviously sensible to consider her future,' Hamilton told the Commons in January 1993. To replace *Britannia* would cost at least £80 million.

The yacht had become 'a geriatric waste of money,' said Labour MP Alan Williams. 'It should be retired as soon as possible.' The Conservative Peter Viggers, chairman of the Commons Defence Committee, believed it would be 'a tragedy to lose it. If it is too expensive to run, why don't they use it for trade more often?' For several years, the government had been developing the notion of 'sea days' aboard the yacht to coincide with royal visits abroad. Businessmen and dignitaries were to be taken on a day's cruise, in the hope that the yacht's magnificent interior would impress upon them the merits of British design and technology. 'It earns colossal sums overseas,' claimed the Queen's perennial financial apologist, Lord Wyatt, when *Britannia* came under attack in 1993. 'American and other foreign businessmen come aboard and sign multi-million contracts after lunch or dinner on board.' In truth, as the Ministry of Defence confirmed, *Britannia* had undertaken precisely three 'sea days' in 1991, and three in 1992.

The oldest vessel in the British Navy, after Nelson's flagship *Victory, Britannia* is decorated in manor-house style, with oak panels, hand-woven rugs, antique chairs and hand-picked flowers from around the royal residences. While the royals are aboard, the crew wear a special uniform to show they are about royal duties: their jumpers are tucked inside their trousers, which are trimmed with a black silk bow. White-coated stewards are on round-the-clock duty to serve drinks and meals either in the royal cabins or in the elegant dining room, whose antique walnut table scats forty. The dining room doubles as private cinema with seating for twenty.

The crew are trained to look away when a royal comes in sight. Silence is compulsory; the staff communicate by hand signals and wear rubber soles so as not to disturb the royal slumbers. 'The royal family are treated better on board *Britannia* than they are at the Palace,' said one former crew member. 'Everything has to be just right.' In the Caribbean, there was even a twenty-six-strong Royal Marines band on board for the royal princes' entertainment.

Philip flew to meet *Britannia* aboard a British Aerospace 146 jet of the Queen's Flight (at a return cost to the taxpayer, as has been seen, of more than a dozen times the first-class return fare aboard British Airways). The royal fleet consists of three 146s bought by the Ministry of Defence for the Queen's Flight in 1986 for £16.4 million each, and two Wessex helicopters. They are used primarily by the Queen, Prince Philip and the Prince of Wales ; other family members may use the aircraft only on royal business and with the Queen's permission. In 1993 the future of the Queen's Flight, like that of the royal yacht, was officially declared 'under review' by the Ministry of Defence, who had been asked to 'make savings'. One idea under discussion was to cut back the fleet to just one aircraft for official trips. Public criticism had grown since 1990, when Charles used one of his mother's jets to go skiing; the cost to the taxpayer was £20,000, compared with a commercial fare of less than £500. In March 1993, while his estranged wife flew by scheduled aircraft for an official aid visit to Nepal, Charles flew to another skiing holiday in Klosters in a jet of the Queen's Flight, which returned to collect him a week later.

On her first trip abroad following her separation, the Princess of Wales took her sons to the Caribbean aboard a scheduled flight, herself travelling economy. The same month, January 1993, prime minister John Major dispensed with the RAF VC10 used by his predecessors and travelled around India in a 747 chartered from British Airways. The prime minister, said Downing Street, covered the costs of the trip by charging members of the press who came along for the ride. Besides, he was determined to 'fly the flag'. Many Britons now seem to think that the royals should be doing the same.

A Gallup poll for *The Daily Telegraph* in February 1993 showed that a majority of the British people, at all levels of society, thought the monarchy had 'lost touch with ordinary people', and wanted the royals to drop their 'over-lavish' lifestyle. Although 87 per cent still thought the Queen did 'a good job', three out of four of her subjects felt that 'too many members of the family lead an idle, jet-set kind of existence.' Even after the Queen's agreement to pay some taxes, only one in three Britons believed the monarchy gave 'good value for money', and only one in four wanted the institution to stay as it was. Less than a quarter thought the taxpayer should continue to fund the royal yacht, with only a handful more supporting continued public subsidy of the palaces, train and planes.

Prince Edward may dismiss estimates of his mother's wealth as 'absolute crap', but *The Wall Street Journal* has recently calculated that the British monarchy costs the taxpayer almost double the *combined* cost of the monarchies of the Netherlands, Sweden, Spain, Belgium, Denmark and Norway.★ The Queen's tax concessions will not be the end of the debate, believes Philip

★To the Palace response that the British monarchy was 'international in scale', the Queen being 'head of state of seventeen countries and Head of the Commonwealth to boot', a *Sunday Times* reader wrote from Gwynedd, Wales, to ask what financial contribution – 'if any' – was made towards the cost of the monarchy by any of these seventeen countries or by the rest of the Commonwealth. 'Not a penny, I suspect, otherwise we would have been told about it *ad nauseam* by the royal apologists, as a further point to try to convince us that the cost to the long-suffering taxpayer here is negligible.'

Hall, the man who started it. Sticking firmly to his £400 million estimate of the monarch's private wealth (on which he calculated tax due at £8.5 million a year), Hall summed up: 'The Queen has decided to remain above the law. The principle that holds true is that people expect the Queen and the royal family to pay tax according to the same rules as everyone else.

'If a future King Charles or King William does not pay inheritance tax on what he inherits from the Queen, his reign will start off in the type of controversy that her tax announcement was supposed to avoid.'

PART TWO
LONG TO REIGN
OVER US?

CHAPTER 6

A 'FAMILY' MONARCHY: 1917–52

'A family on the throne is an interesting idea.'
WALTER BAGEHOT,
The English Constitution

THE YEAR IS 2021. TWELVE MONTHS AFTER THE DEATH OF
Queen Elizabeth II at ninety-four (almost as old as her revered
mother at the time of her death), the coronation of King Charles
III is taking place in Westminster Abbey. The King has failed to
persuade parliament to pass legislation enabling him to divorce
his estranged wife, Diana, and deprive her of the title of Queen
Consort; but he has still denied her the right to attend his
coronation. When the Queen turns up at the Abbey anyway,
with a large retinue of enthusiastic supporters, she is refused
admission. Riots are but narrowly avoided.

This unlikely-sounding scenario would in fact be an action
replay of the scene exactly two hundred years before, when the
new King George IV attempted to deal with the consequences of
a twenty-four-year separation from his immensely popular wife
Caroline. The new *status quo* of today's junior royals – by which
the Princess of Wales lives an overtly separate life, both public
and private, from her husband – offers the House of Windsor
the prospect of an equally divisive, potentially terminal future.

A month before their formal separation was announced, Diana made a stern declaration of intent on 14 November 1992, her husband's forty-fourth birthday. Far from spending the day baking him cakes at Highgrove, she was in Paris taking the French by storm – not least President Mitterrand, with whom she enjoyed a forty-minute audience. A meeting with Hillary Clinton, Diana's unelected equivalent across the Atlantic, seemed inevitable. Not content with emulating Mother Teresa's charitable work, Diana seemed intent on moving in on her husband's diplomatic patch and cornering his international *gravitas*. It was one way of gaining revenge for what she saw as his betrayal of their marriage vows.

Unlike George and Caroline, Charles and Diana seem likely to get divorced with almost unseemly speed – probably during 1995, little more than two years after their formal separation. If not, Charles should urgently re-read his Cambridge history books to learn from George IV's bitter experience. Although Caroline's attempt to gatecrash her husband's coronation ended in her public humiliation, she was quite within her legal rights. Constitutionally, as John Major has told the House of Commons, an undivorced Diana would also be perfectly entitled to claim her share of the throne.

George IV's first act on becoming King was to remove Caroline's name from the traditional prayers for the royal family in *The Book of Common Prayer*. For several years, in anticipation of his accession, he had been seeking ways to discredit and divorce his wife. Although himself well-known to be a copious adulterer, George had devoted much of his energy as Prince of Wales to compiling evidence of Caroline's extra-marital activities. *Plus ça change.* Those around the present Prince of Wales have mounted a desperate campaign, in the wake of the Camillagate tape, to marginalize the princess as part of their programme to rehabilitate the prince. The clandestine methods involved are detailed later in these pages; at the time of writing, they do not appear to be working.

Even in an age before tabloid newspapers, mobile phones and sophisticated scanning equipment, George's 'dirty tricks' also succeeded only in increasing the huge popular support enjoyed by his wife, whom he was perceived to have cruelly wronged. When public outcry had caused his measures against her to fail in the House of Lords, prompting his dilemma over a joint coronation, huge crowds had cheered her regal procession to a thanksgiving service in St Paul's. Three weeks after his coronation, the King was 'gayer than might be proper to tell' when Caroline's sudden death, attributed to years of suffering at his hands, solved all his problems.

Fifty years later, the whole episode was still fresh in the mind of William Gladstone, prime minister when Queen Victoria's dissolute son Bertie (the future King Edward VII) became entangled in the Mordaunt divorce case. 'So long as the nation has confidence in the personal character of the sovereign,' he told the then Prince of Wales, 'the throne of this empire may be regarded as secure. But the revival of circumstances only half a century old must tend rapidly to impair its strength and might bring about its overthrow.'

The republican movement of the 1870s was fuelled less by outrage at the Prince of Wales's sexual misconduct than resentment of Victoria's reclusive widowhood, during which she performed few public engagements to 'justify' her Civil List subsidy. Even if Elizabeth II ends the century paying her taxes, however, will her heir care to be booed while his wife is cheered, as were Bertie and Princess Alexandra? Will he sleep easy as toastmasters again call for glasses to be raised separately: 'For the Princess'?

Charles's appetite as a libertine may scarcely rival that of some of his Hanoverian ancestors. But his contribution to the conspicuous collapse of the royal family's domestic stability, along with the widespread public ill-feeling about the royal finances, has recently conspired to create a distinctly rebellious atmosphere, chipping remorselessly away at the foundations of an institution traditionally expected to set a moral example. Seventy-five years of royal stability had been undone in as many weeks; for the Royal House of Windsor had relied for its popular appeal on the notion of a 'family' monarchy, symbolic of the nation's public and private virtues, ever since it changed its name from Saxe-Coburg-Gotha in 1917.

★

King George V managed to reign over a nation at war with Germany for three blood-stained years before being persuaded of the insupportable irony that most of his family, not to mention he himself and his dynasty, bore distinctly German names.

A shy if irascible man, George was 'sensitive to criticism and prone to self-doubt', in the words of his official biographer, Harold Nicolson (who was told that he would be expected to 'omit things and incidents which were discreditable to the royal family'). The King apparently 'started and grew pale' when told of whispers that he and his close relatives were suspected of pro-German sympathies. The Kaiser was, after all, George's cousin; and the King's private secretary, Lord Stamfordham, was gravely obliged to admit that many members of the royal family did indeed bear distinctly Teutonic names. Of those then residing in England, the King's brothers-in law were the Duke of Teck and Prince Alexander of Teck; his cousins were Prince Louis and Prince Alexander of Battenberg. Others were Dukes and Duchesses of Saxony and Princes and Princess of Saxe-Coburg and Gotha – the very name of the royal house itself.

It had to be changed – but to what? Truth to tell, the King was not even sure what his own surname was. Coburg, perhaps, as in the abbreviated name of the royal dynasty? Called upon for advice, Mr Farnham Burke of the Royal College of Heralds also displayed some doubt. He was sure it was not 'Stewart'; it might perhaps be 'Guelph'. Most likely was either 'Wipper' or 'Wettin', neither of which would do at all. There was only one thing for it: a wholesale change of names.

As the British army floundered at Passchendaele, the summer of 1917 saw George V 'much occupied' with the matter of choosing a new dynastic name to ring through subsequent British history. The Duke of Connaught suggested 'Tudor-Stewart', but political advisers such as Lord Rosebery and H. H. Asquith felt that the name might have 'inauspicious associations'. 'Plantagenet', 'York', 'England', 'Lancaster': many more noble names were considered and rejected, even exotica such as 'D'Este' and 'Fitzroy' (which the King rather liked until told that it meant 'royal bastard'). Then Stamfordham came up with the name of the pleasant and unassailably English town in which the royal family spent its weekends.★ On 17 July 1917, a royal proclamation formally approved by the Privy Council duly announced that King George V had decided to change the name of his dynasty, his family and their descendants to Windsor.

For good measure, the King was further persuaded that all his relatives should undergo similar cosmetic metamorphoses. The Duke of Teck became the Marquis of Cambridge, Prince Alexander of Teck the Earl of Athlone. The Battenbergs anglicized their family name to Mountbatten, Prince Louis becoming the Marquis of Milford Haven and Prince Alexander the Marquis of Carisbrooke. It was 'tacitly accepted' within the terms of the proclamation that in accepting peerages of the United Kingdom, and thus becoming members of the House of Lords, members of the royal family 'would not identify themselves with any political party'.

For the fiercely proud King, the birth of the Royal House of Windsor was a moment of unexpected and humiliating defeat after several years of stout resistance. Since the outbreak of war with his first cousin, Kaiser Wilhelm II of the House of Hohenzollern, he had turned away angry demands for the removal of certain Garter banners from St George's Chapel at Windsor, arguing that they were symbols of past rather than present history. But the Kaiser himself was among eight German Knights of the Garter whose well-being was still prayed for, at the height of the war, during Garter services. Even the King's mother, the Danish-born Queen Alexandra, urged him to 'have down those hateful German banners in our sacred church'.

The argument, to the King, was 'petty and undignified', as was the nationwide rash of anti-German sentiment, which had seen the First Sea Lord, Prince Louis of Battenberg, forced to resign because of the 'painful' truth that 'at this juncture my birth and parentage have the effect of impairing in some respect my usefulness at the Board of Admiralty.' Next to go was the

★Stamfordham's son, Sir Michael (later Lord) Adeane, was private secretary to Queen Elizabeth II, 1953–72; Lord Adeane's son, Edward, became private secretary to the present Prince of Wales in 1979. Although apparently destined to follow his father and grandfather as private secretary to British kings, Edward Adeane abruptly resigned after only six years, thus ending more than a century of unbroken service by his family to the royal dynasty whose name his grandfather had chosen.

Lord Chancellor, Lord Haldane, hounded from office after rashly describing Germany as his 'spiritual home'. (What Haldane actually meant was that he had pleasant memories of his student days at the University of Heidelberg; on his resignation, the King promptly signalled his sympathy by appointing him to the Order of Merit.) Even Asquith himself, while prime minister, was criticized for maintaining a German governess in Downing Street. Soon he insisted to the King that those Garter banners had to go. In a letter to the Dean of Windsor, deploring this 'dramatic action' in response to 'hysterical clamour', the King nevertheless refused to countenance the removal of the German names inscribed on the brass plates above their Garter stalls.

But other anomalies still abounded for his discomfort. The Kaiser and his son, for instance, figured in the British army list as the holders of honorary commands. Again the King resisted demands that they be publicly erased, or 'drummed out'; a quiet, inconspicuous removal of their names would suffice. Early in 1917 the report of a parliamentary committee then led to the Titles Deprivation Act, which stripped the German Dukes of Cumberland and Brunswick of their British rank. It was only a matter of time before the 'witch-hunt' reached the royal doorstep.

George was horrified when informed by his new prime minister, David Lloyd George, of a campaign of anonymous letters to Downing Street demanding to know how Britain expected to defeat Germany when the sovereign himself was German. At the same time as this unwelcome pressure came the even less welcome news from Russia of a revolution – greeted with excited approval in Britain by such prominent socialists (and republicans) as H. G. Wells and Ramsay MacDonald, the future prime minister. Amid calls for the establishment of Workers' and Soldiers' Councils came demands for the abolition of the 'alien and uninspiring' court. 'I may be uninspiring,' the King retorted, 'but I'll be damned if I'm alien.'

The Royal House of Windsor was thus a child of political necessity, delivered with some pain after considerable labour: not, perhaps, the most auspicious of births. For the King's comfort,

Stamfordham found a historical precedent dating back to King Edward III, who had also used the title 'Edward of Windsor'. But no royal dukes had commandeered the name of the pleasant Berkshire town identified with so many moments of English history; there were Dukes of Lancaster and Cornwall, York and Edinburgh, Gloucester and Kent, but none – as yet – of Windsor. Less comforting, however, was the Kaiser's immediate response. On hearing of his cousin's sudden metamorphosis, Wilhelm snorted that he was off to the theatre to see a performance of *The Merry Wives of Saxe-Coburg-Gotha*.

Although George V felt that he had been pressured into an unnecessary piece of window-dressing, he was subsequently obliged to admit its success. The novelty of the patriotic new dynastic name encouraged the British people to forge its twentieth-century habit of coalescing around the monarchy in time of war; and the King himself, having made a self-denying gesture towards popular feeling, enjoyed a new wave of almost universal respect. Eighteen years later, even he was taken by surprise at the now familiar outpouring of national affection on the occasion of his Silver Jubilee in 1935, the year before his death. 'I had no idea that I was so popular,' he told his friend Robert Menzies, the future prime minister of Australia. 'I am beginning to think,' he added to his nurse that night, 'that they must really like me for myself.'

Though a martinet within his family, George appeared to his people a decent but thoroughly average, none-too-bright naval man, characterized by simple pleasures such as fishing and stamp-collecting. It was an image which would set the tone through three generations for the royal house he had founded: a more down-to-earth, unpretentious monarchy, the 'First Family' of the land rather than an hereditary elite with pretensions to political power. Yet the picture is a deceptive one. Apart from the reluctant disavowal of its German origins, George V's reign saw at least three instances of a lingering constitutional role for the monarchy which could still come into play today.

When her grandson came to the throne, it was only thirty years since Queen Victoria had felt free to follow her personal

whims in vetoing some of her prime minister's major cabinet appointments and quibbling with his lesser ones (which Gladstone
had shown her, he complained to a colleague, 'only as a matter
of courtesy'). Not born to be King – he had inherited both the
succession and his wife from his older brother, Prince Albert
Victor ('Eddy'), who died of pneumonia in 1892 – George
also inherited from his father a constitutional crisis of major
proportions: a clash of wills between the government and the
House of Lords that touched on the very hereditary principles
which enshrined the institution of monarchy.

The protracted struggle between the Houses of Commons and
Lords had begun in 1909, with the Lords' rejection of Chancellor
Lloyd George's 'People's Budget', designed to raise money for
old-age pensions. Asquith, the Liberal prime minister, was constitutionally correct in his complaint that this was a breach of a
250-year-old convention whereby the upper, unelected chamber
did not interfere with financial legislation. When he held an
election on the issue, he was returned to power (though with
a reduced majority) hell-bent on reform of the Lords. The resulting Parliament Bill, limiting their Lordships' powers of veto,
presented Edward VII with an unpleasant dilemma: what to do
if the hereditary chamber, its powers dependent on the same
principle as his own, chose to veto the loss of its veto? Asquith
demanded of the King a guarantee that he would create enough
Liberal peers – three hundred, if necessary – to push the bill
through. 'We have never been nearer a revolution since 1688,'
wrote Lord Esher to his son. 'If the King says yes, he mortally
offends the whole Tory party to which he is naturally bound. If
he says no, he lets loose all the radical gutter press at his position
as sovereign and his person as a man. A charming dilemma, full
of revolutionary possibilities . . . '

George, Prince of Wales, as yet wholly ignorant of affairs of
state, had every confidence in his father's ability to tiptoe his
way through this potential minefield. But the issue remained
unresolved the following year, when he found himself the newest
of nine kings leading his father's funeral procession. After a
brief moratorium, Asquith demanded the same guarantee of the
new King George V, despite doubts as to whether he had the

constitutional right to do so. 'Most reluctantly,' George gave a 'contingent' guarantee to create hundreds of Liberal peers, his condition being that the deal remain secret. When the mere threat was made known to the Lords, they dutifully voted for their own emasculation to avoid dragging the monarchy into party politics in a cause that was already lost.

George V hated the whole experience. A lifelong naval officer, accustomed to giving and obeying unequivocal orders, he detested the complex machiavellian scheming of day-to-day politics – especially when it required of him secret undertakings, divulged not even to the cabinet, which seemed to him underhand. The niceties of Asquith's argument about an undertaking given during one parliament for possible use in the next, after an election, were also lost on this political innocent. Certain details of the affair, notably an offer by the Tory leader, Arthur Balfour, to form a government and force a general election, had been kept from the neophyte King by his private secretary, Lord Knollys. Just as well, perhaps, for they would have involved him in even deeper complexities.

George's second intervention in the political process followed more than a decade later, in 1923, when his national standing had been greatly enhanced by the shared trauma of the First World War. Following a post-war period of disturbing social unrest, Lloyd George's coalition government had broken up, to be replaced by a Conservative administration under Andrew Bonar Law. When, after only six months in office, Bonar Law discovered he was mortally ill, the King was forced to make a choice between Lord Curzon and Stanley Baldwin, both of whom enjoyed strong support in the party. Called in as an elder statesman for his advice, Lord Balfour considered Curzon 'an old friend whom he could not bear', Baldwin 'a nobody'. But he persuaded the King that the government should be led from the House of Commons, rather than the Lords (despite Baldwin's lack of 'special gifts' or 'exceptional ability'). Thus did George V exercise his royal prerogative to nominate a prime minister. Although he could not know it, he was appointing the very man who would be called on to save the monarchy from the unconventional aspirations of his oldest son, the Prince of Wales.

Baldwin had lost power by the time of George's next and great-est political crisis, in 1931, when the collapse of the pound led to a financial crisis which split the Labour government of Ramsay MacDonald. After a stormy cabinet meeting, MacDonald went to the Palace to tender his resignation – only to discover that the King had already received Baldwin, the Conservative leader, and Sir Herbert Samuel, acting leader of the Liberals during Lloyd George's long illness. To his surprise, MacDonald found himself being asked to form a national coalition government; Baldwin and Samuel, he was told, had already indicated their willingness to participate. He agreed, of course, precipitating a split in the Labour Party which would haunt it for many years. This constitutional tinkering on the King's part is still seen as the last, dubious hurrah of the royal prerogative (though there have been moments when Elizabeth II has been forced perilously close to intervention; *see* Chapter 7). As recently as 1960, the Labour elder statesman Herbert Morrison argued that George V had acted unconstitutionally in inviting MacDonald to form a government; the correct course would have been to send for Baldwin, leader of the next largest party, to form a government with Liberal support. Not to put too fine a point on it, there was widespread suspicion that the King had deliberately precipitated the split in the Labour Party which would keep it out of power for many years. This was certainly the view of Sir Stafford Cripps, a future member of Churchill's wartime coalition and Attlee's post-war Labour government, who said two years later: 'When the Labour Party comes to power we must act rapidly . . . There is no doubt that we shall have to overcome opposition from Buckingham Palace as well as other places.'

These constitutional arguments were wholly lost on George's heir, the dashing Edward, Prince of Wales (known to his family as David), who was a very popular figure with the public despite his undisguised taste for a life of idle pleasure. His wartime service in France was taken as an indication that his sense of duty would eventually override his all-too-evident hedonism. But when Britain expected Edward to do his duty, and find himself a future queen, he chose rather to launch himself upon the 1930s with an abandoned self-indulgence none of his younger brothers displayed. Albert ('Bertie'), the Duke of York, had married Lady Elizabeth Bowes-Lyon, daughter of the 14th Earl Strathmore, in 1923; George, Duke of Kent, married Princess Marina of Greece in 1934; Henry, Duke of Gloucester, married Lady Alice Montagu Douglas Scott the following year.

It fell to the Duke of York and his wife to keep the Windsor dynasty's 'family' image afloat. Their two daughters, Elizabeth and Margaret Rose, had been largely shielded from publicity until the events of 1936 thrust them centre-stage. For the first ten years of Elizabeth's life, the York household had enjoyed a cosy fireside glow of which we have a vivid, if saccharine portrait via the celebrated indiscretions of Miss Marion Crawford ('Crawfie'), who spent fifteen years with the family before publishing the book which would see it disown and ostracize her.

Amid today's controversy over Elizabeth's raising of her own children, it is intriguing to read her governess' evidence that 'no-one ever had employers who interfered so little'. As Lord Rees-Mogg has recently observed, this was 'the end of the period in which children were brought up, whether royal or not, in the traditional British values, that strange mixture of stoicism, Christianity and class deference which was the underlying ideology of the British Empire.' When their parents were leaving for a tour of Canada, for instance, Elizabeth told her younger sister: 'Your handkerchief is to wave, not to cry into.' Wrote 'Crawfie' herself: 'I often had the feeling that the Duke and Duchess, most happy in their own married life, were not over-concerned with the higher education of their daughters. They wanted most for them a really happy childhood, with lots of pleasant memories stored up against the days that might come and, later, happy marriages.'

In later life, as Duke of Windsor, King Edward VIII proved himself at least aware of the image his father had pioneered, and had wished him to maintain: 'The King himself, in the role of the bearded paterfamilias, his devoted and queenly wife, their four grown sons and a daughter, not to mention the rising generation of grandchildren – he transformed the Crown as personified by the royal family into a model of the traditional family virtues.' Edward himself would never preside over such an idyllic royal group – and his dying father seemed to know it, displaying some sixth sense of the crisis which would follow his demise. One of the last pleasures of the old King's life had been looking through his binoculars from Buckingham Palace to 145 Piccadilly, where little Princess 'Lilibet' would be waiting at the window to wave to him. On one such occasion, with uncanny foresight, the dying King had said: 'I pray that my eldest son will never marry and have children, and that nothing will come between Bertie and Lilibet and the throne.'

Throughout the 1930s the Yorks' relaxed family life at Royal Lodge, Windsor, was a far cry from the goings-on down the road at Fort Belvedere, where Edward, Prince of Wales was conducting only semi-discreet affairs with older, married women. Most of fashionable society knew of the prince's liaisons with Mrs Dudley-Ward and Lady Furness. Soon they were to hear, too, of a Mrs Wallis Simpson, whom he had first met at the Fort late in 1930. Such a mythology has come to surround this first encounter that doubts have been cast even upon their own respective accounts of it. The least likely small-talk to have passed between them, however, is that most often repeated:

The prince, on realizing that Mrs Simpson is an American: 'Do you not miss the comforts of central heating here in England?'

Mrs Simpson: 'I'm sorry, Sir, but you have disappointed me. Every American woman who comes to your country is always asked the same question. I had hoped for something more original from the Prince of Wales.'

In the words of Lady Furness, who had introduced them, and was herself American-born: 'Had this been true, it would have been not only bad taste but bad manners.' The truth is that Mrs Simpson, an American divorcee newly married to an Englishman, was delighted to be introduced into princely circles – and quite as excited as the next mere mortal on first catching sight of, let alone meeting, the royal family's most glamorous member. This is probably why neither of them could remember precisely what, if anything, was actually said. Edward, for his part, was simply meeting a friend of a friend, and turning on his instinctive, *ex-officio* charm. The couple would meet socially, with increasing regularity, for the best part of three years before anything more than an acquaintanceship developed.

Wallis Warfield, daughter of an old and prosperous Baltimore family, had been born in Pennsylvania on 19 June 1896. When only nineteen she had married an American naval officer, Earl Winfield Spencer Jr – a surprising choice, given her own unconcealed ambition 'to marry money'. Spencer had neither much money nor much prospect of making any, but the young Wallis was apparently of a mind to marry ('to get away from her family,' said a friend) and did so impetuously. It did not last long. Spencer turned out to be neurotically jealous; his wife's public vivacity, whether flirtatious or merely high-spirited, soon turned him into an alcoholic, then a sadist. (He would lock her in the bathroom, sometimes all night.) It is extravagantly ironic, in light of subsequent events, that when she told her family she wanted a divorce, these proper Baltimore people threw up their hands in horror and asked her to reconsider. Said her Uncle Sol, who cut her off without a penny: 'The Warfields in all their connections since 1662 have never had a divorce.' What, he demanded, would people think?

People knew just what they thought when Wallis surfaced in England ten years later, now married to the wealthy, bookish and beetle-browed figure of Ernest Simpson, himself half-American and already once divorced. She was thought – not to put too fine a point on it – pushy. It is a long-standing misconception that the British aristocracy's aversion to Mrs Simpson was due either to her being American or to her being divorced. Many well-born Englishmen had already taken American brides, Nancy Astor and Emerald Cunard being prominent examples; and high society had learnt, since the days of King Edward VII's offstage antics, to tolerate not just the royal habit of hijacking other men's wives but the divorces which often resulted. What people disliked about Mrs Simpson was that she didn't know the proper way to behave in polite society. She combined all the worst hallmarks of determined social climbing with a haughty, self-assertive, very unBritish disregard for propriety. By so publicly taking command of her prince, and behaving with scant respect towards other members of his family, she committed a social crime far more heinous than possessing merely the wrong citizenship or marital status.

It was early in 1934 that the prince realized he was in love with Mrs Simpson, and late the following year that he must marry her, regardless of the consequences. In his memoirs the Duke of Windsor pleaded with posterity that he would have confided in his parents, sought their guidance, had not 1935 been the year of his father's Silver Jubilee, with an unusually heavy public schedule aggravating the King's already poor health. It is questionable whether this particular father and son could have discussed such a matter constructively, if at all. What is revealing is the duke's confession that he was contemplating the marriage, resigned to the fact that it would probably put his brother on the throne, at least a year before it actually did so. And he had never breathed a word to anyone, least of all poor Bertie. The Prince of Wales's brother and his wife were quite oblivious to the gathering drama around them.

King George V died just before midnight on 20 January 1936, his demise accelerated by a lethal injection from his doctor, Lord Dawson of Penn, to be in time for the 'respectable' morning papers rather than the 'less desirable' evening journals. There are those in the royal family who believe to this day that distress over his eldest son's liaison with Mrs Simpson hastened his end; the Prince of Wales had brought her, outrageously in his father's eyes, to his Silver Jubilee ball only a few months earlier. Shortly before his death, the King voiced his fears to his prime minister, Stanley Baldwin: 'After I am dead, that boy will ruin himself within twelve months.'

In fact, King Edward VIII's unsuitability for the crown went far beyond the instinctive hypocrisy of his famous remark to un-employed Welsh miners that 'Something must be done'. (What he actually said was that something must be done 'to see that they stay working', because 'agitation and Bolshevism' were behind the coalfield crisis.) His innate prejudices extended to racist sentiments 'even beyond the norm for his generation', to his biographer, Philip Ziegler; he once wrote to his mother, Queen Mary, of his 'disgust' at being offered communion by a black priest in Sierra Leone. Later, Edward's instinctive Fascism would lead him into sympathy with Germany's distinctive new breed of National Socialism. So Britain was mercifully relieved of a potentially disastrous sovereign when Edward VIII's reign lasted only 325 days – almost managing, even in that short time, to bring down the House of Windsor on the eve of its twentieth anniversary.

The suddenness of George V's death, almost as soon as his Jubilee Year was over, had in itself speeded the fulfilment of his dying prayer that nothing would come 'between Bertie and Lilibet and the throne'. Such a fate was emphatically not the wish of Bertie himself, let alone his nine-year-old daughter. As heir presumptive, however, and brother of a man who showed no immediate intention of settling down to the breeding of heirs, Bertie now had to square up to the fact that he or his elder daughter might one day inherit the crown. But it seems not to have crossed his mind, as he and David joined their two younger brothers to stand ceremonial guard over their father's coffin, that 1936 might turn out to be a year in which Britain had three kings, the last of them himself.

The second of those kings was more than aware of the possibility. Later that day, as he processed behind his father's body through the streets of London, Edward caught sight of 'a flash of light dancing across the pavement'. It was the Maltese Cross which surmounted the Imperial Crown, which a jolt of the gun carriage had sent toppling down from the catafalque into the gutter of the Strand. 'I wondered,' he said later, 'whether it was a bad omen.' At the time he was heard to exclaim, 'Christ! What will happen next?' The MP who reported the remark, Bob Boothby, turned to his companion and suggested that it was 'a fitting motto for the coming reign'.

King Edward VIII started in a spirit of innovation. On the very night of his father's death he ordered all the Sandringham clocks, kept half an hour fast by the punctual George V, to be restored to the correct time. He then undertook the first flight by a British monarch – to London, to preside over his inaugural Privy Council. That day he insisted on Mrs Simpson's presence at his side for his proclamation ceremony at St James's. He then caused further offence by receiving overseas ambassadors *en masse*, rather than individually (as was traditional on the accession of a new king), and by abolishing the wearing of ribbons at the monarch's birthday parade. Those who saw all this as a breath of fresh air were further heartened on St David's Day, 1 March, when a broadcast by the new King to his people marked the first time a British monarch had dispensed with the royal 'we'.

But all this betrayed an interest in trivial, symbolic matters at the expense of weightier ones. By April, Downing Street was horrified to hear that cabinet papers were being left lying around at Fort Belvedere, open to the perusal of Mrs Simpson and the King's other guests. Some were never returned; and the rings on those that were appeared to come less from the royal pen than the wet bottoms of wine glasses. Regular visitors to the Fort reported that Mrs Simpson had taken charge of the place, tactlessly forcing change upon royal servants dating back to Queen Victoria. She had been known to kick the King under the table if she wanted him to stop talking, and was not averse to contradicting him in public. All pretence, as in the past, that she was a 'joint' guest with her husband (albeit a *mari complaisant*) had been abandoned. Mrs Simpson, here as in the other royal residences, had established herself as the King's official hostess.

The gravity of the situation seems to have been lost on the Duke and Duchess of York, who simply hoped against hope and reason that the stories emanating from the Fort were untrue. One weekend that summer the King drove over to Royal Lodge to show off his new American station wagon, complete with American passenger. 'It was a pleasant hour,' the Duchess of Windsor later recalled, 'but I left with a distinct impression that, while the Duke of York was sold on the American station wagon, the Duchess was not sold on David's other American interest.' She was right. Elizabeth was never to receive Mrs Simpson again – nor, for the rest of her life, to take anything less than a wholly unforgiving attitude. Even today, the Queen Mother can refer privately to the Duchess of Windsor as 'the woman who killed my husband'.

The Yorks were never regular guests at Fort Belvedere, but those who were included their diary-writing friend Harold

Nicolson, to whom life at court had now become 'really rather second-rate'. To J. H. Thomas, the pugnacious union leader who had joined MacDonald's coalition cabinet, it spelt disaster. ' 'Ere we 'ave this obstinate little man with 'is Mrs Simpson,' he told Nicolson. 'Hit won't do, 'arold. I tell you that straight. I know the people of this country. They 'ate 'aving no family life at court.' Thomas was not the only politician sensing mortal danger to the throne. The prime minister, Stanley Baldwin, although outwardly cordial in his relationship with the King, was privately a very worried man. 'When I was a little boy in Worcestershire,' he told his private secretary, 'I never thought I should have to interfere between a king and his mistress.' But interfere he would have to – and soon.

Thus far British press barons had agreed to maintain an extraordinary silence on this sensational story, which had been appearing for months in newspapers and magazines on the continent and across the Atlantic. Even when the King forsook the royal ritual of summering at Balmoral, taking Mrs Simpson on a highly indiscreet Adriatic cruise, the British press refrained from reprinting the lurid coverage of their transatlantic and European cousins. There was the King, his married mistress on his arm, wading ashore shirtless (with pained, pinstriped officials in tow) to lunch with foreign princes and potentates in quayside cafés – and Fleet Street breathed not a word. It could not, to be sure, happen today.

Even then, Baldwin knew the press's silence could not last much longer. He had hoped that someone in the royal family – Queen Mary, perhaps, or the Duke of York – might speak to Edward about the impossibility of maintaining this *status quo*. When he returned on 14 September, however, it was to a private dinner with his mother at which the matter went quite undiscussed. 'Didn't you find it terribly hot?' was about the most searching question the old Queen asked him. 'David got back looking very well,' was all she told even her diary. 'We had a nice talk.'

For their own private reasons, even the most senior members of the royal family either could not or would not confront the King. So the government was forced to step in. Nearly a month later, on 2 October, Baldwin sought an audience with his monarch at which he showed him letters received from all over the empire, deploring his relationship with Mrs Simpson, the publicity it had earned everywhere but in Britain, and the constitutional consequences of his apparent wish to marry her. At the time the lady herself had retreated to Suffolk, the more discreetly to file her divorce proceedings against her husband. Baldwin begged the King to get her to drop the case; the newspapers' legal right to report it would inevitably open the floodgates of publicity and force the whole issue into the public domain, where they would both lose control of it. Edward irritably replied that it was not for him to interfere in other people's business. The divorce case must go ahead.

KING'S MOLL RENO'D IN WOLSEY'S HOME TOWN was the headline in one American paper which greeted the granting of Mrs Simpson's decree nisi in Ipswich. A French paper preferred the more romantic L'AMOUR DU ROI VA BIEN. Amazing though it may seem, the British public still lived in ignorance of the whole business. Still Edward hoped that the cabinet would agree to a morganatic marriage before the British public knew a thing. His family being unwilling to talk the King round, and his government unable, it fell to his private secretary, Major Alexander Hardinge, to risk a dramatic, carefully worded letter which tersely summed up the state of play. The silence of the press, he argued from inside knowledge, could not be maintained much longer. The choices were thus bleak: either the King must face the possible resignation of his government – and a general election 'in which Your Majesty's personal affairs would be the chief issue' – or Mrs Simpson must be sent abroad 'without further delay'. It was the only way to buy time for a considered decision and to avoid 'the damage which would inevitably be done to the Crown'.

'Shocked and angered' by this document, Edward never spoke to Hardinge again. But the letter did at least make him realize the bleakness of his situation. Whether or not he must abandon his hopes of marrying Mrs Simpson *and* remaining King – even if the marriage were, as had been suggested, a morganatic one – it was time to make his intentions clear to the prime minister. Two days later Edward summoned Baldwin and told him categorically that he proposed to marry Mrs Simpson as soon as she was legally free. He hoped to do so as King; but if the government remained irrevocably opposed, he would abdicate.

Not expecting such single-mindedness, the prime minister replied merely, 'Sir, this is most grievous news, and it is impossible for me to make any comment on it today.' Back at Downing Street Baldwin decided to sleep on it, telling a colleague: 'I have heard such things from my King tonight as I never thought to hear.' Edward, by contrast, sensed a sudden mood of release. That same evening, he went to tell his mother of his unshakeable resolve. Next day he told his brother Bertie, hitherto wholly unconsulted in a matter which had so direct and drastic a bearing on his own personal future. 'I feel,' the Duke of York told his private secretary, 'like the proverbial sheep being led to the slaughter.'

Still there were those who thought abdication could be avoided. Winston Churchill, in his romantic way, made a plea for 'time and patience'. Other, more outlandish solutions were canvassed while still the press kept its corporate finger in the dyke. Then came the event which, in its unlikely way, yanked that finger out – 'the spark,' as Edward himself put it, 'that caused the explosion'.

On Tuesday 1 December the Bishop of Bradford, meaning to make a veiled but stern criticism of the King's infrequent churchgoing, told his diocesan conference: 'I commend the King to God's grace – for the King is a man like ourselves. We hope that he is aware of his need. Some of us wish that he gave more positive signs of his awareness.' Jumping to the wrong conclusion, the Yorkshire press reported the Bishop's remarks as breaking the establishment silence on the King's relationship with Mrs Simpson. The national press could not but pick up where the provincials had left off, and the floodgates were opened. Newspaper placards soon carried a tantalizing shout of THE KING'S MARRIAGE.

Now, as Mrs Simpson was spirited out of the country and the crisis could be put off no longer, the Duke of York's stammer ('God's curse upon me') returned with a vengeance. The Yorks' greatest grievance, which still smarts with the Queen Mother to this day, was that her 'Bertie' was so little involved in the toings and froings between King, prime minister and intermediaries during Edward's days of decision in the autumn of 1936. Even in the fateful December week which ended it all, the Duke of York made appointments to see his brother only with the greatest difficulty, and even then most of them were cancelled without explanation at the last minute. But there were hidden reasons.

Thanks to his official biographer, Sir John Wheeler-Bennett, we have King George VI's own handwritten account of his side of the events leading up to his reluctant assumption of that title. On the evening of Thursday 3 December, Bertie noted in his diary a 'dreadful announcement' to the family by his brother: 'David said to Queen Mary that he could not live alone as King and must marry Mrs S—.' (He could never bring himself, whether in conversation or the privacy of his diary, to mention Mrs Simpson's name.) The King's last words that night were to ask Bertie to come and see him at Fort Belvedere the next morning. But again the appointment was cancelled. Saturday . . . Sunday . . . Monday . . . appointments were made, appointments were cancelled. Often the King would not even come to the phone. All weekend the Yorks waited – he constantly telephoning his brother and constantly being stalled, she relapsing into a particularly virulent bout of her annual dose of 'flu.

Finally, on the Monday evening, after a devastating series of rebuffs, Edward telephoned his brother at 6.50 p.m. to say, 'Come and see me after dinner.' At last showing some resolve, Bertie insisted on coming at once. 'I was with him at 7 p.m. The awful & ghastly suspense of waiting was over. I found him pacing up & down the room, and he told me his decision that he would go. I went back to Royal Lodge for dinner . . . ' Why had he been so painfully excluded from the deliberations of that long and dramatic weekend? It seems that his older brother, his own hopes and certainties coming and going almost as frequently as the prime minister, was being cruel only to be kind.

It was a time of growing political anxiety in Europe. If Britain were to have a new monarch, at a time of constitutional crisis, then it deserved the best available candidate. The plain fact is that both King and government were considering by-passing the shy, stammering, ill-at-ease Duke of York – *and* Harry, Duke of Gloucester, a rather dim career soldier none too devoted to what he called 'princing about' – and offering the throne to their younger brother George, Duke of Kent, a dashing and much more confident thirty-four year old with the added advantage of a male heir. There is nothing in the British constitution to specify that, after an abdication, and especially in the absence of an heir apparent, the throne must pass to the next in the line of succession. It is merely customary, after the death of one monarch, for the heir apparent or presumptive to succeed. Abdication, by contrast, requires an act of parliament, in which event it is up to parliament to specify the succession.

The Duke of Kent, as events transpired, was to be killed on active service in 1942; had he become King in 1936, however, he would presumably not have been allowed to serve. Either way, the present Duke of Kent would now have been King and the Queen merely a princess royal. It is a subject – scarcely surprisingly – which you raise in royal circles today at your peril. Details of recent political history are for the most part revealed after thirty years, when the relevant cabinet papers become available at the Public Records Office; anything pertaining to the royal family, however, is still subject to a hundred-year embargo (always assuming the papers have not already 'disappeared'). Posterity already knows, however, unlike either monarch or government at the time, that the Duke of Kent was seriously addicted to cocaine – which would indeed have made for an interesting reign.

The Duke of York's record of poor health told against him, as did his inexperience in affairs of state, his public nervousness (symbolized by his stammer) and above all his unconcealed reluctance to take on the job. There seems little doubt that the proven virtues of his wife swung the balance in his favour. After thirteen years in the royal family, Elizabeth was immensely popular with the public; she had worked hard and effectively in her chosen spheres of royal patronage; she had left a lasting impression upon the empire and dominions (a vociferous group in the anti-Simpson faction); she was known by church leaders to be devoutly religious; and she had won the heart of every politician who had met her. Her husband might be a bit of a risk as king, but Elizabeth was certain to be an accomplished queen consort.

So, thanks to her, Bertie won the day after all. These deliberations, and indeed the decision, had taken place not merely without his participation but without his knowledge. It is far from certain how much he ever knew of the matter. It was an act of kindness on the part of his brother to attempt to ensure that Bertie would never know the full extent to which his abilities had been so doubted. All the King revealed, when he finally saw Bertie that Monday evening, was that he had decided to 'go'. Next day, by the Duke of York's own account, 'I broke down and sobbed like a child.' Another forty-eight hours and there dawned 'that dreadful day', Friday 11 December, which brought a distressingly deadpan telegram from his brother in Boulogne, *en route* to Austria: HAD A GOOD CROSSING. HOPE ELIZABETH BETTER. BEST LOVE AND BEST OF LUCK TO YOU BOTH. DAVID. Bertie still could not get over the fact that his brother's last act, as they parted at Windsor, was to bow to him. The 'unthinkable' had happened. The Duke and Duchess of York were now King and Queen. 'If someone should come through on the telephone,' Bertie asked Elizabeth over lunch, 'who should I say I am?'

'Dickie, this is absolutely terrible,' the new King confided to his cousin and friend, Lord Mountbatten. 'I'm quite unprepared for it. David has been trained for this all his life. I've never even seen a State paper. I'm only a naval officer – it's the only thing I know about.' Mountbatten, himself of course a naval man, replied: 'There is no finer training for a king.' As despatch boxes full of cabinet papers began to flow into his office, Bertie sorely regretted his father's insistence on refusing him access to these and other aspects of the constitutional process. At first the new monarch was unable to conceal from his intimates the full extent of his bewilderment. Crisis, however, brought out the best in him.

The gravity of that crisis is not to be underestimated. In those first few unreal days of the new reign, there was a distinct

INSTRUMENT OF ABDICATION

I, Edward the Eighth, of Great Britain, Ireland, and the British Dominions beyond the Seas, King, Emperor of India, do hereby declare My irrevocable determination to renounce the Throne for Myself and for My descendants, and My desire that effect should be given to this Instrument of Abdication immediately.

In token whereof I have hereunto set My hand this tenth day of December, nineteen hundred and thirty six, in the presence of the witnesses whose signatures are subscribed.

SIGNED AT
FORT BELVEDERE
IN THE PRESENCE
OF

Edward RI

Albert

Henry

George

possibility that the whole 'fabric' of the monarchy, as the King
himself privately put it, might 'crumble'. Having been let in so
late on his secret, the British people were still torn about the
fate of their last, short-lived monarch. In the absence of clear
information, there were many who believed – as the ex-King
himself eventually came to – that sinister plots by Baldwin and
others had hounded him from the throne. There was also widespread doubt as to whether his diffident, stammering brother
was really up to the job. When the Abdication Bill came before
the House of Commons, even the staunchest of Conservative
MPs, Sir Arnold Wilson, feared that fully one hundred members, given a free vote, would support the abolition of the
monarchy in favour of a republic. Leading republicans were
seizing the hour to create that chance.

One radical Labour MP, James Maxton, thundered that 'the
Humpty Dumpty' of royalty had fallen from the wall, and
no power could put him back again. 'We are doing a wrong
and foolish thing,' declared Maxton, a respected and popular
parliamentarian, 'if we do not seize the opportunity of establish-
ing in our land a completely democratic form of government,
which does away with our monarchical institutions and the
hereditary principle.' The vote went heavily in the government's
favour; but it remains an indication of the House's mood that
such sentiments were heard there at all. Equally striking, barely
sixty years later, is the evidence of a December 1936 poll that
almost half of Britain favoured the monarchy's abolition.

It is only a few centuries since the British people believed that
the touch of their monarch could cure people of disease. Even
during the present reign, surveys have shown that as many as a
third of the subjects of Queen Elizabeth II believe her possessed
of some sort of divine authority. In a country where the numbers
of regular churchgoers have never been lower, the monarchy has
taken on a quasi-religious role, replacing orthodox beliefs with
faith in the royal family as incarnate symbols of those moral and
ethical standards to which its followers aspire.

The physical presence of royalty certainly reduces most be-
lievers to a state of incoherence akin to a religious experience. So

when these earthly idols turn out to have feet of clay, the sense of disillusionment is all the more shattering. The recent breakdown of the family monarchy has been a classic case in point, a critical phase in the demythologizing of the House of Windsor. But the abdication of King Edward VIII began that process, perhaps irreversibly, if only with what one commentator has called 'a downgrading of expectations'. The abdication, wrote Robert Lacey, 'would have been a disappointment in any monarch, but it hurt especially from one whose career had started out so glitteringly as Prince of Wales. Britons were shocked to discover in 1936 that Edward VIII could love anything more than being their King.' After all those years of promise, Edward's abrupt farewell to his obligations was 'an admission of selfishness which people expect royal persons to rise above'.

With the outpouring of national affection during her Silver Jubilee in 1977, it appeared that it had taken a mere forty years for Elizabeth II and her father to restore the monarchy to a popularity and security as strong as it had ever known. The seeds of the present crisis had, however, already been sown. Although the Second World War was to prove the making of Edward VIII's uncertain successor – repairing the umbilical link between crown and people, always at its strongest in time of national crisis – the institution would need something more substantial than a smiling corporate family image for long-term survival. Edward's abdication had shown a face of monarchy which its subjects did not want to see; yet it was shown them again just two generations later, when a whole set of supposedly archetypal figures proved just as fallible as their subjects. How could any royal expect to be treated as 'special' when each was revealed to be the same 'poor, bare, fork'd animal' as the rest of us?

The crisis of 1936 afforded Bertie, who was not naturally given to intellectual inquiry, little time for reflection. The reluctant new sovereign found immediate salvation in his sheer pragmatism. On the very first evening of his reign, he surprised his most experienced courtiers by outsmarting them on a couple of knotty constitutional problems. How, for a start, to style the outgoing King for his farewell broadcast from Windsor? Sir John Reith, director-general of the BBC, who was to introduce the broadcast, proposed to call him Mr Edward Windsor. 'Quite wrong,' snapped the new King at his assembled protocol experts, who had themselves failed to come up with an acceptable alternative. He would be announced tonight, his brother ordered, as Prince Edward; and henceforth he would formally be known as His Royal Highness the Duke of Windsor.

Bertie was being as cunning as he was practical. Edward had been born the son of a royal duke, and was therefore entitled to the rank of prince. The rank of plain Mr would entitle him, should he choose, to return to Britain and stand for parliament – the implications of which, given the lingering support for a pro-Edward 'King's Party', were unthinkable. As a duke, he would be entitled to speak freely on all political subjects in the House of Lords; but as a royal duke, with the rank and dignity of HRH, he would not. In view of the Duke of Windsor's subsequent flirtation with Hitler and the Nazi Party, these were decisions of more consequence than his brother could know.

The new King showed equal canniness in the choice of his own public name. Rather than keep the one by which he was known, thus granting Victoria's dearest posthumous wish by becoming King Albert I, he shrewdly chose to take his father's name and style himself King George VI in the interests of continuity and stability. For the same reason, when asked if he wished to wait the customary year before being crowned, he opted for the imminent date already scheduled for his brother's coronation. 'Same date, different King' was the laconic message he sent to the Lord Chamberlain's office.

In naming himself after his father, George VI was quite consciously attempting to return to the values and aspirations of King George V's reign. Even his official signature, his friend and adviser Lord Wigram was touched to note, was almost indistinguishable from his father's. Over the Christmas of 1936 at Sandringham, as he and Elizabeth enjoyed a brief respite in the bosom of their family, they were already beginning the return to the family values which would become the hallmark of his reign, and recover the fortunes of his royal dynasty. 'I am new to the job,' he wrote revealingly to Baldwin on the eve of his coronation, 'but I hope that time will be allowed to me to let me make amends for what has happened.'

As 'head of our morality', George VI overrode the wishes of churchmen with the symbolic decision that his coronation be broadcast – in striking contrast to his refusal, fourteen years before, to admit the BBC to his wedding. Any national sense of rededication was marred, however, by his exiled brother's decision to marry Mrs Simpson only three weeks later, on 3 June, their father's birthday. Bertie was seen as yet as a 'rubber-stamp' monarch, under the thumb of his government, while there was still considerable fascination in the 'king across the water'. Whether it was a political or a personal decision, however, an anxious George VI now asserted himself by personally decreeing that the new Duchess of Windsor would not be accorded the style and rank of Royal Highness. It fell to Walter Monckton, the lawyer who had acted as Edward's emissary, to deliver this royal kidney-punch to the wedding party at the Château de Candé, near Tours. It was, said the duke, 'a damnable wedding present'.

The long-running debate over the humanity and morality of this decision still rages in some circles, twenty-one years after the Duke of Windsor's death and seven after that of his duchess. Given that the situation was without precedent, and that the rank of Royal Highness is entirely within the monarch's gift, its legality was not in question. But if Edward had forsaken his throne to marry a woman unacceptable as Queen, might he not have had the consolation of sharing with her the rank accorded him *in lieu*? George VI thought not. If Mrs Simpson had proved unacceptable as Queen, she was for the same reasons unacceptable as a Royal Highness. He simply did not believe, moreover, that the marriage would last. Like his mother, Queen Mary, Bertie was still unable to believe his brother's priorities. 'It seemed inconceivable to those who made such sacrifices during the war,' Queen Mary wrote to the exiled duke, 'that you, as their King, refused a lesser sacrifice.' These were George VI's sentiments entirely. He believed that Mrs Simpson had temporarily 'deranged' his brother, and feared the consequences of awarding the rank of HRH to a woman who already had three living husbands and may before too long have yet more. The present Duchess of York might well be interested to note what King George VI wrote to his prime minister, Baldwin, at the time: 'Once a person has become a Royal Highness, there is no means of depriving her of the title.'

As George grew into the job, Baldwin soon felt enough confidence in the new regime to tender his long-postponed resignation. 'He's coming on magnificently,' the former prime minister, Ramsay MacDonald, rather patronizingly told the Queen as they watched George VI making a speech. By the first anniversary of his accession, the Archbishop of Canterbury wrote to him that the British people's initial feelings of 'sympathy and hope' had now warmed to 'admiration and confidence'. Just as well, with Hitler advancing across Europe and the King's brother paying court to him in Berlin. Suddenly a visit by the King and Queen to Roosevelt's Washington had more than merely the cosmetic effect of showing that it was not Mrs Simpson's nationality which had prevented her becoming Queen; it established a bond which, according to Churchill, was to assist his long struggle against American isolationism. It also solidified the couple's reputation at home as competent ambassadors for Britain. 'This,' they agreed on their return, 'has made us.'

During the Second World War, in the words of Frances Donaldson, one of Edward VIII's biographers, the King and Queen restored the stability of the crown 'not by what they did but by what they were'. There were times when the King's eagerness to help betrayed his lack of political sophistication. His appearance with Neville Chamberlain on the balcony of Buckingham Palace after the 1938 Munich agreement had already proved George not merely unwise, but capable of 'a grave constitutional impropriety', as it had yet to be the subject of a party vote in the House of Commons. Now his offer of a personal mission to Hitler was tactfully declined by his government. When a similar offer arrived from the ex-king-in-exile, he was confined to the Military Mission in Paris. But there soon followed sightings of the Duke of Windsor on the prowl around Europe, wandering from Madrid to Lisbon, in frequent contact with emissaries from Ribbentrop and Hitler. The duke was said to have declared himself 'against Churchill and the war', to have described his brother as a man of 'copious stupidity', and to have accepted the role of Pétain-style pawn in the event of a successful German invasion of Britain. As he still tried to negotiate his wife an HRH in return for good behaviour, he was finally bundled off to the Bahamas for the duration – governor of the least relevant dominion available.

The young princesses were moved away from London, at first to Balmoral and then to Windsor, where they would see out the war. When it was put to her that her daughters should be shipped to America for the duration, the Queen declined. 'The children will not go without me,' she said. 'I won't leave the King. And of course the King will never leave.' George and Elizabeth resolutely stayed on in Buckingham Palace – an act of defiance to the German bombers that came to symbolize their place at the head of an embattled nation, sharing every aspect of its ordeal. When Eleanor Roosevelt visited in 1942, she testified that conditions in the Palace were no more comfortable than in any other home around the land. The Queen had given America's First Lady her own bedroom, which had wooden boards instead of windows and was heated by a one-bar electric radiator. The food was 'very sparse,' Mrs Roosevelt wrote to her husband, and the Palace 'enormous, and without heat. Both the King and Queen have colds.'

The royal couple's conduct throughout the war amounted to monarchy at its most potent: among the most effective royal images of this century are the King's secret visits to his troops, the Queen's to bomb victims and evacuees, the broadcasts and whistle-stop tours to boost national morale, but above all the refusal to leave London even when Buckingham Palace itself was bombed. After one near-miss in 1940, when two bombs fell just thirty yards from them in the Palace courtyard, the Queen memorably observed: 'Now I can look the East End in the face.' It was a remark which would reverberate through subsequent debates about the nature of monarchy, distilling a sense of shared suffering and fellow-feeling which it had taken a major crisis, itself following hard upon a more technical crisis, to provoke. As Churchill wrote to them when the Palace had been bombed for the ninth time: 'This war has drawn the throne and the people more closely together than ever before, and Your Majesties are more beloved by all classes and conditions of people than any princes of the past.'

Before the outbreak of war, the King had supported Neville Chamberlain's policy of 'appeasement' towards Germany and Italy. After Chamberlain was forced to resign in May 1940, George VI would personally have preferred Halifax over Churchill, and took some time to warm to his new prime minister. But circumstances forced them to form a working relationship described by Churchill, not without a note of self-aggrandizement, as 'unprecedented since the days of Queen Anne and Marlborough'. It was not, intriguingly, without its rivalries. In the spring of 1944, when King and prime minister were privy to the planning of D-Day, both decided they wanted to be there. When neither would give way, the King's horrified private secretary, Sir Alan Lascelles, caustically asked if eighteen-year-old Princess Elizabeth had been fully versed in both the rites of succession and the procedures for appointing a new prime minister. The King took the point and reluctantly withdrew, only to be dismayed by Churchill's refusal to follow suit. He wrote his PM a tetchy, rather jealous note:

> I am a younger man than you, I am a sailor, and as King I am the head of all three services. There is nothing I would like better than to go to sea but I have agreed to stop at home. Is it fair that you should then do exactly what I would have liked to do myself? You said yesterday afternoon that it would be a fine thing for the King to lead his troops into battle, as in old days; if the King cannot do this, it does not seem right to me that his Prime Minister should take his place . . .

Churchill failed to answer the note and left Downing Street for Eisenhower's headquarters at Portsmouth. When George discovered this, he made ready to drive down personally at dawn next day, either to prevent Churchill sailing with the fleet, or to insist on accompanying him. But Lascelles managed first to get hold of the prime minister by phone and at last persuade him to call off his bravura performance.

This curious story vividly illustrates George's inborn sense of the symbolism of monarchy, not to mention the dangers of surrendering it to a prime minister in the early stages of megalomania. On 8 May 1945, however, the King generously invited Churchill to join the royal family on the Buckingham Palace balcony for no fewer than eight VE-Day 'curtain calls'. Princess Elizabeth and her sister had earlier been out in the crowd, enjoying the victory ritual of knocking people's hats off. The moment has been recalled, not least by her, as one of the most poignant in her life – perhaps the only time at which she has truly been at one with the British people.

Like so many recent reigns, George VI's will perhaps best be remembered for the achievements of his politicians: the conduct of the war, the transition from empire to Commonwealth, the development of the welfare state – even Attlee's craven submission in July 1945 in accepting his monarch's choice of foreign secretary, Ernest Bevin, over his own, Hugh Dalton. His already poor health (the King was a heavy smoker) never really recovered from the strains of the war, after which he lived only another seven years, dying in February 1952 at the age of just fifty-six. The 'little princess' never born to be Queen, but now his successor while still only in her mid-twenties, was embarked on a reign which would prove far longer than those of her father, uncle and grandfather combined. She was also to face a period of greater difficulty for the monarchy than any of them could ever have foreseen.

CHAPTER 7

QUEEN ELIZABETH II:
THE LAST BRITISH MONARCH?

'The best mode of testing what we owe to the Queen is
to make a vigorous effort of the imagination, and see how
we should get on without her.'

WALTER BAGEHOT,
The English Constitution

SHE IS SHORTER THAN YOU EXPECT — ONLY 5FT 4IN — BUT
Queen Elizabeth II comes across as very feminine, sharp rather
than bright, direct rather than engaging. Years of avoiding controversy have rendered her conversation rather bland, although
she admits to enjoying 'unmalicious' gossip. Her social exchanges are in any case inhibited by the need for propriety
and protocol; overstep the mark, and she will have moved on
before you can blink. From an early age it has been drummed
into her that she can never be weak, vulnerable or emotional.
To meet her even briefly is to encounter someone so distinctly
from another world that she might as well be a temporary (and
very reluctant) visitor from Mars.

The apparent embodiment of common sense, devotion to
duty, and middle-of-the-road wholesomeness, this very ordinary
upper-middle-class woman is also the repository of a nation's

aspirations. Dreams, even; for so deeply is she embedded in the national sub-conscious that surveys have shown that more than half her subjects regularly dream about her – sipping tea, more often than not, in a tableau of decorous English gentility. Once she was a glamorous young figure symbolizing the nation's future; now she has metamorphosed into the national mother-figure so many Britons seem to need.

It is Elizabeth II's most striking achievement that even opponents of the monarchy offer her a grudging respect, and that all recent debates about abolition presuppose her demise. How has she managed it? She was not, after all, born to be Queen. When the former Lady Elizabeth Bowes-Lyon gave birth to Princess Elizabeth Alexandra Mary by caesarian section on 21 April 1926, the infant was simply the first daughter of the second son of King George V, who had blessed the line of succession with four sons. Though third in line to the throne, behind her uncle and father, Elizabeth did not seem likely to remain so for long. The Prince of Wales would surely marry and have children of his own; the Duke and Duchess of York might well themselves soon have a son. Only some freak turn of events could ever see the crown pass to young Elizabeth.

When that freak duly came to pass, she was readied for office only with a crash course in the constitution from an elderly Eton schoolmaster, Sir Henry Marten. Though heir presumptive from the age of ten, Elizabeth was never even to attend school, let alone have the chance to forge natural relationships with other children her own age. The chatty reminiscences of her governess, Miss Crawford ('Crawfie'), make it clear that preparations for the burdens of monarchy were the last thing on the Yorks' curriculum for their daughters. The extent of the princesses' formal education is summed up in their mother's aspirations for Elizabeth and her sister, Margaret: 'To spend as long as possible in the open air, to enjoy to the full the pleasures of the country, to be able to dance and draw and appreciate music, to acquire good manners and perfect deportment, and to cultivate all the distinctively feminine graces.' Even their grandfather, the King, was concerned about nothing so much as their handwriting. 'For goodness sake,' he told Crawfie, 'teach Margaret and Lilibet to

write a decent hand, that's all I ask of you. None of my children
could write properly. They all do it exactly the same way. I like
a hand with some character in it.' A generation later, Elizabeth
would make very different – to her, revolutionary – decisions
about the upbringing of her own children, especially her
first-born, the only heir to the throne in British history to be
educated beyond the Palace walls.

But that decision had more to do with Lieutenant Philip
Mountbatten, the strong-willed prince of Greece and Denmark to whom Elizabeth has now been married for more
than forty-five years. Son of the divorced King and Queen
of Greece, his restless character shaped by a rootless childhood wandering Europe, Philip was determined that his sons
would attend the same austere, far-flung Scottish outpost as
himself: Gordonstoun, modelled on the Spartan precepts of
his German mentor, Kurt Hahn, who believed that the path
to spiritual fulfilment lay via a curious combination of physical
discipline and community service.

Young people, Hahn believed, had to combat the five-fold
decay of a sick civilization: 'The decay of fitness, the decay
of initiative and enterprise, the decay of care and skill, the
decay of self-discipline, the decay of compassion.' A lifelong
bachelor, assumed to have been a repressed homosexual, Hahn
was uncomfortable with women and forbade any discussion of
sex among his boys. 'Philip couldn't help but be affected by this
attitude,' wrote Fiammetta Rocco in a perceptive profile, 'and his
sons' failure to form sustainable relationships with women may
stem directly from it.' Although she would have preferred her
sons closer to home, at Eton, Elizabeth let Philip have his way.
Out of concern for the considerable ego of a husband who must
always take second place to her, in private as in public, she has
always been careful to let him rule the domestic roost, of which
he has proved a highly demanding *paterfamilias*.

In the remote Pacific islands of the New Hebrides, there is
a 200-strong native tribe called the Iounhanans who worship
Prince Philip as their god. A signed photograph he once sent
them is now the centre-piece of an altar before which they
prostrate themselves. One day, they believe, Philip will come

to live among them and rule over them, blessed with the power of healing. The closest their Messiah has come to fulfilling this prophecy was in 1974, when he sailed straight past their island with his wife in her yacht *Britannia,* on their way elsewhere.

However much royal merriment this curious slice of anthropology may have caused over the years, it is intriguing to note that Elizabeth II's husband has done little to discourage his hapless disciples. In his time he has even sent them gifts: a clay pipe, for instance, in return for which he received a fearsome weapon for sticking pigs (not to mention a penis gourd). Perhaps, in their remote, endearing way, these innocents offer Philip some consolation for the lifelong frustrations he has had to endure as an eternal Number Two – a husband who takes second place to his wife in all matters of precedent and protocol, often third place to a son in whom he has shown ill-concealed disappointment. The problems faced by Sir Denis Thatcher during just one decade of the Queen's reign pale into insignificance beside the continual strain on Prince Philip's male ego. It is not easy, and never has been, to be famous only for being a husband.

A man of fierce masculine pride, himself born a prince, Philip is self-styled chairman of what he has called the 'Back Seat Club'. It is more than merely having to walk a pace or two behind his wife whenever they appear in public. There are many other constitutional niceties that hurt. Philip is not permitted access, for instance, to the state papers which his wife peruses every day, and to which his oldest son has been privy since his teens. He is excluded from the weekly audience between monarch and prime minister. On state occasions such as the opening of parliament he plays merely a walk-on role as a royal appendage, there to be seen but not heard. (Only in recent years has he been given a throne alongside his wife's; for years he was made to stand.) Even in private, in front of family friends, he must apologize to his wife, addressing her as 'Your Majesty', if he arrives in the room after her.

'I've never dared press the subject with him,' says another male member of the royal family. 'But I get the very strong impression that even today, even after all these years, Prince Philip often finds this reversal of his natural male role a terrible strain.' One method of compensating has been to flaunt his acerbic streak, to develop a reputation for outspokenness which he relishes in private as in public. A man of forceful views, impatient when frustrated, he can be testy and overbearing behind closed doors. The Queen loves it whenever Philip is challenged in argument by one of their few close friends prepared to risk it. 'That's right,' she'll say, 'you tell him!' It comes of years of living with Philip's single-minded stubbornness. Their marriage has passed through periods of turbulence, especially in the 1950s and early 1960s, when his long and frequent absences abroad raised eyebrows. There were times when Buckingham Palace felt constrained to deny rumours of a 'rift' in the monarch's marriage, and rumours of Philip's infidelities have always lurked not far beneath the surface of tabloid propriety. It has always been his good fortune that to attack the Queen's consort is in effect to attack the Queen herself, whom even the tabloids have considered off-limits until very recently.

Princess Elizabeth fell in love with the first man she ever met. She was just thirteen when she accompanied her father on a visit to the Royal Naval College at Dartmouth, where the young rating assigned to entertain her was (in Miss Crawford's description) 'a fair-haired boy, rather like a Viking, with a sharp face and piercing blue eyes'. Eighteen-year-old Philip was a nephew of the King's friend 'Dickie' Mountbatten. According to Crawfie, Elizabeth 'never took her eyes off him' throughout the visit, at the end of which a huge flotilla of small boats escorted the royal yacht down the river and out to sea. Fearing for their safety, the King instructed that they be signalled to turn back. But one solitary rower, so legend has it, struggled manfully to keep up in the yacht's wake, exasperating the King – 'The damned young fool', he exclaimed – while delighting the princess, who 'watched him fondly through an enormous pair of binoculars' until Mountbatten at last ordered his nephew back to shore.

Immediately interrupted by the Second World War (during which Philip's exiled father died a penniless gambler in Monte Carlo), their developing courtship then had to survive a severe testing by Elizabeth's doting parents, not to mention the awkwardness of British involvement in the Greek civil war.

It was a still-rationed, food-couponed Britain which celebrated their marriage in November 1947, described by Churchill as 'a flash of colour along the hard road we have to travel'. Five kings and six queens came to London for the ceremony, among them King Michael of Romania, whose countrymen took advantage of his absence to abolish the monarchy and declare themselves a republic.

Less than five years later Elizabeth was Queen, at the age of just twenty-five. Those present at that celebrated moment in Kenya on 6 February 1952, when the news arrived of King George VI's death during the night, have described how Philip sat slumped behind a copy of *The Times*. Said his private secretary and close friend Mike Parker, the first to tell him the news: 'I'll never forget it. He looked as if half the world had dropped in on him.' Another friend recalls: 'He didn't want it at all. It was going to change his whole life, take away all the emotional stability he'd finally found.'

In the first few years, according to one of the Queen's private secretaries, Lord Charteris, Philip 'came to being the consort of the sovereign as opposed to being the husband of the princess with a certain amount of antipathy and impatience. He sulked quite a bit.' There are ways in which Philip seems never really to have adjusted to his wife's having become monarch, and the subsequent extent to which he has been shut out of so large a part of her life. Even today, staring wistfully out of his window, he confesses to visitors that he resents the loss of his maritime career: 'It was not my ambition to be president of the Mint Advisory committee. I didn't want to be president of the World Wildlife Fund. I was asked to do it. I'd much rather have stayed in the navy.'

He was not formally made a Prince of the United Kingdom until 1957, ten years after his marriage, and five after his wife had become Queen. While granting him this honour, she nevertheless accepted Churchill's advice not to add his surname (or, to be precise, the anglicized version of the surname he had borrowed from his mother's side of the family) to that of her dynasty. Her own descendants would still be members of the House of Windsor, although she did decree that those not accorded the rank of Royal Highness – those, in other words, remote from the prospect of inheriting the throne – should use the family name of Mountbatten-Windsor. Small wonder that in those early years, when refused permission to enter his wife's study, he exclaimed: 'I'm just a bloody amoeba, here to procreate members of the royal family.'

In his seventies Philip has suddenly aged, his skin flecked with liver spots, his hands swollen and twisted by arthritis. Though less publicly voluble, he is as cantankerous as ever in private, where the ferocity of his criticism can still reduce his eldest son to tears. Constitutionalists occasionally express surprise that the Queen, who took so long even to make him a prince, has not created her husband Prince Consort – even King, which is perfectly within her powers. The first title, so the official line goes, is too closely associated with Victoria's beloved Albert. As to the second: either the Queen is sexist (her own mother having automatically been made Queen Consort), or she is reluctant to detract from her own hard-won authority.

Queen Elizabeth II is now by far the longest-serving head of state in the Western world. Her forty-one years on the throne have seen the comings and goings of nine British prime ministers, ten American presidents, six Russian leaders, five French presidents and five Popes. By February 1992, the fortieth anniversary of her accession, the Queen's reign was the sixth longest in English history – just three years short of that of her legendary name-sake, Elizabeth I, and exceeded only by those of Edward III (fifty years), Henry III (fifty-six), George III (fifty-nine) and Victoria (sixty-three).* At the age of sixty-five, with a mother still going strong in her nineties, Elizabeth II seemed set to break Queen Victoria's record.

Just six weeks before, however, she had been reduced to a bit part in a television soap opera. In the Christmas 1991 special edition of *Coronation Street*, British television's longest-running series, the unexpected arrival of Alma Sedgwick's lover made her

---

*James I logs fifty-eight years if his period as James VI of Scotland, before the union, is included.

late for Christmas lunch with Alf and Audrey Roberts. 'Where on earth has Alma got to?' ranted Alf. 'I'm starvin'.' Angrily snapping on the television set, he told his wife: 'We'll give her till after the Queen's speech. Then we'll start without her.'

At which the screen filled out and a fanfare of trumpets signalled the real thing. Unbelievably, the Queen's traditional Christmas Day broadcast to Britain and the Commonwealth had been downgraded to an interlude in *Coronation Street*. In her familiar flat monotone, Elizabeth II enthused about the changing face of Eastern Europe and a meeting of Commonwealth heads of government in Zimbabwe, while declaring herself distinctly unhappy about warfare. She also dropped an unexpected hint, for viewers still in any doubt, that she had no intention of abdicating in favour of her son Charles.

Scarcely had Her Majesty's subjects received her festive greetings than they were returned, without interval, to a still fuming Alf Roberts, who switched off his set, donned his paper hat and demanded his turkey, Alma or no Alma. 'Right, then, that's it!' was all he had to say about Her Majesty's performance – presumably speaking, as is the function of leading soap characters, for millions of working men throughout the land.

How could the Palace have allowed it? The monarchy had been definitively demeaned, with the Queen a mere pawn in the ratings game. Independent television traditionally struggles in the Christmas airwaves war, for the curious reason that most Britons feel it somehow more proper to watch their monarch on the BBC. But subsequent figures did indeed show that, by inserting Her Majesty into *Coronation Street*, the independent network had boosted its audience for the Queen's speech from 4.3 million the previous year to 10.5 million – achieving parity, for once, with the BBC. Total audience figures for the broadcast were 23.3 million, up by 10 per cent from 1990. 'The Queen can be grateful to the schedulers who planned independent television's Christmas programmes,' reported *The Times*. 'Astute scheduling halted the continuing decline in the audience for the Queen's speech.'

But at what price? Would next year see a commercial break, with the autocue prompting Her Majesty to promise: 'I'll be right back after these messages'? That same Christmas saw the advent of *Pallas*, a now seasonal parody in which news film of the royals is overlaid with caricatures of their voices in less than regal scenarios. *Lèse-majesté* was no longer an adequate term to describe the mass media's sudden irreverence for the British crown; its portrayal on television that Christmas offered a stark measure of the speed of the monarchy's headlong fall from grace. Britain's obsessive interest in its royals was no less intense than ever; but recent events had seen habitual deference decline via disillusion into crude mockery.

If the year ahead was to prove Elizabeth II's 'annus horribilis', 1991 had carried dire auguries. What should have been a celebratory year – marking her own sixty-fifth birthday, her husband's seventieth and her heir's tenth wedding anniversary – began instead with the young royals under fire during the Gulf War (*see* Chapter 4). Soon civil war had been openly declared in the Wales marriage, while an unruly 80 per cent of the Queen's subjects supported a parliamentary bill for their monarch to join them in paying taxes. In the midst of it all, she was even bitten by one of her own corgis – badly enough to need three stitches in her leg, another sharp reminder that the Queen was only human. While visiting the United States, where she was visibly shaken by a spontaneous hug from a large black matron in Washington DC, Elizabeth II was asked by a schoolchild how long she had reigned. 'Too long!' she replied. 'Wait and read about it in the history books.'

For one rare moment, the royal mask seemed to have slipped. 'Many a true word has been spoken in jest,' observed the *Daily Mail,* whose loyal columnist Lynda Lee-Potter sensed 'a powerful unease' in Middle England. The Queen was going through 'some of the most traumatic and dangerous days of her reign'. The world-weary note in Elizabeth II's voice that day seemed to go beyond her own immediate problems, betraying some sixth sense of the national decline which was already beginning – if, as yet, imperceptibly – to drag the monarchy down with many another British institution. For forty years, give or take the odd reverse, the Queen had reigned happy and glorious. Now, though it was scarcely her fault, Britain's belief in itself was revealed to have faltered dramatically during the latter half of her time on the throne. In a stark Gallup poll for the British-as-roast-beef *Daily Telegraph* in February 1993, the most striking finding was that half the nation wanted to emigrate. The worst news for the House of Windsor was a 60 per cent drop over the previous twenty years (from 86 per cent to 26 per cent) in the number of Britons who thought their monarchy 'something to be proud of'. Only 7 per cent chose the monarchy as 'the single thing about Britain [which] gave them most pride'.

To Elizabeth Longford, one of the monarchy's most impassioned recent defenders, the Queen symbolizes more than the nation's history; she 'represents the people's aspirations' and 'personifies the country's unity [even] in diversity'. If so, either Elizabeth II has been landed with a task incongruous with the times, or recent years have seen her pay as heavily for her subjects' disenchantment with their government as for her own family's misconduct. In tandem with its gloomy prognosis for the monarchy, the *Telegraph* poll revealed deep-seated disillusion at all levels of society about almost every aspect of British life. Only 5 per cent of Britons thought the streets 'safe to walk at night', as opposed to 85 per cent twenty years before; only 6 per cent (as opposed to 82 per cent) thought there was 'no need to fortify [their] homes against burglars'. There were equally large declines over the previous two decades in the number of Britons who thought children were 'usually polite and well behaved', that 'foreigners looked up to us', that the education system and the National Health Service were 'something to be proud of', even that 'a British gentleman's word is his bond'. Fifty per cent fewer considered British sportsmen 'well-behaved, on and off the field', 42 per cent fewer believed Britain to be 'a well-governed country'. Only 9 per cent thought the United Kingdom 'free of racial strife'. Confidence in parliament and political leaders, the law courts and the police, the BBC and the Civil Service had all declined by similarly grim margins. The only arm of the state to have retained broad confidence, at 84 per cent as opposed to 89 per cent twenty years ago, was the armed forces – still 'among the most professional and well-trained in the world'.

Their Commander-in-Chief could take as little consolation from this statistic as from W.S. Gilbert's quip that the British are renowned for praising 'all centuries but this and every country but their own'. As the titular head of the political, legal and ecclesiastical branches of state, already aware of a crisis of faith in the monarchy, Elizabeth II was said to have been 'personally hurt' by the *Telegraph*'s grim conclusion that 'pride in Britain and confidence in British institutions are at their lowest levels since records began'. Only days later, as John Major found himself required to mount a public defence of the monarchy on his first visit to Clinton's Washington, a MORI poll for *The Times* of London showed fully 80 per cent of Britons 'dissatisfied' with the way his government was running the country. The savage murder that week of a two-year-old Liverpool boy, and the arrest of two ten-year-old suspects, provoked a wave of emotional soul-searching over the state of the nation. Within days there followed another collective spasm over the premature death of the captain of the English soccer team which had won the World Cup in 1966. Suddenly, 'Gentleman' Bobby Moore seemed to symbolize a far better, bygone age.

Britain had entered the 1990s in a state of seemingly irreversible decay. By late 1992, only six months after its fourth consecutive election victory, it was a very weary-looking, thirteen-year-old Conservative government – under new leadership, but seemingly bereft of new ideas – that presided over the worst recession for sixty years. By April 1993, John Major's first year as an elected prime minister in his own right had been marked by a parlous series of U-turns – on the job security of adulterous cabinet ministers, the devaluation of the pound, interest rates, pit closures and the infinite complexities of the Maastricht Treaty. Even one of Major's most senior Conservative colleagues, Viscount Whitelaw, deputy prime minister during the Thatcher years, called it 'the worst first year of any government I can remember'.

It certainly made a stark contrast with Churchill's 'new Elizabethan era', when post-war Britain had taken hope for its future from the coronation of a young new Britannia, showing the world a fresh, confident shine on the face of its oldest democracy. Ten years later, as a Labour government was about to end thirteen years of Tory rule, a national opinion poll showed that 30 per cent of Britons still believed their monarch to be a figure specially chosen by God. At the heady climax of the 'Swinging Sixties', when England's capacity for self-deception was aptly symbolized by its emergence on home turf as world soccer champions, this belief in the monarch as a semi-divine figure had fallen by only four per cent over twenty years. A similar survey today, just three decades later, would provoke little more than hollow laughter.

If Britain's problem is that it has changed beyond recognition during the forty and more years of Elizabeth II's reign, the monarchy's problem is that it has not. Yes, the winsome young Queen, symbolic of a proud old nation's lingering aspirations, quickly broke with tradition by abolishing the ceremony at which debutantes – the eligible young daughters of high society – were annually presented at court. Yes, she pioneered the royal 'walkabout', through which she has personally met more of her subjects than any British monarch before her, and private lunches for select subjects at Buckingham Palace. Yes, she adapted to the age of jet transport, swiftly becoming the most travelled monarch in history. But no, she has not otherwise seen fit to permit the ancient, irrational institution in her care to bend sufficiently before the prevailing post-war winds.

In that 1991 Christmas broadcast, as Alf Roberts waited impatiently for his turkey and trimmings, she admitted as much. 'Over the years,' said the Queen, in her curiously world-weary tone, 'I have tried to follow my father's example.' Quite, thought some commentators; far too much so. 'The beloved figure of King George VI has cast a long shadow over his elder daughter's reign,' wrote Hugh Massingberd in *The Daily Telegraph*. 'So much does the Queen like things to go along as they did in her father's day that the structure of the "Royal Firm" has virtually become ossified in the 1940s.' Elizabeth II was 'a shining example of the undoubted merits of that austere, stiff-upper-lip decade . . . but the blunt truth is that her inflexible, old-fashioned rectitude is having a stifling effect on the monarchy'.

To Massingberd, the occasional attempts to 'modernise' and 'democratise' the royal image had been 'bogus and footling'. He went on to reiterate one of the most familiar, forty-year-old themes of Elizabeth II's reign: 'Her advisers and her household are stuffy, servile, unimaginative and, frankly, second if not third-rate.' Thirty-five years before, in August 1957, Elizabeth II's honeymoon on the throne had come to an abrupt end with a hail of very similar charges. 'The Queen's entourage,' wrote the then Lord Altrincham, 'are almost without exception the "tweedy" sort [who had] lamentably failed to move with the times.' The court surrounding the thirty-year-old Queen was 'a tight little enclave of English ladies and gentlemen . . . second-rate . . . lacking in gumption', who put into the Queen's mouth utterances which made her sound like 'a priggish schoolgirl, captain of the hockey team, a prefect and a recent candidate for confirmation'.*

Altrincham's reflections earned him a public slap in the face from a member of the League of Empire Loyalists, and a bellyful of obloquy from all sides. The Duke of Argyll did not mince his words: 'I'd like to see the bounder hanged, drawn and quartered.' An Italian monarchist even challenged him to a duel; though he later apologized with a bunch of roses on realizing that he was 'a good monarchist'. Altrincham's famous tirade has ever since been misunderstood and misinterpreted.

Owner-editor of a journal called the *National & English Review*, whose entire August 1957 issue he devoted to the subject of the monarchy, this son of a former minister in Churchill's government was in fact a devout royalist, whose only mistake was to assume that the court and its attendant aristocrats might perhaps include figures large enough to heed and respond to constructive criticism. Thirty-five years later, as plain Mr John Grigg (having disclaimed his father's peerage in 1963), he blamed the disproportionate response to his article on 'something uncomfortably akin to Japanese Shintoism'. In post-Coronation Britain, public

*Massingberd chose to exempt from his charge the Queen's former private secretary, Lord Charteris of Amisfield – the same courtier, as it happens, who offered Lord Altrincham minority support in 1957, privately assuring him that his article was 'the best thing that had happened to Buckingham Palace in my time'.

attitudes towards the monarchy had been marked by 'a degree of blandness and servility quite alien to the British national tradition . . . Britain seemed to be compensating for loss of power in the world by relapsing into a state of collective make-believe, in which the hierarchical aspects of the monarchy were grossly exaggerated and the healthy habit of criticizing office-holders was ceasing to apply to the monarch.'

Back in 1957, soon after Altrincham's well-meant assault, less friendly criticism came from the playwright John Osborne, whose play *Look Back in Anger* had sent shock-waves through the British theatre and anointed him unofficial leader of a group of radical writers known to the press as the 'Angry Young Men'. Osborne objected to the decline of the monarchy into a soap opera, compromising itself with its 'puzzled impression of modernity' and 'looking foolish into the bargain':

> It bores me, it depresses me that there should be so many empty minds, so many empty lives in Britain to sustain this fatuous industry. My objection to the royal symbol is that it is dead; it is a gold filling in a mouth full of decay. When the mobs rush forward in the Mall, they are taking part in the last circus of a civilisation that has lost faith in itself and sold itself for a splendid triviality.

The first commentator to characterize the House of Windsor as a soap opera – 'a sort of substitute or ersatz religion' – had in fact been the journalist Malcolm Muggeridge, writing the previous year in the then influential left-wing weekly *The New Statesman*. To Muggeridge, it was 'duchesses, not shop assistants' who found the Queen 'dowdy, frumpish and banal'; compared with the cost of nuclear submarines or guided missiles, the monarchy could not be considered expensive, 'though there are those who find the ostentation of life at Windsor and Buckingham Palace not to their taste.' Given its mild enough strictures, the article attracted little attention until late the following year, when, in the wake of Altrincham's attack, it was reprinted in the American magazine *Saturday Evening Post* on the eve of a royal

visit to Washington. But *The New Statesman*'s headline 'The
Royal Soap Opera' now became the *Saturday Evening Post*'s
'Does England Really Need A Queen?' In the face of such
transatlantic provocation, the British press blithely removed
Muggeridge's remarks from their true context; now it was the
writer, not the duchesses, who thought the Queen 'dowdy,
frumpish and banal', Muggeridge himself who considered life
at court 'ostentatious and tasteless'. Nowhere to be found was
his original conclusion that the Queen, with her 'charming personality', played a necessary role: 'The British monarchy does
fulfil a purpose. It provides a symbolic head of state transcending
the politicians who go in and out of office.'

Although his article had originally been the first to appear,
it was only now that Muggeridge too suffered from what
Altrincham called 'a tendency to regard as high treason any criticism of the monarch, however loyal and constructive its intent'.
Excrement was shoved through Muggeridge's letter-box; he was
banned from appearing on the BBC; and his contract to write a
weekly column for *The Sunday Dispatch* was cancelled. In vain did
he protest to the Press Council, which ruled that 'the impression
of the article conveyed [in the British press] was honestly held and
those papers had a right to put their case that the article contained
a number of unfair, untimely and wounding disparagements of
the royal family'. No doubt there were knighthoods at stake.

Once Muggeridge's old age rendered him increasingly eccentric, it was Altrincham's remarks which lingered in the national
memory, especially those concerning the courtiers with whom
the Queen chose to surround herself. Her choice of advisers has
remained a running sore to this day. To a worried British press,
whose incomes depend so heavily on the continuance of the
monarchy, the series of miscalculations made during her 'annus
horribilis' was always laid at the royal household's (if not John
Major's) door. 'It is more than time that it was shaken up,'
wrote, for instance, *The Independent* (which had long since abandoned its original policy not to write about the monarchy*).

---

*The evolution of *The Independent*'s policy on royal coverage was described to the
author by one courtier as 'rather like a virgin's attitude to sex: frightening until you
first try it, but then you can't get enough'.

'The Queen's advisers are drawn from a narrow circle of people with little experience of the way most of the nation lives, or thinks. They continue to demonstrate their inability to anticipate new problems or to cope with them when they occur. As a result, the Palace is wrong-footed, time after time.' According to *The Observer*, it was 'a preoccupation with loyalty guaranteed by personal friendship (not the same thing as snobbery or bigotry) that limits recruitment to the royal household. A handful of fashionable regiments, the older merchant banks, estate management – that's the catchment area, augmented now and then by a presentable middle-class civil servant . . . Social in-breeding is unhealthy for a bureaucracy – and not a good advertisement if you're coming on as the people's friend.' To *The Mail on Sunday*, 'Much of the blame [for the Palace's "inertia and arrogant naivety"] can be levelled at the courtiers and other puffed-up flunkies who are supposed to guide the royal firm. . . The Palace team must be reorganized. Independent managers should be brought in. Blue-blooded connections must no longer be accepted as prime qualifications for a top job.'

Thirty-five years on, Grigg himself returned to the theme in a meditation upon the lessons to be learnt from 1992: 'The first is that the assumption which has so far largely governed recruitment of new members to the royal household, or indeed the royal family, during the present reign has to be discarded once and for all. That assumption has been that only people from a very restricted social and ethnic background could be trusted to stick to the rules. How very absurd.' He was echoed by the playwright (and former Conservative Party adviser) Michael Dobbs:

> The real damage has been inflicted by the friends and advisers who hang around the palaces. All too frequently they seem to have been inexperienced, unworldly and often competitive, even at times appearing to be divided into rival camps for the purpose of heaping abuse on each other . . . A modern monarchy needs to be surrounded by an effective administration, and not rely on gossip queens for friends and three wise monkeys for media advice.

To Bernard Levin of *The Times*, concerned in early 1993 about the Queen's decision to sue his colleagues on *The Sun*, the royal advisers should have been 'hanged at the yardarm and buried five fathoms deep'.

The quality of the advice offered to the Queen carries a resonance far beyond mere shifts in public perceptions of the monarchy or royal family. That is a matter largely left to the Buckingham Palace press office, whose qualities have yet to rival those of Madison Avenue. The Queen's senior advisers are also there to whisper in her ear when Her Majesty's government wishes to exercise the 'Royal Prerogative' – by which it may, without reference to parliament or the electorate, declare war; make peace; sign and ratify treaties; grant pardons; recognize foreign governments; grant charters; confer patronage appointments; establish commissions; and make (or amend) law via Orders in Council. These, at the end of the twentieth century, all remain acts within the scope of Britain's hereditary head of state.

When John Major committed British forces to war in the Gulf in January 1991, he did not need parliament's authority. But he was obliged to 'inform' the Queen. 'The authority to commit our forces in direct conflict is vested in the crown,' explained Downing Street at the time. 'It is part of the royal prerogative, and that can be exercised only on the basis of advice from ministers. It does not need any legal preliminary approval from parliament.' The prerogative is also available, *in extremis*, for even less democratic use. In February 1993, when Major was at the height of his difficulties over the Maastricht Treaty, experts in European Community law made it clear that the royal prerogative gave the prime minister the legal right, if he so chose, to ratify the treaty by going directly to the crown, over the heads of a dissenting parliamentary majority.

Although he is not yet through the Maastricht woods, Major has thus far opted to soldier on by more traditionally democratic methods. Had he chosen the more direct and drastic route, however, would the Queen have heeded the wishes of parliament and people by refusing him the exercise of the prerogative? This must remain, in the time-honoured political evasion, a hypothetical question. In the words of the historian Lord Blake, however: 'The crown does still remain, despite its greatly diminished constitutional status. . . a sort of reserve power which in certain circumstances might affect the way in which the prime minister operates.' As Blake is himself a constitutional adviser to the Palace,★ it is significant that he chose to add: 'We live in an era when many of our time-honoured constitutional usages are being scrutinized and questioned.'

No legislation passed by parliament becomes law until it bears the Queen's signature. Under a constitutional democracy, the theory goes, she would be obliged to sign her own death warrant, should any parliament choose to lay it before her. Until she did so, however, to put the will of the people's elected representatives into practice would be illegal. Blake's constitutional gloss would suggest that, in the absence of any written rules, a monarch who has seen the comings and goings of nine prime ministers might well begin to consider herself a more seasoned political veteran. Indeed, it may be thought that the lingering powers of the crown go well beyond the familiar, century-old definition of Walter Bagehot: 'The right to be consulted, the right to encourage, the right to warn.'

One obvious example is the right of the sovereign to refuse a prime minister a dissolution of parliament – to refuse him, in other words, permission to call a general election. The issue would arise if he or she perceived the prime minister's strategic reasons for an election to be against the national interest. In October 1992, only six months after a general election, Major threatened to call another if the House of Commons reversed its original vote on the Maastricht Treaty. 'There can be little doubt,' adjudged John Grigg at the time, 'that if he were to ask for a dissolution, the Queen would grant his request.' On the other hand: 'If all or most of his cabinet colleagues were to tell him they were utterly opposed to an appeal to the country in present circumstances, he might decide to resign as prime minister rather than ask for a dissolution.'

★Another is Blake's successor as Provost of The Queen's College, Oxford, Dr Geoffrey Marshall.

As it was, Major backed down on his threat, intended to concentrate the minds of 'Eurosceptic' rebels within his own party, many of whom would probably have lost their seats in a Labour landslide. Had he proceeded with the tactic, however, Elizabeth II might well have thought it against the national interest to hold a second general election within six months, at a time of economic crisis – designed merely to gratify a prime minister's remote hopes of self-preservation, or to take his enemies down with him.

In theory, the Queen would have had to decide whether to agree to the dissolution of parliament and a Christmas poll. The monarch is obliged by the constitution to look for a prime minister who can command a majority in the Commons. It was widely suggested at the time that her advisers were ready to call Major's bluff by finding his replacement from the current government. The Queen would have consulted senior Conservatives such as the leader of the Lords, Lord Wakeham; Lord Whitelaw; Lord Pym; and perhaps Lady Thatcher (unless, of course, she were an interested party intent on a return to office). Elder statesmen such as Sir Edward Heath, the former chief whip Michael Jopling and the chairman of the 1922 committee, Sir Marcus Fox, would have been asked for advice. Knowing the probability of a Labour victory, they would certainly have insisted that an election was not needed since a successor could be found within the party.

The problem would have been that the three most likely contenders – Douglas Hurd, Kenneth Clarke and Michael Heseltine – were all, like Major, Euro-enthusiasts; so their succession would not have solved the original problem. The two eligible Eurosceptics who would have halted the Maastricht process were the former party chairman Kenneth Baker and the chief secretary to the Treasury, Michael Portillo. For Elizabeth II to have invited either of them to form a government in Major's place would surely have questioned the monarchy's future as much as the prime minister's, by creating a highly contentious constitutional crisis at a time when the monarchy was already an unpopular, discredited institution.

★

'Advice,' wrote Harold Macmillan in his memoirs, 'in the long run, the crown must today accept.' As he went on to point out, however, a prime minister's request for a dissolution 'the crown can agree to or not'. Macmillan called this 'the last great prerogative of the crown' – which, in his view, 'must be preserved . . . It might be of vital importance at a time of national crisis.' Subsequent prime ministers – among them John Major – might not thank 'Supermac' for reminding the monarch of her power to thwart their schemes, long after his own scheming days were over. He himself had been a major player in the first two of several episodes in the present Queen's reign when the constitutional monarchy flexed muscles generally supposed to have atrophied with King George III. Holding her hand through the first, as if to prove Lord Altrincham's point, was the latest scion of a family who had lurked around the throne for the best part of four centuries.

The Cecils, who had proved so influential with the first Queen Elizabeth, were still busy advising the second in 1957, when ill-health in the wake of the Suez crisis forced the resignation of her prime minister, Anthony Eden. In the absence of any established electoral procedure – these were the days when Conservative leaders were still allowed to 'emerge', usually from smoke-filled rooms – the thirty-year-old Queen, on Eden's advice, asked the current Cecil at court, the Marquess of Salisbury, to take soundings. With the Lord Chancellor, Lord Kilmuir, Salisbury summoned cabinet members one by one to the Lord President's room in the Privy Council offices and asked each the subsequently celebrated question, 'So which is it to be? Wab or Hawold?'

Through his speech defect, Salisbury was offering a choice between R.A. ('Rab') Butler, who had been acting prime minister during Eden's illness, and the Chancellor of the Exchequer, Harold Macmillan. The latter, Salisbury reported back to the Queen, appeared to command a narrow majority in the cabinet. Macmillan himself recalled how he spent that morning reading *Pride and Prejudice* in his sitting-room at Number 11 Downing Street – 'very soothing' – until interrupted by a phone call from the Queen's private secretary, Sir Michael Adeane, asking him to go to the Palace at two o'clock. 'So it was settled.'

Yes, but most unsatisfactorily. The process had been handled with aristocratic disdain for mainstream Conservative Party opinion, leaving the monarch open to the serious accusation that she had been unduly influenced by Salisbury and the small coterie of noble advisers huddled around her. The royal prerogative appeared to have been wielded in careless, high-handed fashion. No other parliamentarians at all had been consulted – not even the Whips' Office (then led by Edward Heath), the traditional nerve-centre of party opinion in parliament. Had they been, the final outcome might well have been the same; but it would have carried a great deal more conviction. 'I suffered much at this time,' Butler later admitted, still smarting at his reputation as 'the best prime minister we never had'. There was (and still is) dark talk of an aristocratic conspiracy to steer the premiership the way of Macmillan, a denizen of the grouse moors who had married into the landed gentry, at the expense of an opponent of modest social standing.

As prime minister, Macmillan was not above using the monarch, often without her knowledge, for political gain. The cabinet papers for 1962 (released, after the customary thirty years, in January 1993) reveal, for instance, that he shamelessly 'played the royal card' to squeeze US aid for Black Africa out of President Kennedy at the height of the Cold War, in the hope of thwarting Soviet ambitions in the region. At a time when Algeria and the Congo were in the grip of bloody civil wars, Macmillan arranged for the Queen to make a royal tour of Ghana, Liberia, Sierra Leone and the Gambia; then, with nearby Upper Volta apparently ripe for Communist take-over, he urged Kennedy to purchase Western influence in the region. The transcript of a 'hot line' phone call from Downing Street to the White House has Kennedy describing the situation in the Upper Volta as 'awfully unsatisfactory', and showing reluctance to pour millions of dollars into a country 'which is so unstable and which would involve a threat to the whole of our aid program'.

'Yes,' said Macmillan, 'but we must not lose it to that fellow Khrushchev. I have risked my Queen. You must risk your money.'

'Well, I won't be ungallant,' replied Kennedy. 'You made the greater risk.' Later that year, in another phone call with Macmillan, the president signalled that the US was prepared to 'go ahead' with Upper Volta. (All their efforts were to prove vain; in 1984 Upper Volta underwent a socialist revolution, becoming the independent republic of Burkina Faso.)

By the time Macmillan himself fell ill, after six years in office, no lessons had been learnt from the manner of his own appointment. Hospitalized in October 1963 for an operation on a prostate tumour, he told various cabinet visitors that he would remain prime minister only until a successor could be found.* This time there was a veritable throng of eligible contenders, chief among them Butler again; Iain Macleod, the leader of the House of Commons; Reginald Maudling, the Chancellor of the Exchequer; and, from the Lords, Viscount Hailsham (the former Quintin Hogg). To become prime minister, Hailsham would have had to make use of legislation recently secured by a Labour peer, Viscount Stansgate, to enable him to renounce his peerage and stand for the House of Commons as plain Mr Anthony Wedgwood Benn (later shortened to the even plainer Tony Benn). So would the foreign secretary, the Earl of Home, who was slowly beginning to emerge as a reluctant compromise candidate.

The protagonists' memoirs all carry conflicting accounts of the wheeler-dealing which ensued, as senior politicians shuttled between the prime minister's hospital bed in London and the Conservative party conference in Blackpool. 'I fear,' Macmillan told the Queen, 'that all kinds of intrigues and battles are going on.' He was himself, of course, in the thick of them, said by Macleod to be 'determined that Butler, although incomparably the best qualified of the contenders, should not succeed him'. Macmillan was pressing the case of Home, who had not even entered the race until urged by the outgoing prime minister to do so; he had been quite happy, he said, as foreign secretary, with no thought of leaving the Lords.

---

*It was a decision Macmillan was later to regret, when the tumour was found to be benign and he was fully restored to health.

Butler's supporters were outraged. A midnight cabal at the home of one pro-Butler cabinet member, Enoch Powell, wondered quite how the parliamentary party was to be persuaded that not one of its 363 members of the House of Commons was as suited to be prime minister as a faded aristocrat in the House of Lords, not noted for his knowledge of domestic or economic affairs. Still Butler could have won the day; a group of his followers, including Maudling and Hailsham, told him they would join him in refusing to serve under Home, which would make it impossible for the Earl – even when downgraded to Sir Alec Douglas-Home MP – to form a government. Ever the political gentleman, Butler told them he had already pledged Home his support. 'We handed Rab a loaded revolver,' as Powell later put it, 'and told him all he had to do was pull the trigger. He asked if it would make a noise and we said, "That is in the nature of guns, Rab." He asked if it would hurt him and we said, "That too is in the nature of guns, Rab", and he said, "I don't think I will. Do you mind?" '

On the morning of 18 October, Macmillan's private secretary delivered his formal letter of resignation to Buckingham Palace. That afternoon, in a scene without precedent in British history, the Queen went to visit him in hospital, where he read her a memorandum detailing his conclusions; he was 'not strong enough,' he told her, 'to trust myself to speak without a text'. After Macmillan had argued the case for Home, entrusting the Queen with the necessary documentation 'to prevent mistakes or arguments in the future', she replied that she did not feel it necessary to take any advice but his. Upon her return to the Palace, she immediately sent for Home and invited him to attempt to form a government. Even so, he was unable to give her more than an undertaking to try. Once Butler and Hailsham agreed to serve, he was secure; but Macleod and Powell still declined to join his cabinet.

Again, it was unwise of the monarch not to take further soundings. An outgoing prime minister has no constitutional right to nominate his (or her) successor. Even under the Conservative Party's informal system of 'emergence', a more secure consensus was required than merely the results of a backstairs conspiracy fuelled by personal prejudice. Macmillan's suitability to advise was compromised not only by his ill-health, but also by his personal involvement in the intrigues which followed his resignation. Even the Salisbury method was preferable to this; at least the man taking soundings was not a directly interested party.

To Powell, Macmillan had 'played fast and loose with the royal prerogative'. An outgoing prime minister cannot offer both his resignation *and* advice as to his successor; he must do one or the other. The effect of Macmillan's conduct 'was in fact to take away the crown's prerogative, and was incompatible with the nature of binding advice'.

Whether or not Macmillan was trying to enhance his own reputation by ensuring the least effective successor available, Douglas-Home managed within the year to lose the only election he ever fought, letting Labour back into power for the first time in thirteen years. Had Butler become prime minister, he might well have beaten Labour's Harold Wilson in 1964. Either way, the dubious episode which saw Douglas-Home installed in Number Ten had one salutary consequence; during his brief tenure of office, he commissioned a more formal system for electing Conservative leaders – the very system that would precipitate the downfall of Margaret Thatcher in 1990. While confessing himself sad to see the end of the time-honoured Tory tradition of 'emergence', Douglas-Home thought it wise to adopt a system 'where, from start to finish, everything was seen to be open and above board'. In so doing, he performed an inadvertent service to the monarch, who would henceforth be spared further such embarrassments at the hands of Tory mandarins.

They could, nevertheless, find plenty of other ways to embarrass her. That same Edward Heath who had not been consulted over the Eden succession, as chief whip back in 1957, proved the next Conservative prime minister to bring the Queen perilously close to intervention in the political process. The general election which Heath called in February 1974 resulted in a 'hung' parliament. Though Labour had won the most seats, with 301, it had no overall majority; the Conservatives, with 296 seats, could have clung to power if Heath were able to form a coalition with the fourteen Liberals led by Jeremy Thorpe, or sufficient of the twenty-four seats held by other parties: the Scottish and Welsh Nationalists, and the Ulster Unionists.

The Queen returned hastily from Australia, boarding a plane to London immediately after performing the opening of its parliament, to be informed by Heath that he proposed to stay on in Downing Street in the hope of forming a coalition. A very long weekend ensued, with much toing and froing through the door of Number Ten, while Harold Wilson waited patiently in the wings to claim another term in office. Four days later, by Monday 4 March, the deadlock was curdling to crisis; still without the support he needed, Heath showed no sign of giving way to the Labour opponent who had defeated him. It was already being whispered in some quarters that the Queen had given the defeated prime minister more time than constitutionally permissible; the monarch appeared to be bending the rules to accommodate the Conservative Party. Had that Monday evening not seen Heath finally give up, and go to the Palace to tender his resignation, the sovereign would soon have had to step in and demand it. As it was, she was able to send for Harold Wilson, who immediately formed a minority government. For four days, as Wilson later put it, British democracy had stood still.

Uncertain political situations like these will become much more frequent if and when Britain adopts a system of proportional representation, in common with many of its European partners. In the absence of any written constitution, the monarch can rely only on precedent, and the advice of leading historians of the day (such as Lord Blake). But anomalies will always abound, as in the case of Elizabeth II's next uncomfortable political period, three years after the Heath episode, when Wilson informed her in confidence during the autumn of 1975 that he intended to resign the following March. For six months, the monarch was in possession of information vital to the country's political stability, which Wilson filtered out to his political friends at strategic intervals along the way. Not until mid-March did he give his favoured successor, James Callaghan, a few days' notice that he would be making a formal announcement to the cabinet on the sixteenth. On the advice of Sir Martin Charteris, the Queen's private secretary, Wilson resigned as leader of the Labour Party, remaining as prime minister during the three weeks it took for a leadership contest to be held under the party's established rules. On the same night that he won the final ballot, 5 April 1976, James Callaghan visited the Queen at Buckingham Palace and became prime minister on the spot.

Although he was in office only three years, Callaghan became one of Elizabeth II's favourite prime ministers. Though of course a natural Tory herself, she has in recent years preferred the affable informality of her Labour prime ministers, Wilson and Callaghan, to the stiffness of some Conservatives. According to Anthony Sampson, the weekly meetings between the Queen and Mrs Thatcher were 'dreaded by at least one of them', and Thatcher would return to Downing Street 'in urgent need of a drink'. The relationship grew more difficult once their roles became confused: 'The Queen's style is more matter-of-fact and domestic, while it is Mrs Thatcher (who is taller) who bears herself like a queen.' As Thatcher became increasingly autocratic, she even took to using the royal 'We' – most famously in her announcement outside Number Ten that 'We have become a grandmother'.

Even with a real queen in place, to Sampson, Thatcher had become 'alarmingly regal; without a queen, she would have been terrifying'. Significantly, the Falklands victory parade saw the prime minister instead of the usual royal on the saluting platform; disaster victims (such as survivors of the 1987 Zeebrugge ferry disaster) grew accustomed to the hasty arrival of Thatcher in advance of the usual posse of royal sympathizers. But rumours of a strained relationship were discounted by Thatcher's biographer, Hugo Young, who cited Heath as the only one of her prime ministers with whom the monarch never managed to develop an 'easy' relationship. This, remarked Young, was 'a failing which gave Her Majesty something in common with much of the human race'.

The Queen's relations with Thatcher certainly began somewhat tensely, when Britain's first woman prime minister was horrified to find, at her first weekly audience in the spring of 1979, that she was wearing the same colour dress as the monarch. On her return to Number Ten, she immediately tried to set up an early-warning system whereby the Palace would each week notify Downing Street what the Queen was wearing, and the prime minister would adjust accordingly. There would be no need for any such arrangement, came back the immortal reply from the Palace, as 'Her Majesty does not notice what other people wear'.

Within three months, Elizabeth II was also giving her new prime minister lessons in diplomacy. The main issue before the Commonwealth heads of government meeting in Zambia in the summer of 1979 was the continuing crisis in Rhodesia, almost fourteen years since the government of Ian Smith had made its unilateral (and illegal) declaration of independence. Mrs Thatcher went to her first Commonwealth summit sceptical about the prospects of success; her instinct that an internal settlement was the best option, aided by the lifting of sanctions, was expressed with an aggression which was to become familiar – but which, at the time, alienated several Commonwealth prime ministers, notably Kenneth Kaunda of Zambia. Having known Kaunda for years, unlike Thatcher, the Queen personally intervened, persuading him to take a more optimistic view. She was, said Kaunda at the time, 'a tower of strength . . . Leaders in the Commonwealth, of all sorts of different political persuasions, are agreed on one thing. They can trust her.' Kaunda was not alone in giving the credit to the monarch, rather than the prime minister, for the subsequent preliminary agreement which paved the way to a solution which had eluded British governments for fifteen years. Within nine months Rhodesia gained its independence as the Republic of Zimbabwe, and joined the Commonwealth.

The British Commonwealth was again at the centre of a dispute between Thatcher and the Queen – through no fault, as it happened, of either – during a brief but dramatic US military excursion in 1983. Since the tiny Caribbean island of Grenada had come under Marxist rule, it had been regarded with suspicion by the United States, like Cuba and Nicaragua, as a possible source of trouble in what successive American presidents liked to call their 'back yard'. On 19 October 1983 events came to a head with the ousting and murder of the Marxist leader,

Maurice Bishop, by an even more extreme leftist group, who seized power.

With law and order on the verge of apparent breakdown, neighbouring Caribbean countries such as Barbados and Dominica feared a swift spread of disorder, and appealed to their allies for help. At the British Foreign Office the request caused little stir; the Foreign Secretary was away in Greece, and the matter was shelved for the weekend. In Ronald Reagan's White House, by contrast, with a thousand American nationals on the island, the threat was taken seriously enough to prompt plans for a 'benign' invasion – which duly took place on 24 October, with the minimum of fuss and bloodshed. The attack was already under way when Congressional leaders were called to a White House briefing. The then Speaker of the House, Tip O'Neill, reminded Reagan that Grenada was a British dominion, and asked what prime minister Thatcher thought about the invasion. 'She doesn't know about it,' replied Reagan.

Nor did Queen Elizabeth II, who also happens to be Queen of Grenada. The United States, supposedly Britain's oldest and closest ally, had invaded one of its dominions without so much as a by-your-leave. If Margaret Thatcher was furious with Reagan – the president's own memoirs describe her as 'adamant' (if, alas, too late) that the operation be cancelled – the Queen was furious with Thatcher. It was for her, as Queen of Grenada, an abject humiliation that the first she heard of the American invasion of her country was on the BBC's television news. Her private secretary telephoned Downing Street to demand Mrs Thatcher's immediate presence at the Palace, only to be told that the prime minister was in a meeting. At the Queen's insistence, he called back immediately to say that the head of state demanded that she leave her meeting at once. Moments later, Thatcher was duly seen hurrying to her car and heading for Buckingham Palace. When she arrived, the Queen clearly signalled her displeasure by not inviting her prime minister to sit while explaining why she had not passed on details of her conversation with Reagan.

That there was no love lost between Elizabeth II and Margaret Thatcher was suggested in no uncertain terms to readers of *The Sunday Times* in the summer of 1986. Two weeks before a

Commonwealth summit, the paper reported that the Queen, also head of the Commonwealth, disagreed 'to the point of outrage' with Mrs Thatcher's policy towards South Africa, possibly even with her refusal to impose sanctions. But that was not all. The paper also stated that, as British head of state, she was also distressed by the government's apparent lack of compassion for the underprivileged; she had disagreed with Thatcher's handling of the miners' strike in 1984; she bore 'misgivings' about British co-operation with the US air force in the 1986 bombing of Libya; and Thatcher's overall strategy was causing a corrosive divide between the north and south of her kingdom, undoing the consensus approach which had served the country so well through the entire post-war period.

The source of this remarkable information, most unusually, was named in the article as the Queen's press secretary himself, Michael Shea. The implication was clear. By authorizing her senior staff to make her views known to the press, the monarch was indulging in a deliberate intervention in the political process – an astonishing breach of her clearly defined constitutional role. 'For one brief weekend,' as Hugo Young put it, 'the British public was invited to transport itself back to the eighteenth century or earlier, with a Royal Party apparently mobilizing to overturn the coalition of forces now in charge.'

What could have provoked this extraordinary outburst? Was the Queen launching a pre-emptive strike against any move to reform the monarchy by an iconoclast who had taken on most other British institutions? Were the senior members of the royal family 'worried paternalists' (in Young's description) 'who instinctively spoke for the kind of society that Mrs Thatcher felt it necessary to challenge'? In a letter to *The Times* the Queen's private secretary, Sir William Heseltine, described as 'preposterous' any suggestion that a member of the Royal Household would reveal such details to the press, 'even supposing that he or she knew what Her Majesty's opinions on government policy might be'. Whatever personal opinions the monarch might hold, she was constitutionally bound to accept and act on the advice of her prime ministers. 'She is obliged to treat her communications with the prime minister as entirely confidential between the two of them.'

To *The Times*'s leader writer, the report signified the escape from captivity of 'some monstrous caged beast' in the shape of the monarch's political opinions. It was understandable that the Palace wanted the beast re-caged with all speed. If the Queen's opinions of her government coincided with those of a majority of her subjects – which was not inconceivable – then a breakdown of constitutional democracy could swiftly ensue. The editor of *The Sunday Telegraph*, Peregrine Worsthorne, believed the Queen's displeasure with her prime minister had made 'an indelible impression on the public imagination', with the result that Mrs Thatcher 'might actually have her spirit broken'.

Although they were almost exact contemporaries in age, monarch and prime minister displayed clear differences of style and emphasis. To Mrs Thatcher, the ambitious daughter of a Lincolnshire alderman, Queen Elizabeth II had always been a role model. Two weeks after her accession, on 17 February 1952, the would-be MP had written in *The Sunday Graphic*: 'If, as many earnestly pray, the accession of Elizabeth II can help to remove the last shreds of prejudice against women aspiring to the highest places, then a new era for women will indeed be at hand.' As prime minister thirty years later, a courtier told Young, Thatcher had always behaved with excessive reverence in the royal presence: 'Her curtsies before even the remoter royals reached lower than anyone else's' (which remained the case 'even when the passage of a decade might have made the habit more perfunctory'). Thatcher was always fifteen minutes early for her weekly audiences; because she came from a different background, however, because she didn't hunt, shoot or fish, her staff always found it difficult to occupy her time during the prime minister's annual weekend at Balmoral. While the royal family was out braving the elements, Mrs Thatcher would usually content herself with working on state papers.

Thatcher's forthcoming memoirs seem less likely to throw much light on these mysteries than to add further to the pile of deferential tributes already paid Elizabeth II by her long succession of prime ministers. Harold Wilson has not been alone in confirming Bagehot's suspicion that 'in the course of a long reign, a sagacious king would acquire an experience with which few ministers could contend.' At one of his early audiences, according to Wilson, the Queen had remarked that it was 'very interesting, this idea of a new town in the Bletchley area'. Wilson had 'smiled, blinked,' and later confessed that he had not himself read the cabinet paper documenting plans for the new town of Milton Keynes. Telling the story in the Queen's presence, at a Downing Street dinner to mark his retirement in March 1976, Wilson concluded that he would 'certainly advise my successor to do his homework before his audience'.

That same successor, James Callaghan, told Elizabeth Long-ford that the Queen was 'very interested in the political side – who's going up and down'. Her prime ministers received 'friendliness but not friendship' and also 'a great deal of under-standing of their problems – without the Queen sharing them, since she is outside politics. . . Of course she may have hinted at things, but only on the rarest occasions do I remember her ever saying "Why don't you do this, that or the other?" She is pretty detached on all that.'

Less charitable intermediaries blame this on a lack of regal imagination. 'Like her mother,' wrote Lord Altrincham of Elizabeth II, 'she appears to be unable to string even a few sentences together without a written text.' This was echoed in 1990 by Tony Benn, recalling a presentation by the cabinet to mark her silver jubilee in 1977: 'The Queen, who can't say good morning without a script, referred to bits of paper and said "Mr Prime Minister, thank you very much indeed".'

John Grigg, the former Lord Altrincham, remained cruel to be kind even at the height of her 'annus horribilis': 'As for departures from routine, the Queen has tended to avoid them as a matter of principle. Unscheduled gestures have been comparatively few, and the power of the monarchy to appeal to the imagination has, in this respect, been seriously underused.' He cited the Queen's failure to pay a hospital visit to a policeman recently shot while pursuing IRA terrorists – a curious omission in view of the ensuing furore over which royal should comfort IRA bomb victims in Warrington (*see* page 261–4). But Grigg, overall, was appeased. He was gratified that Elizabeth II had heeded some of his earlier advice (specifically, the abolition of the presentation at court of debutantes). 'If the Queen can move into a higher rather than a lower gear in the years ahead,' wrote one of her sternest critics late in 1992, 'her reign, already in so many ways good, may become great.'

The greatness of Elizabeth II's reign currently seems to be an open question. If history eventually rules in her favour, however, the Queen herself would cite 'training' as the secret of her success. 'You can do a lot if you've been properly trained – as I have,' she has said. 'If you live this sort of life' (she managed, *en passant*, to acknowledge that 'not many people do') 'you live very much by tradition and by continuity. This is what the younger members of the family find difficult: the regimented side of it . . .'

Ay, there's the rub. When everything unravelled in 1992, and even *The Daily Telegraph* suggested that it was time to hang up her crown, the Queen was deemed in some quarters to have failed in her one cardinal duty: presenting the nation with an acceptable successor. 'The changes that badly need to be effected in the style and purpose of the monarchy would actually be facilitated,' Hugh Massingberd had written that summer, 'were the Queen to hand over the reins now to the Prince of Wales.' Within months of that commendation, however, Charles's reputation was also under threat, as he began 1993 a thoroughly discredited figure.

One of the most potent arguments in defence of the monarchy is the supposed direness of the alternative: President Callaghan, President Major, even President Thatcher. Now one of the strongest arguments for remembering Elizabeth II as the last British monarch is the prospect of the royal alternative: King Charles III.

CHAPTER 8

CHARLES: THE HEIR APPARENT

————◆————

'The only fit material for a constitutional king
is a prince who begins early to reign.'
WALTER BAGEHOT,
The English Constitution

JANUARY 1993, AS EVERY JANUARY, SAW THE PRINCE OF
Wales taking his ease with friends at Balmoral, killing off the
last Scottish hind of the season, when across the world his worst
fears were realized. Since the battering he had taken throughout
1992, as the man who had betrayed the affections of the world's
most popular woman, Prince Charles had been well aware that
'a sword of Damocles' (as he put it to his house guests) still
hung menacingly over his princely brow. Above all else he
had dreaded the one thing which now came to pass. At first in
Australia, then in America, then in newspapers and magazines
all over Europe, the transcript of the notorious Camillagate tape
was published in full. The would-be king was revealed to be a
puerile, bawdy, hot-blooded adulterer.

'I want to feel my way along you, all over you and up and
down you and in and out,' the future Defender of the Faith
told the wife of one of his oldest friends. 'I fill up your tank!

I need you several times a week,' said the heir to the throne to Mrs Silver Stick-in-Waiting.

None of Charles's contemporaries would wish to have their late-night phone calls broadcast to the world. Few of them, come to that, have reached middle-age without the odd indiscretion: some conversations they would not wish others to hear, some meetings, perhaps liaisons they would prefer to keep to themselves. As was already under public debate at the time of Charles's embarrassment, democratic societies regard such privacies as a basic human right – although in Britain, with no written constitution and thus no Bill of Rights, no such right is enshrined in law.

None of Charles's contemporaries, however, aspire to be head of the church and a symbol of moral probity to the nation and the Commonwealth. None have lived a pampered life of luxury as consolation for the burdens of being born royal, let alone enjoyed an *ex-officio* pulpit from which to deliver moral homilies to the nation. Fairly or unfairly, the Prince of Wales could not hope or expect to be judged as other men. Even those prepared to indulge human frailty felt obliged to measure him by higher standards. As Charles himself was only too ruefully aware, the transcript of that raunchy late-night phone call was now set to haunt the rest of his life. Coming from one of the leading characters in the world's ultimate soap opera, moreover, it was sure to prove the most widely-read royal document since Magna Carta.

Most of the mainstream British press funked publication in full – staying their hand, perhaps, because that very week they were fighting off the threat of legislation to curb press freedom.* But photocopiers and fax machines whirred samizdat copies from Fleet Street to the City of London, from Whitehall to Downing Street, from Land's End to John o'Groat's. The wonders of modern technology thus averted a repeat of the Establishment conspiracy of 1936, when the rest of the world knew all about King Edward and his Mrs Simpson while the British were kept in ignorance. In Friday night pubs and clubs

---

*Five days after its publication in Australia, the transcript was printed in full in the *Sunday Mirror* and *The People*. Other British papers found roundabout ways of printing the spiciest extracts, such as having them analysed by 'Agony Aunts'.

around the land, loyal subjects pored over this latest insight into the character of their future king.

'Oh God,' moaned Fred to his Gladys, 'I'll just live inside your trousers or something. It would be so much easier.'

'What are you going to turn into?' she giggled. 'A pair of knickers or something?' Both giggled. 'Oh, you're going to come back as a pair of knickers!'

'Or, God forbid, a Tampax,' ventured the would-be Head of the Church of England. 'Just my luck to be chucked down a lavatory and go on and on forever swirling round on the top, never going down.'

That weekend Charles was summoned to a summit with his parents at Sandringham. Never had the reputation of the Queen's son and heir, or indeed that of the monarchy, sunk quite so low. Though she had long known of Charles's friendship with Mrs Parker-Bowles – even endorsed it by publicly embracing Camilla – she had never raised its precise nature with her son. Even with her family, she has a habit of avoiding personal conversations, preferring to stick to safer subjects such as the weather. The Duchess of York once took a long walk with her mother-in-law at a time when she was desperate to discuss her failing marriage; every time Sarah broached the subject, the Queen found a more urgent talking point among the corgis at their feet. On this occasion, however, her son's behaviour amounted to family business. The future of 'the firm' was at stake. Upon Charles's arrival, Elizabeth II made it very clear to her son that she was distinctly unamused.

Previous Princes of Wales had of course kept mistresses, while also keeping the golden establishment rule of not getting caught. There was thus a certain retrospective romance to Edward VII's dalliance with Lily Langtry, and a generous grace in his wife's invitation to his favourite mistress, Mrs Alice Keppel, Camilla's great-grandmother, to visit the king on his deathbed. But neither he nor his adulterous grandson, Edward VIII, had been caught in public with their trousers down. Charles's love of his mobile phone was to prove far more damaging than his love of a homely Gloucestershire housewife, devoted enough to beg for sneak previews of his speeches. No previous Prince of Wales had publicly presented his credentials for office in the form of soft-core pornography.

Even more damaging than the sex-talk, for the man aspiring to the nation's moral leadership, was the open and unashamed deception of his friend, the hapless brigadier, Andrew Parker-Bowles. 'Not Tuesday,' says Camilla. 'A's coming home.' Complex arrangements are then discussed for clandestine meetings at the homes of friends. Amid frequent declarations of love, the couple finally display a winsome teenage inability to hang up.

'Press the button,' says Camilla.

'Going to press the tit,' says Charles.

'All right, darling, I wish you were pressing mine.'

'God, I wish I was. Harder and harder.'

That same week had seen revelations that Charles had himself been 'managing' the very press coverage of his marital difficulties that had been denounced in his name. Undeterred, the prince immediately resorted to a desperate newspaper campaign of damage containment via his ever-talkative staff and friends. 'THEY WILL FORGIVE ME' proclaimed the front page of the *Daily Mail* on the heir to the throne's behalf, after an 'emotional' chat with 'a member of his circle'. Although twenty-seven more such tapes of Charles–Camilla sex-talk were rumoured to be in circulation, the prince apparently believed that the worst was over. 'Things,' he was quoted as saying, 'can only get better.' By 'distance and silence', his private secretary told *The Times*, he hoped to 'douse the fires of a nine-day wonder'. Time, his advisers believed, was on his side: 'He still has many years in which to prove his worth as the next monarch.'

His future subjects were not so sure. 'If Prince Charles does believe [the British people] will forgive him,' wrote Denis Evans of Cheshire to the *Mail*, 'he may be in for a rude awakening.' There was 'no way,' agreed John Everard of Devon, 'that after his lapses Prince Charles can command the respect due to a monarch . . . What example is this to the nation?'

An equally pertinent question was raised by Major Anthony Dryland of the Royal Electrical and Mechanical Engineers, until recently a serving officer with the British army on the Rhine.

In February 1992 Dryland's former wife had admitted killing his German fiancée. Six months after she was sentenced by a court martial to one year's probation under medical supervision, Dryland himself was charged with misconduct and eventually required to resign his commission after thirty-one years of 'loyal and meritorious service'. The Army Board, he was informed, held him responsible for the embarrassing publicity his former wife's actions had caused the Army.

By January 1993, not unreasonably, Dryland declared himself 'interested to hear of the Army Board's attitude' in respect of the conduct of his brother officer, the Prince of Wales, whose own case had itself attracted considerably more publicity. (That very weekend the Camillagate tape was broadcast throughout America and Australia.) 'I refer,' said Dryland, 'to the much publicized alleged affair with Camilla Parker-Bowles, herself the wife of a serving brigadier.' Politicians, ministers and members of the royal family were 'getting away with all sorts of things,' he added, accusing the Army of 'double standards'.

Annex C of Chapter 62 of the Army's General Administrative Instructions specifically forbids affairs with the wives of fellow officers. Among eight rules under which officers can be called upon to resign or retire for misconduct, Rule D cites adultery with 'a spouse of a serving member of the armed forces'. The previous month a forty-year-old major had been thrown out on precisely this charge.

The Prince of Wales was Colonel of the Welsh Guards and Colonel-in-Chief of the Parachute Regiment, the Royal Dragoon Guards, the Royal Regiment of Wales, the Gordon Highlanders, the Cheshire Regiment and the 2nd King Edward VII's Own Gurkha Rifles. 'You cannot have one rule for the serving Army officer, and another for the honorary colonel-in-chief,' said a senior military man who preferred, for obvious reasons, to remain anonymous. 'The Army has got to lead by example, and Prince Charles is clearly not doing so.'

At the time, the prince was still in hiding at Sandringham, considering his future tactics with his coterie of friends and advisers. On the same day that he and Mrs Parker-Bowles both declined an invitation from the Press Complaints Commission to lodge a formal protest over the transcript's publication, he also remained silent on demands for his resignation from the Army. Not that he had become newspaper-shy. The previous day, a royal aide was reported in *The Observer* to have telephoned the paper on the prince's behalf, denying a front-page story by its political editor suggesting that Charles had abandoned hope of becoming king.

On the front page of the same day's *Sunday Telegraph* (whose editor, Charles Moore, had consistently maintained that the royal family's private life was not a matter of public concern), the prince was given above-the-fold prominence to suggest, again via unnamed 'friends', that his affair with the brigadier's wife was over, that he would become celibate for the rest of his life – anything, it seemed, to ensure that he could still inherit the throne. Charles would meanwhile be carrying on with his schedule 'as normal'; the very next day, as planned, he would be meeting local worthies in King's Lynn.

Alas, the meeting never took place. Charles was struck down overnight by a convenient bout of gastro-enteritis. Lest anyone wonder just how convenient, the Palace was quick to stress that numerous other Sandringham residents had caught the bug, including the Queen herself. After two days Charles was said to have made a full recovery. But still he cancelled his engagements – unlike his mother, also fully recovered, who accompanied her own mother to the local Women's Institute.

Charles did not show his face in public again until ten days later, when he visited a North London housing development. Buckingham Palace sent advance orders to the prince's hosts that he did not want to meet 'too many people'. Children, especially, were to be kept away from the Prince of Wales 'because they tend to ask awkward questions'. They duly were. The following day, however, as Charles left a health centre in Whitechapel, East London, a cockney pensioner shouted : 'Have you no shame?' Looking shaken, the prince climbed into his limousine and sped away. 'What right has he got to come to the East End after what he's been up to?' demanded the feisty old man, who refused to give his name to reporters. 'He's a disgrace.'

Any doubts about the public significance of Charles's adultery had now been dispelled by the Church of England's second most senior clergyman, the Archbishop of York. Speaking while the Archbishop of Canterbury was abroad, and thus with the authority of the Church's 'day-to-day leader', Dr John Habgood said he certainly considered it a matter of public concern. 'Looking back over history, the nation has been extraordinarily tolerant of all sorts of behaviour among its monarchs, but all tolerance has its limits and I would not want myself now to say where those limits might lie.' A week later, from South Africa, the Archbishop of Canterbury signalled his agreement: 'We expect our leaders at every level to embody Christian values.'

Although neither Archbishop said as much, it was beginning to look as if Charles might have some difficulty finding a prelate prepared to crown him. Said the Archdeacon of York, the Venerable George Austin: 'I've been a monarchist all my life, but I must say my support is not what it was. If Prince Charles divorces and remarries, I would have very great difficulties.' The prince's adultery would seem to 'disqualify' him from heading the Church of England, added the Revd David Streater, head of the influential Church Society.

It did not look as if Charles's 'nine-day wonder' was going to disappear quite as fast as he had hoped. Amid his constitutional woes, the prince had by now become the laughing-stock of Britain, Europe and the world. 'My shares have gone down more often than Jug Ears on Camilla,' said the comedian Rick Mayall in the popular ITV series *The New Statesman*, watched by six million Britons. A box of tampons became 'a box of Prince Charlies' in the award-winning comedy *Drop the Dead Donkey,* watched by 4.5 million. When the American film of Andrew Morton's book was shown on British satellite television, watched by an estimated two million viewers, Tampax was the leading product advertised between segments.

Italy's *L'Indipendente* called Britain's future head of state 'the Porno Prince', while *La Stampa* of Turin dubbed him 'Il Tamponcino'. In America, Mick Jagger dressed as a bewigged butler in a period sketch on TV's *Saturday Night Live* to present 'Camilla' with a present from the Prince of Wales on a silver tray – a gift box of tampons. Thanks to Charles, Jagger told the BBC, the royal family were in 'a right old mess . . . They've

shot themselves in the foot. There's not a lot you can say in their support.' When a brief trip to the United States took Charles to Williamsburg, Virginia, on St Valentine's Eve, the local radio rebroadcast the Camillagate tape, dubbing him 'the phone-sex prince', and students at the College of William and Mary celebrated its 300th anniversary with fancy dress 'Charles and Camilla slumber parties' – somewhat overshadowing their honorary fellow's sombre call for a return to 'traditional values'.

Among young British women, a 'Charlie' was now a synonym for a Tampax. It was mischievously suggested that the manufacturers should be allowed to embellish their distinctive blue boxes with a 'By Royal Appointment' crest. *The Sun* carried a cartoon showing Charles entering his greenhouse to find his plants begging: 'Talk dirty to us.' It was reported that the Privy Council had endorsed arrangements whereby Princess Anne would become Regent if the Queen died before Prince William reached eighteen, the age at which he could accede to the throne. The plan had apparently been initiated by Prince

Philip 'who has accepted for some time now that his eldest son is not king material'. The inevitable Palace denial served only to strengthen belief in the story.

By February 1993, a Gallup poll in *The Daily Telegraph* showed that Charles was losing the propaganda war with his estranged wife. Where she remained the royal family's most popular member – on 22 per cent, exactly the same figure as eighteen months before – Charles's rating had slumped from 15 per cent to just 4 per cent, moving him down the royal charts from second to fifth.* As he put a brave face on a visit to Mexico, a poll for Sky Television showed that more than a third of Britons considered him 'most to blame' for the breakdown of his marriage, with 11 per cent blaming Diana (24 per cent the press and 25 per cent 'the royal family as a whole'). Most damaging of all, the Sky poll showed that 42 per cent of Britons now thought Charles should 'never become king'. Asked if he should take over the throne 'within the next couple of years', a resounding 81 per cent said no.

Charles's apparent self-restraint in declining to sue those papers which had printed the Camillagate transcript was meanwhile diminished by two unlikely lawsuits launched by the mighty – the prime minister, John Major, over allegations in the left-wing weekly *The New Statesman* about his private life, and the Queen herself, over the leaking to *The Sun* of the text of her Christmas broadcast.

The rogue prince revealed by the tape could, however, boast one maverick school of thought rallying to his aid. In the 1968 American presidential campaign, the personal popularity of the Democratic presidential candiate, Senator Hubert Humphrey, had soared when President Richard Nixon's 'dirty tricks' department falsely accused him of an affair with his secretary. 'It's the first interesting thing I've heard about him,' ran the argument. 'Adds some colour to a pretty grey guy.' The same syndrome

*The poll rated the royals' respective popularity as follows (June 1991 figures in brackets): **1** The Princess of Wales 22 (22) **2** The Princess Royal 20 (15) **3** The Queen 15 (12) **4** The Queen Mother 14 (14) **5** The Prince of Wales 4 (15) **6** The Duchess of York 2 (3) **7** The Duke of York 2 (2) **8** The Duke of Edinburgh 1 (2) **9** Princess Margaret 1 (1) **10** Prince Edward 1 (0) **Other** 2 (2) None of the above 17 (11). (*Source*: Gallup poll for *The Daily Telegraph*, London, 9 February 1993.)

had boosted the personal ratings of Paddy Ashdown, leader of the Liberal Democratic Party, when he was forced to admit to an affair with a former secretary on the eve of the 1992 general election campaign. Now mischievous columnists such as Peter McKay of the London *Evening Standard* declared Charles their kind of king. The 'silly, touching and filthy' conversation had made McKay 'think better' of Charles: 'He comes out of it as a daft romantic dying to leap under the duvet, fond of terrible sex jokes.' (Eight months before, the same columnist had written of Morton's revelations about Charles and Camilla: 'We are entitled to be furious that Charles, who cultivates so careful an image of gentle, sensitive concern, has treated his young wife in this way . . . This is a very serious matter.')

Other monarchists wielded equally desperate arguments in the prince's defence. Readers of *The Sunday Express* were told that the 'best' English kings – Charles II, George IV, Edward VII – had been even greater philanderers. 'One of the ablest medieval kings, Henry I, holds the record. He is believed to have fathered at least thirty-five bastards, by a wide range of mistresses.' Charles II, with eighteen, took second place. 'Four of the current dukes owe their titles to their descent from Good King Charles and his mistresses.' Back in the *Standard*, the novelist A. N. Wilson begged to differ with his colleague McKay: 'The prince is very unlikely to be king because he won't outlive his mother. If he did so, he would not be very popular. This has nothing to do with what he might have said on the tapes to Mrs Parker-Bowles, but rather more to do with the fact that he is a diminutive bore with protuberant ears.'

Once widely admired – regarded as a well-meaning and compassionate man, with all the makings of a reforming royal – Charles had spent his early forties drifting into self-caricature. Even the proverbial London cab driver, who had volubly shared his views on such matters as the evils of modern architecture, began to see the ever more thinly spread prince as a remote and effete pedant, out of touch with the real world of his fellow Britons, notoriously fond of talking to his plants and reliant on the advice of like-minded, elderly gurus. Throughout the early 1990s Charles's failure to achieve much of substance – which

had grown to dog him as much as his admirers – was suddenly set alongside evidence of even more damaging domestic
inadequacies, as both husband and father.

History has a tendency to feel sorry for Princes of Wales,
who seem to have made a habit of failing to fulfil their early
promise. Whatever the caprices of their parents, however, heirs
apparent have always borne an unavoidable stake in the current state of the monarchy's reputation. During the Windsor
crisis of 1992–93 it became clear that the current monarch-in-
waiting must shoulder a major share of responsibility for the
loss of public confidence in the future of the institution which
amounts to his birthright.

The British constitution defines no role for the heir to the throne.
Its unwritten rules are eloquent as to what the Prince of Wales
should *not* do, unhelpfully silent as to what he should. British
history has thus seen some monarchs-in-waiting set themselves
up as rivals to their royal parents, acting as unofficial leaders of
the opposition, barely disguising their eagerness to take over;
others have taken the chance to make themselves useful, as
patrons of the arts or activists in other non-controversial fields.
Rather more, denied any role in affairs of state, have used the position and its perks to enjoy lives of self-indulgent dissipation.

The history of the office is not, as a result, a particularly distinguished one. Charles Philip Arthur George, the twenty-first
English Prince of Wales in seven hundred years, entered his
thirties intent on changing all that. One of the better-educated
heirs to the throne, endowed with a strong sense of history,
Charles seemed by disposition more earnest, reflective and conscientious than the majority of his predecessors. In his early
adulthood, his modest intelligence appeared to belie all genetic
theory. Heir to the throne since the age of three, but unlikely
to inherit it until he was a grandfather in his sixties, he had
spent most of his youth frustrated by the prospect of so long
and tiresome a wait in the wings, and increasingly irritated
by continual taunts that he should get 'a proper job'. In the
mid-1980s he made a conscious decision to turn necessity to
advantage by earning himself a niche as a crusader Prince of

Wales, riding a populist white charger to the rescue of disadvantaged minorities around his future realm.

For a few years he succeeded. From architecture to conservation, employment to the inner cities, race relations to other urgent social concerns of the day, the prince boldly used his office to launch worthy initiatives like grapeshot. The mid-1980s saw him ready to ride to the rescue of any underprivileged minority with whom he could sympathize without incurring the wrath of Margaret Thatcher. Under pressure from right-wing backbenchers, the then prime minister steered him away from tacit criticism of the government, striking unemployment and the inner cities from his agenda; but a philosophical jigsaw nevertheless appeared to be falling into place, its disparate pieces fusing the wild profusion of causes he had espoused.

While still in the Navy, in the mid-1970s, Charles had founded an organization called the Prince's Trust, designed to make small financial grants to unemployed youths intent on community service. The Trust's work was worthy but dull stuff to a tabloid press intent on chronicling the 'macho' lifestyle of the playboy prince, playing the field as he open-endedly postponed his choice of bride. Having entered his thirties a frustrated and somewhat embittered figure, he was finally liberated by his eventual marriage from the long and powerful shadow of his parents. Free to pursue an increasingly idiosyncratic range of interests, he had soon turned virtually vegetarian ('Oh Charles, don't be so silly,' said his mother) and started exploring the virtues of holistic, homeopathic and other less conventional forms of medicine.

An attack on orthodox medicine in 1982, at the 150th anniversary dinner of the British Medical Association, brought him his first, unexpected taste of criticism. When he formally opened the Bristol Centre, an 'alternative', drug-free cancer clinic, orthodox cancer specialists wrote outraged letters to *The Times* and indeed to the prince himself, eliciting a highly defensive, even apologetic reply. Such is the power of royal patronage that the BMA felt obliged to institute an official inquiry into the virtues of 'complementary' forms of medicine, the case for which was found distinctly unproven in its 1986 report. Some 'alternative' treatments promoted by Charles, such as

herbalism, were found to be 'positively harmful'. The doctors had given the prince a taste of his own medicine; and he
didn't much like it. Little has since been heard from him on the
subject of alternative medicine.

Charles had meanwhile begun to practise organic farming on
the Duchy of Cornwall acreage adjacent to his Gloucestershire
home, Highgrove; his attempts to make Highgrove 'a model
of environmental soundness' were proudly chronicled in a 1993
book, *Highgrove: Portrait of an Estate.* Window-sills and door-
frames had been draught-proofed and disused chimneys blocked,
it proclaimed, to conserve heat. Low-energy light-bulbs have
been installed. Charles was frustrated in his wish to introduce
straw-fired central heating, which proved impractical, but converted the swimming-pool heating system from electricity to
oil. He introduced a 'reed-bed' sewage-disposal system, har-
nessed to solar power, and a 'short rotation coppice system'
to prevent his trees degenerating through cross-breeding. All
this, plus his 1,000-acre organic 'crop rotation' programme,
were lovingly chronicled in a television film to plug the book.
As the cameras lingered longingly on the façade of Highgrove
House, a Grade II listed building, no mention was made of the
fact that he had tacked on a neo-classical pediment without
planning permission.

Charles's habit of disappearing for a few days to 'live' the
life of a Cornwall dairy farmer or Highland crofter, often with
only a television crew for company, had long since earned him
the tabloid nickname of 'the Loony Prince'. Similar satire had
greeted his trips to Africa, under the tutelage of the veteran
traveller Laurens van der Post, to study the primitive, unspoilt
ways of the Kalahari bushmen. Throughout the 1980s – to the
disgust of his father, who considered his oldest son a 'wimp'
in need of 'toughening up' – the prince emerged as an embryo
'green', worrying about what he ate and drank, banning aerosol sprays from the royal residences, persuading his mother to
convert the fleet of royal cars to lead-free fuel. From there it
was but a short step towards espousing fashionable, if urgent,
concerns about the planet: the ozone layer, global warming, the
destruction of the tropical rain forests.

Britain, its future king believed, was becoming a selfish, consumer-oriented society in a state of increasing spiritual decay. The Thatcher years were creating an every-man-for-himself rush for wealth in which the devil was palpably taking the hind-most. Homelessness, urban blight and inner-city decay were, to Charles, the inevitable products of a post-industrial society, in which too little care was taken to regenerate once prosperous areas now fallen on hard times. He especially admired the work of an organization called Business in the Community (BiC), founded in 1981 by a group of enlightened businessmen to per-suade major companies to donate money, personnel or resources towards trusts, projects and enterprise agencies, designed to foster business initiatives and thus create new jobs. A catalyst for local action, inspiring rather than managing partnership projects, BiC acted as honest broker between companies and communities, creating mutual goodwill as much as mutual advantage. In 1984, after placing his diffuse array of initiatives under BiC's umbrella, Charles was persuaded to become its president.

Despite this long overdue pragmatism, his speeches were still peppered with references to the decay of the modern world, its loss of spiritual values, the injuries modern man was inflicting on himself and his planet. Often his heartfelt sentiments went unre-corded amid excited newspaper coverage of his wife's latest hat or hair style; so, to the disappointed groans of waiting crowds, he stopped taking her with him. As their marriage moved into a distant *froideur*, Charles grew more confused than ever about the curious hand dealt him by fate. Plunging deeper into philosophy and spiritualism, his pronouncements about the meaning of life became increasingly eccentric; his trademark references, amid much half-hatched metaphysics, to such Jungian concepts as 'the mirror of the soul' were invariably lost on his listeners all over the Commonwealth. Combine this with his candid confession that he was in the habit of talking to his plants, and the Prince of Wales had finally lost his audience.

By the time of his fortieth birthday in 1988, Charles's public work was not merely drowning in tidal waves of negative pub-licity about his marriage. Equally damaging was his failure to give any central focus to what seemed like a different obsession every week. When a series of polo injuries and back problems caused a period of unwonted silence, there was an almost audible sigh of relief around a land which had been green and pleasant long before he had nagged it comatose. After books and television films on architecture and ecology, he published collections of his water colours and his treatise on organic farming. The Palace fought to prevent tens of thousands of unsold copies winding up on the shelves of remainder shops. Renaissance Man had become the pub bore; the crusader prince on his white charger had metamorphosed into Don Quixote on Rosinante, tilting with his polo mallet at politically incorrect windmills.

Charles and his admirers had reckoned without one of the crueller enigmas posed by the history of his office: that, given the constraints of the job, the more successful Princes of Wales have tended to be the less assertive ones. 'Sensitive to criticism and prone to self-doubt' (very like his great-grandfather, George V, in the description of his official biographer), Charles also has a short fuse and an even shorter attention span. His butterfly mind is easily distracted. Readily discouraged, he has allowed frustration or overt opposition in one field to divert him too easily towards another. Shrinking from private as well as public challenge, he has chosen to surround himself only with like-minded advisers; notoriously bad at taking advice, he has seen three private secretaries resign in five years. It is a characteristic part of this process that many initiatives launched with great fanfare during the 1980s have subsequently been left to fend for themselves, often to wither and die. Without the prince's active support, such causes are indeed hopeless.

Take the case of Inner City Aid, the prince's urban answer to Bob Geldof's Band Aid, launched under the prince's patronage in November 1986 at a community architecture conference in London. Its aims were ambitious: to raise £10 million in its first year of operation, under the chairmanship of Charles's friend Rod Hackney, then president of the Royal Institute of British Architects, and to provide grant aid, in cash and kind, for development and rehabilitation projects initiated by community self-help groups. 'This is about regenerating Britain's inner cities,' trumpeted Hackney at the launch. Benefactors would be investing in nothing less than 'the renaissance of the United Kingdom from the inner cities outwards,' he declared, hailing the Prince of Wales as 'our champion, patron and friend'. Clause Two of the charter deed of Inner City Aid's parent body, the Inner City Trust, summarized its objectives as: 'to relieve need, hardship and distress among persons living in deprived and decayed urban areas . . . to provide such persons with adequate housing . . . to improve their environment and to relieve poverty among such of their number who are unemployed.'

Two years later, wholly ignored by the prince since the day of its launch, Inner City Aid fired its remaining staff and closed down without having achieved a thing. In its first year of operation, abandoned by Charles, it raised just £33,000 of its £10 million target – much of it from a book of royal cartoons compiled to mark the prince's fortieth birthday by Inner City Aid's founder-director, Charles Knevitt, the proceeds of which he donated to the Trust. Less than a year after the launch Knevitt resigned amid some rancour; and one of the trustees, Lord Scarman, warily conceded that 'enthusiasm had tended to get in the way of sensible planning'. Scarman also remarked that 'a great mistake' had been made – namely, the launch on the very same day of yet another worthy cause bearing Charles's name: the Prince's Youth Business Trust, headed by Lord Boardman, chairman of the National Westminster Bank. While the Trust has flourished, under the auspices of BiC, Inner City Aid was left by the prince to wither on the vine. In October 1988 Tom Shebbeare, the director of the Prince's Trust, confirmed that it was being 'phased out to make way for other initiatives'.

Those who volunteered considerable time and energy to the cause of Inner City Aid remain in bitter despair at the prince's indifference from the very moment of its widely-publicized launch. A letter to Hackney less than four weeks later, signed by the prince's deputy private secretary, Humphrey Mews, thanks him for invitations 'to attend a meeting with the Trustees of the Inner City Trust, to be briefed on housing/architecture matters on a bi-monthly basis and to attend a ball in the Docklands in August', but informs him that his royal patron would be unable to accept any of them. 'As you know better than most, the

problem is quite simply one of time.' It was also a problem
of pressure from a prime minister, Margaret Thatcher, not at
all amused by implicit royal criticism of her government's urban
policies (or the lack of them); not even breakfast with a plain-
spoken Geldof in August 1987 could persuade Charles to give
the slightest support to an organization whose launch had won
him a great deal of positive publicity. He simply allowed it to
curl up and die – and, along with it, the aspirations of those
genuinely concerned to ameliorate the plight of the homeless
and unemployed in Britain's inner cities, notably Knevitt and
Geldof. When they suggested dumping the prince and carrying
on without him, fellow Trustees closer to Charles – among
them Sir Evelyn de Rothschild and Sir Hector (now Lord)
Laing – would hear none of it.

Prince Charles's relish for delivering moralistic homilies, on
subjects from medicine and architecture to the ozone layer and
the Queen's English, has remained just that; it is hard to identify
a single constructive result to have flowed from any of his in-
numerable tirades. Once his trade mark was the self-deprecating
jest, a self-conscious attempt to forestall criticism; now it is the
over-confident gaffe. In 1988, after deploring the 'irresponsible'
use of aerosol cans, he presented an enterprise award to a group
of Rastafarians for spray-painting graffiti; in 1990, as he made
a speech deploring gas-guzzling cars, his 9 m.p.g. Bentley was
being driven 600 miles across Europe for his use the following
week in Prague; in 1993, visiting the United States, he bemoaned
'the technical ease of modern life, the effortlessness and speed of
modern communication' within hours of stepping off a super-
sonic Concorde, pride of British Airways' fleet.

Early in 1992, Charles braved a new round of satire after
an impassioned speech in favour of French cheese. Later that
year, back in France at the height of the monarchy's difficulties,
the prince mounted a vehement defence of protectionist French
farmers – thus compromising Britain's position in the already
embattled GATT talks, and alienating the UK farming community of which he considers himself an enlightened leading
member. 'It was,' to one observer, 'a characteristic contribution:
well-meaning but, in political terms, breathtakingly ill-judged.'

The previous week, on a solo visit to France, the Princess of Wales had wowed *le tout Paris* and enjoyed a forty-minute meeting with President Mitterrand. The contrast was not lost on the couple's respective followings in Britain. Literary circles were appalled to hear from Bernard-Henri Levy, the fashionable French philosopher, of a dinner conversation in Paris during which Charles had launched into an attack on the British writer Salman Rushdie – then approaching his fifth year in hiding, under sentence of death since the Ayatollah Khomeini's *fatwah* over his book *The Satanic Verses*. Rushdie, insisted the prince, was a bad writer. Well, said Levy, Charles was entitled to his view. 'But he added that Rushdie costs the taxpayer too much, which struck me as a bit steep. So I replied: "And the Crown of England? Have you never asked yourself how much the Crown of England costs the British taxpayer?" ' Charles did not, apparently, come up with an answer.

The stylish *faux pas* had become the prince's hallmark, symbolic of his dogged determination to wander way out of his depth. A speech attacking the standards of English teaching in state schools was itself full of grammatical and syntactical errors. Rather than simply criticize the standards of state education, as one political columnist observed, he might actually improve it by setting an example and putting his children through it. 'I doubt whether the prince even knows anyone, socially or professionally, whose offspring are being educated in the schools used by 90 per cent of his subjects.'

'Dear God, how he screws things up,' wrote the cultural commentator Brian Appleyard. 'The man is a meddlesome fool who has now to be stopped.' On this occasion, in August 1991, Charles had resigned his position as patron of the Museum of Scotland, complaining that he had not been adequately consulted over its development plans; in truth, he was peeved that a modernist scheme not to his taste had been named winner of the design competition for the museum's extension. By accusing the prince of 'outrageous' and 'disgraceful' conduct, amounting in this case to 'deliberately inflicting damage on a national institution', Appleyard gave voice to the impotent rage of a large cross-section of the architectural profession, at their wits' end

over Charles's naive and destructive interventions. The prince
was behaving 'like some sulky child; if the game were not
played by his rules, he would take his ball home'. It was difficult to see how he could now sustain any position with any
organization: 'There will always be the danger that, at the slightest whiff of a building project, he will appear on the scene,
grinning and whingeing, ready to screw things up . . . His way
of conducting his campaign began merely as speech making,
but he has moved on to covert subversion of any modernist
scheme with which he is even distantly involved.' There were
many examples – well-known in a profession still reluctant
to risk its livelihood by overt public protest – of architects
being 'sacked or blacklisted because the prince expressed his
displeasure with their designs'. The royal track record was 'a
malignant cocktail of smear and bigotry'.

The prince has recently maintained an uncharacteristic silence
on the subject of architecture, at one time his great hobby-horse.
Perhaps his fingers have been burned once too often. Much of
his ill-informed interference has been attacked by architects as
misguided, at best; at worst, as in the case of his celebrated
outburst over the 'monstrous carbuncle' planned for London's
Trafalgar Square, an unjustified assault causing commercial damage to a British company.

When Charles criticized Peter Ahrends' design for the National
Gallery extension in his famous Hampton Court tirade of 1984,
he was not merely abusing the hospitality of the Royal Institute of
British Architects at what was supposed to be a celebratory dinner on the occasion of their 150th anniversary. He was insulting
the distinguished Indian architect Charles Correa, whom he
completely ignored throughout the evening, although he was
there to present Correa with the RIBA's Gold Medal for his
outstanding work for the Third World homeless – precisely
the kind of work that the prince has otherwise claimed as his
own. He was also defying the advice of his private secretary,
Edward Adeane, to the point of precipitating his resignation
– the beginning of a lemming-like procession.

The speech was typical of Charles's failure to understand
the intricacies of the architectural process – which is not merely

about style, but about the handling of space and scale, interminable negotiations with planners and developers, and the immense complexities of designing modern, high-technology buildings to last at least a century or more. Had the prince done adequate research before launching a vicious public assault on a man's reputation, he would have realized that the design he criticized was in fact a compromise between the National Gallery's trustees and the architect, then at an interim stage about which Ahrends himself was less than happy. At the request of the trustees, he had completely redesigned his original scheme to meet the gallery's needs. So when the prince questioned, by implication, the sacrifice of gallery space to office space, he was in fact attacking the brief given Ahrends by his client, the gallery's trustees (of whom Charles himself would soon be one). At the time of the prince's speech a public planning inquiry was, in any case, under way, after whose report the Secretary of State for the Environment, Patrick Jenkin, was due to make a final ruling. But the views of the public became irrelevant from that moment. Jenkin happened to be in Charles's audience at Hampton Court; as the prince was still speaking, he whispered to his neighbour: 'Well, that's one decision I don't have to make!'

Peter Ahrends' distinguished career was badly damaged that evening. For the next several years his practice, one of Britain's leading architectural partnerships, lost millions of pounds in potential commissions. Developers who feared the prince's veto no longer invited the 'carbuncle architects' to enter competitions, the meat and drink of the upper echelons of their profession. Next day, in the heat of the moment, Ahrends gave vent to his feelings; the prince's remarks, he told attendant journalists, were 'offensive, reactionary, ill-considered . . . if he holds such strong views, I'm surprised he did not take the opportunity offered by the public inquiry to express them.' Ever since, however, Ahrends has displayed great dignity by holding his peace, though described by colleagues as 'the victim of a public mugging' who had 'every right to feel aggrieved'.

Seven years later, in July 1991, the Prince of Wales watched

his mother open the building hastily commissioned to replace
the British architect's design: the new Sainsbury Wing of the
National Gallery, the work of the American architect, Robert
Venturi. Could Charles *really*, asked one architectural critic,
admire this 'limp, sub-classical' result of his intervention? 'For
those committed Classicists whose work the prince has endorsed,
this building is not so much a joke as a crime - an insult to the
hallowed tradition of Vitruvius and Palladio.'

More such *ad hominem* attacks from the prince followed, reinforced by a highly selective book and television film, before
he finally learnt his lesson and stopped putting British architects
out of business. But there were tragic casualties *en route*, notably
Lord (Peter) Palumbo's plans to erect a Mies van der Rohe
masterpiece in the City of London. At a time when Britain
could boast three of the world's greatest living architects –
Richard Rogers, Norman Foster and James Stirling – the prince's
bad-mouthing was forcing them to do their best work abroad,
while cowering British planning authorities kowtowed to their
future king by sanctioning a 'Toytown' suburban landscape, full
of hypermarkets and superstores artificially clad in lurid brick
and embellished with cutesy bell towers, Corinthian columns
and dormer windows. The Museum of Scotland's extension
looks like a rare example of a stylish and sensitive contemporary
design which will be built despite a fit of princely pique. But
the most dubious example of his handiwork as an unauthorized,
self-appointed national planning officer now threatens to engulf
one of the most important sites in the nation: the Paternoster
Square area around St Paul's Cathedral.

A dinner-table of London architects recently guffawed at one
guest's vision of Charles riding in state to his son's wedding at St Paul's, early in the next century, to arrive on
global television at a waste-land of crumbling reproduction
chaos around Sir Christopher Wren's masterpiece – entirely
the product of the would-be king's arbitrary interference. His
involvement with the rebuilding of Paternoster Square is a long,
complex saga of princely scheming: at first to exclude Richard
Rogers's work from contention, then to see off the developers'

chosen 'masterplanners', winners of a public competition, and replace them with architects more to his own personal (and highly traditional) taste. Since his so-called *Luftwaffe* speech of December 1987, in which he argued that British planners had done more damage to the London skyline than Nazi bombers during the Second World War, Charles has used his office to undo several years' work by leading British architects, notably Sir Philip Dowson's team at Arup Associates, which led to this huge project going the way of his preferred (though considerably less experienced) architect, John Simpson.

Somewhat against their will, Dowson and his colleagues bent over backwards to accommodate the prince, organizing a series of meetings to explain their thinking and two elaborate exhibitions in the cathedral crypt to bring their plans to life. Not merely did Charles fail even to visit the second exhibition; in his 1989 book, *A Vision of Britain*, it took him just two picture-captions to dismiss the immensely complex, sophisticated Arup plans as 'a rather half-hearted, grudging attempt to accommodate public concern about the national importance of this great site'. Given to dismissive one-liners about contemporary British architects, the prince accused Arup of wanting 'to put St Paul's in a prison camp, surrounding it with [a] spiky roof-line'. Thus were many months of painstaking and expert work dismissed with a frivolous flick of the royal pen. In October 1989 the site was sold for £158 million to its present owners, an *ad hoc* British-Japanese consortium calling itself Paternoster Associates, who are now implementing Simpson's scheme.

A leaked memo to the prince from one of his architectural advisers, Dr Brian Hanson, revealed just how much time and money Arup Associates were wasting by reluctantly courting his approval. 'The absolute minimum requirement of the meeting,' Hanson suggested, 'is to show them YRH [Your Royal Highness] is taking a *very* close interest in developments (which will unsettle them).' In other words, in Appleyard's gloss: Use your position to terrorize these people. 'The word "dirty" does not even begin to capture the sheer cowardly nastiness at work here.'

The scale of the prince's dubious victory in Paternoster Square became apparent in February 1993, when another Environment Secretary, Michael Howard, announced that he would not be ordering a public inquiry into the royally endorsed Simpson scheme, declaring himself 'satisfied that the current proposals meet the needs of this nationally important site'.

With construction due to begin in 1994, it will be the late 1990s before the prince's personal vision of the London skyline is ready for inspection. But will it stand the test of time – as the potential backdrop, perhaps, to his sons' weddings? Many leading experts have their doubts. Deyan Sudjic, editor of the architectural magazine *Blueprint,* has described the prince's intervention – overturning a democratic selection process, subverting statutory planning procedures and denying the public any say – as 'a gross abuse of the royal prerogative'. To Sudjic, the prince was 'lurching from one half-digested piece of received wisdom to another, abandoning each as he has discovered a new enthusiasm, moving from fiasco to fiasco'. It had become Charles's habit 'to adopt as his own the views of the last person he has talked to'.

Oblivious to the chorus of protest, Charles proceeded to found architectural schools in London and Italy to put into practice the 'Ten Commandments' laid down in his book and television film. He also began to develop ambitious plans to build a 'model' village on Duchy of Cornwall land at Poundbury in Dorset. For this project he called in the latest in an ever-changing succession of architectural gurus, a Luxemburg-born theorist named Leon Krier, noted for favouring 'monumental classicism'.

Krier had also been enlisted by Charles to advise on Simpson's rival scheme for Paternoster Square. Now he was told to design a model for 'an alternative, kinder city which would somehow manage to be classical, community-based and green'. But things got off to a bad start when Krier arrived for a 'consultation' session with the locals carrying a set of already completed plans. 'We don't want to live next door to a factory. It's barmy,' said one local worthy, as public opposition grew to the princely notion of mixing housing with jobs. 'Let him

Matriarch: Queen Victoria with four of her great-grandchildren, including the future Kings
Edward VIII (standing) and George VI (on cushion).

Queen Alexandra stood loyally by her husband, King Edward VII, throughout his affair with Mrs Alice Keppel – great-grandmother of Prince Charles's friend, Mrs Camilla Parker-Bowles.

913: George V rides out with his cousin, Kaiser Wilhelm (left), a year before the First World War. 1935: The Duke and Duchess of York with their daughters, lizabeth and Margaret, at George's silver jubilee service. 1936: The Duke of York nd King Edward VIII, flanked by the Dukes of Kent (left) and Gloucester (right) at heir father's funeral.

1936: *Before the abdication*: King Edward VIII and Mrs Simpson go night–clubbing and cruising in the Adriatic. *After the abdication*: The Duke and Duchess of Windsor meet Hitler, and weekend with him at Berchtesgaden.

The 'family monarchy' survives as the Duke of York becomes King George VI and his ten-year-old daughter heir to the throne. 1940: The bombing of Buckingham Palace reinforces the bond between crown and people. 1955: Churchill hails 'a new Elizabethan era'.

1953: A new Queen is crowned and gets down to work on her 'red boxes'.

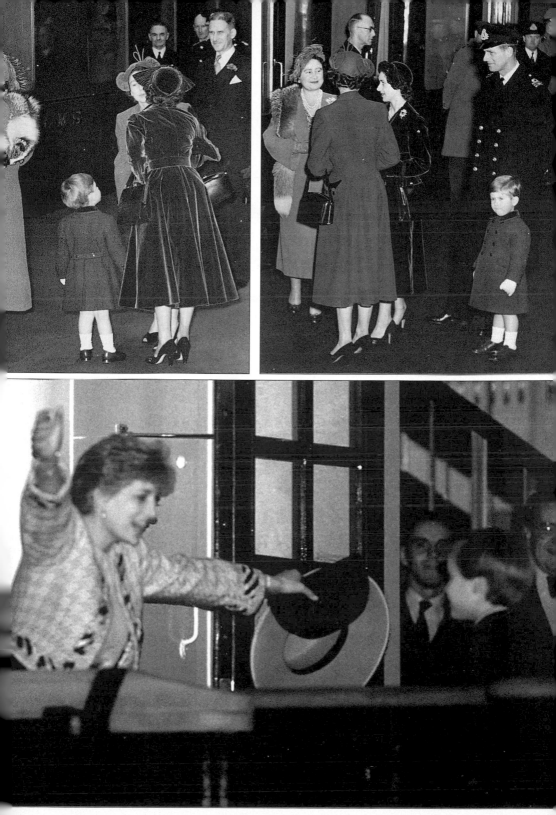

ternal styles: A forlorn young Charles is ignored as his parents greet the Queen Mother and *ncess Margaret on their return from Canada, 1951, while Diana has William (and Harry, out picture) flown out to join her in Canada, 1991.

A united royal family celebrates the Queen's silver wedding in 1972, nine years before the marriage of Charles and Diana.

come and live here himself,' muttered another. 'See how he'd like it.'

Indefinitely abandoned in 1990 thanks to a combination of planning objections, local opposition and lack of finance, a corner of the scaled-down Poundbury scheme has recently resurfaced under the auspices of the Guinness Trust. A row of dinky little princely cottages may yet come to pass – thanks more to the Guinness Trust than the Duchy, and regardless of the wishes of those who would have to live there. In architectural terms, to Sudjic, it would be 'the equivalent of his embracing faddish diets and alternative medicine. As a model for a city it not only doesn't work, it is turning out to be unbuildable.'

If either part-Poundbury or the Simpson vision of Paternoster Square is ever in fact built, Prince Charles might finally have something concrete to show (if he'll pardon the expression) for his many years of much-resented meddling. To date, as in so many other areas of his life, he has managed to get nothing off the drawing-board. 'Slammed by his enemies as a merely destructive critic, and challenged to do better than the modernists whose past mistakes he has so mercilessly catalogued,' as *The Daily Telegraph*'s architectural correspondent put it, 'the prince has failed to come up with the goods . . .   Given the extent of his personal wealth and of his influence, this seems more than unfortunate.'

Even Charles's great-grandfather, King George V, who as Prince of Wales showed no particular interest in architecture, managed as Duke of Cornwall to build his own 'model' village of handsome and durable neo-Georgian houses around the Surrey cricket ground, the Oval, in Kennington, South London. The development began on Duchy land in 1909, following complaints about seriously substandard housing. In 1992 the present Duke of Cornwall, scourge of so much twentieth-century architecture, was said to take a particular pride in his predecessor's achievement.

He must also have envied it. All Charles had to show for his own decade of subversive activism was a style of supermarket architecture ingloriously dubbed 'Caroline Tescoism'. As Brian Appleyard observed in late 1992, surveying the princely scene

as the Wales marriage formally ended: 'His role in architecture
has been more damaging than he can possibly realize . . .
His ignorance of the real workings of real politics has resulted
in a planning nightmare in which "Wrenaissance" belfries or
cornices can be glued to any old hyperstore in the name of
his whims.'

The distinguished British architect Sir Richard Rogers has
accused Prince Charles of declining all invitations to take part
in public debate on his pet subject, preferring to exercise his
unearned prerogative as the nation's aesthetic arbiter more
surreptitiously, with secret visits to developers and private
conversations with the juries of competitions. 'The claim to
be defending a democratic approach does not sit easily with
his own inherited authority,' argued Sir Richard, architect of
the Lloyd's building in the City of London and the Pompidou
Centre in Paris. 'The prince might like to consider whether
the charges of paternalism and unaccountability, with which
he criticizes architects, might not more aptly be directed at
his own way of doing things.'

As a man with 'strong public views about architecture, a
high public profile and enormous private wealth,' suggested
Rogers, the prince enjoyed 'an extraordinary opportunity' to
commission important buildings, but had 'yet to produce a
noteworthy construction'. Where were the royal commissions to compare, for instance, with Inigo Jones's Queen's
House for King James I, Nash's Royal Pavilion in Brighton for
the Prince Regent or the Crystal Palace in London for Prince
Albert?

To Sir Richard, Charles's 'Disneyland' approach was defending a past which had never existed. 'If the conservative principles
favoured by the Prince of Wales and his followers had been
applied throughout history, very little of our "traditional" architectural heritage would ever have been built.' Charles's insistence
that buildings conform to the height of those around them,
for instance, would have ruled out most of the great Gothic
cathedrals, not to mention the massive Italian stone *palazzi* so
favoured by the prince on his frequent excursions to paint water
colours. His argument that 'adventurous' work was 'certainly

inappropriate in rural areas' would have deprived posterity of the very masterpieces of Palladio and Vanbrugh which he now cited as his ideal. Most of the great buildings in the classical and Gothic traditions which he now valued so highly were, as Rogers pointed out, 'in their own time, revolutionary'. Most ironic of all, Wren's design for St Paul's – itself a watered-down version of his original scheme, which had been rejected by royalty as too avant-garde – had been so controversial at the time that Wren had had to build an eighteen-foot perimeter fence around the construction site to prevent his critics from seeing and again frustrating his plans.

Would a seventeenth-century Prince Charles have allowed Wren to proceed with his daringly modernist plans for St Paul's Cathedral? It seems highly unlikely.

Those who enjoy dishing it out must also be able to take it. To a man surrounded all his life by sycophants and flatterers, the first waves of expert opposition to his views – from doctors, architects and teachers – came as an unwelcome shock. Publicly voiced resentment that he was interfering in areas beyond his expertise further unnerved the prince, as did the inevitable damage which his assaults caused British businesses. At times like these, Charles crumpled. 'There's no need for me to do all this, you know,' he told a radio interviewer in the mid-1980s. 'If they'd rather I did nothing, I'll go off somewhere else.'

During a lunch designed to win over influential journalists, he went further: 'I've had to fight every inch of my life to escape royal protocol. I've had to fight to go to university. I've had to fight to have any sort of role as Prince of Wales. You're suggesting that I go back and play polo. I wasn't trained to do that. I have been brought up to have an active role. I am determined not to be confined to cutting ribbons.'

Charles was apparently 'incandescent with rage'. His tirade, according to one of those present, was delivered with 'frightening intensity'; the prince was 'either going to have a public function, or a nervous breakdown'. In its forlorn way, that passionate outburst symbolizes all the contradictions inherent in both Charles's character and his position. If, for instance, he has fought 'every inch of his life' to escape royal protocol, he has fought with very little success. He did *not*, however, have to 'fight to go to university'; that decision was made on his behalf at a Buckingham Palace dinner party on 22 December 1965, at which he was not invited to be present. He *has* had to fight to have 'any sort of role' as Prince of Wales, but he *was*, alas, trained to play polo, to which he has since devoted quite as much time and enthusiasm (not to mention money) as to any other activity – to the exclusion of other potential interests, not least his wife and children. The result of all this sorry confusion, to his dismay, is that an increasing number of Britons have now begun to wish that he *could* be 'confined to cutting ribbons'. If that.

One early symptom of the monarchy's current malaise was growing resentment of the condescending lectures delivered to the nation by Prince Charles and his sister, Princess Anne. If they couldn't manage to lead stable, contented lives of their own, what right had they to lecture their fellow-citizens on parenthood, morality, the pursuit of pleasure? When Charles broke his arm in a polo accident in 1990, and retired from public duties for four long months, the nation became uncomfortably aware for the first time of the prince's capacity for acute self-pity. Subsequent back troubles accentuated Charles's conviction that, through no fault of his own, he is a somehow ill-starred figure. To quote his favourite lines from Shakespeare's *Henry V* (which he never appreciated, he says, until he saw his friend Kenneth Branagh's film version):

> 'What infinite heart's-ease
> Must kings neglect, that private men enjoy!'

It is this deep-dyed depressive streak which may yet see the prince confound all early expectations, resign himself to the inevitable, and abandon the destiny which he has always made to seem such a burden.

Born on 14 November 1948, Charles was only three when his grandfather died and his mother was propelled on to the throne much earlier than she would have wished. The new Queen made one homespun concession to young motherhood – asking her prime minister, Winston Churchill, to put back his weekly audience by one hour so that she could be with her children at bathtime. Otherwise, the young Charles's world was one of closed doors and restraining hands, constantly reminding him that his ever-more remote mother had an important job to do.

In May 1954, when the five-year-old prince greeted his mother on her return from a six-month world tour, their reunion consisted of a formal handshake. His nannies, Helen Lightbody and Mabel Anderson, testified to a highly strict nursery routine, already training the young man for kingship. Far from receiving hugs from his parents, or even his gentle-hearted grandmother, Charles was required to bow to them when entering or leaving their presence. When children of the Queen's friends came to stay at Balmoral or Sandringham, they ate separately from the royal children (who themselves ate separately from the adults) and were allowed to play with them for only two hours a day, one before lunch and one after. This regime was imposed on the personal instructions of the Queen.

For most of her long reign the public and private character of Queen Elizabeth II have both been beyond criticism; even during the House of Windsor's recent woes, commentators have repeatedly intoned that she alone stands unimpeachably above the fray. As all three of her children's marriages failed, however, a chink of vulnerability appeared, with the raising of obvious questions about the way she brought up her children.

It was well-known that Charles had suffered at the hands of one domineering parent. He had been 'gravely damaged', in the verdict of Lord Rees-Mogg, by 'one of those unhappy fathers who fail to see how frightening they are to small children'. Even when he had himself become a forty-year-old father-of-two, Charles could still be undone by his own father's wrath. Philip has publicly, if obliquely, mocked Charles's taste in architecture ('It would be a pity,' he told an urban planning conference, 'if regeneration created eighteenth-century cities in the twenty-first century'); and he has made no secret of his impatience with his oldest son's inability to 'stick at things'. In the words of one courtier: 'Charles starts with great enthusiasm. Then he dithers and procrastinates, and he won't make up his mind. His office is a mess. No-one knows what the priorities are. So things hang around, and just don't get done. That's what gets up Philip's nose the most.'

When the writer Tim Heald was researching his authorized biography of Prince Philip, published in 1991, he approached the Queen Mother, Princess Margaret, Prince Charles and Princess Anne for interviews. Only Charles refused to co-operate. Speaking in December 1992 at the Age Resource Awards, a ceremony to promote 'solidarity between generations', the prince warmly recalled chats with his grandmother, the Queen Mother, and his 'honorary grandfather', the late Lord Mountbatten; but he conspicuously failed to mention either of his parents. 'Sadly,' said the prince, 'so often nowadays there is less and less contact between generations.' In her determination to train her son for kingship, had the Queen proved as damaging a parent as her husband – erring, in her case, on the side of ice-cold formality?

It is very difficult to find a photograph of the young Charles, at the age his own children are now, in which his mother is even looking at him, let alone touching him. Usually he resembles a forlorn young Fauntleroy, a solitary waif in velvet-collared coat and brightly polished shoes, left to one side while his mother's attentions are all devoted to her fellow-adults. In one sequence of photographs, the Queen steps off a train after two months away, kisses her mother, greets an unctuous welcoming committee, then adjusts her five-year-old son's collar before offering him, once again, just a handshake.

Compare this with most contemporary pictures of his own sons: smiling boys with brightly shining eyes, in unpretentious T-shirt and jeans, rapt by whatever their mother is saying to them, her arm around their shoulders as she moves them to laughter about some unseen detail of their mutual foreground. From the age of three, the devoted son of an unfailingly competent mother, Charles has been ready to recognize that his and her duties all too often took them in different directions. His own sons have been far from ready to recognize any such thing, needing and receiving all the warm attentions of a mother with some knowledge of a world beyond inherited obligations. Their father, like his, has largely been absent from the picture.

By his own account, the prince was miserable at school. The great royal experiment in education – sending the heir to the throne to school with other children his age, albeit at expensive, all-male institutions for the sons of the wealthy – proved double-edged. Hounded by the press at Hill House and Cheam, he also made no lasting friendships: a naturally shy boy, accustomed only to the company of sycophantic courtiers, he was doubly wary of those over-eager schoolboys who offered him friendship. Once despatched to Gordonstoun, in the far north of Scotland, he began a long life in the shadow of his father, whose name was engraved on the sporting trophies; although, like Philip, he made it to Guardian, or Head Boy, Charles's natural inclinations were rather more studious. Indeed, he became the first heir to the throne in history to win himself a place at Cambridge, and subsequently the first to win a reassuringly average university degree.

By then, however, 'royal protocol' was already intervening. His Cambridge studies were interrupted by one cynical term at the University College of Wales, Aberystwyth, in a token attempt for the Prince of Wales to be seen learning a few words of Welsh before his investiture in 1969 at Caernarvon Castle. Like so many of the trappings of contemporary royalty, the ceremony was not at all the ancient, historic institution it appeared. After more than six centuries of disuse, it had been revived as recently as 1911, for the last Prince of Wales, by a Welsh-born prime minister in political difficulties.

It was at Caernarvon in 1282, after slaughtering Prince Llewelyn-ap-Gruffydd, that the English invader King Edward I had declared his infant son the first English Prince of Wales. For more than 600 years, most subsequent monarchs had been wise enough to invest their sons in parliament, palaces or the safety of English county towns. In 1911, however, during the painful disestablishment of the Welsh church, Lloyd George had talked King George V into a ceremony supposedly designed as a demonstration of Welsh unity. More likely to enhance the prime minister's political prestige, and to appease the opponents of his regular assaults on inherited privilege, it went ahead over the strenuous protests of the nineteen-year-old prince himself. The 'preposterous rig' he was required to wear, Edward complained to his father, would make him a laughing-stock among his friends in the Navy. But the naval officer King, ever the martinet, decided that his son's 'mini-coronation' would make a fitting climax to his own coronation tour of Britain.

In 1969, as Lord Snowdon prepared to turn Charles's own mini-coronation into the world's biggest television event to date, Welsh MPs launched a sustained Commons campaign against a ceremony to be held 'in a castle built by Welsh slave labour under the orders of the intruder, the conqueror'. Half the Queen's Welsh subjects declared the ceremony 'a waste of money'; its mounting costs, declared one Welsh MP, were 'a cunning ploy' to justify an increase in the Civil List. Plaid Cymru, the Welsh Nationalist Party, dissociated itself from 'this piece of English trickery', while the Welsh Language Society daubed revolutionary slogans over roads, bridges, and traffic signs throughout the principality. During the six months before the ceremony, fifteen bomb attacks were mounted on government and military buildings, post offices and pipelines by a motley terrorist group calling itself the Free Welsh Army, two of whose members were killed planting another device on the very morning of the investiture. Secretly, BBC Television prepared an obituary of the twenty-one-year-old Prince of Wales – just in case.

In conjunction with the official television film, *Royal Family*, Charles's investiture at Caernarvon was consciously designed as his launch into public life. As a piece of public relations, it was brilliantly effective, thanks in large part to the fact that his then private secretary, Sir David Checketts, was an experienced PR professional – working in tandem with William Heseltine, the most innovative courtier of the Queen's reign. Over the subsequent two decades, he has been nothing like so well served. By employing a mix of administratively efficient military men, like-minded aristocrats and third-rate media men craven enough to turn gamekeeper, Charles has personally precipitated the singular plight in which he now finds himself.

After seven years of unabated (and largely unchallenged) negative publicity about his marriage, he has emerged from the final separation the villain of the piece – the discredited partner, blamed for its breakdown and perceived as a cruel, callous deceiver. As for his work: in the public mind, it scarcely exists. The prince's own capacity to theme-hop, compounded by a series of unforced errors, have conspired to have him resembling a latter-day King Canute, failing to keep at bay an ill-defined tide of contemporary evils. Charles's regal assumption has always been that it is his duty to protect his future subjects from those aspects of the modern world they seem to find most appealing; their response, not unnaturally, has been to write him off as an interfering, out-of-touch royal busybody. Contemporary Britain has remained determined to continue pursuing what few pleasures it could afford, undeterred by his stream of princely health warnings.

Come 1993, and the revelations of Camillagate, even Charles realized that 'something' (in the celebrated words of the last Prince of Wales) 'must be done'. Fearful of Madison Avenue techniques, and thus wary of calling in the likes of Saatchi & Saatchi, he decided, characteristically enough, to appoint himself his own 'spin doctor'.

Among the guests greeted by the Prince of Wales at a Kensington Palace reception in 1990 was the Labour Party's then director of communications, Peter Mandelson. 'Ah, the red rose man,' said the prince, showing some appreciation of the recent efforts of one of the country's most dynamic strategists to modernize Labour's image. Their meeting led to others, among them one between the prince and the Labour Party's rising stars, John Smith, Gordon Brown and Tony Blair. It also left Mandelson with a clear fix on Charles's problems: 'Somewhere between his natural urge to "do something" and the pressures on him not to get too involved, he is suspended in a half-committed, half-thought-out, half-professional limbo.' A Labour MP by the time Charles's marriage broke up, Mandelson blamed the

prince's image problems on weak material ineptly managed. 'If
you don't define yourself, others will do it for you, and not
usually the way you would like . . . '

No doubt he had in mind persistent (and highly articulate) critics like Brian Appleyard, who had recently written of Charles's
speeches: 'The general mood is familiar: anti-progressive, fearful
of the effects of unbridled profiteering, suspicious of technology and possessed of an inchoate yearning for some sort of
holistic vision. His place in the popular imagination is clear:
he is dreamy, ineffective and hopelessly unrealistic to an almost
infantile degree . . . His ideas tend to emerge flavoured with
something of the all-embracing gullibility of a New Age catalogue.' Writing in the same paper a week later, in the wake of
the Waleses' formal separation, Mandelson's advice to the prince
was clear-cut: 'His new communications action plan must be
to examine what exactly he is trying to do, to look at how he
is trying to do it and to start to co-ordinate his activities and
messages more effectively to the public . . . The opportunity
for change will not last long. If the prince fails to grasp it, it
will be a personal tragedy for him.'

Within days – even before publication of the Camillagate
transcript – Charles's media machine was working overtime.
His first task was to repair his image as a failed family man by
offering incessant photo opportunities with his sons. Mother-
less at Sandringham over Christmas, the young princes were
paraded with their father to church, on the grouse moors, even
co-opted into television specials – as walk-ons in a programme
about press intrusion for the BBC (whose van was chauffeured
by the prince's press secretary) and playing a bizarre game of
televised Happy Families in the manner of Charles's story for
children, *The Old Man of Lochnagar*. Perhaps the boys wondered
why their father had written a story for his younger brother,
Edward – and published it amid much fanfare, minus the countless farts and burps edited out by his then private secretary,
Edward Adeane – yet had failed to write any such children's
story for them.

As the campaign to discredit his estranged wife got under way
– counterpointed by the prince's offer to *The Sunday Telegraph* to

turn celibate and his denial of defeatism to *The Observer* – there followed some extraordinary rewriting of recent history. With bad timing and worse taste, for instance, the suddenly ubiquitous 'friends' of Prince Charles used the premature death from lung cancer of one of his staff, a forty-three-year-old executive of the Prince's Trust named James ('Jock') Barr, to 'correct' the negative publicity caused by Charles's abandonment of Diana at her father's funeral almost a year before. The prince had been obliged to leave Earl Spencer's funeral early, the story now went, to go to the bedside of his sick friend. Yes, later that afternoon he *had* taken tea with the Sultan of Brunei. But before tea he had visited Barr in St Mary's Hospital, Paddington. And later in the summer Charles had even sent him organic plums from Highgrove; when Barr wrote back saying that plums weren't quite what he had in mind, the prince had sent over a bottle of champagne.

This was royal revisionism at its most bizarre. Innocent readers of this widely published story were naturally moved to ask various questions arising. Is the illness of an acquaintance *really* reason enough to walk out of a father-in-law's funeral? Could royalist headlines like that, for instance, in the London *Evening Standard* – CHARLES RUSHED TO DYING FRIEND – really be justified in view of the fact that Barr's life was not immediately threatened, while Earl Spencer's was over?

To what extent was this a conscious echo – culled from the file labelled 'Caring Prince' – of the celebrated story of Diana's overnight dash from Balmoral to London, braving the Queen's wrath for leaving without her permission, to fulfil her promise to be at the deathbed of her friend Adrian Ward-Jackson? And was it pure coincidence that the same day's *Standard* carried another article trashing the princess? On the adjacent page an unnamed 'senior source in the Church of England' called the Princess of Wales 'a little girl lost' and speculated about her capacity for adultery.

Where on earth were these 'friends of Prince Charles' getting their material, let alone their instructions? Not, to be sure, from Peter Mandelson. By the time of the prince's visit to Mexico in February, his first overseas trip since the separation, Charles and his entourage appeared to have re-read Mandelson's piece. On the fourth and last day of the visit, at the invitation of some excited Mexican farmers, he hooked up two oxen to an ancient wooden plough and determinedly steered it through two hard-wrought furrows. Another dream photo-opportunity, duly relayed home by an unusually large posse of travelling press – though not, perhaps, with quite the effect intended. Blazoned in colour across the English papers, the pictures bespoke an uncomfortably apt metaphor for the prince's life at that moment. His marriage over, his reputation in tatters, Charles had many more long, hard furrows to plough before any reassessment could be made of his standing in Britain and around the world.

In the meantime, although drained by a combination of jet lag, polo and pollution, he chose the end of his visit to Mexico to clarify his objectives, along Mandelsonian lines, by unveiling his immediate aspirations. The tour had included a meeting with 100 business leaders, from whom he had wrung promises of a wide range of environmental and social projects. It was the fourteenth such gathering under the auspices of his Business Leaders Forum, set up in 1990 primarily to offer assistance to the fledgling democracies of Eastern Europe. Positively publicized back home, the Mexican tour had proved quite a contrast with that in South Korea three months before, where Charles's attempts to set up a waste-recycling programme had been obscured by saturation coverage of his visibly failing marriage. Now even the tabloids were reporting his Mexican speeches – hammering home a call, as *The Times* distilled it, for 'sustainable development, quality of life and the need for a spiritual dimension in a technological age'. Charles left Mexico, according to briefings from his staff, convinced that 'his future lies as a leading player on the world environmental stage'.

The prince had apparently taken a conscious decision to 'bury himself in his work' and 'rededicate himself to his perceived messianic role as an ecological prophet of the new world order'. How long was this process expected to take? The new, remodelled Prince of Wales would be re-presented for public approval in July 1994, on the twenty-fifth anniversary of his investiture as Prince of Wales. Though scarcely likely to provoke dancing in

the streets, it was a milestone of great personal significance to
the prince. Already he had secured the services of a respected
television journalist, Jonathan Dimbleby, to mark the occasion
with an officially sanctioned book and television film about his
public work. On the ski slopes, at his various homes, even on
on the overnight sleeper from Scotland: a film crew is already
at work shaping a mature, purposeful prince-with-a-heart to be
presented for public re-evaluation, in the hope of winning back
the affection and trust of the British people.

In Mexico, the only problem was that everywhere Charles
went, people asked where his wife was. British children were told
by the Palace advance party not to mention Diana's name; but
the inevitable happened when an eleven-year-old Mexican girl
tried to take his photograph. Charles asked her not to, bizarrely
explaining that he did not photograph well. 'Diana does,' replied
innocent little Maria, like a child in an H. M. Bateman cartoon,
mentioning the unmentionable – who that day was busying
herself back home, fighting off 'flu to deliver another speech
about AIDS, a rather more relevant contemporary issue than
ox-ploughs.

Would reed-bed sewage disposal systems and third-world
waste recycling plants be enough to bring the British flocking
back to their prince's banner, forgiving him his trespasses against
their favourite princess? Though the jury will be out for some
years yet, the omens do not look good. The real question is
whether, in the meantime, the would-be king in the dock will feel
obliged to plea-bargain. In the absence of diminished responsibility, it will need a dramatic improvement in his fortunes to avoid
a sentence of prolonged seclusion – stepping aside, when the time
comes, in favour of an unblemished candidate to be king.

In the longer term, Charles has his own private contentment
to consider. Ahead of him lies a struggle between his devotion
to inherited duty and his natural human instinct for a settled,
rewarding life. At present, the price he must pay for the throne
would indeed appear to be celibacy; those around him wish to be
friends of a future king, not a future Duke of Windsor. Charles
will not go down without a fight. But nor would it surprise some
of his circle if the struggle were to prove too much, eventually

seeing the prince's fierce pride surrender to circumstances. A quiet life at Highgrove, as the future King Father, can at times seem a highly attractive prospect to a man weary of public pressure, who has always wanted to be a farmer.

The stories of England's two previous King Charleses, who bridged the only period of republican rule in British history, have never augured well for the third. Though the British people considered Charles I a principled and serious man, they decided to cut off his head. The putative King Charles III has spent his whole life trying to be taken as seriously; now he seems more likely to wind up wondering, with the adulterous Charles II, how 'God could make a man so miserable for taking a little pleasure'.

CHAPTER 9

DIANA: THE PEOPLE'S PRINCESS

'She's only a bird in a gilded cage,
A beautiful sight to see.
You'd think she was happy and free from care;
She's not, though she seems to be . . .'

TRAD. BRITISH MUSIC HALL SONG

ONE SATURDAY IN FEBRUARY 1993, AS HER ESTRANGED
husband contemplated his future on a lone Caribbean cruise
aboard *Britannia*, the Princess of Wales took their sons to the
Trocadero Centre in London's Piccadilly Circus. For several
hours, amid crowds as astonished as they were delighted, the
junior Waleses had the time of their lives under their mother's
careful watch, enjoying the video games of 'Funland' alongside
equally excited children their own age. Like the previous week's
go-karting near Windsor, or their annual trip to the water slides
of Thorpe Park, it was a great day out – of a kind they had
never known with their father.

Charles is not in the habit of taking his sons with him to
any public place frequented *en masse* by his mother's subjects
– apart, of course, from polo fields. It would not even occur
to him. The princess's Trocadero expedition was not merely
a sign of the 'natural touch' which so endears her to a vast

and resolute band of followers. It was a deliberate display of the way royalty can behave if it chooses. Since her formal separation from Charles, Diana had been pioneering a royal style quite alien to her in-laws – an anathema to the House of Windsor, but a breath of welcome, long-overdue fresh air to its subjects.

Charles's three-day sunshine break that weekend cost the British taxpayer more than a million pounds. When Diana herself went to the Caribbean the previous month, taking William and Harry with her, she had travelled aboard a British Airways flight – herself sitting in the crowded economy cabin with her companions (beside the lavatory, which made for even longer queues than usual). Every so often she went forward to visit the first-class cabin, where she had sat her royal sons to ensure they could enjoy some privacy. Diana has since used scheduled flights for an official visit to Nepal and a skiing holiday in Austria (just after Charles had travelled to and from Klosters by one of his mother's private jets). It would seem 'profligate' of her, she told a friend, to use aircraft of the Queen's Flight.

In February 1993, when the princess travelled to Cardiff Arms Park for the England–Wales rugby international – an official royal engagement, announced in the Court Circular – she passed up the chance to use the royal train, opting instead for a regular seat aboard British Rail's InterCity service. That weekend, she took her girl friends Kate Menzies and Lulu Blackler, plus escorts and detectives, to the Royal Ballet at Covent Garden. Far from arriving in a chauffeur-driven royal Rolls, the party climbed happily out of a (British-made) Ford minibus, which soon became the norm for such visits. At Easter, when Diana took her sons to the European Grand Prix at Donington Park, Derbyshire, she was herself at the wheel of the family's Ford station wagon.

Instinctively, Diana has been pioneering a British version of the Scandinavian-style monarchy which may yet prove the House of Windsor's only hope of salvation. As a tactic in the guerrilla war forced upon her by Buckingham Palace, it has been a typically adroit piece of public relations. The minibus trip to Covent Garden, for instance, came within twenty-four hours of the prime minister's Commons statement detailing the Queen's proposed tax payments. Still dazzled by figures, Britain's twenty-five million recession-hit taxpayers had yet to wake up to the true extent of their monarch's future contribution to the Exchequer. Once they realized that it would come down to a mere one or two million pounds per annum - scarcely enough to make much difference to either the royal fortune or the national debt – they seemed likely to feel much the same about building the Queen a new £80 million yacht as they had about footing the £60 million bill for fire damage to Windsor Castle.

Meanwhile, Diana's trail-blazing continued. On 16 February 1993, while Charles was communing with rural farmers in Mexico, she was effortlessly upstaging him at home. As he, across the world, bemoaned 'a cynical disbelief in the relevance of the past to the present, in the value of what is traditional and timeless', back in London she was talking about a rather more urgent contemporary concern: 'Too many people have used AIDS as an issue to which they could add their own prejudices. If their views were voiced to help fight the disease, that would be fine. However, too often their attitudes reveal only a narrowness of mind and a sad lack of common humanity.'

Was this another coded reference to Charles? If so, she had good reason.

That same week a select group of half a dozen movers-and-shakers was invited to the Prince of Wales's new London home at St James's Palace to sip tax-deductible Duchy of Cornwall champagne. Among those present were the novelist and television heavyweight Melvyn Bragg, the 'Live Aid' impresario Harvey Goldsmith, the patroness of the arts Lindy Dufferin, *Everyman* publisher David Campbell and the editor of *The Times*, Peter Stothard. This distinguished band eagerly awaited the arrival of their prince, recently returned from his high-profile visit to Mexico.

While they straightened their ties, Charles's staff asked the assembled opinion-shapers, themselves no strangers to media controversy, how they thought the post-Camillagate rehabilitation process was going. Was HRH over the, er, Tampax hurdle? Plying their guests with more champagne, the prince's private secretary, Richard Aylard, his (then) deputy Peter Westmacott*, and their assistant Belinda Harley, herself a former public relations consultant, solicited expert views on public perceptions of their boss. That photo-opportunity with the Mexican ox-plough, for instance: it had 'played very well' back home, didn't they think?

'Why Mexico?' asked one guest, wondering where Charles had got to. 'Why not send him to Blackburn?' The atmosphere perceptibly tensed. The prince, explained his aides, was trying to carve out a role on the world stage as an environmental campaigner. That waste-recycling plant in Korea, for instance: how appalling that HRH's achievement had been overshadowed by all that fuss about his marriage. 'I still think he should go to Blackburn,' repeated the unimpressed celebrity, now looking impatiently at his watch. 'If the prince wants to improve his image, he could make a start by turning up here on time.'

But their host, without explanation, never materialized. Although in part convened to plan a joint initiative with Czechoslovakia's President Havel, to raise money for the historic buildings of Prague, the meeting was treated to more praise of Charles, and some snide remarks about Diana, before finally and forlornly petering out. 'Hamlet without the prince,' said one guest afterwards. 'As a PR exercise, it left a very nasty taste in the mouth.' While the group had waited – and waited – the talk had turned to Charles's estranged wife, then about to leave on an official visit to Nepal. 'That trip should be a public relations disaster,' said Charles's staff, with an exchange of knowing looks. 'We expect it to be, anyway.'

When the Princess of Wales arrived in Kathmandu a few days later, escorted by the British Overseas Aid Minister, Baroness (Lynda) Chalker, the Nepalese welcoming band owned up to some disappointment at 'instructions from London' not to play the British national anthem. Travelling journalists

*Westmacott has since returned to the Foreign Office, from which he was on secondment to the Prince of Wales's Office.

reported that Diana had been 'snubbed' by the Nepalese royal family, who would not be hosting an official dinner in her honour.

More instructions from London? That little cocktail party appeared to be firm evidence of the existence of a 'dirty tricks' campaign to rehabilitate Charles by discrediting Diana. What a coincidence, as one party guest observed a few days later, that the missing extract from the Squidgygate tape surfaced just as Diana was making her own bid for solo glory on the world stage. What a coincidence, too, that Charles was by then offering upbeat photo opportunities on the ski-slopes of Klosters, 'getting up smiling' each time he fell down (to quote but one set of mid-market picture captions) and 'looking like a man again enjoying life'.

There followed a flying visit by Charles to British troops in Bosnia; a dash to the bedsides of IRA bomb victims; and, on Easter Sunday, a gauche appearance as a would-be Pied Piper in *The Legend of Lochnagar*, an animated television version of his story for children. The previous Sunday, his mother had been persuaded to leave the parish church at Sandringham via the back door so as not to crowd the photographers' view of Charles and his sons exiting by the front. So even the Queen was in on the strategic planning. Cynical though the Palace's tactics might appear, the prince's camp believed that they were beginning to work, and that Operation 'Caring Prince' was forcing Diana on to the defensive. Then, with the crudest of public gestures, Buckingham Palace managed to give the game away.

Mid-April saw a memorial service in Warrington, Lancashire, for Tim Parry and Johnathan Ball, teenagers killed by an IRA bomb in the town's shopping centre two weeks before. In a disastrous public misjudgement, the Palace overruled Diana's expressed wish to attend, announcing that it would be sending Prince Philip. Pressed for its reasons – and a response to the suggestion that Philip, not noted for his concern for children, was widely perceived as the royal family's least compassionate member – the Palace explained that this was a job for 'the most senior royal available'. In the absence of the Queen – 'who never

attends memorial services, except those of very close friends' –
her husband was next in line.

This had not been its policy in the past; in 1988, for instance,
pre-fall Fergie had been the choice to attend a service for the
victims of the Clapham train disaster. The Warrington ceremony,
as one paper pointed out, was 'precisely the kind of delicate royal
duty that the princess handles so well . . . Diana's presence in
Warrington would have been the best possible advertisement
for a united royal family desperately in need of some positive
publicity. It would also have given the lie to the persistent
rumours that staff of the "born" royals are out to reduce the
princess's public work to an ineffective side-show.'

But the service went ahead without her, and with Philip in
her stead. The night before, it became public knowledge that
Diana had telephoned the parents of the two dead boys to offer
her sympathy, and to express regret that she would not be
able to join them for the service. 'She was ever so nice. It
gave me a big boost to talk to her,' said Mrs Wendy Parry,
who revealed that Diana – as 'one mother to another' – had
said she would like to have given her a hug. 'It is a great
comfort that someone in her position should take the time to
think of us,' said Maria Ball.

Diana's foes immediately began portraying the phone calls
as 'a cheap publicity stunt', further distressing the bereaved
parents. But the facts were that the princess had called the
Parrys, without warning, at 6.20 p.m., and a television crew
had come through the door, by prior arrangement, ten minutes later. Naturally, Diana's expression of sympathy was the
first thing the Parrys mentioned in the television interview.
The next day, on the morning of his son's memorial service,
Colin Parry felt obliged to express regret that he had mentioned
Diana's call to the press. He had not wished to embroil the
princess in the public row which was now developing. 'She
didn't ask us to keep our conversation confidential, but maybe
she thought it was implicit. I hope she doesn't feel we have let
her down by telling the media how much her call meant to
us.' The other father, Wilf Ball, added: 'Our lives have been
empty since Johnathan left us. But it has been really heartening

to know that someone like Diana should want to say a few words mother-to-mother like that.'

The wide airing given the bereaved parents' delight at Diana's phone calls did not deter friends of the Palace, such as Lord Wyatt, from trying to turn the episode against her. Careful to call her condolences 'genuine', to avoid completely losing his audience, Wyatt declared that they were 'mixed up with her vanity'. The princess was 'addicted to the limelight her marriage brought. It's like a drug. To feed her craving she'd do anything. Even if it meant destroying the throne she solemnly swore to uphold.' With a disingenuous plea that he was 'far from anti-homosexual', Wyatt also took the chance for a passing sideswipe at the princess's work for AIDS victims: 'This elevates them to heroes to be copied by the young. It's well known that AIDS stems mainly from sodomy.' Much more in keeping with popular opinion was the outspoken columnist Julie Burchill: '[Diana's] phone calls were utterly in character; Prince Philip's attendance was not. . . Day by day, despite their pathetic PR efforts, the [royal] family seems more and more to be the most unnatural, destructive and loathsome family since Charles Manson's homicidal gang of the same name.'

The city of Warrington itself chose to settle the issue, by inviting the princess to a charity concert for the bereaved families' appeal fund the following weekend. She was unable to go, but sent a message of condolence, offered a 'substantial donation' to the appeal fund, and promised to meet the families privately as soon as possible. The Palace, by general consensus, had shot itself in the foot, undoing all its work to promote the newly 'caring' prince by a clumsy attempt not just to tarnish his wife, but to shut her out of her natural public habitat. It was a tactic which never looked like working with the British people, who had long since recognized Diana's genuine sense of compassion and her rare gift for expressing it. In an action 'quite typical of her', as Burchill wrote, the princess was 'yet again displaying the warmth and spontaneity which comes harder than speaking Swahili to the Windsors'. A survey by the *Daily Mail*, which had mounted a huge operation to 'monitor' the couple 'in minute detail' throughout the four months since their separation, showed that Diana had attracted more than nine thousand spectators to her sixteen public appearances, while Charles had attracted barely four thousand to his thirty-one. 'Diana,' concluded the paper, had 'got the better' of Charles; the Palace's tactics were 'clearly not working' for the heir to the throne.

Where, meanwhile, had Charles been while his father attended the Warrington memorial service? In Spain, at the funeral of King Juan Carlos's father. Although Diana was spending the day alone at home – as by now, thanks to the Palace, the entire nation knew – the prince chose not to send their sons back to their mother during his absence, sticking rigidly to the schedule, by which they were with him until the following evening. Easter weekend saw the dividend for Charles in the television debut of his *Legend of Lochnagar* cartoon devalued by a current affairs programme which broadcast, for the first time in Britain, the Camillagate tape. That same weekend, the royal Easter at Windsor was marred by a distinct absence of royals. Princes William and Harry were with their mother; Prince Edward was in America; Prince Andrew made a hurried exit to spend the day at home with his estranged wife and their children. Apart from Charles, only Princess Anne and her new husband, Tim Laurence, lined up alongside the Queen, Prince Philip and the Queen Mother for the traditional family photos – for which only one of the Queen's grandchildren, Zara Phillips, was on hand. 'It was a smaller royal party than usual,' sighed the Dean of Windsor, the Rt Revd Patrick Mitchell. 'I had got Easter eggs for the children, as always. But there weren't many here this year. . . just the one, in fact.'

On Easter Monday the Queen was spotted wandering Windsor Great Park on her own, deep in thought. She may well have been wondering if the 'Diana problem' was being handled in quite the right way.

The corporate might of the British Establishment had rounded on the Princess of Wales, savagely and shamelessly, within a month of her formal separation from the heir to the throne.

As publication of the Camillagate tapes threatened to damage Prince Charles's reputation beyond repair, leaders of every major British institution were urged to close ranks around the prince and set out to sideline his wife.

To parliament and church, the legislature and the armed forces, all of whom would one day swear oaths of allegiance to him, the prince's relationship with Mrs Parker-Bowles was not the issue. It was Diana's failure to put up with it. 'The Establishment is 100 per cent against the princess,' said one man with his ear to the high ground, Harold Brooks-Baker, the American-born editor of *Burke's Peerage*. 'I believe the royal family will jettison her as quickly as possible. Very soon she will no longer be involved in state affairs and almost without her noticing it, her political importance will be removed.'

Given their deep-dyed instinct for self-preservation, it was entirely predictable that the major pillars of state would set out to save Charles by destroying Diana. Remarkably little attempt was made to disguise the concerted campaign against her. 'Leading members of the Establishment have decided that the cause of monarchy will be best served by extolling Charles and denigrating Diana,' one Sunday paper blandly reported on its front page. 'There is now undisguised animosity towards the princess among the monarchy's prominent supporters in the House of Lords, the Church of England, academe and among royalist pundits and politicians. Their hope is that her demise in public popularity, if it happens, will be conveniently accompanied by a resurge in popular affection for Charles.'

The ubiquitous Lord St John of Fawsley inevitably led the charge. Master of Emmanuel College at Cambridge University (whose Chancellor is the Prince of Wales's father), His Lordship even came up with an elegant new metaphor for the occasion: 'I am reasonably optimistic that, having been through a difficult period, we are moving out of the shadows and into the sunlight . . . All the feeling of loyalty will constellate around the Prince of Wales as heir to the throne.'

Other Cambridge academics did not shrink from personal abuse. 'The public are deceived in the princess,' declared John Casey, a fellow of Caius College. 'They will see that her friends are everything that is shallow and third-rate – a ghastly milieu where she fits in very happily. She will be diminished, especially when she loses her youthful looks.'

Prince Charles, to Casey, had 'long-term qualities' whereas the princess did not 'stand for anything'. The 'great question' about Diana and her friends was whether they had plotted to displace the rightful prince. 'If the public thinks that,' said Casey, 'it will very much turn against her.' The conspiracy theme was taken up, again without any attempt to produce evidence, by Lord McAlpine, former treasurer of the Conservative Party, and a big wheel in government circles. Accusing Diana of fighting a propaganda campaign against the royal family, McAlpine proclaimed that she should not be 'allowed to enjoy the spoils of that victory'.

Could it yet be called a victory? Diana's own step-grandmother, the romantic novelist Barbara Cartland, disowned the princess for the crime of 'outshining' her husband. From the world of knighted media folk, Sir Peregrine Worsthorne predicted that the 'electric charge' between Diana and the public would dissipate once she was perceived as Princess of Wales in name only: 'I don't see her carrying on as a star in her own right, as if she's got some momentous glamour of her own.' Sir Perry at least had some cautionary words for the prince. Predicting 'a rather austere and unworldly' period of transition for the heir to the throne, he recalled the atonement paid by King Henry II for the murder of Thomas à Becket: 'The King ostentatiously had himself lashed on the steps of Canterbury Cathedral. Charles has got to find some equivalent.'

The Church of England was not bothered about penance. To the Bishop of Peterborough, the Rt Revd William Westwood, it was Diana's position which was 'perilous'. Unless she was careful, she would find herself greatly reduced. 'As a friend of mine says, if you live by the media you should die by the media.' Charles had the continuity of his family's lineage and the necessary time to indulge in a period of reflection. 'My honest view is that Prince Charles should really move a bit out of the public eye. Doing ordinary things – openings and visits, that sort of stuff – wins people's hearts.' The former Lord Chancellor,

Lord Hailsham, agreed: 'I think it best for the prince to be left alone. Let it simmer for a bit.'

The bishop's line that Diana had 'lived by the media' emerged from another propaganda campaign against which the princess was powerless. At the time, she was dealing with the much more pressing problems of any recently separated parent: re-assuring the children. After one of their first weekends visiting their downbeat father, morose in the wake of the Camillagate transcript, William and Harry returned to their mother full of questions about why he was so unhappy. Like any devoted mother, Diana herself was putting on an especially cheerful front to her sons, who could not fail to notice the contrast. She seemed OK, so why was Daddy so miserable? Was it all her fault? Even royalty, it seemed, was not above the unforgiveable post-separation tactic of 'using' the children.

Diana was thus less publicly visible than usual just as her name was again being blackened. Lord McGregor, chairman of the Press Complaints Commission, now made his accusation that both the Prince and Princess of Wales had 'used' newspapers to reveal details of their marital problems in what amounted to open warfare. As long ago as May 1991, according to McGregor, he had been told at a private dinner in Luxemburg by Lord Rothermere, owner of the *Daily Mail* and *The Mail on Sunday*, that the prince and princess had each 'recruited national news-papers to carry their own accounts of their marital rifts'. Later he had been told by Andrew Knight, executive chairman of Rupert Murdoch's News International (owners of *The Sun*, *The News of the World, The Times* and *The Sunday Times*), that the princess was 'participating in the provision of information for tabloid editors about the state of her marriage'. Knight had cited as evidence press photographs of Diana visiting her friend Carolyn Bartholomew, one of the sources for Andrew Morton's book *Diana: Her True Story*, in the week the book was published. 'I took further soundings,' said McGregor, 'and was satisfied that what Mr Knight told me was true.'

As a week of controversy and leaks wore on, an embattled McGregor eventually withdrew his charge against the Prince of Wales, maintaining it solely against the princess – about whom he did not mince his words. Her actions, said his lordship, had 'seriously embarrassed the Commission' and 'undermined the purpose' of his 'carefully timed and emotively phrased statement' (about journalists 'dabbling their fingers in the stuff of other people's souls').

The princess has been declared guilty without evidence or trial. How exactly was she supposed to have 'conspired' with tabloid newspapers to publish her version of the Wales marriage? Not one single instance of Diana's 'recruitment' campaign had been offered, beyond the charge that she had set up a specific photo opportunity – itself insubstantiated and, in fact, incorrect. The celebrated photographs to which Knight referred, of Diana kissing her friend Mrs Bartholomew on her front doorstep, were widely interpreted as a tacit endorsement by the princess of the contents of Morton's book. In fact, as Morton publicly admitted, he had never even met Diana. According to the princess's circle, her visit was made to reassure a worried Mrs Bartholomew that the extent of her co-operation with Morton had not endangered their friendship. The photos were the result of a call to the press from a habitually nosey neighbour, hoping for a handsome payday. The pictures, after all, showed Diana *leaving* the house; there had been no photographers there to record her arrival. Equally convincing was the point made by Diana's friends that, if the princess had known she was going to be photographed, she would never have been so scruffily dressed.

Lord Rothermere had asked for his evidence of press recruitment to remain confidential; it would never have become public but for a leak to *The Guardian*. To what, however, could Rothermere have been referring, beyond the leak from Prince Charles's friends to his own employee, Nigel Dempster of the *Daily Mail*, about Charles's spurned offer to throw his wife a thirtieth-birthday party? As McGregor dutifully withdrew his accusations against the prince, leaving Diana to ride an unfair and unpleasant storm, those ever talkative 'friends of the prince' got back to work.

Now Charles's unofficial spokesmen adopted an ugly *ad feminam* line. To the London *Evening Standard,* 'one of

Charles's circle' revealed that Diana was in 'a familiar state of nervous excitement'. This made her 'very dangerous'. The prince's camp could not 'carry on indulging her neurotic tyranny. We have learned that lesson.' In his excitement the *Standard*'s reporter, Rory Knight-Bruce, betrayed his own apparent membership of the Prince's Party: 'It is time for the Establishment to see off the woman who thought that she was more powerful than the royal family.' He wheeled on another 'senior source in the Church of England' to call the princess 'a little girl lost'. But the anonymous cleric proceeded to let the side down with an apparent pang of guilt: 'She may be flirtatious – and she is, I've met her several times – but she is surely incapable of adultery.' Given an uphill struggle, the verbal hit-team parroting their master's voice was showing occasional signs of fatigue.

On the other hand, one of Charles's most vocal media champions, Penny Junor, conceded that the Establishment would not have been too shocked by the revelations of Camillagate: 'His crime was getting found out.' Even in the case of the future Supreme Governor of the Church of England, adultery was no big deal to politicians and lawyers, academics and soldiers, even churchmen. There but for the grace of God, via the tabloid press, might go any of them, any minute.

For once, however, it looked as if the might of the British Establishment might not prevail. The British people were not going to surrender their beloved Diana without a struggle. When she visited the city of Liverpool in mid-1992, thousands of people turned out for a glimpse of her. In the same city, in December of the same year, just eight of his mother's subjects turned up to greet the Prince of Wales.

The scale, persistence and sheer nastiness of the campaign against Diana was a direct indication of the fear and frustration around Charles at her apparently unshakeable public popularity. At the time of her separation from the prince, as before and since, media interest alone has proved Diana the world's most popular woman. The issue of the London *Sunday Times* containing the first extract from Morton's book sold a record 1.38 million copies, up 21 per cent from its regular figure of 1.14 million. In the United States, the issue of *People* magazine containing the first American excerpt sold over four million copies, a record in the magazine's eighteen-year history. When the book leapt to the top of the *New York Times* bestseller list, there were two other books about Diana (both far less reliable) already there. The fascination with Diana, Princess of Wales is far more than a merely British phenomenon.

To the American feminist Camille Paglia it is 'an international obsession whose scale and longevity show that it is more than high-class soap opera or a reactionary wish-fulfilment fantasy for American Anglophiles . . . Diana may have become the most powerful image in popular world culture today, a case study in the modern cult of celebrity and the way it stimulates atavistic religious emotions.' To Professor Paglia, Diana's story 'taps into certain deep and powerful strains . . . that suggest that the ancient archetypes of conventional womanhood are not obsolete but stronger and deeper than ever.' Paglia's list of the archetypal female images evoked by the evolving Diana is worth summarizing in some detail:

Cinderella. Diana once earned money doing odd jobs as a char-lady – 'vacuuming, dusting, ironing and washing'. In Morton's book, she is actually found 'on her knees cleaning the kitchen floor' as she chats with a chum about her weekend plans. Like Cinderella, Diana has two bossy older sisters, a ruthless step-mother, and a father who is both a baron and hard-up. Once in royal circles, she is given a hard time by the snooty family and its hangers-on.
The betrayed wife. Like the character played by Mia Farrow in Roman Polanski's film *Rosemary's Baby*, tricked and manoeuvred into impregnation by Satan, Diana seems 'isolated and conspired against by a faithless husband in league with a secretive, coldly smiling coterie'.
The princess in the Tower. Diana's story evokes 'imperilled or mourning femininity that flourished in Victorian poetry and painting, but that one had thought long dead in this era of aggressively career-oriented feminism'. Once Charles has 'cut

himself off' from her, Diana's friends 'beyond the moat' joke that PoW stands for prisoner of war. Pre-Raphaelite images by Holman Hunt and Millais come to mind, Tennyson's Lady of Shalott or Keats's half-mad young widow, Isabella.

The 'mater dolorosa'. Diana's children give her 'stature'; without them her complaints would seem 'far more juvenile or petulant'. Charles, who plucked her from obscurity, seems helpless in the court of popular opinion against the sorrowing mother or 'mater dolorosa'. His 'philandering attempts to remain himself' have produced, ironically, a Catholic Madonna, 'a modern Mary with a taste for rock'n'roll'.

The pagan goddess. Amid Graeco-Roman echoes, Diana the huntress (pictured reading *Country Life*) becomes a fierce Italian goddess of the woods, ranged against her enemy Camilla, Virgil's Amazon, the militant Volscian horsewoman.

The Hollywood Queen. An exasperated Charles accuses Diana of feigning, even relishing 'martyrdom'. There is an operatic quality to her melodramatic suicide attempts. The House of Windsor comes to resemble a studio in the way it 'sequesters stars and subjects them to inhumane rules that make them more than human'. Diana's celebrity is achieved without words; she expresses herself through dance. Diana may thus be 'the last of the silent film stars'; she exists as 'primarily a visual presence'.

The beautiful boy. Pictures of Diana as a child look almost like soft-core child porn. There is an auto-erotic quality in her boyish androgyny. 'Her charisma springs from a pre-sexual narcissism that is both male and female.' Aquatic shots 'offer all the charms of semi-nudity': a Botticelli's Venus at the poolside. There is a 'persistent, half-conscious provocativeness' in the clothes she chooses for her public appearances, notably the famously low-cut black dress in which she chose to make her very first outing on her fiancé's arm.

To sum up: 'Deification has its costs. The modern mega-celebrity, bearing the burden of collective symbolism, projection and fantasy, is a ritual victim, cannibalised by our pity and fear. Those at the apex of the social pyramid are untouchables, condemned to horrifying solitude . . . Diana the huntress is now the hind paralysed in the world's gun sight.' Charles, by contrast, is 'dogmeat'.

How could Paglia omit the slogan (targeted at women) of Virginia Slims cigarettes: 'You've come a long way, baby'? Diana may have more resonance for American than for British feminists, who apparently still 'cannot find much sympathy for the trials of a young, beautiful and economically privileged celebrity'; but it scarcely seems plausible, looking back to July 1981, that the coy, blushing teenager married in front of 700 million people should now hold the rest of the world in thrall, and the future of the thousand-year-old British crown in the palm of her elegant hand.

Via his friends, Charles has tried to make out that Diana is 'a sick woman' who proved 'a seriously unbalanced wife' and has 'deceived a lot of people' with her public charms. 'In private, she can be a very different woman – irrational and unreasonable . . . hysterical at times.'

According to Penny Junor, billed as 'the author closest to Prince Charles' (who openly admitted that she was 'contacted by his circle and asked to write this article'), the failure of the marriage was quite as much Diana's fault as Charles's. 'She can scream and shout, burst into tears, and flounce out of the room in a display of temper.' Diana's grasp on reality is 'tenuous', went the Junor version, and her 'obsession' with her husband's friendship with Camilla Parker-Bowles 'borders on the paranoid'. Far from Charles's being an absentee father, Diana 'thwarts his attempts to see the children, and increasingly keeps them away from him'.

On 15 April 1993, Princes William and Harry travelled to Balmoral to rejoin their father, after an Easter week with their mother which had included outings to the European Grand Prix, the 'fun runs' of Thorpe Park and a lunch party at one of her favourite restaurants, San Lorenzo. The next day, their first day back with their father, the young princes were left alone with a 'minder', to be taught to shoot rabbits (much to the disgust of campaigners against blood sports). Charles had left them behind while he joined the British Deer Society's annual 'Stalker's Day'. According to a Balmoral estate worker, Charles was 'too busy to spend a lot of time' with his sons throughout their four-day stay. The only moment he was seen with them was the inevitable photo-opportunity when emerging from church on the Sunday morning.

For all their persistence and ferocity, the charges mounted against Diana by the prince's camp carry as much credibility with the British public as Penny Junor's prediction, five months before the couple's formal separation, that 'the hysteria has died down, the hype is over and no doubt the whole business will ultimately be forgotten. It will fade in our memories as just one of the many storms that the royal family has weathered over the years.'

To the British people their wronged princess is more than ever an object of adoration. It has taken a decade of public triumph and private suffering for Diana to reach the unprecedented position in which she finds herself today. To global victims - from lepers to AIDS patients, dying cancer sufferers to deprived children – she is a ubiquitous saint, a devoted guardian angel with the perfect bedside manner. To international feminists, who had previously dismissed her as a pampered sell-out, she has struck 'a symbolic blow for womankind' – at the apex of not merely the British, but the global, establishment.

No longer is Diana just a pretty face. 'I have always been very impressed by the seriousness of her approach,' says Baroness (Margaret) Jay, former director of the National AIDS Trust, who has known and worked with the princess for several years. 'She puts in an enormous amount of time and effort, much of it unpublicised, to meet people involved in every aspect of a problem. She really wants to grasp the complexities. Much more goes on behind the scenes than is apparent from her published list of engagements.' To Lord Rees-Mogg, Diana is 'not academically clever, but she has an intuitive understanding of human nature that is of more use to the world'. In her features His Lordship discerns 'a nose expressive of powerful will, commanding eyes set in strong sockets – a face, like Margaret Thatcher's, not of prettiness but of command'.

Very shrewd, says a former member of her staff. 'Diana has an intuitive grasp of other people's problems, and how to respond to them – more so than any other royal. She would make a much better Queen than the Queen.' He cites Elizabeth II's awkwardness with a hospital patient in *Elizabeth R*, the BBC film made to mark her fortieth year on the throne. 'Diana would have sat down on the bed and held her hand. She would have listened.' From Diana's camp there emerges a more convincing party line: that the princess is much brighter than people have yet had the chance to realize. Highly manipulative, yes, with more than her share of feminine wiles, but neither the dumb blonde nor the temperamental hysteric painted by her foes. As if emerging from a golden chrysalis, the decorative bubble-head of yesteryear has metamorphosed into a dynamic, concerned, contemporary career woman, anxious to use her pulling-power to make the world a better place.

A potential queen more popular and respected than the future king – the *status quo* for the foreseeable future – poses the embattled British monarchy an open-ended nightmare. The effect of the warfare between their staffs has been to force Britain to take sides – to line up behind the Prince's Party or the Princess's. For a young woman who has never passed an exam beyond her driving test, this is pretty heady stuff.

Towards the end of the Middle Ages, when wool was so important to England that the Lord Chancellor presided over the House of Lords while sitting (as he still does) on the Woolsack, the Spencers were among a handful of old English families to make a huge fortune simply by owning sheep. In 1506, under the Tudors, they acquired the 1,500-acre estate of Althorp in Northamptonshire, where they built the stately home which is to this day their family seat. A century later Sir Robert Spencer was reputed to be the richest man, in terms of ready cash, in the country. In 1603 he was made Baron Spencer, one of the first peers of England created by the new Stuart King, James I. The line of descent has remained unbroken ever since.

The former Lady Diana Spencer, in other words, is more English than the royal family, and arguably more royal. On her wedding to the Prince of Wales in 1981, she became the first English girl to marry an heir to the throne for more than three hundred years; she was set to become the first English-born Queen Consort since the days of King Henry VIII. But Diana also brought to the Windsor line the only royal blood it lacked, that of the Stuarts. Her son, Prince William, is thus the first potential monarch in British history to be descended from every British King and Queen who had issue.

Before her separation clouded her future, Diana was also on course to be the first British Queen ever to have worked for her living. The last Princess of Wales, later King George V's Queen Mary, never made a speech or used a telephone in her life. Less than thirty years after Mary's death, her successor set a new style for the monarchy as a girl-next-door princess, wearing off-the-peg clothes from chain stores; more to the point, she had worked as a kindergarten teacher and lived the Chelsea life of a flat-sharing 'Sloane Ranger'. Throughout her eleven years as a royal, one of her primary qualities was that she never lost touch with the 'real' world outside.

Born on the royal estate at Sandringham, in a house rented by her father from the Queen, Diana was literally the girl next door. Althorp, the house in which she later grew up, was bigger than any royal residence except Buckingham Palace. For all her deep-blue blood, however, she was also a thoroughly modern young woman; though no intellectual, she was increasingly savvy, street-wise and smart. No heart-on-sleeve feminist, either, she showed considerable Spencer pride beneath those demurely low-ered eyelashes. All of which was to prove her problem.

Only seventeen when the Prince of Wales first showed a romantic interest in her, Diana fell deeply in love. Few girls her age could have resisted the attentions of the world's most eligible bachelor. Though Charles finally singled her out (if only as his 'brood mare') largely thanks to the restrictions on his choice, she was prepared to put up with all the flummery – even to look on as the antique absurdities of the contemporary British monarchy obliged her uncle to reassure a press conference, in surely the most demeaning such occasion of modern times, that she was a virgin. 'Charles's parents!' says one friend of the family, looking back to that moment. 'They should have known that he needed someone more experienced than that . . . To hell with being a virgin. That was the least important consideration.'

A month before her formal separation Diana herself looked back, giving some clues to her own character in what most observers read as a coded attack on her husband. Earlier that week she had established her own distinct identity, thanks to a forty-minute meeting with President Mitterrand of France – the first time in British history that a Princess of Wales had enjoyed any such 'summit', in her own right, with a senior foreign head of state. Now, back in London, Diana gave the keynote speech of European Drug Prevention Week. Not merely was it one of the longest public speeches she had ever given, another attempt to bulk out her public persona. Given its central theme – lavish physical affection upon your children, and they are less likely to look elsewhere for artificial substitutes such as drugs – the speech was also full of secret messages about her own dilemma, and the apparent inadequacies of her husband.

Herself well-known to be a copious hugger of her sons, Diana seemed to be offering Charles veiled rebukes, in such phrases as: 'Hugging has no harmful side effects . . . There are potential huggers in every household . . .' In passing, she certainly offered some private theories about his personal shortcomings, given a cold and formal upbringing utterly starved of physical affection:

> Children are not chores, they are part of us. If we gave them the love they deserve, they would not have to try so hard to attract our attention. . . Children who have received the affection they deserve will usually continue to recognize how good it feels, how right it feels and will create that feeling around them. We've all seen the families of the skilled survivors. Their strength comes from within and was put there by learning how to give and receive affection, without restraint, or embarrassment from their earliest days.

Significantly, in retrospect, she went on: 'If the immediate family breaks up, the problems created can still be resolved, but only if the children have been brought up from the very start with the feeling that they are wanted, loved and valued.

Then they are better able to cope with such crises . . .'

If it was a message about Charles – at the time, before she had won her formal separation, another cry for help – her heartfelt speech was also about herself. To the former Diana Spencer, her husband's friendship with Camilla Parker-Bowles was but the latest and most devastating in a lifelong series of betrayals. The cycle had begun when she was only six, on the day her mother, Frances, abruptly disappeared from her life. So wretched was Frances' marriage to Johnny Althorp, the future 8th Earl Spencer, that she was prepared to lose custody of her children to escape him.

Although Frances tried to fight for them, suing for divorce on grounds of mental and physical cruelty, Johnny mobilized enough aristocratic character witnesses to see her off with ease. The lurid publicity accorded the high-society divorce case was very hard on a young girl abruptly exiled to a far-flung boarding-school – where, on her ninth birthday, she joined her schoolfriends around the television to watch, live from Caernarvon Castle, the investiture as Prince of Wales of her twenty-one-year-old future husband.

Divorced parents were then much more unusual in Britain than they are now; and schoolfriends can be cruel. Starved of hugs, Diana retreated within herself. Hard though her soft-hearted father tried to create a loving family atmosphere, he was traditional-minded enough to maintain firm discipline. Diana's brother, Charles, has revealed that he and his three sisters were physically punished. One of their nannies, Mary Clarke, testified: 'The children were very strictly brought up in a very old-fashioned way, as if they were still living at the beginning of the century.'

Her mother's remarriage took her to Scotland, while her father's brought to thirteen-year-old Diana's life a stepmother she and her siblings couldn't stand: Raine Dartmouth, ex-wife of another Earl (and daughter of the romantic novelist Barbara Cartland). Although Raine undoubtedly made Johnny Spencer happy, later giving him the will to recover from a near-terminal stroke, her pushy, domineering ways were anathema to his children, who took to calling her 'Acid Raine'. Photographs of the period already show a telling dislocation in the young Diana's eyes. Now her father too had betrayed her.

Five years later, when the eighteen-year-old innocent fell for her prince, friends worried about the thirteen-year age gap, and Charles's penchant for older, wiser company. She was young for her years, he old for his – and very stuck in his bachelor ways. But Diana had every reason to hope that she could create with Charles the happy family life she herself had been denied – the happy family life that he told her he too wanted, that he had enjoyed with his own parents. The denial of that hope, at the very outset of her marriage, was to Diana the ultimate betrayal.

The collapse of the marriage seems, in retrospect, inevitable. Andrew Morton may have exaggerated the five 'suicide attempts' – who on earth tries to kill themselves with a lemon grater? – but they were nevertheless desperate appeals from a wretched young woman alone in a hostile world. As for Diana's bout of *bulimia nervosa*: according to Elizabeth Longford, the Queen believes that 'the stress in the princess's marriage was the result of [this] precondition', dating back to her childhood. But Mary Clarke, who knew her as a child, says Diana became ill 'because of the anger and hurt of finding out she wasn't loved'.

Mrs Clarke first arrived on the scene via an advert in *The Lady*, three years after Frances Spencer's departure. The youngest of the three daughters, and thus the most affected by their parents' separation, Diana had locked one previous nanny in the lavatory and thrown another's clothes on to the roof. What Mrs Clarke learned about Diana during her two years with the family left her in no doubt that it was her parents' divorce which forged the complex character before us today. 'I can see her now, this child with fair hair down to her shoulders, rosy cheeks and downcast eyes, talking about love. She always needed to be loved. It's so sad . . .

'I remember her saying: "I shall only get married when I am sure I am in love, so that we will never be divorced" – and this became something of a theme for her. The abiding ambition of this child was simply to marry happily and have children.' Mrs Clarke described her former charge as 'beautiful, obsessive, every bit an actress, astute, devious, strong-charactered, nonetheless sympathetic, genuine and sensitive, in tune with ordinary folk'.

Diana's sincerity, she said, came from her father, 'whom she adored'.

Mrs Clarke believes that Diana fell deeply in love with Charles, and would never have married him unless she had been convinced that he loved her in return. 'There's no doubt of the tremendous pain and hurt she must have endured when she realized that her husband had never loved her. How betrayed and used she must have felt. No wonder she came to hate him.'

The British public, who had invested so much affection in their 'fairy-tale' couple, tried long and hard not to believe the persistent rumours about the state of the Wales's marriage – until one dramatic night in July 1991, when their eight-year-old son William was rushed to hospital with a fractured skull after an accident at school involving a golf club. As 'Wills' underwent emergency surgery in London, where his mother maintained an all-night bedside vigil, the Prince of Wales stunned the nation by going off to the opera. Charles's friends later argued that the doctors had reassured him all would be well, that they had the number of his mobile phone in the event of emergencies. But no amount of special pleading could alter the astonishment of parents throughout the land at Charles's priorities that night.

It was from that moment, in a growing crescendo via Morton's book to the announcement of their separation in December 1992, that the sympathy of the British people lay overwhelmingly with Diana. In the days before the marriage came to a formal end, as she busied herself reassuring the children before the news was made public, her friends noticed a dramatic change in the princess. At last she was more cheerful and self-confident than they had seen her in a long time. Two months before, when the Squidgygate episode had sapped her morale, she had seemed to lose the initiative in her long negotiations with her royal in-laws and their lawyers. Still she had nursed her bruises from the assumption that she had 'tacitly' assisted Morton, when the truth was that she too had felt betrayed by the extent of her friend's indiscretions. Her sullen display in Korea, followed by the Camillagate tape, had finally won her the independence she sought – but at what cost to her future credibility? Then came the House of Windsor's worst week since 1936.

It was as if Diana lived a charmed life. Even the Great Fire of Windsor and the Queen's 'annus horribilis' speech seemed to work to her advantage. In a poll in *The Daily Express*, 50 per cent said Diana had 'done most to improve the standing of the royal family over the last two years', compared with 29 per cent for the Queen and just 14 per cent for Charles. Asked who was responsible for the collapse of the Wales marriage, Charles was held to blame by twice as many respondents as Diana. Fifty-seven per cent 'sympathized most' with her, a mere 12 per cent with him. To the British public, through thick and thin, Diana was 'the Teflon princess', to whom no mud ever stuck.

Given the distinct note of misogyny in the campaign against her, even indifferent British feminists gave Diana credit for 'speaking out when the pressure to shut up reached dangerous levels'. As the journalist Lesley White saw it, 'She could easily have been frightened off. She could easily have fallen in love with her own perfect image as the untarnished Madonna and kept her fans happy with an illusion of contentment.' That she had chosen otherwise deserved respect. 'She knew she could not carry on with integrity; could not raise two sons in a lie of a marriage; could no longer exist in a bubble of silent rage.' Zuleika Robertson, a psychoanalyst, also applauded Diana's 'courage' for being 'drawn into adult relationships which replicate past unresolved experiences between parents and children'. And the man whose book had proved the catalyst for change in her life, Andrew Morton, paid his own pithy tribute: 'Diana was not prepared to sacrifice her one chance of fulfilment on this earth for the institution of monarchy.'

So what does the future hold for Diana, Princess of Wales? There can now be little doubt that she has abandoned all thought of becoming Queen; lingering hopes of a compromise on this score amount to wishful thinking by her loyal legions of followers. It seems inevitable, whatever the prime minister may say, that a no-fault, 'quickie' divorce (on the grounds of the 'irretrievable breakdown' of the marriage) will follow sooner than the nation may think, leaving both prince and princess free to remarry.

The only significant unknown is which party will be seen to initiate the move – or, to put it more bluntly, which party will be perceived to be to blame.

Still in her early thirties, Diana is young enough to start a new life, perhaps have more children – and at last create for herself, second time around, the genuinely happy family life she so deeply craves. This remains, and always will, foremost among her personal aspirations. If personal happiness can be won only at the cost of her public life, it is a sacrifice she is prepared to make. As her brother Charles has said, 'She may have a wonderful relationship with the British people, but when she gets home she is utterly alone.'

As she watches, waits and wonders, however, the Princess of Wales is determined to continue the public work which has come to mean so much to her. Diana's saving grace through recent trials, apart from her children and friends, has been what she likes to call her job. To her, this has offered the sense of purpose and fulfilment missing from her marriage. To her admirers, it has formed a stark contrast with the parallel public careers of other royals. Where the charitable work of the 'born' royals (with the notable exception of Princess Anne) can so often seem the dutiful price they pay for so much hereditary privilege, Diana's growing portfolio of causes is now more clearly perceived as the personal mission it has become. Within a week of the separation she assured a combined meeting of all the causes she has espoused that it would still be business as usual: 'Whatever uncertainties the last few weeks may have brought, I want you to be certain of this: our work together will continue unchanged.' Since becoming an independent operator, she has added homeless teenagers and 'battered' wives to her widening range of social concerns. With an increasingly mature international schedule ahead of her – she is particularly proud of an invitation to speak at Harvard University in the autumn of 1993 – Diana is also intent on becoming a major force for social change on the world stage. Her partisans have already been heard to wonder how Prince Charles would feel if she were to beat him to the Nobel Peace Prize.

But to remain a substantial public figure, even after the end of

the marriage which conferred that status upon her, there will be
a private price to pay. Diana is well aware that she must handle
her newfound freedom with care. With powerful forces out to
discredit her, popular perceptions of the independent princess
will remain all-important. Desperate though she may be (as is
only natural) to form new alliances, she will have to be careful
not to endanger her popularity by forming any 'unsuitable'
relationships. Although society deems it acceptable for most
estranged wives to be seen on the arms of other men, the case
is somewhat different for the wife – and mother – of future
kings. Even after a divorce, it seems likely that the strength
of feeling Diana arouses among the British people will see any
emergent suitors subjected to the most intense scrutiny by an
anxiously affectionate nation. Though the vast majority wish
her well, a remarriage by their favourite princess might seem,
at least temporarily, to come between Diana and her public. In
a curious way, the sheer scale of her popularity may thus prove
as much a burden as a support.

Meanwhile, she will watch from the sidelines as her estranged
husband agonizes over his future. Just as Diana has been called
a 'bolter' – the women in her family have tended to run away
from problems – so Charles has something of a track record
as a quitter. 'The man who has never made a decision in his
life,' in the words of one informed observer, 'is currently wres-
tling with the biggest decision he will ever face.' If the Parker-
Bowles marriage were to end in divorce – all predictions of
which, unsurprisingly, have so far been denied – will Charles
be caught in the public fall-out? Even Penny Junor has told
us, on his behalf, that 'there is no doubt Charles loves Camilla
very dearly' and that 'the Queen has always been very fond
of her too.' Might Charles contemplate remarriage? Whatever
the church may say (and all other British institutions ready to
change their own rules to save the monarchy), even the prince
recognizes the practical truth behind the impossible dream: that
public opinion would never accept a *second* Princess of Wales
as a future queen. Remarriage, in other words, would mean
Charles overcoming his ingrained sense of duty, and renouncing
the throne he was born to inherit. Although those closest to

him are still trying to steel his nerve, the more realistic of them suspect that Charles may well wind up – perhaps, in the longer run, like Diana – sacrificing public office to private contentment.

Barring a constitutional upheaval of republican proportions, he would always be able to take pride in his son's progress as a dynamic young monarch offering Britain renewed hope for its future. If anything were to happen to the Queen before 21 June 2000 – William's eighteenth birthday, and thus the day on which he could succeed to the throne – Charles would earn warm public respect for assenting to the Privy Council decision that his brother Andrew (not, as rumoured, his sister Anne) will serve as Regent.

Whatever Charles's future may hold, Diana considers her primary long-term duty to be the shaping of her elder son into a happy, well-balanced young man ready to steward the troubled institution of monarchy into a new millennium. By her own relaxed public style, and her good sense in eschewing unseemly royal extravagance, she is already giving both her sons the best possible lead on how to handle their futures. It is heavily ironic that this 'temporary' royal, in and out of the family within such recent memory, should still outscore the born royals in regular opinion polls; if she continues to do so in the longer term, as an independent agent shorn of her formal membership of the royal family, it will be an un-comfortable object-lesson for the Palace. The British people will be demonstrating, in effect, that they prefer the public persona of this ex-royal to the real thing. Where would that leave the House of Windsor?

Diana is nobody's fool. She will continue to show the born royals the kind of royalty Britain wants, in a style they seem quite unable to master or even comprehend. She is unlikely to put a foot wrong as she alone represents to the world – as is one of the central functions of a constitutional monarchy – the young and positive face of Britain, a proud and vigorous country looking to its future rather than coasting on its past. And in any dark moments, she will be able to take comfort in the memory that her late father, Earl Spencer, never warmed to the Prince of Wales, and died thinking that his daughter's husband was not good enough for her.

Diana is not only the most popular of the royals; in her own example, and in the careful upbringing of her sons, she may well be the monarchy's best hope for survival. She is provenly bright enough, despite a lack of expert advice, to maintain her own independent, ever popular public profile, while letting her foes within the royal system make all the mistakes. She has all too few real friends – even her own siblings, especially her sister Jane, are capable of insisting that the royal family's interests must come first – but she can take comfort in sympathy from some unexpected quarters, notably such royal females as Princess Margaret. So it is plainly counter-productive of the royal machine to be conducting its petty warfare against the princess; rather, in the monarchy's own interests, it should be pleading with her to return to the central royal role in which the world wants to see her. If she demurs, the Queen's staff will have only themselves to blame. To treat her with less than the respect the public feels she deserves, meanwhile, will be to forfeit whatever national affection for the monarchy remains – at the very moment when the constitutional debate about its future is getting under way in earnest.

If the end of the Wales marriage were in time to prove the beginning of the end of the British monarchy, history may choose as its text the Prince of Wales's own recent words, published in *The Daily Telegraph* in March 1993, in an extract from his latest book:

> If you treat [something] with love and respect, it will repay you in kind. But if you fail to respect the complex, universal laws to which every living creature is ultimately subject . . .
> in the end the consequences could be painful and deeply destructive.

Charles was writing, with a deeply felt passion, about the organic farmland around his beloved Highgrove. What a pity he did not observe the same principles, and expend the same passion, when it came to his wife.

CHAPTER 10

'WE WILL GO QUIETLY'

'So long as the human heart is strong and the human reason weak, royalty will be strong because it appeals to diffused feeling, and republics weak because they appeal to the understanding.'
WALTER BAGEHOT, *The English Constitution*

KING FAROUK OF EGYPT PREDICTED THAT BY THE END of the twentieth century there would be only five monarchs left in the world: the Kings of England, hearts, diamonds, clubs and spades. Maybe he spoke too soon. During the morning of 4 February 1993, at two North London branches of William Hill, an unnamed middle-aged Briton placed bets totalling £8,000 on the abolition of the British monarchy by the year 2000. If history proves him right, this canny punter stands to win £146,000. 'We don't know who he is,' said William Hill, 'but he didn't have big ears, he didn't have a posh voice, and he certainly didn't have a mobile phone.' In the first two months of 1993, British bookmakers felt obliged to shorten the odds against the monarchy's imminent demise from 100-1 to 5-1.

'We will go quietly' has for years been a standard joke in the Queen's social repertoire, which may yet return to haunt her. 'After all,' as Prince Charles has said, 'if people don't want it, they won't have it.' This simple truth, Charles continued, makes the monarchy 'a kind of elective institution' – a piece of royal semantics which surely stretches contemporary notions of democracy to the outer limits of princely optimism. His more pragmatic father, Prince Philip, speaks less in riddles than in earnest: 'To survive, the monarchy must change.'

Will the House of Windsor, only the eighth dynasty to have sat on the British throne in more than a thousand years,* turn out to be the last? As it flounders amid personal and financial controversy, facing calls for fundamental constitutional reform, the next foreseeable milestone is Elizabeth II's golden jubilee in 2002, when she will be seventy-five years old and her son Charles fifty-three. For the Royal House of Windsor to reach that anniversary intact, it must ensure that the monarchy is perceived as a relevant, contemporary force for good in the modern world, rather than an antique, outmoded repository of hereditary wealth and privilege. As long as its denizens live in extravagant luxury at public expense, hoarding their huge private wealth – and failing, in some cases, to maintain the high moral standards which are the price of such privilege – the monarchy's chances of survival sink daily. The longer it takes the Windsors to set their House in order, the more the crown will be seen as an obstacle to – rather than a safeguard of – basic democratic freedoms. From the demise of the monarchy would flow a written constitution, an elected second chamber of parliament and the separation of church and state. These reforms would pave the way for a Bill of Rights, a Supreme Court, a Freedom of Information Act and all the other civic rights taken for granted in most modern democracies, but denied the British so long as they remain subjects rather than citizens. This constitutional renaissance would be *possible* under a radically reformed monarchy; but it would be *inevitable* if Britain were to become a European republic.

It is not just the failure of several royal marriages, notably that of the heir to the throne, which has wrought the monarchy's

---

*__Saxons__ (802–1066): 264 years; seventeen kings (interrupted by three Danes). __Normans__ (1066–1154): 88 years; four kings. __Plantagenets__ (1154–1485): 331 years; fourteen kings. __Tudors__ (1485–1603): 118 years; three kings, three queens. __Stuarts__ (1603–1714): 111 years; five kings, two queens (interrupted by Cromwell). __Hanover__ (1714–1917): 203 years; seven kings, one queen (including __Saxe-Coburg-Gotha__ 1901–17). __Windsor__ (1917–): 76 years to date (three kings, one queen).

current plight. Nor is it merely the flagrant abuse of their public trust by certain members of the sovereign's family. It is the failure of the hereditary head of state and her advisers to have mirrored national evolution in the institution which is supposed to symbolize it. So long as the monarchy remains redolent of Britain's lost empire – and thus, in Dean Acheson's famous phrase, of her lost role – it will compound rather than amend Britain's failure to face its future as a European nation-state.

Neither crown nor government has yet acknowledged it, but this is the central flaw which has brought the monarchy so low: clinging to a sumptuous imperial past rather than shedding its ermine to face a more realistically modest European future. John Major's supposedly egalitarian Britain is meanwhile expected to muddle through with an unelected head of state, and a narrowly elected prime minister whose 'big idea' is a Citizen's Charter for consumers who are not even citizens.

All the portents of the Windsors' present troubles were apparent during the 1980s, the meritocratic 'Thatcher decade', long before the embarrassments of the Queen's 'annus horribilis' publicly shamed the crown into minor cosmetic change. Unless government is prepared to haul a reluctant monarchy through its expensively subsidized looking-glass, out of that Victorian world of imperial make-believe into the more straitened Britain of the twenty-first century, there is little hope for the House of Windsor – and, more importantly, there is less for Britain.

During the Thatcher years, for all the prime minister's fierce personal loyalty to the crown, the institution of monarchy was already beginning to look dangerously out of synch with the times. By the end of Thatcher's first decade in power, Royal House of Windsor Ltd was at least as bloated and inefficient as any of the nationalized industries she had so ruthlessly privatized. 'Heavily subsidized, monopolistic and unaccountable,' as The Guardian's Joanna Coles pointed out, the monarchy represented everything most loathed by Thatcher's children, 'vigorously schooled in the art of self-improvement', who might be more tolerant of Elizabeth II if she had 'started off life as a chambermaid and worked her way up to the position of Queen'.

Nor was it only *The Guardian*, one of those liberal papers traditionally indifferent to royalty, that was goading Thatcher to square up to the monarchy. For some years her own Conservative backbenchers had been expressing concern about the rising costs of the crown, and demanding (with some success, *see* Chapter 8) that she gag the meddlesome Prince of Wales. In October 1990 the Institute of Economic Affairs (IEA), an influential, free-market group then renowned as Thatcher's 'favourite think tank', issued a policy document calling for the sovereign to be stripped of her remaining constitutional duties and reduced to a merely symbolic role in British life. Power should be transferred, it argued, to 'an officer appointed by parliament'. As long as the monarchy held popular appeal, it would be worth retaining only as 'an emblem of historical continuity in British life' and 'an alternative focus for popular attention away from political leaders'.

With expediency worthy of Bagehot, in other words, the IEA was recommending that the monarchy be reduced to a mere tourist attraction, its only constitutional value being to provide the British voter with a sense of well-being while the politicians did their worst. Drawn up by Frank Vibert, the institute's deputy director, the document's appearance was timed to coincide with early drafts of the Conservative Party's manifesto for the forthcoming general election, which at that time offered every prospect of a 'hung' parliament. The monarch's prime constitutional function – the selection of a senior politician to form a government – becomes 'difficult', Vibert argued, when no party has an overall majority. 'At that moment the crown is politicized and alternative, transparent, non-monarchical procedures become important. In so far as the crown has a wider constitutional significance, it is a negative one – the confusion of the status of the citizen with the status of the subject.'

The IEA document also recommended a written constitution (to help 'buttress' the United Kingdom against the rest of the European Community), and an elected second chamber of parliament, from which hereditary peers would be excluded. Two years earlier, Thatcher had said that her government owed a great debt to the 'leadership' of the IEA; that June, however, she had warned European Community leaders at the Dublin summit against any moves that might have constitutional implications for 'our beloved Queen'. So which way would the lady turn?

The question proved academic. Within a month the document had suddenly been withdrawn, without explanation, and Mrs Thatcher had in any case lost office, giving way to a successor more prone to fine-tuning than wholescale upheaval. On paper, the Queen could breathe again. But an uncomfortable atmosphere prevailed, in which the forces of left and right seemed to be forming an unholy alliance against the crown. 'I am glad that the more commercially-minded New Britons shook us up under Mrs Thatcher,' wrote the conservative commentator Frank Johnson, 'but we could not have expected that to happen without it also shaking up the monarchy and polite society in general.'

Given recent world events, hidden warnings for the monarchy were also coming from other unlikely directions. The collapse of communism, for example, showed a direct correlation between political structures and economic achievement, argued Robert Harris. 'Centralised, secretive regimes were shown to be bad, not only for individual freedom but for the economy, fostering alienation and apathy. That applies with equal force to Britain, which is why right-wing groups such as the IEA have suddenly begun looking at constitutional reform.' Given the chance, Harris also made the libertarian case for abolition:

> How can one have an intelligent, responsive modern citizenry in a nation where men and women are subjects of the crown, without any rights or duties which are written down; where the political system divides the nation between the fiefdom of two big parties; where unelected, titled boobies can have a voice in the legislature by accident of birth; and where a prime minister, sustained by patronage, enjoys almost untrammelled power?

The floodgates were opening. After decades of uncritical deference, a weakened monarchy was under attack from all sides, and its position at the heart of the constitution suddenly under scrutiny. Even at the dawn of 1992, the year which would bring the monarchy to its knees, it was open season on the crown – a subject previously beneath their dignity – among upmarket columnists of all persuasions.

'This country may finally be growing tired of the deception that what you are is more important than what you do,' muttered Janet Daley in *The Times*. The literary editor of the London *Evening Standard*, A.N. Wilson, boldly looked forward to the day an elected president was installed in Kensington Palace, while Buckingham Palace became a conference centre, concert hall and art gallery. It was in *The Spectator*, the radical but traditionally loyal Tory weekly, that Wilson had already outraged royalists (not to mention his host, Lord Wyatt) with a daring exposé of the banality of the Queen Mother's table-talk. Now the same journal sanctioned some extreme *lèse-majesté* from Ludovic Kennedy, who recalled the BBC's famous announcement, as George V lay on his deathbed, that the King's life was 'moving peacefully towards its close' – expressing the hope that 'the same may soon be said of the collective public life of today's royal family.'

Kennedy's sentiments were echoed (also in *The Spectator*) by the political columnist of *The Observer*, Alan Watkins. Detecting 'a whiff of republicanism in the air', Watkins was reluctantly prepared to 'put up with' a sovereign, his or her consort, and an heir to the throne, but 'the rest of the royal family has grown quite out of hand and should be disbanded forthwith'. The Queen should also be 'compelled' to relinquish her role as head of the Commonwealth. Even sacred constitutional cows such as the annual State Opening of Parliament were not *hors de combat*. To Watkins, the ceremony was 'pretty degrading to Queen and Commons alike'. Recalling the days when a senior minister of the Ottoman Empire was obliged to run alongside the Sultan's coach, he mused: 'John Major is not forced to run alongside the royal coach, but Lord Mackay [the Lord Chancellor] has to walk backwards down some steps. The Queen is compelled to read out a lot of claptrap, while they have to trot along to the Lords to hear her . . . The question is how much longer this nonsense can go on. I do not mean the State Opening, but the monarchy itself.'

Come the high summer, and Fergie's toe-sucking at the tax-payer's expense, even *The Daily Telegraph* (in the shape of Hugh Massingberd) was calling on the Queen to retire to Sandringham. With the right in full cry, both up and downmarket, the tabloid 'feeding frenzy' was seen as evidence that the right-wing forces unleashed by the Thatcher years were turning on their own. By the autumn, in apparent despair, Sir Peregrine Worsthorne stood alone on the burning deck: 'So what should British monarchists do? I fear the answer is embrace republicanism – not because we love the monarchy too little, but because we love it too much.'

Paradoxically, Sir Perry was echoing the sentiments of his political antithesis, the left-wing Labour MP Ken Livingstone: 'I'm a republican, but it's not an important issue on the door-steps. I think the royal family should be left to self-destruct.' As their 'horrible' year wore on, the Windsors' capacity for self-destruction duly drove Worsthorne to abandon hope and delighted Livingstone by bringing the issue right on to the doorsteps. With poll after poll showing support for the mon-archy fast eroding, the editor of *Burke's Peerage* also feared for the future: 'The damage is very great. If the royal family doesn't change many aspects of its style, it will simply disappear, like its relations did across the continent.' It took the London cor-respondent of *The Washington Post*, surveying the wreckage with cool transatlantic eye, to go to the heart of the matter: 'The damage has occurred because the royal family, which long ago ceded the job of running the country to parliament, is falling down on its one remaining task – being regal.'

Discussion of the monarchy's future should properly revolve around issues, not personalities; but this time the question had been raised by individual conduct. Most critics – Tony Benn is a rare exception – find it impossible to separate the two. Take the arguments, for instance, behind the view of Alan Clark, a former minister in Thatcher's government, that the monarchy is ripe for 'root-and-branch' reform: 'The Queen is all right, and Princess Diana is a goddess, but most of the rest are so awful that it is quite a work to dredge out of the English language pejoratives strong enough to describe their vulgarity, brutishness and maladroitness. They've become so tainted with the conventions of the showbiz world as to be utterly contemptible. Even Prince Charles is a disappointment. I can see no consistency of purpose or vision there.'

It is hard to avoid an *ad hominem* debate when the capacity of the would-be head of state to handle the job is under question (even, apparently, by his father). Few, as yet, dare question the abilities of the present incumbent – beyond the likes of A.N. Wilson, that unlikely Tom Paine *de nos jours,* whose views have bordered on the abusive: 'All she requires is sufficiently powerful reading spectacles to be able to drone through her speeches written for her by the Prime Minister.' But the personal character of the heir to the throne is central to the monarchy's immediate future. Does a hereditary system require the British people, by definition, to tolerate a head of state whom a majority do not want – in this case a man who, whatever his other qualities, has largely forfeited the two essential prerequisites of a successful monarch: popularity and respect?

'Reposing the flame of our nationhood upon an individual toward whom millions may feel disapproval or disenchantment,' as one commentator remarked, 'has become the modern risk of monarchy.' Philip Ziegler, the official biographer of Lord Mountbatten and King Edward VIII, and one of the very few writers to have been awarded honours by the Queen, observed as long as fifteen years ago that the British 'like their monarchs either old, wise and paternal or young and hopeful'. A sixty-year-old King Charles III would be neither. The logical conclusion, to Ziegler, was for the Queen to hand on the crown to her grandson – then unborn, now the putative King William V. 'The golden jubilee of 2002,' he suggested, 'might be a suitable occasion.' Ziegler ruefully acknowledged that this would require the 'premature disappearance' of the present Prince of Wales, 'the need for which he might consider inadequately proven.'

Not any more. As the Prince of Wales contemplates his personal future, which may well see him make a voluntary surrender to Ziegler's thesis, there are many of his potential subjects who now consider the case for his 'disappearance' proven beyond doubt. It was before the formal end of his marriage, and the subsequent Camillagate scandal, that Massingberd urged the Queen to hand over to her son sooner rather than later, basing his argument on a uniquely British class point: 'The great landed aristocracy . . . has adapted far more successfully [than the crown] to the modern world. It is an axiom of good estate management that the heir should take over while he is still in his prime and the titular head withdraw gracefully to the stables, or wherever. The monarchy should take a leaf out of the aristocracy's book.'

Like King Edward VII, with whom he has so much else in common, Charles will have been waiting since birth for a job he will not inherit until past retirement age, a grandfather pushing seventy. 'I don't mind praying to the eternal father,' muttered Edward during a church service marking Queen Victoria's diamond jubilee, 'but I do mind being the only man in the country afflicted with an eternal mother.' But Elizabeth II will never abdicate in her son's favour. There came a rare sag in Andrew Morton's credibility with his suggestion that Charles sulked for a week after she said as much in her 1991 Christmas broadcast. The prince has always known full well (with reluctant respect) that the Queen regards her job as a lifetime commitment – a sacred trust from God, solemnized in her public coronation vows. Abdication would reduce the throne to a job like any other, to be indifferently abandoned at sixty-five, robbing the monarchy of its *sine qua non* mystique. It would also create an awkward precedent, as in Holland, obliging Charles to hand over to William while still trying on the crown for size.

'Absolutely nothing', as Massingberd rightly points out, has meanwhile been done by 'self-satisfied courtiers' to cope with the 'Edward VII situation': namely, 'repeating the error of having a Prince of Wales kick his heels in the ante-room while his mother reigns for sixty, seventy or even eighty years'. One result of this is that Charles has become like his great-great-grandfather in more ways than appeared likely in his youth, when he seemed so full of promise. Another, in the words of Professor Stephen Haseler, is that 'it now seems unlikely that in the early years of the twenty-first century there will be much of a national consensus in favour of a new reign of Charles III'.

Anthony Sampson, for thirty years Britain's leading 'anatomist', suggests that the royal family have themselves created other obstacles to maintaining popular support in the next century:

> Their narrow old-fashioned life-style, revolving round stables, grouse-moors and large country-houses, has become more closely identified with the class-conscious pursuit of money and status. During and after the Second World War, the monarchy prided itself on being detached from the class arrogance of the aristocracy, and able to move naturally among all kinds of people. But in the eighties, with all the competitive advertising and social ambitions, the royal family became more obviously identified with wealth and privilege, and were helping to sustain the recurring British disease, of class.

The same important point is made from a different perspective by the psychiatrist Dr Anthony Storr:

> As babies get older, they discover that just being is not enough: they no longer get love for nothing. But royals go on being treated as worthy of adoration throughout their lives without necessarily doing anything to deserve it . . . To make such eminence derive from an accident of birth rather than from any excellence of personality or achievement is to perpetuate the class structure and snobbery which other nations find so distasteful in British life.

The various worlds of Sampson, Storr, *The Telegraph* and the royal family all seemed to meet in pitched battle on that ultimate upper-class playing-field, the grouse-moor – or, even more frequently, in hunting pink, with three-quarters of Her Majesty's subjects adding their protest to Sampson's metaphorical placard as the royals obliviously sipped their subsidized stirrup-cup. A recent Gallup poll conducted for the League Against Cruel Sports showed that more than 80 per cent of young Britons disapprove of the royal family foxhunting. Opposition was highest, at 84 per cent, among the 25-34 age range; even among those over 65, however, it was fully 65 per cent. Seventy-five per cent disapproved of the royals shooting game birds. The Prince of Wales takes no notice, and hunts blithely on, bobbing between the Quorn and the Beaufort, the Berkeley and the Belvoir. Recently, in his newfound role as a caring father, he has ensured that his sons begin their killing young.

'The need for the conservation of nature has never been greater,' said Prince Philip recently, after agreeing to continue as president of the World Wide Fund for Nature. A few hours later he hosted the biggest shoot of the season, at which no fewer than fifty-six guns destroyed several thousand pheasant. In the last thirty years, it has been calculated, Philip has killed more than 30,000 birds, not to mention an Indian tiger, two crocodiles and at least sixty wild boar, as well as thousands of stag, roe, rabbits, hares, wild ducks, snipe, woodcock, partridge and teal.

Was it because of its president's love of killing animals and birds that the World Wildlife Fund changed its name to the World Wide Fund for Nature? Not merely is the royal obsession with hunting and shooting an essentially class phenomenon; that Philip should be president of such an organization, and remain a blood sports fanatic over the protests of three-quarters of the country, is all part of the royal 'game' that Britain had been seduced into playing for so long.

Not, perhaps, much longer. 'All that is required of us, as the audience at *Peter Pan*, is to say that we don't believe in it any more,' suggests the critic Selina Hastings. 'How many of us would care if we never again saw Princess Anne scowling at a première or Princess Michael self-consciously photogenic in evening dress, or Prince Edward attending the opening of a tennis court in France?'

Richard Littlejohn, the *Sun* columnist and radio talk-show host, was formally censured by the British Radio Authority in 1992 for calling the royal family 'a tax-evading bunch of adulterers'. In early 1993, to an unabashed Littlejohn, the royals were 'a front for the corruption of the establishment'. Fast becoming a working class hero, named 'Irritant of the Year' in the 1992 British newspaper awards, Littlejohn was among the most outspoken of the tabloid columnists, likening the Windsors to the

Corleone family in their ruthless determination to 'hang on
to their power and perks at all costs'. Day by day, his colleagues in the field – collectively known, even to themselves,
as 'the royal rat-pack' – meanwhile relished the seamy side
of royal life, undoubtedly adding to the pressures on some
already strained royal marriages. It was possible even for some
republicans, like Tony Benn, to sympathize with the unnatural
human pressures upon contemporary royalty, dismissing 'those
who tried to build reputations on sniping at members of the royal
family' (MPs, presumably, included) as 'cheap self-publicists'.
To independent observers like Barbara Amiel, it was 'an awful
sight' to watch the royals 'paraded through the streets in cages
constructed by the tabloid press':

> I cannot understand why any person in the House of Windsor
> today would not immediately renounce title and position and
> take nothing but the private income. What possible pathology
> could make any one of them put up with their degradation
> for another minute? . . . The mobs may have killed the
> French royal family but the tabloid press is doing something
> infinitely worse with the Windsors.

Royalists such as Elizabeth Longford blamed all the royals'
troubles on the tabloid press, wishing that Prince Charles, 'a
kind of Pied Piper', could tempt the rat-pack to 'follow him to
Mount Lochnagar, where, like the Brunswick rats, they would
vanish inside, never to be seen again'. The Queen's former press
secretary, Michael Shea, called the tabloid press a 'cancer in the
soft underbelly of the nation'. They were doing a 'huge disfavour
to our society in terms of the damage they do to individuals, to
institutions, to the body politic, to ordinary people, with their
daily mix of sexual innuendo, hypocrisy and lies'.

The tabloids could be criticized for publishing extracts from
the transcripts of private royal telephone calls; but they could
not be blamed for taping the calls in the first place. That was
the work, it was widely suspected, of a special royal unit at
the Government Communications Headquarters (GCHQ), the

high-security 'listening station' in Cheltenham, Gloucestershire, whose staff had plenty of time on their hands since the end of the Cold War. The writer John le Carré, himself a former intelligence officer, had no time for official denials, even from the prime minister. 'Baloney,' cried le Carré. 'GCHQ could have done it, and the odds are that they did . . . A monitoring service would be derelict in its duty if it didn't. The question is whether, having intercepted the phone calls, GCHQ's servants leaked them. On present evidence, there are too many indications that they did.'

That there were sinister forces at work was certainly a suspicion shared by royal writers whose homes or offices had been burgled (Andrew Morton and the present author among them), and other out-of-favour royal familiars who had also experienced theft from their cars or houses. More evidence came on 12 May 1993, when the so-called Highgrove tape [see Appendix F], of a spat between Charles and Diana, suggested that even their sitting-room was bugged. Government denials of secret-service involvement remained unconvincing. If the press had no motivation other than profit, was there a more high-level conspiracy to destabilize the monarchy? The evidence was still sketchy, but circumstances appeared to point to a combination of mischief-making and commercial gain, rather than a fiendish republican plot, behind the leaking of the tapes.

As the Squidgygate transcript worked its evil spell, the tabloids appeared to find an unlikely ally in *The Daily Telegraph*, which conceded that 'the future of the Prince and Princess of Wales is inextricably bound up with the future of the British monarchy', making it a matter of 'obvious' public concern. Lord McGregor, the chairman of the Press Complaints Commission, then himself argued that 'the royal family's life must be open to scrutiny by newspapers':

> You cannot have a private royal family, you cannot have privacy in a royal family. If the monarchy is to be preserved and protected, this can happen only if the truth is known. When the truth is known, the dangers can be removed. It is a public institution and the reason it carries a magic is because the press reports it all the time.

In his evidence to Sir David Calcutt's review of press self-regulation, the Queen's press secretary, Charles Anson, had said that the monarch did not seek 'special treatment' for herself or her family. Then in January 1993, during the controversy following publication of Calcutt's report, a right-wing press baron directly linked the need for a free, unfettered press with the absence of a written constitution and an enacted Bill of Rights. 'Millions of our countrypeople gave their lives, their health and their happiness in two world wars for the defence of democracy,' said Lord Rothermere, owner of the *Daily Mail* and *The Mail on Sunday*. 'It is a sad state indeed that now our precious freedom could be put in jeopardy by a blinkered lawyer, two sad, lost aristocrats, politicians who have been most fairly and others most unfairly attacked by the press, and the advent of a proletarian press, which, although it occurred during the last war, has not yet been understood apparently by the academic classes.'★

There can be no doubt that the tabloid press, self-appointed tribunes of the people, have played a large role in forcing the monarchy to contemplate change, and to let it be forced upon them. But they cannot be blamed for precipitating the end of already unstable marriages any more than they can be blamed for protesting, on behalf of the hard-pressed taxpayer, about the cost of repairing Windsor Castle or building a new royal yacht. For reflecting popular opinion, as evidenced by a stream of polls, they can regard themselves with some justice as messengers blamed for the message – as did Andrew Neil, editor of *The Sunday Times*, when under fire for serializing Morton's book.

Other complaints could be laid at the tabloids' door: their obsession with Fergie's frolics, for instance, at a time of ethnic cleansing in Bosnia, or with the royal tour of Korea on a historic day in recent American history. But that is a price tabloid readers are apparently prepared to pay in vast numbers, preferring the charms of a 'Page Three Girl' to the latest nuances of the

★Rothermere's 'blinkered lawyer' was presumably Calcutt, and the 'sad, lost aristocrats' the Prince and Princess of Wales. The maligned politicians, whether 'fairly' or 'unfairly' attacked, may well have included John Major's star-crossed friends David Mellor and Norman Lamont, and/or, quite possibly, Major himself.

Maastricht debate. Collectively, the tabloid press has merely
reflected the British people's irrational obsession with royalty
– its insatiable relish, however shamefaced, for the latest royal
indiscretion and tittle-tattle. 'Reason takes a holiday in Britain's
relationship with the royal family,' as *The Independent on Sunday*
observed after the separation of the Duke and Duchess of York.

Six years earlier, to the day, an *Independent* journalist had been
wandering down Piccadilly on the day the couple's engagement
had been announced. Seeing three middle-aged women 'burst
into tears of joy' as they read the news in the evening paper, he
was moved to ponder the role of the press in contemporary perceptions of royalty, and its universal view that no other subject
could so kindle the interest of its readers. 'Are we right, or are we
mad?' asked Alexander Chancellor. 'If we [the press] are right,
are you [the reader] then mad? Or are we all equally mad?'

Although they may have fomented it, profiting hugely in the
process, the tabloids could not be blamed for this national madness. Nor could they be accused, as they frequently were during
1992–93, of a deliberate campaign to undermine the monarchy.
For one thing, they would be depriving themselves of their main
source of income; for another, they would be defying the wishes
of their formidable, much-feared proprietors, titled royalists to
a man, jealously proud of their access at court.

The one exception, of course, is Rupert Murdoch, owner
of five newspapers accounting for more than a third of total
national circulation,* as well as a satellite television station claiming to reach three million British homes. It was Murdoch's *Sun*
which earned a belated lawsuit from the Queen, its fourth in
ten years, a month after leaking the text of her 1992 Christmas
broadcast. Spurred on by legal doubts about the wisdom of the
Queen's move, *The Sun*'s belligerent editor, Kelvin MacKenzie,
combatively greeted his monarch: 'See you in court!' He had
good reason to be confident. With Elizabeth II seeking damages

*On March 1993 figures, Murdoch controls 34.1 per cent of total weekly newspaper cir-
culation in Britain. Daily papers: 31.4 per cent (*The Sun* 25.0 per cent, *Today* 3.8 per cent,
The Times 2.6 per cent); Sunday papers: 36.79 per cent of Sunday circulation (*The News
of the World* 28.92 per cent, *The Sunday Times* 7.87 per cent). [Source: Audit Bureau of
Circulation]

in cash – another less than judicious tactic, given the running controversy over her untaxed wealth – legal authorities wondered how she could sue for breach of copyright over a document long since released into the public domain, and quite what financial damage she could claim to have suffered. Were *The Sun* to lose the case, moreover, the copyright laws could thereafter be used to stop more serious investigative journalism as effectively as any ban on phone-tapping and intrusion. If the monarch chose to bring this particular suit, having for years avoided the law courts because they are 'her' courts, would she not henceforth be obliged to sue every inaccurate newspaper story?

All these dilemmas were swiftly and unexpectedly resolved when *The Sun* abruptly caved in, apologized to the Queen for spoiling her Christmas, and agreed to pay £200,000 to Princess Anne's Save the Children Fund. It was so out of character for MacKenzie to eat his words – he had only recently terrorized a Commons select committee on press freedom★ – that explanations were required. According to internal sources, the royal climbdown had been made on orders from the very top. 'It is Rupert Murdoch who feels we should make this very handsome gesture,' said *The Sun*'s assistant editor, Chris Davis. 'It has been discussed at the very highest level.'

Neither Murdoch nor his editors are out to destroy the British monarchy. It is merely another British institution that they choose, quite rightly, to subject to constant scrutiny. The Australian-born magnate's republican sentiments (*see* page 101) stop short of Heathrow's immigration desk, where he turns into a man much more interested in profit and power. A few days before his 1992 weekend with the Queen at Balmoral, for instance, the prime minister went to a dinner party at Murdoch's London flat where the guests included Kelvin MacKenzie. That week's *Sun* was full of damaging stories about Major's embattled colleague and friend, David Mellor; but that little contretemps does not seem to have been the only matter of state on the Murdoch menu. As Major left for Balmoral, *The Sun* ran a

★Referring to the proposed arrangements for a 'watchdog' press tribunal, MacKenzie told MPs that he was 'not going to have some clapped-out judge and two busybodies deciding what our readers want to read'.

leading article calling on the Queen to trim the Civil List and take 'a firm line' with her family. The advice (in due time, of course, accepted) was self-evidently in the royal interest.

Murdoch and his *Sunday Times* editor, Andrew Neil, were called 'moral dwarves' by *The Sunday Telegraph* for serializing Morton's book, while *The Daily Telegraph* charged that Murdoch's papers had 'never made any secret of their republican leanings, nor of their indifference to whether the British throne continues to possess an occupant'. But it was 'a bum rap', Murdoch told his biographer, William Shawcross; Neil was 'a chippy Glaswegian who thinks the whole system is rotten'. Asked if he would like to see the end of the monarchy in Britain, Murdoch replied:

> I'm ambivalent about that. I think you'd have to say No, because I don't think the country has the self-confidence to live without it . . . But is the system holding the country back in this new competitive, open, global village that we

talk about? Is it inhibiting the country's growth? I think it's debatable at least. And I think there is nothing wrong in debating it. But if you show yourself even to be thinking about it, that makes you a figure of hate, because some people get very excited about it.

Another of Thatcher's legacies, symbolized by the Murdoch press and its tabloid brethren, was a diminution of deference among the 'lower' orders to their supposed superiors, the monarchy foremost among them. Most saw this as a distinctly healthy trend. 'The greatest benefit from the current royal troubles would be if they helped to root out that loathsome English vice, deference,' declared the Conservative MP George Walden. 'In its present form the monarchy remains the peak of a stultifying system of deference that still runs through British society, and which takes many forms. Americans defer to money, Frenchmen to brains, and the English to social status.'

As Disraeli wrote to Matthew Arnold: 'Everyone likes flattery; and when it comes to royalty, you should lay it on with a trowel.' Typical of the prevailing deference among parliamentarians was the remark of Edward Heath, the former Conservative prime minister, that the demise of the Wales marriage was 'one of the saddest announcements made by a prime minister in modern times'. Sadder than Black Wednesday? Or Bloody Sunday? Or the deaths of 255 British troops in the Falklands conflict? Heath's fawning was reminiscent of the reveries of the Archbishop of Canterbury after Elizabeth II's coronation: 'Last Tuesday this country and Commonwealth were not far from the kingdom of heaven.' Or of the day in 1977, when the Queen went to Westminster Hall on the occasion of her silver jubilee, to receive a 'loyal address' from both houses of parliament: a velvet curtain had been discreetly drawn across the plaque recording that it was here that King Charles I was sentenced to death.

Such cringing towards the monarchy now jars all the more because of the speed with which that built-in British deference is eroding. 'Magic no longer rules, tradition and Ruritanian pomp are no longer sufficient,' to Professor Haseler. 'People want to know the *rationale* for institutions, particularly those they fund and to which they supposedly owe loyalty.' More ominous still for the royal family were the changing attitudes of Britain's commercial and media élites. 'They reflect a growing sensibility that the monarchy, with its antique social habits and its indifference to merit, sets the wrong values for a country trying to compete in the modern world.'

The generation of Britons who will soon be running the country does not share its parents' uncritical, tribal deference toward the crown. 'Anyone in authority who does not understand that huge swathes of the nation, mostly those under forty and by no means on the left, have had it up to here with royalty, is putting the future of the monarchy at risk,' thundered Walden. 'What sort of country do we want? Reproduction antique?'

If the notion of monarchy initially emerged in primitive tribal society, reflecting mankind's instinctive need for leadership, it seems understandable that after a thousand years the tribe is at last getting restless. But human society is still governed by 'the emotions and instincts of the first hunting primates', maintains Sir Antony Jay, one of the most effective of recent royal exegetists. In Jay's scenario, the Queen is thus the tribal chief of her subjects, to whom popular allegiance is rooted in 'our earliest needs as animals for security and a sense of belonging'. Ceremonies like the Trooping the Colour and the State Opening of Parliament are not empty shows of pomp and circumstance but 'important rituals which affirm tribal membership and celebrate tribal unity and tribal values'.

Even Dr Storr, to whom 'royalty is the apotheosis of the commonplace', grants that human beings, like many social animals, are hierarchical creatures, 'bound to put some of our number at the top of the tree, and to regard such people with a measure of special respect or even awe'. But an anthropologist observing our tribe for the first time, suggests Christopher Hitchens, would be bound to note 'a strongly marked and continuous adherence in the first place to a fetish, and in the second place to a taboo on the discussion of it'.

Of late, however, the decline of deference has combined with that of the Windsors' credibility to break that taboo. The British tribe of the 1990s has become, at the very least, schizophrenic about its monarchy. To Hitchens' fellow republican, Professor Haseler, 'we live a double constitutional life, officially as loyal subjects owing fealty to a medieval institution, unofficially as modern people in a republic. We proclaim all the republican values, believing in government by the people while possessing no entrenched rights against the state and being owned by the crown; we talk incessantly of that most republican of ideas, citizenship, yet remain *subjects* of Her Majesty; we believe in the separation of church and state while continuing with an established church.'

Again, the personalities are inextricably intertwined with the points of principle. On the one hand, there are the Windsors themselves, still stuck in a Victorian time-warp – failing to 'connect up with contemporary life', in Anthony Sampson's view, to an extent which now threatens their survival. 'The immense Victorian apparatus, from glass coaches to palaces, remains largely intact,' creating illusions for the occupants as much as for the public. Sampson calls as witnesses the three very different 'commoners' whose royal marriages have failed because they found it impossible to adapt to the Windsors' 'rarefied and antiquated style of life'. After their departure, the royals themselves are left 'high-and-dry, curtseying to each other even in private, with a court of flatterers, hangers-on, soothsayers and rich layabouts to protect them from reality.'

On the other hand there is the institution of monarchy, entrusted to the Windsors' care, and so equally out of touch with contemporary notions of democracy. Modernizing the monarchy, however, is seen by ardent royalists as a contradiction in terms. To Worsthorne, it is 'a conservative institution or it is nothing'. Does Britain, he muses, want to retain such an institution? Would there be any politician prepared to champion it on these terms; and would the present heir to the throne ever be content to head such an anachronism? 'Only when these questions can be answered affirmatively will the monarchy's future be secure, which is another way of saying that its prospects have seldom been bleaker.'

★

John Major sees the monarchy as 'a very precious part of our way of life – a rock of stability in a changing world'. But he also thinks that the Queen's offer to pay a modest amount of income tax has 'brought the monarchy up to date'. To Major, that one concession is enough to make it 'an institution relevant to the 1990s, just as a hundred years ago it was an institution relevant to the 1890s . . . The monarchy has evolved and changed. I think the Queen has judged it very well.'

The current atmosphere suggests otherwise: that the monarchy will have to 'change and evolve' rather more to ensure even its medium-term survival. As Roy Hattersley, the senior Labour politician, has warned: 'The Establishment always responds to the threat of real reform by making some concessions to the reformers.' On the financial front alone, little has happened to outdate the view expressed in 1911 by the early feminist Vera Brittain, the mother of Baroness (Shirley) Williams, that the royals are 'expensive lunatics kept in motors and stables by an industrious nation's toil'. The heir to the throne surely realized Worsthorne's worst fears when he told a recent interviewer that 'members of the royal family should be allowed to take a job when they want'. Or join a dole queue? Someone should perhaps brief the prince that it is not quite as simple as that in Major's Britain, where there are currently more than three million subjects of the crown who would very much like to be allowed to 'take a job when they want'.

Charles also raised again the question of financing the monarchy from the Crown Estate (*see* Appendix D).

> I think it of absolute importance that the monarch should have a degree of financial independence from the state. I am not prepared to take on the position of sovereign of this country on any other basis. I must have independence, and you can only have that through financial independence.

Lest it be thought that his family's personal wealth might in itself guarantee such independence, he went on: 'Misunderstanding of the situation is *enormous*. People understand the basics but have no idea of the details.' Perhaps, in that case, they might be made public. Until they are, a majority of Britons will continue to believe that the Windsors are quite capable of financing their own palaces, yachts, planes and trains without the taxpayer's ever more reluctant assistance.

Among the many critics less satisfied than Major by the royal tax concession of 1992 was the former MP Robert Kilroy-Silk, now a talk-show host and *Daily Express* columnist, who considered that the Queen's exemption from inheritance tax wrought 'the worst of all worlds'. If the monarch was to be treated like everyone else, as the prime minister had affirmed, then she must be subject to the same tax rules as the rest of her subjects.

> Why is it acceptable, in John Major's supposedly fair and classless society, for those with relatively little, but hard-earned wealth, to have it taken from them bit by bit until there is little left to pass to their children? But why is it *not* acceptable to apply the same rules to the very wealthy, who have never had to work for a penny of their great riches?... If the Queen was really as sensitive to public opinion as it is claimed, and if she had really volunteered to pay tax instead of being forced into it by hostile criticism, she would have offered, no, insisted upon, being treated exactly like the rest of us.

Popular support for the republican movement of the 1870s derived partly from disenchantment with the adulterous Prince of Wales, more from outrage at the huge public subsidy paid an elderly Queen who did not appear to need it. As the historian Colin Matthew has observed, however, protests over the royal finances in the 1990s have even more in common with the anti-corruptionalist republicanism of the 1820s. Writing in mid-1992, Matthew suggested that it was 'more worrying for the monarchy', in an age when the Labour Party had long since shed any vestige of its republican tradition, that 'the most effective assaults on the monarchy are coming from the right'.

Nine months and one tax concession later, the Labour Party finally moved on to the offensive. In mid-January 1993, amid the heir to the throne's Camillagate embarrassments, a leading member of Labour's shadow cabinet finally lost patience and broke ranks. Britain could soon become a republic unless the royal family 'changes its ways', warned Jack Straw, widely regarded as a potential Labour prime minister. Its only hope of survival was as 'a much tighter and more limited constitutional monarchy' like those of the Netherlands or Sweden, where 'a more democratic royal family underpins rather than undermines the monarchy's constitutional role'.

Support for the monarchy as presently constituted, said Straw, was 'palpably declining' in Britain. Most people accepted the justification for a constitutional monarchy - 'that the state, the rule of law and the stability of its institutions should be embodied in a different identity from the partisan politicians of the day' – but they were increasingly questioning the utility of eighteenth-century institutions such as the House of Lords and the judiciary (which had 'sheltered conveniently behind the monarchy'). Those institutions, he warned, 'depend powerfully on deference and obfuscation. Neither is compatible with a fully functioning democracy.' The latest crisis had left the present system 'without a serious future'. As Her Majesty's Opposition, the Labour Party had to think about constitutional reform 'as a matter of priority'.

There was no shortage of suggestions. Although the Labour leader, John Smith, was quick to emphasize that Straw was speaking in a personal capacity, he was soon joined on the barricades by another shadow cabinet member, Marjorie ('Mo') Mowlem, the party's spokesman on the Citizen's Charter. 'I would suggest that we need to look at tax, removal of much of the pomp and ceremony, and an examination of the constitutional role and the accountability of those who advise.' The weekly audience between the Queen and the prime minister was 'surely out of date'; the Queen could be kept informed by other means. And there was 'clearly a need to review the role of the monarch in the event of a hung parliament. I do not believe it should be the Queen's role effectively to decide who should govern.'

Both Straw and Mowlem were members of Labour's constitutional committee, chaired by the shadow Home Secretary,

Tony Blair, which was already committed to reviewing the
royal prerogative, reforming the House of Lords, introducing
a Bill of Rights and incorporating the European Declaration
of Human Rights into the British constitution. 'I am not a
republican,' said Mowlem. 'I don't want to see an end to the
monarchy.' But there was a need to look at how respect for the
royal family could be rebuilt.

A survey now revealed that 24 per cent of Labour MPs believed
Britain should become a republic, while 32 per cent said the royal
family should be reformed along the lines of their more modest
Dutch and Swedish counterparts. Only 14 per cent wanted no
change. Michael Meacher, Labour's overseas aid spokesman,
said: 'I would like to see an end to the mystique of the royal
family – the way in which it is used to underpin a class system
in this country. Although I don't see us becoming a republic
yet, things are moving in that direction.' Clive Soley, former
housing spokesman, said he favoured a republic. 'I don't think
we can any longer justify the royal family. We need a radical
overhaul of the British constitution. In the long run, with the
move towards a federal Europe, I think it is inevitable that we
will become a republic.' From Labour's back benches, Joe Ashton
said he would 'get rid of' the royal family: 'I wouldn't exile them
or do them any damage. They could live like all the other nobility
and have a peaceful time at Sandringham with their heads on the
pound note but without any power. Sadly, it is not going to
happen unless we have a revolution.'

Now Labour's leader had something of a revolution on
his own hands. Mounting a 'damage containment' operation,
fearing Conservative attempts to paint Labour as a republican
party, Smith strenuously denied that he was in favour of
abolishing the monarchy, diverting attention to the party's
policy on the House of Lords: 'The hereditary element has
got to go. I've never understood how it was remotely possible
to defend it.' Labour would institute 'a House of Lords of life
peers'. But the troops were restless. Another Labour MP, Bob
Cryer, now called for the Queen to take shorter holidays and
provide 'better value for money', urging her to 'set an example
to the nation' by agreeing to accept a 'performance-related

contract'.* As a Gallup poll showed that 65 per cent of the public wanted the monarchy reformed along more democratic lines, Tony Banks MP called for a referendum on the monarchy's future: 'We should look at the whole institution, and look at ways to ensure that the Queen comes in line with everyone else paying tax.'

An emboldened Straw now went further, calling the royal family 'deeply decadent'. Namesake of one of the leaders of the 1381 Peasants' Revolt, executed for trying to overthrow King Richard II, Straw said the Windsors were 'at the apex of a separate society of extremely rich people'. A less than ringing intervention by Major – expressing 'a growing fear that we may lose so much that is precious to this country' and emphasizing the need for 'an unbroken chain of community linking the monarchy to the humblest household' – did not prevent more senior Labour figures throwing caution to the winds. 'We have to ask the question: is it right to exempt the Queen from inheritance tax?' said the shadow Chancellor of the Exchequer, Gordon Brown. 'The challenge to the government is to explain why it has exempted the monarchy from inheritance tax but done nothing to honour its election promise to cut tax for millions of ordinary home-owning families.' Labour frontbenchers now privately conceded that the Queen's private wealth would 'undoubtedly' become liable to tax if they came to power. Indeed, they 'relished the prospect' of the royal wealth being eroded. 'Of course I want the Queen to pay inheritance tax,' said one. 'That will ensure that the monarchy gradually becomes more like the Scandinavian model some of us want.'

Even the Liberal Democratic Party now got in on the act as its leader, Paddy Ashdown, foresaw 'a radical overhaul' of the monarchy if it was to 'fend off challenges to its position'.

*In this Cryer was echoing the monarchist critic John Grigg, the former Lord Altrincham, who the previous year had described references in the film *Elizabeth R* to the Queen's holidays as 'short' as 'disingenuous, to say the least. They are by any standards long.' The six weeks she was said to spend at Balmoral each summer 'are in fact ten weeks . . . Her six weeks at Sandringham in the winter were passed off in the film as just Christmas and the New Year.' In addition, there was a 'substantial' break in the spring. 'Altogether these probably constitute the largest amount of holiday taken by any major and active public figure in the world.'

Simon Hughes, the Liberal Democrat who had originally led the campaign for the Queen to pay tax, agreed with Labour that the exemption from inheritance tax was 'indefensible'. It was time for a Labour heavyweight, the former deputy leader Roy Hattersley, to reclaim the high ground by elevating the level of the debate. The existence of a hereditary monarch was 'a proclamation of the belief that some human beings are – by their nature and their origins – superior to others.' The royal family did not exist outside the class system. 'It stands at the pinnacle of our social hierarchy, simultaneously challenging the arguments in favour of both equality and morality.' To believe that one family possesses hereditary virtue was 'an innately unreasonable conviction . . . To build a constitution on such a fatuous proposition can only serve to create a society which, at best, is firmly rooted in the past.'

As left and right reunited on this unlikely ground, the debate was best summed up by the Conservative, George Walden: 'What is needed is clear: a greatly scaled-down institution where essentials are retained and unhealthy accretions dispensed with; reform of the House of Lords; and – most difficult of all to achieve – an adult attitude to royalty.'

Britain may not yet be ready to dispose of its monarchy, but it is certainly in a mood to dictate terms for its continuance. As the movement for reform gathers strength, there is little doubt where to start.

By the end of April 1993, five months after the Great Fire of Windsor, the British public had contributed a grand total of £25,000 to an appeal fund aiming to raise £40 million towards the cost of repairing the castle. Contrary to all expectations, the Queen herself has made no offer to contribute out of her own pocket – merely opening Buckingham Palace to the public for a temporary period, at £8.00 a head, thus charging Britons to visit a building which they already pay millions to maintain. She regarded her income tax concession, it seemed, as a *quid pro quo* not merely for more sympathetic treatment from the press, but for an end to the universal carping about her wealth. Which royal aspiration was the more hopelessly optimistic? It was hard to tell, royalists having argued for six months that the British people would overdose on anti-royal propaganda, that public opinion would soon 'turn around' and revert to its traditionally tacit deference. The Windsor fund had been envisaged by the Palace as a financial 'sympathy vote' for the Queen, in the expectation that 1993 would see the public anger of late 1992 melt back into the usual reverence, even fellow-feeling. On that measure, the hard-pressed British taxpayer was as angry as ever. The money raised so far, said one expert, would not be enough even to pay for the curtains. The restoration committee chaired by Prince Philip – not, to the vocal relief of architects, Prince Charles★ – was going to have to look elsewhere for its money.

As time wore on, it would again fall to the hapless Peter Brooke to announce that the bulk of this vast amount – estimates kept varying from £40 million to £60 million – would be coming out of the government's 'contingency fund': in other words, the taxpayer's pocket. Next up would be the Armed Forces Minister, Archie Hamilton, on the pressing (and even more expensive) subject of a new royal yacht. How much would the public voluntarily contribute towards the £80 million estimate for a new *Britannia*? It was a ministerial task none of his government colleagues envied.

If the monarchy is to descend to a plane remotely commensurate with the times, the royal yacht, trains and aircraft will clearly have to go. To be deprived of the world's biggest private yacht, maintained at the expense of people who cannot themselves afford to go on holiday, is not yet to be reduced to the level of the 'bicycle kings' at whom the British royal family have sneered for so long. It is to acknowledge that the globe is no longer one-quarter pink; that the UK is extremely lucky to be considered one of the G-7 countries, let alone one of the 'Big Five'; and that the institution of monarchy is supposed to symbolize the Britain of the 1990s, not the 1890s.

★'Prince Philip is one of the unsung heroes of British architecture,' Michael Manser, a past president of the Royal Institute of British Architects, told *The Independent on Sunday*. 'He has a solid background knowledge about design and designers. Unlike his son, who is deeply emotional and prejudiced when it comes to architecture, Prince Philip has an open mind.'

The future of the royal train is in any case threatened by the government's plans to privatize British Rail. Before a new company is set up (as planned) to operate the luxuriously furnished, 14-coach train, the cost should be as closely scrutinized as the symbolic merits of travelling British Rail. The jets and helicopters of the Queen's Flight should be sold off, or made over to the RAF, and the royal family should begin the scaling-down process forthwith by following the example set by both the Princess of Wales and the prime minister. To fly British Airways is not merely much cheaper; it is to 'fly the flag'.

As for the royal yacht, fast approaching the end of its working life: it has been suggested that *Britannia* should be handed over to the Royal Navy – which would seem just, as it is entirely financed by the Ministry of Defence. But it would surely be much more constructive (and cost-effective) to sell *Britannia* to the tourist industry to become a floating hotel-cum-museum, perhaps alongside Tower Bridge, not unlike the *Queen Mary* at Long Beach, California. That way, the monarchy could really begin to earn the tourist dollars so often quoted these days as the last unassailable defence for its survival.

Most Britons believe that the monarchy's 'greatest value' is as a tourist attraction, according to a Harris poll conducted for *The Daily Express* in July 1992. An astonishing 30 per cent rated its tourist appeal 'the best argument for having a monarchy', followed by 21 per cent for its provision of a non-political head of state. (Ten per cent voted for 'pomp and ceremony', 9 per cent for 'continuity', 8 per cent for 'the link it provides with the Commonwealth', 7 per cent for the royal family's 'personal qualities' and just 3 per cent for the 'good example they set'. Six per cent voted for none of the above.)

Richard Branson, founder of Virgin Atlantic airlines, has recently expressed the view that the abolition of the monarchy would be 'a financial disaster' for the British tourist industry. 'If we became a republic,' said Branson, 'the future for tourism here would be incalculable. It would certainly result in the loss of hundreds of millions of pounds in revenue.' The royals, he believed, 'pay for themselves ten thousand times over'. Branson found support from a perhaps unexpected quarter, the vice industry. 'The Queen does a great job of attracting tourists to Britain,' said Janet, a hooker in London's Paddington district, to an enquirer from Rupert Murdoch's *News of the World*. 'Prostitutes are part of the tourist industry. We would be hard hit if the royals weren't around.'

More than 17 million foreign tourists visit Britain each year, spending an annual average of more than £7 billion. Almost half watch the Changing of the Guard and two million visit the Tower of London (technically a royal palace, where 1993 saw the display of the Crown Jewels undergoing 'Disneyfication', to shudders of protest from the Queen and the Prince of Wales). But even the most ardent royalists were somewhat reluctant to see tourism become the last, best defence for the institution supposedly somewhat more central to the British way of life. 'Britannia would have come to a pretty pass,' as Elizabeth Longford put it, 'if tourists were to be the arbiters of her constitution.'

Even the tourism defence falls, however, in light of a remarkable new survey of American tourists conducted in the summer of 1993 by the New York-based travel magazine *Condé Nast Traveler*. Its startling findings completely undermine the received wisdom on the monarchy's powers as a tourist attraction, hitherto deemed 'immeasurable'. Over three-quarters of American tourists, 77.2 per cent, said that their interest in the royal family 'does not at all influence' their decision to visit Britain. Almost nine out of ten, 87.7 per cent, would still visit Buckingham Palace and Windsor Castle even if they were not occupied by royalty. And the vast majority, 93.5 per cent, said that it 'would not affect their decision to visit Britain' if the monarchy were abolished.

Nine out of ten respondents, 90.9 per cent, said that it 'would not affect their opinion of Britain' if the Prince and Princess of Wales got divorced; nearly all of those surveyed, 99.3 per cent, said the end of the royal marriage would not 'make them less likely to visit Britain in the future'. (A third, 33.3 per cent, said they would like to meet Diana, as opposed to 8.7 per cent for Charles.) Although 72.8 per cent of American tourists said they were 'interested' in the British royal family, only 15.6 per cent were 'very' interested, with 57.2 per cent 'somewhat'. A mere

13.8 per cent said that they would be likely, while visiting London, to buy a souvenir bearing a likeness of the Queen or any member of her family.

Buried away in the small print of the £75 million of public money spent to finance the monarchy in 1991–92 was the sum of £210,000 for 'the administration of the honours system'. It is not, in the scheme of things, a huge amount: the same, for instance, as the cost of royal equerries, though rather less than the publicity budget (£380,000) and rather more than was spent on computers (£123,000) or stationery (£139,000). But the figure is surrounded with mystery – given, for instance, that the Queen is not obliged to pay for the postage stamps which bear her head through the mail-boxes of those being offered peerages, knighthoods, or membership of the Order of a long defunct Empire.

The figure becomes even more mysterious in light of the discovery – not hitherto known to the taxpaying public - that those receiving honours are these days invited by Buckingham Palace to pay £55 for a twenty-minute videotape of their investiture. The video in fact amounts to their own thirty seconds of glory stitched into a standard tape of the Queen handing out awards. With a fixed camera in place throughout the proceedings, the former BBC cameraman in charge of the operation does not even have to work too hard for his percentage.

But the crown's financial interest in the honours system is far less important than its role in entrenching the class distinctions which bedevil British society. 'It is hard to imagine the social pyramid enduring as long as it has,' says Hitchens, 'without a crown at its apex'. The honours system, he suggests, would look 'tawdry and corrupt if it were not sanctified by the mystery of the crown.'

In the 1993 New Year Honours, announced at the end of the Queen's 'annus horribilis', Elizabeth II gave a knighthood to her doctor, Dr Anthony Dawson, and the Royal Victorian Medal to the boss of the firm which cleans the windows of Buckingham Palace. In a list which also knighted Anthony ('Hannibal the Cannibal') Hopkins and the television interviewer David Frost, Royal Victorian Medals went to the Prince of Wales's senior chef, Mervyn Wycherley, and the woman who looked after the Princess of Wales's clothes for ten years, Evelyn Dagley. Sir Antony Jay, already knighted for his services to the monarchy, was made a Commander of the Victorian Order for writing the script of the official film *Elizabeth R*, as was its director, Edward Mirzoeff; the cameraman, Philip Bonham Carter (who also made the royals' home movie of Anne's wedding to Tim Laurence), and the sound engineer, Peter Edwards, were made mere Lieutenants. Chief Inspector John Askew, a former protection officer to the Duke and Duchess of York, was made a Member of the Order, as was Tom Corby, the recently retired court correspondent of the Press Association news agency.

So much for Prime Minister John Major's self-professed goal of a classless society. Even *The Times*, long regarded as 'the noticeboard of the Establishment', quoted Aristotle ('Dignity does not consist in getting honours, but in deserving them') *en route* to concluding that honours 'cheapen society and divide the classes'. Despite Major's declared intent to reform the system, this was the same old 'hierarchical, huge, craftily networked, petty pyramid of baubles to reward the boys and girls who have pleased their political masters.' The size and complexity of the orders 'dished out' reflected 'the last doubtful enchantments of the gang warfare of the Middle Ages.' The British Empire Medals, which accounted for roughly a third of all such awards, were named after an empire that had ceased to exist thirty years before. In a recent radio interview Major had said he believed 'honours should reflect merit'; to *The Times*, this was 'like an American televangelist bearing witness that he is against sin.'

As long as the crown, 'the fount of all honour', so jealously guards its powers of patronage, it will continue to be tainted by a system grown complacent and corrupt. There is nothing wrong, *per se*, with rewarding genuine service to the community; but the system as presently constituted has long caused widespread offence. It sanctions, for instance, unacceptable distinctions between ranks, with the grander gongs reserved for officers and gentlemen, while sports and showbiz stars are fobbed off with lower degrees of an Order invented for servants of the British Empire. Only the upper-echelon professions – High

Court judges, army officers, senior civil servants - *automatically* bring certain honours with each rung of the career ladder.

Worst of all, political knighthoods have become rewards for undistinguished backbenchers who have always toed the party line but failed to make government rank – those who, in *The Times*'s phrase, 'have never thought of thinking for themselves at all'. In recent years the purchasing of titles via contributions to the funds of political parties – often by captains of publicly quoted industries, without reference to their shareholders – has become as blatant as Lloyd George's practice of selling knighthoods and peerages *à la carte*. Since the creation of life peerages to balance the hereditary presence in the House of Lords, moreover, the phrase 'working peer' has too often proved a contradiction in terms. 'Honours are by nature political,' as *The Times* summed up, 'from the warlord kings who rewarded their magnates with titles to James I refreshing his Treasury by flogging baronetcies . . . [But] a reforming government, which wanted to make Britain a country at ease with itself, would see that its honours did less to cheapen society and divide the classes.'

Major's promises of reform have so far resulted only in minor tinkering with the system. By coming up, meanwhile, with the 'Charter Mark', an award given to individuals and organizations approved by his Citizen's Charter, the prime minister is inadvertently in danger of setting up his own personal system to rival the royal honours. 'It is a complete threat to the honours system,' says no less a figure than Lord Scarman, the former Appeal Court judge, and president of the Constitutional Reform Centre. 'I have no doubt about that.'

If reform of the honours system would reflect well on the monarchy, allying it with service and merit rather than mere rank and wealth, disestablishment of the Church of England would help remove several more layers of hypocrisy. The paradox of an 'established' state church in a multi-denominational society probably exercises as many Britons as are these days regular Anglican churchgoers: something less than 3 per cent. But to those directly involved – church leaders, royal family and, to a lesser extent, politicians – it is of central significance. There's very little divinity hedging a late twentieth-century king; but this institutionalized link between crown and church lends the monarchy a useful if spurious dignity, while enabling the Anglican hierarchy to maintain political and financial advantages over its rivals. The price to be paid by the church is the surrender of its senior appointments to Downing Street; that to be paid by the crown is at least some semblance of Christian conduct. Were the monarch no longer the Supreme Governor of the Church of England, her heir might have been spared many of the embarrassing questions – and answers – recently on constitutional lips.

Could the established church, for instance, crown a divorced, even adulterous monarch, and accept him as its titular head? 'We don't change the constitution,' said Dr Edward Norman, an authority in ecclesiastical law, 'because people have marital problems.' Less rigid churchmen have been more outspoken. 'It has to be asked whether a man who has cheated on his wife so consistently could properly become Supreme Governor of the Church of England,' wrote the Archdeacon of York, the Venerable George Austin. 'Perhaps by the time Charles ascends the throne, the Ten Commandments will have been reduced to a more manageable number.'

A 1992 survey showed that a majority of MPs now believe that the church should be disestablished, moving one church lawyer to warn: 'I cannot see how there would be any role left for the monarch. The two go together.' On the contrary, there would be obvious advantages to a reformed constitutional monarchy; if it focused on 'the official duties of the sovereign rather than the private morality of a dynasty,' as *The Times* perceived, the royal family 'might fare rather better'. To the columnist Simon Jenkins, the coronation service which symbolizes the umbilical link between church and state is a 'compote of show business, piety and paganism', as anachronistic as the concept of a nation state imbued with religious, let alone sectarian, significance:

> Tell me that church and state achieve this symbiosis through an anointed hereditary line, biased towards males, and I despair of reason. I will watch the resulting spectacle with patriotic tears in my eyes; but forgive me if I afterwards lunch with Voltaire.

Again, the point of principle cannot be discussed in isolation from the personal dilemma which has brought it back on to the national agenda. Were a divorced Prince Charles to contemplate remarriage, he would be bound by the Church of England's Act of Convocation (1957), which ordained that 'in order to maintain the principle of lifelong obligation which is inherent in every legally contracted marriage, and is expressed in the plainest terms in the marriage service, the church should not allow the use of that service in the case of anyone who has a former spouse living'. Under the 1701 Act of Settlement, Prince Charles could not leave the Anglican communion or marry a Roman Catholic. Under the 1772 Royal Marriages Act, he could not remarry without the consent of the monarch and parliament.

In a better Britain, with a reformed constitution, it would be possible to wish the Prince of Wales well in any second marriage he might care to make – which would no more prevent him becoming king than environment secretary, president of the Royal Institute of British Architects or manager of the England football team. The only difference is that the first job would be his by virtue of parentage, while the others would require some evidence of ability, in competition with other candidates. As it stands, the defence of the constitution requires displays of hypocrisy as breathtaking as that of a legal adviser to the General Synod of the Church of England, who has baldly declared that there is 'nothing in statute law to say that a monarch can't be divorced and Supreme Governor' – thus sweeping aside most canon law to preserve the church's handy alliance with the crown.

If either church, crown or indeed government wishes the monarchy to reflect a twentieth-century Britain, there is urgent need for repeal of both these eighteenth-century statutes. The Act of Settlement (which ordains that any royal who 'shall profess the popish religion or shall marry a papist' must be treated 'as if said person were naturally dead'*) is clearly offensive in today's heterogeneous society – especially at a time of schism in the established church, when 'the greatest upheaval since the

*The Queen's permission was required for the Earl of St Andrews, elder son of the Duke of Kent, to marry a (lapsed) Roman Catholic divorcee in an Edinburgh register office in 1988. He was obliged to renounce his right of succession to the throne.

Reformation' is driving increasing numbers of both clergy and laity to take their faith elsewhere.

Although the Act's repeal would endanger the House of Windsor's legal claim to the throne, even as staunch a royalist as Lady Longford wishes to be rid of it. Lord Tebbit's complaint that it would 'signal the end of the British monarchy by bringing it under the reach of Rome' she rightly dismisses as 'out of touch with the Europe of the future'.

The Europe of the future, whether federal or not, holds different challenges for the monarchy. The Queen may not share her subjects' concern about the potential loss of national sovereignty ('her family,' a courtier explained to Anthony Sampson, had 'long ago come to terms with losing their own political power'); but she should perhaps concern herself with other aspects of the Maastricht Treaty. Professor David Cannadine, for instance, finds it 'difficult to envisage a serious role for the British royal house in any tighter form of continental federation'.

To take Cannadine's point, it is not necessary to rouse Lord Wyatt's familiar apoplexy by joining the 'lacklustre defeatists who see Britain ever dwindling in importance, a cipher on the world stage'. Nor is it just to read the treaty, wherein it appears that the British monarch will henceforth join her subjects as a mere citizen of Europe. It is to acknowledge that integration into 'the very heart of Europe' – the course on which John Major is determined to lead Britain, even against its will – may well involve constitutional arrangements more in line with those of our new democratic partners. If Britons are to be citizens of Europe, might it not be time they became citizens of Britain?

Where else in Europe is the citizenry part-governed by people who *inherit* their seats in parliament, unaccountable to any electorate? As Britain adapts to the European way of democracy, a stream of new and revised legislation should at last prove the need for a written constitution for this country, complete with a Bill of Rights. Were it to include provision for a Supreme Court, it might be possible to pursue civil and human rights cases without resort to the European Court at The Hague. Were

it to lead to a Freedom of Information Act, the British disease
of secrecy might join that of class on the list of threatened,
if not yet endangered species.

Have Major's protracted negotiations ensured that his monarch will receive immunity from European employment and
discrimination laws, as she does from her own? Has he seen
to it that no European court will be able to summon her as
a witness, even a defendant, as is the case in her own British
courts? Will our European partners be content for the British
sovereign to travel without a passport, drive without taking a
test, own numerous dogs without buying a licence?

Which European monarch's face will appear on the integrated
European currency, the federal European stamp? Rampant stan-
dardization throughout the community seems certain to force
the British royal family to adapt to the ways of the 'bicycle
kings' of Europe. Nothing could seem more likely to secure
their future – unless, of course, they expect the taxpayer to pay
for the bicycles.

If the twenty-first century sees King William V performing
the State Opening of Parliament in a suit and tie, rather than
a crown and ermine robes, then the British monarchy will
have been saved by the Maastricht Treaty. If His Majesty arrives in a Rolls-Royce rather than a golden horse-drawn coach,
refers to himself in the singular rather than the plural, and
does not expect elderly aristocrats to walk backwards before
him, bearing five-hundred-year-old relics on velvet cushions,
Britain will at last have emerged from the long shadows of its
past and woken up to its future.

Queen Beatrix of the Netherlands gave the 'bicycle kings' their
name when, as a child, she cycled each day from the royal palace
to the local grammar school (as, in due time, did her three sons,
all educated at state schools). A political science and law graduate,
Beatrix pays all the same taxes as her fellow-citizens on all her
sources of income, from her state allowance to her income as a
professional sculptor. After tax, Beatrix pays for everything from
electricity (free of charge to the British royal palaces) to security
(paid by the Home Office at some £20 million a year). Her fleet

of royal cars consists of two Ford Granadas. Now fifty-five, the Queen will retire at the age of sixty, to be succeeded by Crown Prince Willem-Alexander. Holland takes great pride in Beatrix and her family, who are immensely popular.

In a recent conversation with Elizabeth Longford, Prince Charles insisted that Britain had 'a great deal to learn from the Europeans'; the trouble with his fellow-countrymen was that they were too 'insular to learn from foreigners'. If he still wishes to be their head of state, he now has a chance to set an example by learning from that of Holland's Queen Beatrix – or of Denmark's Queen Margrethe, who holds open court at least once a month, listening to the problems of as many as sixty people per session. Or of the Queen of Spain, who manages to make do without any ladies-in-waiting. Or of the Swedish monarchy, which has done away with the rule of primogeniture – also offensive to a civilized contemporary society – so that the succession now passes to the eldest child of the sovereign, whether male or female.

Back home, there is always a plentiful flow of good advice from John Grigg, the former Lord Altrincham, who believes that the monarchy should patronize the public sector more than it does. The late Prince William of Gloucester, for instance, was the first royal this century to serve in the diplomatic corps. Today there are many more options which the royal family has, as yet, shown no disposition to take up, including the National Health Service and the state schools: 'It would surely be good for morale if a prince were to become a state school-teacher, or a princess a NHS nurse.'

The Queen is head of state not just of the United Kingdom, but of fifteen other countries, including Australia, New Zealand, Canada and Jamaica. She is also head of the Commonwealth, a political association comprising nations in every continent, with a combined population approaching 1,500 million. It may now be too late for Elizabeth II to establish residence in any of the Commonwealth countries, as Grigg has suggested, but it is not too late for the Prince of Wales.

Take, for instance, India. During her entire reign the Queen has spent less than a month, in total, in a country which, though formally a republic, is still 'at heart profoundly monarchist'.

Hence Grigg's suggestion that the Prince of Wales, if he wishes to follow his mother as head of the Commonwealth, should make his home in India for a while, even learn Hindu – thus creating 'a vast new constituency, as it were, for the head of the Commonwealth'. The prince 'would gain immeasurably, and so would the institution he serves, if he were to become less conservative and more genuinely independent'.

With Australia on course to discard the monarchy by the end of the Queen's reign, and look to its future as an independent republic, it cannot be long before other major Commonwealth nations such as Canada, New Zealand and the former British colonies of the Caribbean follow suit. Where, after all, is the logic in loyalty to a monarch who is not merely a foreigner, but chooses to live thousands of miles away? As the Queen's dominions fragment, so inevitably will the Commonwealth which binds them. To many Britons, in any case, it is these days an increasingly irrelevant political grouping, uncomfortably redolent of the days of empire; and the human rights record of some of its members has led more than one recent commentator to dismiss it as 'a collection of more or less corrupt dictatorships'.

So it is hardly surprising that the Queen's unique links with the Commonwealth, and her especial concern for its members' interests, have become a growing source of potential trouble between crown and government in Britain, most recently during the contretemps over South African sanctions. At the end of the present reign, it would seem more than time to sever the link. Contrary to popular belief, the British sovereign is not the Commonwealth's *ex-officio* head; the position, though not formally elective, is held by invitation rather than hereditary right. A twenty-first-century Commonwealth may well choose to institute its own electoral system, or approach a more obviously suitable candidate, such as an elder statesman from an African or Asian member-country.

Closer to home, there are increasing numbers of Britons now beginning to question the hereditary principle as a logical twentieth-century method of choosing their own head of state. So much is done in his or her name, supposedly on their behalf, that they are asking whether they should not, perhaps, be entitled to some say in the choice of the individual purporting to represent their corporate identity and aspirations.

At present, the politicians elected by the British people are pleased to call themselves Her Majesty's Government and Her Majesty's Loyal Opposition. The Queen's peace is kept by the Royal Navy and the Royal Air Force. It is illegal to mail a letter which does not bear the Queen's head, and inelegant not to speak the Queen's English. Even if separate parliaments are eventually won by the Scottish and Welsh Nationalists, not to mention the embattled inhabitants of Northern Ireland, they and the English will all still co-habit a federal state called the United Kingdom.

There are even those who wonder whether Britain needs a head of state at all. 'Why,' asks one such, Matthew Parris, 'do we need mascots, bones, relics, arks of the covenant, princes or presidents, pieces of honorific fluff to be for us the nation? Our ancestors and our descendants, our past and our future, are the nation! We are the nation.' In less apocalyptic moments, he confesses that he would 'rather be ruled by people who make embarrassing phone calls than by people who tape-record them'. To Parris, however, a political columnist and former Conservative MP:

> Royalty, in an age of reason, is a lie. Royalty in Britain asks us to believe things which are not true: to show a deference for which there is no honest basis. Royalty, placed at the apex of aristocracy, legitimizes habits of deference to qualities other than merit. Royalty in Britain is the single most potent symbol of class, and all the unfairness and all the waste of human potential that goes with it.

Are the British ready to put their heads before their hearts – their understanding, in Bagehot's terms, before their feelings – and choose their head of state, by democratic means, from among their own number? Though self-evidently logical, it is a leap of faith which still seems out of the national character. 'Monarchy is neither necessary nor sufficient to a democratic constitution', conceded *The Times* recently, reaching the less-than-inspiring conclusion that 'the strength of the British constitution lies as much in surviving the monarchy as in benefiting from it'.

This British gift for paradox – or is it, perhaps, self-punishment? – will surely remain the crown's best hope for survival. No matter how reasonable, how phlegmatic, how polemical the arguments advanced in favour of an elected head of state – in favour, in other words, of that dread word 'republic' – the British still clap their hands to their ears, ever dreaming of pageantry and princesses. Take the eminently reasonable voice, for instance, of the psychologist Dr Anthony Storr:

> There is something to be said for a head of state who can carry out ceremonial functions and represent Britain without also representing a political party. But surely we can choose such a head of state rather than having one thrust upon us. Our psychological need for a representative leader ought to be met democratically.

Or the phlegmatic tones of Professor Stephen Haseler, chairman of *Republic*, who leavens his pragmatism with a dash of romance:

> Over the next few years we should outline a written re-publican constitution to be implemented when the reign of Elizabeth II comes to an end. It will be a liberating experience to be a citizen of the republic of Britain. In Walter Bagehot's great phrase we can walk 'by the light of our own eyes' . . . Such a cultural revolution may even help the economy. Little else does.

Or the megaphone polemics of Christopher Hitchens, the pamphleteer with his seat long since booked on the barricades:

> The British monarchy inculcates unthinking credulity and servility. It forms a heavy layer on the general encrustation of our unreformed political institutions. It is the gilded peg from which our unlovely system of social distinction and hierarchy depends. It is an obstacle to the objective

political discussion of our own history. It tribalizes politics.
It entrenches the absurdity of the hereditary principle. It
contributes to an enfeeblement of the national intelligence . . .
It is, in short, neither dignified nor efficient.

Somewhere in their midst, not wholly unused to the role of
prophet in the wilderness, stands the majestic figure of Tony
Benn – the reluctant peer-turned-constitutional reformer. On
his hitherto empty horizon, Benn has recently sighted 'a new
and significant, though diverse, body of opinion in Britain today
which favours ending the monarchy'. For years republicans have
been safely dismissed as unrepresentative. But now they are
receiving support from some unexpected quarters: 'Eurofanatics'
(backed by the City of London); newspaper proprietors; Scots
and Irish in pursuit of devolution and home rule; political
scientists alarmed by a series of increasingly undemocratic British
governments; constitutional reform groups such as Charter 88;
and, of course, the great British public, in the shape of disgruntled
taxpayers.

Heartened by these developments, Benn has picked up the
word 'Commonwealth' (in its Cromwellian rather than post-
imperial sense) and substituted it for 'kingdom' in a remarkable
personal vision of Britain's future. With his Commonwealth of
Britain Bill (see Appendix C), drafted over fifteen years 'without the help of a single lawyer', Benn not merely replaces the
monarch with an elected president; he shows how wholesale
constitutional reform would flow from one heady division in the
House of Commons. The Lords would be replaced by an elected
'House of the People'. Each parliamentary constituency would
have two MPs – one male, one female – with Wales and Scotland
granted their own separate parliaments and British jurisdiction
in Northern Ireland ended. Judges would be confirmed in office
and magistrates elected. Benn would institute a Bill of Rights,
disestablish the church and replace the honours system with a
more acceptable means of recognizing service to the community.
Along the way he would lower the voting age to sixteen, do away
with the offence of blasphemy and liberate the laws relating to
official information, the armed forces and the security services.

And that's just for starters. Central to Benn's Bill – introduced in the House of Commons in December 1992, but denied any chance of debate – is a constitutional oath to replace the oath of loyalty to the crown currently sworn by all MPs, judges, civil servants, members of the armed forces and other servants of the Queen. In this he finds common cause with Charter 88, one of the most effective groups currently campaigning for constitutional reform, whose credo runs: 'Instead of us belonging to the monarchy as its subjects, the monarch will belong to the citizens – governed by the constitution'. Like other European monarchs, in other words, the sovereign of this brave new Britain would swear an oath of allegiance to a written constitution.

On other details, Benn and Charter 88 part company. Where Benn would have a president elected by both houses of parliament from among their own number, Charter 88 is prepared to see the continuance of the monarchy along properly democratic, 'European-style' lines; but it believes that the choice between constitutional monarchy and elected republican presidency should be left to the popular will via a national referendum. At present, says the group's co-ordinator, Anthony Barnett, the crown is 'in the unfortunate situation of symbolizing a much wider failure of our governing institutions, and the crisis in our public values'. In May 1993 *The Times* newspaper and Charter 88 joined forces to organize a major debate on the monarchy's future, to re-examine 'those genuine constitutional problems which have been focused in such an unhealthy way on to the royal family'.

Were the monarchy to fall, there would be several potential methods of electing a head of state; but most republicans envisage a range of candidates way beyond Benn's parliamentary tunnel-vision. During the House of Windsor's recent difficulties, royalists have constantly tried to regain the initiative by painting a grim picture of the alternative to a hereditary monarch: a retired – or failed – politician in Buckingham Palace, reducing the office of head of state from 'a glamorous symbol of British glories', in Ludovic Kennedy's words, to 'a shabby sinecure for long-serving lackeys of the government of the day'. In a spirited retort, Kennedy advocates a 'non-political' presidency, citing lawyers, academics and diplomats as ideal candidates. Their private lives, as he points out, 'would scarcely provide much salacious material for the tabloids'. Given the disestablishment of the church, moreover, 'their religious views would have no bearing on either their qualification for office or their fulfilment of their duties'.

Even as ardent a monarchist as the Cambridge historian John Casey allows that there are strong arguments for republicanism. 'Many of the best political theorists in European history have held that a republic is the ideal form of government,' he grants. 'They have thought that civic virtue, intellectual freedom, even military courage do not flourish best under monarchies.' But Casey also suggests that a throne more than a thousand years old does not find its future in question 'unless something has gone really wrong'. It took a world war lasting four years to bring down the ancient Hapsburg dynasty of Austria-Hungary, the Romanov Czars of Russia and the German Kaiser. Sundry minor monarchies around Eastern Europe went down with them, virtually unnoticed. The Shah of Iran later succumbed to megalomaniac heedlessness of his subjects' religious feelings. The last Emperor of China was 'a moral defective whose chief pleasure in life was whipping his servants'.

Has the House of Windsor, for all its efforts at self-destruction, yet reached quite such a pass? It would surely be wrong for the British throne to fall because of the shortcomings, moral or otherwise, of its transient, hereditary occupants. Rather, it should give way, with as much dignity as logic, to the will of a people anxious to better their future with more appropriate constitutional arrangements.

Given the longevity of all the royal women of this century, not least the Queen's own mother, the present reign seems likely to last long enough for the British people to make a considered choice for their future. Either the royal family will use the time to ride out its current notoriety, perhaps even to embody the national way of life by finally beginning to share it. Or a popular consensus will see through its romantic longings to greater realism and a greater democracy: entrusting its national dignity and dreams to an elected, accountable worthy, in office briefly enough to enhance it, rather than a random and fallible family.

With a monarch-in-waiting apparently unsure of his own future, this has to be the hour for his potential subjects to consider theirs. Britain is long overdue a profound and vigorous reappraisal of its constitution. Whatever the resulting reforms, and whenever they are implemented – upon the death of Queen Elizabeth II, or at the time of her golden jubilee in 2002 – it is a debate which must begin in earnest now.

PART THREE
APPENDICES

CHRONOLOGY OF 1992:
THE QUEEN'S 'ANNUS HORRIBILIS'

January (16) *The Daily Mail* reveals the existence of compromising photographs of the Duchess of York on holiday with a Texan oil millionaire, Steve Wyatt, found by a cleaner on the bookshelves of a London flat Wyatt had been renting. **(26)** Fergie puts a paper bag over her head and throws bread rolls at the press on a flight home from a jaunt to Miami. In a poll in *The Daily Express,* just 2 per cent of respondents think she 'sets a good example' (with Prince Edward on 3 per cent, Prince Andrew on 9 per cent and Princess Michael of Kent on 5 per cent).

February (6) The fortieth anniversary of the Queen's accession to the throne, though marked by her first major BBC documentary since 1969, is overshadowed by a sex scandal involving Paddy Ashdown, leader of the Liberal Democratic Party. British newspapers celebrate the event by questioning the royal family's public subsidy, and strongly criticizing the monarch's exemption from income tax. **(11)** On an official tour of India, the Prince of Wales reneges on a promise to take the princess to the Taj Mahal, leaving her to go alone while he stays behind in Delhi to address trainee journalists. As the visit ends with the couple flying in separate directions, after staying in separate suites, rumours over the state of their marriage resurface. **(24)** Australian Prime Minister Paul Keating puts his arm round the Queen during an official visit, and hints that upon her death Australia will abolish the monarchy.

March (14) *The Spectator* reports that Prince Philip has abandoned the Church of England for the Greek orthodoxy of his roots. **(19)** During the first week of the British general election campaign, Buckingham Palace announces the separation of the Duke and Duchess of York. The Queen's press secretary criticizes the duchess; amid the subsequent furore, he apologizes to her and the Queen. **(23)** Andrew and Fergie reunite for their daughter Eugenie's second birthday. **(29)** The Princess of Wales's father, Earl Spencer, dies of a heart attack. She rushes home from her skiing holiday for the funeral. Charles arrives late, Diana having driven alone from London, and leaves early for tea with the Sultan of Brunei.

April: The royal family reportedly tries to buy the Duchess of York's silence, as America's *National Enquirer* offers her £1 million for her story. **(12)** Australia cancels plans for a coin bearing the Duchess of York's head. **(23)** The Duchess of York flies off to the Far East for a thirty-six-day holiday with her children, escorted by her financial adviser, Johnny Bryan. **(23)** Anne, the Princess Royal is granted a divorce from her husband, Captain Mark Phillips.

May (1) The Princess Royal is first seen in public with her friend Tim Laurence. **(12)** The Queen's first speech to the European Parliament is criticized by right-wing Conservative backbenchers. **(16)** The Princess of Wales is photographed poignantly alone at the Pyramids during an official visit to Egypt, while Prince Charles goes on a private visit to Turkey. The spotlight now switches from Fergie to Diana with the first rumours about the sensational contents of Andrew Morton's forthcoming book. **(18)** Andrew and Fergie are seen 'celebrating' in a fashionable London restaurant. **(19)** The Duchess of York moves out of her marital home.

June (3) The Queen Mother is criticized for unveiling a statue of Sir Arthur 'Bomber' Harris. **(4)** Australian Prime Minister Keating announces he is removing the Union Jack from the Australian flag. **(7)** *The Sunday Times* begins its five-week serialization of Andrew Morton's book *Diana: Her True Story* with the disclosure of her five apparent suicide attempts. At Windsor the Queen welcomes Prince Charles's friend Camilla Parker-Bowles into the royal enclosure. **(12)** Diana weeps publicly when given an affectionate reception in Southport, Lancashire. **(13)** After the Trooping the Colour ceremony, Diana returns home with her sons while Charles goes to play polo. **(17)** The Queen invites Brigadier Andrew Parker-Bowles to join her (and Diana) in the royal box at Ascot, where Andrew and Fergie wave from the crowd as the royal procession passes. Charles and Diana leave together, only to be seen getting into separate cars a mile down the road. Amid tabloid uproar, it is reported **(22)** that Prince Charles has told his parents he believes he may never be King, and **(28)** that he has discussed with them the prospect of divorcing his wife. **(30)** Captain Mark Phillips is seen dining with his new 'love', Jane Thornton.

July (1): The Princess of Wales spends her thirty-first birthday alone. **(6)** Prince Charles's 'friends' begin to trash Diana to the tabloids. **(13)** A *Daily Express* poll shows that the public blames Charles for his marital problems, with Diana far and away the most popular royal (on 34 per cent, with Princess Anne second on 12 per cent, the Queen third on 11 per cent and Charles fifth on 9 per cent). **(14)** A sex scandal involving Heritage Secretary David Mellor temporarily removes the spotlight from the troubled royal family. **(17)** An intruder who breaks into Buckingham Palace is released without charge. **(18)** The Duchess of York is excluded from the wedding at Windsor Castle of Lady Helen Windsor, daughter of the Duke and Duchess of Kent. **(26)** The Waleses spend their eleventh wedding anniversary apart.

August (2) Former Conservative minister Alan Clark attacks the royal family as 'vulgar and brutish'. There is speculation about a reconciliation between the Yorks, dented by a denial from Johnny Bryan that he has moved in with the duchess at her rented home near Windsor. **(13)** The Queen is revealed to have applied to the Forestry Commission for a £300,000 grant to fence in her privately-owned estate at Balmoral. **(20)** In the first week of the royal family's holiday at Balmoral, the *Daily Mirror* publishes photographs of a topless Duchess of York canoodling with Johnny Bryan in front of her children during a holiday in France the previous week. Despite Bryan's attempts to obtain an injunction, the *Mirror* splashes the photos over seven pages. The Duchess leaves Balmoral, apparently in disgrace. **(25)** *The Sun* publishes transcripts of an affectionate phone call apparently between Diana and her friend James Gilbey. More than 60,000 people spend some £100,000 listening to the tape-recorded conversation on a telephone 'hotline'. The National Society for the Prevention of Cruelty to Children refuses to accept the proceeds. A *Sun* photographer crashes into Gilbey's car while pursuing him in Norfolk. **(29)** *The Daily Telegraph* calls for the Queen's resignation and describes the royal family as 'a sentimental Victorian concept with progressively little basis in reality'. **(30)** The week's developments are interpreted as a concerted Palace 'plot' to discredit Diana. The royal family is reported to be 'freezing out' the princess.

September (1) A document purporting to be an internal Palace memo attacking Diana is exposed as a fake. *The Sun* claims that Diana enjoyed a relationship with Major James Hewitt, who taught Prince William and Prince Harry to ride. **(2)** Major Hewitt sues *The Sun* for libel, while the London *Evening Standard* reports that Diana enjoyed secret rendezvous with James Gilbey at a 'safe house' in Norfolk. **(3)** It is rumoured that the Princess Royal is about to announce her engagement to Tim Laurence. **(4)** *The Daily Mail* reports that Diana persuaded police protection officers to stand down during six secret meetings with 'close friends' including James Gilbey. **(5)** Scotland Yard, at Buckingham Palace's behest, denies the story. The Duchess of York's mother, Mrs Susan Barrantes, alleges a campaign to discredit her daughter, implying secret service involvement in the topless photos. **(6)** Diana takes William back to school; Charles turns up for Harry's first day but fails to participate in a 'happy family' photo-call. A major ITN documentary chronicles the collapse of the marriage of the Prince and Princess of Wales. **(9)** Charles and Diana show no signs of *rapprochement* during a rare joint outing in Nottingham, after which they again go their separate ways. **(10)** In advance of John Major's visit to Balmoral, a Downing Street briefing suggests that the Duchess of York will be stripped of the rank of HRH, and that the Queen and the prime minister will reappraise the future of the monarchy over the weekend. **(12)** The Duchess of York is seen checking into a therapy clinic. **(13)** As Major weekends at Balmoral, the 'quality' Sunday papers lead with speculation that the 'fringe' royals are to be axed from the Civil List. **(16)** On 'Black Wednesday', the government pours away billions from the national reserves in a vain attempt to save the pound, before removing it from the European exchange rate mechanism, thus reneging on its commitment not to devalue. **(21)** 'Mindful of the recession,' the Princess of Wales gives up her £72,000 red Mercedes in favour of British-made cars from the Palace 'car pool'. **(28)** *The Guardian* reports that the Civil List is to be slimmed down to four (including Prince Andrew), while seven 'fringe' royals are to be axed.

October (4) *The Sunday Express* reports (a) that Charles has 'dropped' Camilla, and (b) that the Queen has overruled her staff in accepting Major's proposals about cutting the Civil List. **(26)** A gala evening at Earl's Court celebrates the Queen's fortieth anniversary on the throne. **(26–27)** The tabloids are astonished as Charles and Diana attend functions together two nights in a row for the first time in three years.

November (1) A Gallup poll for the League Against Cruel Sports shows that more than 80 per cent of young Britons disapprove of the royal family fox-hunting. **(2)** As Charles and Diana fly off to Korea, revelations from the paperback edition of Morton's book suggest that she has had monumental rows with Philip. **(3)** Every tabloid front-page shows Charles and Diana openly at war on official visit to South Korea. **(4)** More Morton revelations, more front-page sullenness in Korea (despite the historic US election result), while

Chancellor of the Exchequer Norman Lamont quietly announces that the government has 'no plans' for the Queen to pay tax. **(5)** A Palace spokesman in Korea admits for the first time that 'all is not well' with the Wales marriage. Charles flies to Hong Kong as Diana returns to the UK. **(6)** The Princess of Wales issues a statement denying that the Queen and Prince Philip have been 'anything other than sympathetic and supportive'. **(13)** The existence of a sixty-minute Camillagate tape, containing intimacies apparently between Prince Charles and Camilla Parker-Bowles, is revealed in the *Daily Mirror* (and reprinted in *The Sun*). **(14)** Charles spends his forty-fourth birthday alone while a more cheerful Diana visits Paris, including a forty-minute meeting with President Mitterrand. **(15)** The Sunday tabloids allege that Charles denied Diana a third child. **(16)** The *Daily Mirror* alleges that MI5 made both the Squidgygate and Camillagate tapes; Geoffrey Dickens MP demands a government inquiry. **(17)** Diana makes a major speech (including coded sarcasm about her husband) for European Drug Prevention Week. **(20)** On the Queen's forty-fifth wedding anniversary, which her husband spends in Argentina, Windsor Castle is ravaged by fire (six years after a disastrous fire at Hampton Court). **(21)** National Heritage Secretary Peter Brooke promptly says that the £60 million bill will be footed by the taxpayer. **(22–23)** Labour MPs demand that the Queen pays for the damage herself. **(24)** A grim-looking, croaky-voiced Queen laments her 'annus horribilis', and seeks public sympathy, but makes no mention of contributing to costs of Windsor damage. Prince Andrew is given his first naval command. **(25)** The House of Commons orders a General Audit Office inquiry into the 'value-for-money' of the financing of the royal palaces (£24.6 million p.a.), but refuses demands that it be widened to include all payments to the royal family. The GAO report 'could take a year'. **(26)** John Major announces that the Queen and Prince Charles have agreed in principle to pay income tax, and that all but the Queen, the Queen Mother and Prince Philip will be dropped from the Civil List.

December (1) The Queen's former press secretary, Michael Shea, writing in *The Times*, calls the tabloids 'a cancer in the soft underbelly of the nation'. Dr Julia Schofield is not allowed to take her guide-dog into corgi-infested Buckingham Palace while receiving an MBE from the Queen. **(3)** The Prince of Wales announces that he will not be taking his wife with him to US and Mexico in February. **(4)** In France, Charles angers MPs and disrupts the GATT talks by making a speech in support of French farmers. MPs are unconvinced by a one-and-a-half-page report blaming the Windsor fire on a badly placed 'spotlight'. **(5)** Buckingham Palace announces that Princess Anne will marry Commander Tim Laurence the following weekend. **(6)** It appears that the Queen Mother won't be going to the wedding.

(7) A row in the House of Commons over safety checks on royal palaces maintained at public expense. **(9)** John Major announces the formal separation of the Prince and Princess of Wales. **(11)** Diana sits next to Mitterrand, at the Queen's (top) table, at the European Summit dinner aboard HMY *Britannia*; Charles and John Major are relegated to Table Three. **(12)** Princess Anne marries Laurence in a virtually secret ceremony at Crathie Kirk on the Queen's Balmoral estate. **(14)** In the House of Commons, Tony Benn reintroduces his bill to abolish the monarchy and introduce a 'Commonwealth of Britain' with an elected president (*see* Appendix C). **(15)** The Princess of Wales tells a joint meeting of all her charities that 'business as usual' will continue. **(21)** Diana publicly turns down the Queen's invitation to Christmas at Sandringham – but her sons, William and Harry, *will* be going. **(22)** *The Sun* publishes a transcript of the Queen's Christmas Day broadcast, claiming it was leaked via the BBC. **(25)** The Queen delivers her Christmas broadcast as planned. **(30)** Pursued by paparazzi, Diana takes her sons to the Caribbean island of Nevis for a six-day holiday. **(31)** New Year Honours go to Charles's chef, Diana's dresser and the man who cleans the windows of Buckingham Palace, as well as the teams who ran the Anniversary Trust and made the film *Elizabeth R*. The Queen, for the first time ever, is seen out riding in a hard hat. The royal family's New Year celebrations are overshadowed by a rumour that someone, somewhere, is about to publish the transcript of the notorious Camillagate tape; in an attempt to contain the damage, the Prime Minister brings forward publication of the Calcutt Report, which recommends legislation to curb the activities of Britain's supposedly free press.

THE LINE OF SUCCESSION TO THE THRONE

In the event of the Prince of Wales renouncing his right to the throne, the succession would pass to his older son, Prince William Arthur Philip Louis (assuming that William reaches eighteen, the age of majority, before the death of his grandmother, Queen Elizabeth II). Until William himself has male heirs, the next in line will be his younger brother Harry, formally Prince Henry Charles Albert David. In June 1993, on the fortieth anniversary of Elizabeth II's coronation, the following were the first one hundred people in the line of succession to the British throne:

1 The Prince of Wales (b. 1948)
2 Prince William of Wales (b. 1982)
3 Prince Henry of Wales (b. 1984)
4 The Duke of York (b. 1960)
5 Princess Beatrice of York (b. 1988)
6 Princess Eugenie of York (b. 1990)
7 Prince Edward (b. 1964)
8 The Princess Royal (b. 1950)
9 Peter Phillips (b. 1977)
10 Zara Phillips (b. 1981)
11 Princess Margaret, Countess of Snowdon (b. 1930)

12 David, Viscount Linley (b. 1961)
13 Lady Sarah Armstrong-Jones (b. 1964)
14 The Duke of Gloucester (b. 1944)
15 Alexander, Earl of Ulster (b. 1974)
16 Lady Davina Windsor (b. 1977)
17 Lady Rose Windsor (b. 1980)
18 The Duke of Kent (b. 1935)
19 Edward, Baron Downpatrick (b. 1988)
20 Lady Marina Charlotte Windsor (b. 1992)
21 Lord Nicholas Windsor (b. 1970)
22 Lady Helen Taylor (née Windsor) (b. 1964)
23 Lord Frederick Windsor * (b. 1979)
24 Lady Gabriella Windsor * (b. 1981)
25 Princess Alexandra, the Hon Lady Ogilvy (b. 1936)
26 James Ogilvy (b. 1964)
27 Mrs Marina Mowatt (née Ogilvy) (b. 1966)
28 Zenouska Mowatt (b. 1990)
29 The Earl of Harewood (b. 1923)
30 David, Viscount Lascelles (b. 1950)
31 Hon Alexander Lascelles (b. 1980)
32 Hon Edward Lascelles (b. 1982)
33 Hon James Lascelles (b. 1953)
34 Rowan Lascelles (b. 1977)
35 Tewa Lascelles (b. 1985)
36 Sophie Lascelles (b. 1973)
37 Hon Jeremy Lascelles (b. 1955)
38 Thomas Lascelles (b. 1982)
39 Ellen Lascelles (b. 1984)
40 Amy Lascelles (b. 1986)
41 Hon Gerald Lascelles (b. 1924)
42 Henry Lascelles (b. 1953)
43 The Duke of Fife (b. 1929)
44 David, Earl of Macduff (b. 1961)
45 Hon Charles Carnegie (b. 1989)
46 Hon George William Carnegie (b. 1991)
47 Lady Alexandra Carnegie (b. 1959)
48 King Harald V of Norway (b.1937)
49 Crown Prince Haakon Magnus of Norway (b. 1973)
50 Princess Martha Louise of Norway (b. 1971)

*Offspring of Prince Michael of Kent, who does not appear in this list because he renounced his right of succession to the throne upon his marriage in 1978 to a Roman Catholic divorcee, Baroness Marie-Christine Agnes Hedwig Ida von Reibnitz (now Princess Michael of Kent).

he Crown in Parliament: An attendant walks backwards before his sovereign as she performs
e annual State Opening.

The monarch as politician: Elizabeth II with five of her nine prime ministers; and with Presidents Mitterrand and Reagan at a D-Day memorial service.

The extended family makes a ritual balcony appearance.

As Head of the British Commonwealth, the Queen endures the touch of the Australian prime minister (above), and enjoys a ritual African welcome.

As Diana begins to steal his limelight, Charles seeks consolation in plants and architecture.

An increasingly powerful public speaker, Diana is determined to continue her work for such 'unroyal' causes as leprosy and AIDS.

Royal Perks: The Queen's private yacht costs the British taxpayer £12.5 million a year, and her three private jets £2,000 an hour.

Above: Part of the royal car pool at Ascot. Right: The Queen's jewels are valued in millions.

Overleaf: The future King Mother will continue to play a vital role in the upbringing of King William V.

51 Princess Ragnhild, Mrs Lorentzen (b. 1930)
52 Victoria Ragna Ribeiro (b. 1989)
53 Ragnhild Alexandra Lorentzen (b. 1968)
54 Princess Astrid, Mrs Ferner (b. 1932)
55 Alexander Ferner (b. 1965)
56 Carl Christian Ferner (b. 1972)
57 Cathrine, Mrs Johansen (b. 1962)
58 Sebastien Johansen (b. 1990)
59 Benedikte Ferner (b. 1963)
60 Elisabeth Ferner (b. 1969)
61 Princess Margarita of Roumania (b. 1949)
62 Princess Helen of Roumania, Mrs Medforth-Mills (b. 1950)
63 Nicholas Medforth-Mills (b. 1985)
64 Elisabetta Medforth-Mills (b. 1989)
65 Princess Irina of Roumania, Mrs Kreuger (b. 1953)
66 Michael Kreuger (b. 1985)
67 Elisabeth Angelica Kreuger (b. 1986)
68 Princess Sophie of Roumania (b. 1957)
69 Princess Maria of Roumania (b. 1964)
70 Prince Peter of Yugoslavia (b. 1980)
71 Prince Philip of Yugoslavia (b. 1982)
72 Prince Alexander of Yugoslavia (b. 1982)
73 Prince Tomislav of Yugoslavia (b. 1928)
74 Prince Nikola of Yugoslavia (b. 1958)
75 Prince George of Yugoslavia (b. 1984)
76 Prince Michael of Yugoslavia (b. 1985)
77 Princess Katarina of Yugoslavia, Mrs de Silva (b. 1959)
78 Victoria de Silva (b. 1991)
79 Prince Christopher of Yugoslavia (b. 1960)
80 Prince Vladimir of Yugoslavia (b. 1964)
81 Prince Dimitri of Yugoslavia (b. 1965)
82 Princess Maria Tatiana of Yugoslavia (b. 1957)
83 Princess [called Grand Duchess] Maria of Russia (b. 1953)
84 Prince Georg of Prussia (b. 1981)
85 Emich, Prince of Leiningen (b. 1926)
86 Karl Emich, Hereditary Prince of Leiningen (b. 1952)
87 Princess Cacilia of Leiningen (b. 1988)
88 Prince Andreas of Leiningen (b. 1955)
89 Prince Ferdinand of Leiningen (b. 1982)
90 Prince Hermann of Leiningen (b. 1983)
91 Princess Olga of Leiningen (b. 1984)
92 Princess Melita of Leiningen (b. 1951)
93 Princess Stephanie of Leiningen (b. 1958)
94 Prince Karl Boris of Leiningen (b. 1960)

 95 Prince Hermann Friedrich of Leiningen (b. 1963)
 96 Prince Friedrich of Leiningen (b. 1938)
 97 Princess Kira Melita of Leiningen (b. 1930)
 98 Princess Mechtilde of Leiningen, Mrs Bauscher (b. 1936)
 99 Ulf Bauscher (b. 1963)
100 Berthold Bauscher (b. 1965)

TONY BENN'S PARLIAMENTARY BILL FOR A COMMONWEALTH OF BRITAIN

The following abbreviated version of Tony Benn's Bill was provided to the author by Mr Benn, and is reproduced here with his kind permission.

A
BILL
TO

Establish a democratic, federal and secular Commonwealth of England, Scotland and Wales dedicated to the welfare of all its citizens; to establish fundamental human rights within that Commonwealth; to lower the voting age to 16 years and to make other provision with respect to elections, including equal representation for women; to prescribe a constitutional oath; to establish a Commonwealth Parliament consisting of the House of Commons and the House of the People and to make provision for the term of a Parliament and for legislative and other procedure; to establish the office of President, and a Council of State, and to prescribe the powers of each; to provide for the formation of governments; to amend the law

relating to official information, the armed forces and
the security services; to make fresh provision for
the participation of Britain in the United Nations
Organisation and the European Communities; to
make the basing of foreign forces in Britain dependent
upon the approval of the House of Commons; to make
new provision with respect to the judicial system
and to establish a National Legal Service; to set up
national Parliaments for England, Scotland and Wales;
to amend the law relating to local government, the
district auditor and the accountability of police forces;
to end the constitutional status of the Crown and
to make certain consequential provision; to abolish
the House of Lords and the Privy Council, to end
the recognition in law of personal titles, and to
provide for the acknowledgement of service to the
community; to disestablish the Church of England,
abolish the offence of blasphemy, and to provide for
equality under the law for all religions and beliefs;
to end British jurisdiction in Northern Ireland; to
provide for constitutional amendment; and to make
transitional and related provision.

Presented by Mr Tony Benn
AD 1991

PART 1: THE COMMONWEALTH OF BRITAIN

THE ESTABLISHMENT OF THE COMMONWEALTH: Britain shall be a
democratic, secular, federal Commonwealth, comprising the Nations
of England, Scotland and Wales, in association with such islands as
have historically been linked to the United Kingdom.

THE RIGHTS OF THE PEOPLE: (1) The Commonwealth shall be
dedicated to the maintenance of the welfare of all its citizens, in
whom all sovereign power shall be vested, to be exercised by them
and, on their behalf, by the representatives whom they shall elect.
(2) Schedule 1 to this Act shall have effect for the purposes of providing
for and entrenching certain basic and fundamental human rights.

THE COMMISSIONER FOR HUMAN RIGHTS: (1) It shall be the duty
of the President, the Government and the Courts to use their best
endeavours to secure and safeguard these rights. (2) The House of
Commons shall appoint a Human Rights Commissioner, responsible

to the Parliament ('the Commissioner'), who shall be responsible for monitoring the observance of these rights.

THE FRANCHISE: (1) A British citizen who has not been resident abroad for more than the immediately previous five years shall be entitled to register and to vote in all parliamentary, assembly and local elections. (2) A person who has been resident in Britain for more than five years may register and shall have the right to vote in all parliamentary, assembly and local elections. (3) A person who is eligible to vote may exercise that right from the date of that person's sixteenth birthday.

THE CONSTITUTIONAL OATH: All oaths of allegiance not taken by any person to the Crown, or by the Crown on the occasion of the Coronation, and all other oaths taken by any person in authority, including judges, magistrates, bishops, members of the armed forces or civil service, members of parliament and Privy Counsellors are hereby declared to be null and void, and, where appropriate, are replaced by the words set out in Schedule 2 to this Act.

PART II: THE COMMONWEALTH PARLIAMENT

THE ESTABLISHMENT OF THE COMMONWEALTH PARLIAMENT: (1) The Commonwealth Parliament (a) shall consist of two Houses, the House of Commons and the House of the People; (b) shall be elected for a fixed term of four years; and (c) shall not be dissolved before the expiry of that period, unless pursuant to Part V below. (2) All elections shall be conducted on the basis of one person one vote from the age of 16, and all electors shall be eligible to be candidates, subject only to any disqualification for which the Commonwealth Parliament may provide.

THE HOUSE OF COMMONS: The House of Commons shall (a) decide its procedure; (b) elect its Speaker; (c) exercise the supreme legislative power; and (d) elect the government.

THE HOUSE OF THE PEOPLE: (1) The House of the People shall be elected so as to represent England, Scotland and Wales in proportion to their populations. (2) Half of the members of the House of the People shall be women and half shall be men.

LEGISLATION: (1) Bills may be introduced in either House of Parliament. (2) Bills of a character now requiring the recommendation of the Crown shall require the consent or recommendation of the

Government before they are debated, but the House of Commons may, by resolution, proceed with such a bill or motion without that consent. (3) Primary legislation shall be considered by each House in turn. (4) (a) The House of the People may amend bills brought from the House of Commons; and (b) Bills brought from, and amendments made by, the House of the People may be accepted or rejected by the House of Commons, and its decision shall be final. (5) The House of the People may reject a bill brought from the House of Commons, whereupon the bill shall be returned to the House of Commons which may, after one calendar year has elapsed, again pass the bill without amendment which shall constitute the final consent, and the Speaker of the House of Commons may issue his certificate to that effect and the bill shall be presented to the President for assent forthwith . . . Each statutory instrument passed by the House of Commons shall be referred to the House of the People, which shall have the power to delay it for a maximum of one month after which it shall have effect, provided that the House of Commons so further resolves.

THE SUPREMACY OF PARLIAMENT: Where legislation passed by the Commonwealth Parliament conflicts with any directive, or regulation issued or approved by the Council of Ministers, or the Commission of the European Communities, British legislation shall prevail, and shall be so accepted by the British courts.

PART III: THE PRESIDENCY

THE PRESIDENT: There shall be a President elected from amongst their number, by a two thirds majority, by both Houses of Parliament sitting together, to serve for a three-year term and to be eligible for re-election for one further three-year term.

PRESIDENTIAL POWERS: (a) All the powers now exercised under Crown Prerogative shall be exercised by the President, who shall act solely upon the advice of the Prime Minister, or of a resolution of the House of Commons (which shall prevail if such resolution is in conflict with the advice of the Prime Minister); (b) the exercise of such powers shall require the assent of the House of Commons before having effect; and (c) the powers of the President shall include: to give Assent to the passage of legislation; to dissolve Parliament; to invite a person to attempt to form an administration; to make orders for any purpose for which Orders in Council were required before the coming into force of this Act; to declare war; to order British forces into armed conflict; to make peace.

PART IV: THE COUNCIL OF STATE

ESTABLISHMENT OF THE COUNCIL OF STATE: (1) There shall be a Council of State consisting of 24 persons, of whom 12 shall be men and 12 shall be women. (2) Half of the members of the Council of State shall be elected by the House of Commons and half by the House of the People. (3) Each member shall serve for a period of two years.

POWERS: In the event of no government being in place, the powers of government shall be vested in the Council of State, and all decisions made by the Council of State shall be subject to confirmation by the House of Commons.

PART V: THE EXECUTIVE

THE GOVERNMENT: (1) The House of Commons shall by a simple majority elect one of its members to form a government as Prime Minister, and that person shall present the Government to the House of Commons for approval as a whole, by resolution, before he or she takes office. (2) All executive power shall be vested in the government for so long as it enjoys a majority in the House of Commons, or until the day of first meeting of a new Parliament. (3) In the event of a government being defeated in the House of Commons on a matter of Confidence, the Prime Minister shall tender his or her resignation forthwith to the President who shall consult widely to determine who might best be able to form a new administration, and shall issue an invitation to that person to attempt to do so, and to present his or her government to the House of Commons for approval. (4) Parliament shall be dissolved before the expiry of its term only if (a) no person attempting to form a government has secured the approval of the House of Commons for that government; (b) the President recommends a dissolution; and (c) the House of Commons itself votes in favour of a dissolution; and in such a case there shall be a general election to elect a new Parliament, for the unexpired term of the previous Parliament.

FREEDOM OF INFORMATION: (1) In the Public Records Act 1958 references to 'four years' shall be substituted for references to '30 years'. (2) Notwithstanding Section 1 above, a Minister may certify that a paper should remain secret, and any such certificate shall be laid before the House of Commons for approval by resolution.

(3) The Official Secrets Acts 1911, 1920, 1939 and 1989 are hereby repealed. (4) All official information shall be published, or made available on request save that categories of information relating to the following subjects may be protected by order subject to approval by Resolution: (i) defence and security matters; (ii) economic policy; (iii) international relations; (iv) personal data. (5) It shall be a criminal offence to disclose protected information.

THE ARMED FORCES: (1) The legal status of all the armed forces of Britain shall depend upon the passing of an annual authorisation order by the House of Commons. (2) The Chief and Vice-Chief of the Defence Staff, and Chiefs of Staff of the three Services shall be nominated by the Government and confirmed by the Defence Committee of the House of Commons, before they are appointed.

THE SECURITY SERVICES: The security services of the Commonwealth shall be accountable to Parliament through the responsible Minister or Ministers, who shall make a report annually to the House of Commons containing the information set out in Schedule 3 to this Act.

PART VI: FOREIGN RELATIONS

THE UNITED NATIONS: (1) The British representative attending the Security Council of the United Nations shall be elected by the House of Commons. (2) No veto may be cast by the British representative on any issue which touches upon the interest of the planet; that is, in respect of United Nations proposals for the control of nuclear weapons, chemical weapons or environmental protection, without specific approval from both Houses of Parliament.

THE EUROPEAN COMMUNITIES: (1) No vote may be given by a British Minister at the Council of Ministers of the European Communities, unless and until the House of Commons has given its approval. (2) The British members of the European Commission shall be nominated by the government and elected by the House of Commons.

FOREIGN FORCES IN BRITAIN: No armed forces of any foreign country, nor any weapons or equipment, shall be (a) based in the Commonwealth of Britain or its territorial waters; or (b) used from British territory, air-space or territorial waters in any armed conflict without the prior consent of the House of Commons.

PART VII: THE HIGH COURT

THE ESTABLISHMENT OF THE HIGH COURT: There shall be a High Court, independent of the Commonwealth Government and Parliament . . . The responsibilities of the High Court shall include the safeguarding of the Commonwealth Constitution and its judgements shall be binding on the Government.

JUDICIAL APPOINTMENTS: Nominations to the High Court shall be made by the President, and shall be confirmed by the Select Committee of the House of Commons for the time being having responsibility for judicial matters, before having effect. (2) High Court, Appeal Court and County Court judges shall retire when they reach the age of 60. (3) Members of the High Court and other judges shall be removed only by a resolution of both Houses of Parliament.

ELECTION OF COUNTY COURT JUDGES: The High Court may nominate persons to serve on a panel from which the County Court judges shall be elected by those who are on the electoral register for the House of Commons constituencies which cover the areas for which they are to exercise jurisdiction.

ELECTION OF MAGISTRATES: Magistrates shall be elected by those who are on the electoral register for the House of Commons constituencies which cover those areas for which they are to exercise jurisdiction, shall hold office for four years, and shall be eligible for re-election, up to the age of 60.

NATIONAL LEGAL SERVICE: A National Legal Service shall be established giving to each person the right, free of all cost, to be represented in Court on matters of direct personal concern to themselves or their families; and such a right shall not extend to commercial, industrial or financial enterprises.

PART VIII: THE NATIONAL PARLIAMENTS

ESTABLISHMENT OF THE NATIONAL PARLIAMENTS: There shall be National Parliaments elected for England, for Scotland and for Wales.

COMPOSITION AND ELECTION: (1) Half of the members of each Parliament shall be men and half shall be women. (2) National

Parliaments shall be elected by those who are registered upon the electoral register in England, Scotland and Wales respectively, at the same time, and for the same four-year period, as the elections for the Commonwealth Parliament, with the exception of any election under Part V above.

POWERS: Each Parliament shall enjoy the power to legislate in all matters save only defence, foreign affairs and Commonwealth finance, which shall remain within the sole authority of the Commonwealth Parliament.

RELATIONS WITH THE COMMONWEALTH PARLIAMENT: The Commonwealth Parliament may enact legislation applying to the Commonwealth as a whole, and where such enactments conflict with any enactments of the National Parliaments, the Commonwealth legislation shall have precedence.

PART IX: LOCAL GOVERNMENT

POWERS: (1) Each local authority shall, after the passage of this Act, enjoy, in addition to the powers which it now enjoys, the power to act as it thinks fit in respect of the activities specified in Schedule 4 to this Act. (2) Nothing in this section shall empower any local authority to take any action that is explicitly prohibited by Act of Parliament, and if such an action is taken the Council shall be collectively liable in the courts, but no individual councillor shall be personally penalised for that decision, excepting only where he or she may be convicted of any breach of the criminal law.

PART X: THE CROWN

THE ENDING OF THE CONSTITUTIONAL STATUS OF THE CROWN: The legal status of the Crown is hereby ended and the Monarch for the time being and his or her heirs and successors, shall cease to enjoy, or exercise as Monarch, any political or personal power of any kind, either directly through the person of the Monarch, or by prerogative, or through Ministers.

CROWN PROPERTY: The ownership and control of all Crown lands, buildings and property which are held by the Monarch for the time being, as a consequence of his or her occupancy of the Throne, or their position as heirs to the Throne, shall be transferred forthwith to the Commonwealth Government.

COMPENSATION: (1) A payment shall be paid from public funds to the person occupying the Throne at the coming into force of this Act, to dispose of as he or she thinks fit. (2) A pension shall be paid to the person occupying the Throne at the moment of coming into force of this Act. (3) Accommodation shall be made available for such members of the former Royal Family, in such Royal Palaces as shall be determined by Parliament.

LIABILITY TO TAXATION: All members of the Royal Family shall be liable for the payment of taxes and charges paid by a citizen of the Commonwealth, or a person residing in the Commonwealth, as the case may be.

THE HOUSE OF LORDS: The House of Lords is hereby abolished and from the coming into force of this Act no person shall thereafter enjoy any legal status as a Lord Spiritual or Temporal, and any person who was formerly a member of the House of Lords shall enjoy the right to stand for Parliament.

THE PRIVY COUNCIL: The Privy Council, and the style and precedence of Privy Counsellor, are hereby abolished.

HONOURS AND AWARDS: (1) No personal title or rank, whether hereditary or not, shall be recognised in law. (2) No personal title, rank or dignity shall be conferred, nor shall any admission be made to a rank or class of an order of chivalry or any similar order. (3) The Commonwealth Parliament and the National Parliaments may express gratitude to those citizens who have distinguished themselves through service to the community by Resolutions of Thanks.

PART XI: RELIGIOUS FREEDOM

DISESTABLISHMENT OF THE CHURCH OF ENGLAND: The Church of England is hereby disestablished, and all the powers over faith, doctrine, liturgy, property, discipline and appointments now exercised over that Church by the Crown, Parliament or private patrons, shall forthwith be transferred, in their entirety, to the General Synod of the Church of England to be exercised in accordance with any rules determined by that body.

ABOLITION OF THE OFFENCE OF BLASPHEMY: No criminal prosecution shall be instituted against any person for the offences of blasphemy, blasphemous libel, heresy, schism or atheism.

EQUAL STATUS FOR ALL RELIGIONS AND BELIEFS: (1) Members of all religious denominations and holders of other beliefs including atheism, agnosticism or humanism, shall have equal status before the law and the legal ban on election of Priests in the Anglican and Roman Catholic faiths to the House of Commons is hereby repealed. (2) The House of Commons (Clergy Disqualification) Act 1801 is hereby repealed, and it is declared that a priest, deacon or minister of the Church of England or any other Christian denomination may stand for election to the House of Commons or the House of the People.

PART XII: NORTHERN IRELAND

TERMINATION OF JURISDICTION: Two years after the passage of this Act, or on such earlier date as the Commonwealth Parliament may determine, the jurisdiction of Britain in Northern Ireland shall cease, and from that date no legislation passed by that Parliament shall apply in Northern Ireland.

ARRANGEMENTS FOR WITHDRAWAL: Orders under this Act shall make provision for the withdrawal of all British troops and personnel, and the disposal of premises or equipment which up to the coming into force of this Act belong to Her Majesty's Government . . . before, during or after the appointed day, but no such order shall purport to give powers to make laws or to enforce them in Northern Ireland, after the day upon which British jurisdiction ends.

PART XIII: IMPLEMENTATION

THE CONSTITUTION: The provisions of this Act shall form a Constitution for the Commonwealth of Britain, subject to approval by referendum.

AMENDMENT OF THE CONSTITUTION: After approval in a referendum, the Constitution shall be amended only with the agreement of both Houses of the Commonwealth Parliament and the endorsement of the people in a referendum.

SCHEDULE 1: THE CHARTER OF RIGHTS

1. All citizens of Britain shall be entitled to enjoy, and to campaign for, universal, democratic and enforceable rights, both individual and collective, enshrined in law, adhered to in practice and respected by society, as a precondition of self-government and the achievement of full political, social and economic emancipation within a civilised society.

2. Every citizen shall have the following political rights: to freedom of speech; to freedom of assembly and of association for the purpose of expressing an opinion, without interference from the state; to organise for common political, social or economic ends; to practise, or not to practise, any or all religions; to vote in all elections, participate in all electoral processes and institutions, and to contest all elections; to privacy and the protection of personal information and correspondence from surveillance or interference; to information about public, political, social or economic affairs; to freedom of movement, unhindered by arbitrary interference, and to be given asylum from political, social or economic oppression; and to conscientious objection to service in the armed forces.

3. Every citizen shall have the following legal rights: to personal freedom from arbitrary arrest, detention or harassment; to a fair and impartial hearing by a jury of the citizen's peers if accused of any unlawful activity; and to equal treatment before the law and equal access to legal representation; to be presumed innocent until proved guilty, to be informed of all charges laid and the evidence in support of them, and the right to silence in court; to freedom from torture or cruel and degrading treatment, and from capital punishment; to legal advice and services, free at the point of use; and to equal treatment before the law, and in the community without discrimination and regardless of race, sex or sexual preference, colour, religious or political conviction or disability.

4. Every citizen shall have the following social rights: to adequate and warm housing and comfortable living conditions; to rest, recreation and leisure, to a limitation of working hours and to holidays; to enjoy access to literature, music, the arts and cultural activities; to good health care and preventive medicine, free at the moment of need; to lifelong and free educational provision; to dignity and care in retirement; to control, in the case of women, of their own fertility and reproduction; to free and equal access to child care; to free, effective and

equitable means of transportation; to a healthy, sustainable, accessible and attractive environment and to clean water and air; to media free from governmental or commercial domination; and to full access to personal information held by any public authority, subject only to a restriction order signed by a Minister and reported to Parliament.

5. Every citizen shall have the following economic rights: to useful work at a fair wage that provides an income sufficient to maintain a decent standard of living; to belong to a trade union and to withdraw labour in pursuit of an industrial dispute; to participate in all decisions, including health and safety, affecting the workplace, and to information and representation and expression of opinion for all employed persons; to full and equal access to all state or social benefits at a level sufficient to meet basic needs; and to freedom from taxation in excess of an ability to pay.

SCHEDULE 2 : THE CONSTITUTIONAL OATH

The Oath shall be in the following terms, and shall be declared in the presence of another person who has taken the Oath, who shall report the names of all those who have taken the Oath before him or her to the President.
'I do solemnly declare and affirm that I will be faithful to the Constitution of the Commonwealth of Britain, and will respect its laws, as enacted by Parliament; will preserve inviolably the civil rights and liberties of the people, including the right to self-government, through their elected representatives, and will faithfully and truly declare my mind and opinion on all matters that come before me without fear or favour.'

SCHEDULE 3 : ANNUAL REPORT ON THE SECURITY SERVICES

1. The responsible Ministers shall lay before the House of Commons a report on the work of the security services, setting out the following information: (a) the total budget of those services, divided into the following categories: (i) wages and salaries; (ii) equipment and offices; (iii) expenditure in Britain; and (iv) expenditure abroad; (b) the total number of persons employed directly and on contract; (c) the total number of names held in records kept in any form by the service in question; (d) the number of telephones intercepted during the

course of the previous year; (e) the number of persons whose mail was intercepted and opened for examination; (f) the broad categories under which interceptions mentioned in paragraphs (d) or (e) above were made; (g) the number of arrests made and convictions obtained as a result of such interceptions; (h) the nature of the suspected crimes or subversive or other activities considered to justify such interceptions.

2. (a) A draft order to renew authority for the legal status of the security services shall be laid together with the report required by section 20 of this Act and this Schedule, and shall be amendable. (b) The authority for the legal status of the security services shall lapse six months after the laying of a draft order under sub-paragraph (a) above if the draft order has not previously been approved by resolution of the House of Commons.

APPENDIX D

SCHEDULE OF CROWN ESTATE PROPERTIES JULY 1988

NOTE: Where an estate comprises both agricultural and non-agricultural portions an entry has been made in the schedule both under 'Agricultural' and 'Urban', as the case may be. All estates treated in this way are marked with an asterisk (★).

AGRICULTURAL

County	Estate	Acreage	Remarks
ENGLAND			
Bedfordshire	Chicksands	282	Purchased in 1936. Bulk of estate sold to farm tenants between 1959 and 1962. Remainder is woodland leased to Forestry Commission.
Berkshire	★Windsor		Ancient possession considerably increased by purchases. Includes agricultural property at Ascot, Datchet and Bagshot.
Buckinghamshire	Wotton	7	Purchased in 1930. Bulk of estate sold between 1976 and 1979.
Cambridgeshire	Holmewood	5,191	Purchased in 1947.
Cheshire	Delamere	183	Ancient possession, original part of Delamere Forest.

AGRICULTURAL

County	Estate	Acreage	Remarks
Cumbria	Aldingham	987	Ancient possession (part of Manor of Muchland) supplemented by purchases in the 19th century.
	Manor of Muchland and Torver	2,594	Forfeited to the Crown in the 16th century. Hill and waste lands subject to rights of common.
Devon	North Wyke	619	Purchased in 1981. Let to the Grassland Research Institute.
Dorset	Bryanston	4,646	Bulk of estate purchased in 1950.
Essex	*Stapleford Abbots including Hainault	2,779	Partly ancient possession partly allotted under enclosure awards and partly purchased. Part of the estate is in Greater London.
Gloucestershire	Clearwell	1,208	Purchased between 1907 and 1912.
	Hagloe	721	Purchased between 1853 and 1902.
Hertfordshire	Gorhambury	3,457	Purchased in 1931.
	Putteridge	3,506	Purchased in 1932. Part of the estate is in Bedfordshire.
	Wallington	837	Escheated to the Crown in 1956 and 1962.
Humberside	Derwent	2,725	Some ancient possession but mainly purchased in 1947/48.
	Gardham	1,086	Purchased in 1950.
	Sledmere	2,017	Purchased in 1981.
	Sunk Island	12,420	Largely reclaimed from the Humber estuary during the 17th, 18th and 19th centuries and partly purchased in 1913, 1947 and 1981.
	Swine	4,637	A small part is ancient possession, the bulk being purchased in 1859, 1871 and 1962.
Kent	Bedgebury	155	Purchased in 1919. Bulk of the estate sold 1983.
	Neats Court (Isle of Sheppey)	774	A small part is ancient possession, the remainder being purchased between 1850 and 1900.
	Romney Marsh	8,595	Purchased from 1958 onwards. Part of the estate is in Sussex.
Leicestershire	Gopsall	8,064	Purchased in 1932.

AGRICULTURAL

County	Estate	Acreage	Remarks
Lincolnshire	Billingborough	11,869	A small part is ancient possession, the bulk being purchased in 1855 and since.
	Croft	193	Ancient possession.
	Ewerby	4,618	Purchased in 1948.
	Whaplode	6,409	Partly ancient possession partly allotted under enclosure awards and partly purchased.
	Wingland	8,802	Greater part reclaimed from the Wash mainly in the last 100 years. Latest reclamations in 1972.
Norfolk	Croxton	8,018	Purchased in 1930. Major part of estate is leased to Forestry Commission.
	Kings Lynn	1,718	Part purchased in 1964. Part reclaimed from the Wash in 1965 and 1966.
North Yorkshire	Boroughbridge	3,194	Partly ancient possession and partly purchased between 1860 and 1876.
Nottingham	*Bingham	8,030	Purchased in 1926 and 1938.
	Laxton	1,870	Purchased in 1981 from M.A.F.F.
Oxfordshire	Wychwood	1,680	Ancient possession – originally part of Wychwood Forest disafforested after 1850.
Somerset	Dunster	9,230	Purchased in 1950.
	*Taunton	11,090	Purchased in 1944 and 1952.
Staffordshire and Shropshire	Patshull	3,865	Purchased in 1959.
Surrey	*Oxshott	1,641	Purchased mainly in 19th century.
Sussex	Poynings	62	Escheated to Crown at the end of the 18th century.
Wiltshire	Devizes	9,798	Purchased in 1858 and 1962–64.
	Savernake	10,448	Purchased in 1950.

WALES

Gwent	Tintern	248	Purchased in 1901.
Powys	Bronydd Mawr	568	Purchased in 1983.

AGRICULTURAL

County	Estate	Acreage	Remarks
Dyfed	Aberystwyth	91	Purchased in 1985 and 1987.
	Plynlimon	2,974	Mainly ancient possession.
		173,976	

SCOTLAND

Central Region
District of Stirling: Arngomery — 46 — Purchased in 1962 under the terms of the will of the late owner. Bulk of estate sold.

County	Estate	Acreage	Remarks
	Fintry	1,445	Purchased in 1930. Two sheep farms and some fishings. Bulk of estate sold.
	Stirling	445	Ancient possession added to in 1972.

Dumfries and Galloway Region
District of Annandale and Eskdale: Applegirth — 17,493 — Purchased from 1963 onwards.

Grampian Region
District of Moray: Fochabers — 13,290 — Purchased in 1937.

Glenlivet — 50,040 — Purchased in 1937. Includes considerable areas of hill and moorland, plus forests purchased in 1985.

Highland Region
District of Caithness: Lythmore — 1,050 — Ancient possession

Scotscalder — 590 — Purchased in 1909. Bulk of estate sold.

Lothian Region
District of Midlothian: Whitehill — 3,461 — Purchased from 1969 onwards.

87,860

URBAN

County	Estate	Acreage and *Sq ft of Commercial Space†*	Remarks
ENGLAND			
Berkshire	Ascot	500 7,000 *(R)*	Partly ancient possession, partly allotted under enclosure awards. Residential, and includes the racecourse.

URBAN

County	Estate	Acreage and *Sq ft of Commercial Space†*	Remarks
Berkshire (cont.)	Bracknell	47,000 *(O)*	Former Crown Estate Office purchased in 1969 and refurbished in 1985/6. Office development funded and purchased in 1985/6.
	Datchet	78 45,000 *(I)*	Purchased at various times. Residential, a golf course and miscellaneous lettings.
	Swinley	673 284,000 *(I)*	Formerly part of Windsor Estate acquired mainly by purchase and exchange and from enclosure awards. Residential lettings, two golf courses together with light industrial areas and proposed light industrial/headquarters development.
	★Windsor		Partly ancient possession, partly allotted under enclosure awards and partly acquired by purchase. The estate may be divided as follows:
	(a) Parks and Woods	12,378	The Great Park and Home Park (public).
	(b) Lands adjoining	211	Residential.
	(c) Town	55 60,000 *(O)*	Chiefly residential but with some commercial including a prestige headquarters office block (acquired 1988).
Buckinghamshire	High Wycombe	3 100,000 *(R)*	Covered shopping centre with offices above, funded and purchased in 1985/7.
	Milton Keynes	48,000 *(I)*	Purchased 1982, industrial.
Cambridgeshire	Cambridge	6 27,000 *(I)*	Hi-tech development part funded and developed since 1985.
Essex	Tilbury		Ferry rights only.
Hampshire	Portsmouth and Gosport	1	Ancient possession.
Herefordshire	Hereford	2 71,000 *(R)*	Retail with ancillary storage and offices plus 300 car parking spaces, purchased in 1986.
Hertfordshire	Hemel Hempstead	2.33 55,000 *(I)*	Business park funded and purchased in 1985/6.

URBAN

County	Estate	Acreage and *Sq ft of Commercial Space†*	Remarks
Isle of Wight	Osborne	28 *20,000 (I)*	Residential and industrial.
Kent	Dover		Ancient possession residential.
London	City of London	*994,000 (O)* *41,000 (R)* *1,000 (I)*	Ancient possession, supplemented by purchases in latter part of 19th century and since. Mainly blocks of offices in Holborn Viaduct, Ludgate Hill and Leadenhall Street.
	Oxford Street	*402,000 (O)* *121,000 (R)* *43,000 (I)*	Ancient possession, supplemented by purchases. Mainly office buildings and shops in New Oxford Street and Wardour Street. Includes quadrangle office development and adjacent shops on corner of Oxford Street and Wardour Street.
	Regent Street	*1,432,000 (O)* *1,192,000 (R)* *3,000 (I)*	Largely purchased in early 19th century for formation of new (Regent) street. Mainly shops and offices. Includes Meridien Hotel, Piccadilly and Regent Palace Hotel.
	Regents Park	*511,000 (O)* *46,000 (R)* *80,000 (I)*	Originally part of the Manor of Tyburn, acquired in 1544. Comprises about 800 buildings surrounding Regents Park together with a number of Regency Villas, the Royal College of Physicians and Royal College of Gynaecologists and Obstetricians, and a housing estate at Cumberland Market.
	Kensington	*90,000 (O)* *471,000 (R)*	Partly acquired in the 19th century supplemented by purchases in late 19th century and since. Residential property and embassies in Kensington Palace Gardens. Palace Green and Kensington with shops in Kensington High Street. Includes Kensington Barracks.
	Millbank	*696,000 (O)* *11,000 (R)* *39,000 (I)*	Mainly purchased in 1799. Housing estate and business premises.
	Victoria Park	*11,000 (O)* *5,000 (R)* *34,000 (I)*	Mainly purchased between 1842 and 1845. Housing estate and business premises.

URBAN

County	Estate	Acreage and *Sq ft of Commercial Space†*	Remarks
London (cont.)	Lower Regent Street and Haymarket	1,216,000 (O) 346,000 (R)	Mainly acquired in 16th century supplemented by purchases. Shops and offices in Piccadilly, Lower Regent Street, Haymarket, Jermyn Street, Waterloo Place, Pall Mall, Suffolk Street and Whitcomb Street.
	St James's	603,000 (O) 243,000 (R) 1,000 (I)	Mainly acquired in 16th century. Clubs, offices, shops and flats in Piccadilly, St James's Street, King Street, Ryder Street, Bury Street and St James's Place.
	South of Pall Mall	725,000 (O) 157,000 (R) 3,000 (I)	Ancient possession supplemented by purchases between 1961 and 1964. Clubs, offices and some residential property in Carlton House Terrace, Warwick House Street, Cockspur Street, Spring Gardens and Pall Mall.
	Trafalgar Square and Strand	206,000 (O) 75,000 (R)	Partly ancient possession and partly purchased. Offices and shops in Trafalgar Square, Strand, Orange Street, Cranbourne Street and St Martin's Lane. Includes Canada House, South Africa House and the Strand Palace Hotel.
	Whitehall and Victoria	706,000 (O) 12,000 (R)	Partly ancient possession and partly purchased. Mainly offices and shops in Whitehall, Great Scotland Yard, Northumberland Avenue, Buckingham Palace Road, Buckingham Gate, Queen Anne's Gate and Victoria Street. Includes Whitehall Court.
	Park Lane	31,000 (O)	Ancient possession. Hotels, offices and clubs in Piccadilly, Hamilton Place, Park Lane. Includes the Intercontinental and Inn on the Park Hotels.
	Fulham – Flats St Katherines and Cartwright Street		Purchased for commercial development.
(Greater London)	Blackheath	1	Ancient possession, residential.
	Eltham	496	Ancient possession. Residential estate with some commercial properties. Includes Royal Blackheath and Eltham Warren golf clubs.
	Lee Green		Residential.
	*Hainault	1	Residential.
	Hampton	57	Ancient possession. Mainly residential.

URBAN

County	Estate	Acreage and *Sq ft of Commercial Space*†	Remarks
London (cont.)	Hornchurch		Purchased in 1962. Business premises.
	Richmond	375	Ancient possession. Residential with some light industrial premises. Includes the Old Deer Park, Royal Mid-Surrey Golf Club and parts of the Old Palace of Richmond.
	Sudbrook	109	Purchased in 1841. Residential. Includes Richmond Golf Club.
Nottinghamshire	*Bingham	15 *126,000 (I)*	Formerly part of agricultural estate.
Somerset	*Taunton	30 *123,000 (I)*	Formerly part of agricultural estate.
Surrey	Bagshot	90 *45,000 (O)*	Partly ancient possession, partly allotted to Crown under enclosure awards and partly acquired by purchase and exchange. Includes Bagshot Park.
	Egham	5	Partly ancient possession, partly purchased. Residential and common land.
	Guildford	14 *310,000 (O)*	Business park being funded and purchased. Phase I – 1987/8, Phase II – 1988/9.
	Horley	*41,000 (O)* *47,000 (R)*	Town centre retail and office development with 270 space car park funded and purchased in 1985/7.
	*Oxshott		Purchased mainly in 19th century. Mainly residential.
Sussex	Hastings	5	Formerly foreshore reclaimed from the sea. Shops and residential.

SCOTLAND

Lothian Region

City of Edinburgh:	Charlotte Street	*16,000 (O)*	Offices including Crown Estate Office and further buildings purchased in 1985.
	Nicolson Street	2 *3,000 (O)* *41,000 (R)*	Acquired in 1978. Reconstructed. Shops, offices and residential.
	Princes Street Gardens	12	Amenity land comprising part of Princes Street Gardens and including the Castlebanks. Ancient possession.
	John Watson's School	12	Being converted to gallery use. Purchased 1977.

URBAN

County	Estate	Acreage and *Sq ft of Commercial Space†*	Remarks
Strathclyde Region			
City of Glasgow:	Blythswood Square	*68,000 (O)*	Offices purchased in 1986 and 1988 and an office development in the process of being funded and purchased.

†O – Office
 R – Retail
 I – Industrial

WINDSOR ESTATE (14,000 acres)

Windsor Great Park and the Home Park; the Savill and Valley Gardens; dedicated woodland (7,500 acres); residential property in Windsor Town, Datchet, Swinley, Bagshot and Ascot, and the Royal Ascot Racecourse.

FORESHORE AND SEABED

About half the foreshore around the coast of the United Kingdom and in tidal rivers. Foreshore is that part of the seashore lying between mean high and low water, except in Scotland, where spring tides apply. Only where grants have been made by the Crown and in counties of Cornwall and Lancaster (where the foreshore is owned by the respective Duchies) and parts of the Northern Isles (where udal tenure applies) does United Kingdom foreshore not prima facie form part of the Crown Estate. All seabed lying below mean low water (or spring in Scotland) is Crown Estate property as far as the limit of territorial waters.

MINERALS

Sand and gravel from the sea; limestone, chert and slate quarries in Wales; tin mines beneath the sea off Cornwall; potash off the Yorkshire coast; salt at Teeside; stone quarries in Dorset, Gloucestershire, Gwent and Cumbria; brick clay pits in Leicestershire and Berkshire; sand and gravel working in Cheshire; gravel in North Yorkshire; peat in Cambridgeshire; sea coal collection in Durham; and rights exercisable in the United Kingdom Continental Shelf, other than those in respect of coal oil and gas (as defined in the Continental Shelf Act 1964) are vested in the Crown Estate. The Crown also has a prerogative right to all mines royal i.e. gold and silver.

MISCELLANEOUS

Revenue from certain sporting rights and fishing, salmon fishing in parts of Scotland including the commercial net fishing at the mouth of the Spey. Additional revenue is obtained from sales of timber from the forestry estates.

APPENDIX E

SELECT BIBLIOGRAPHY
AND SOURCE NOTES

————— •••• —————

BIBLIOGRAPHY

There follows a select list, largely culled from the infinite array of royal
books published in recent years, of works which may prove of interest
to the reader in search of greater detail. The edition cited in each case is
that consulted by the author. Material drawn directly from these books
is acknowledged either in the text or in the source notes that follow.

Allison, Ronald and Riddell, Sarah: *The Royal Encyclopedia* (London:
    Macmillan, 1991)
Bagehot, Walter: *The English Constitution* (London: Fontana/Collins,
    1978)
Barry, Stephen P.: *Royal Service* (New York: Macmillan, 1983)
Beaverbrook, William Maxwell Aitken, Lord: *The Abdication of King
    Edward VIII* (London: Hamish Hamilton, 1966)
Billig, Michael: *Talking of the Royal Family* (London: Routledge,
    1992)
Boothroyd, Basil: *Philip: An Informal Biography* (London: Longman,
    1971)

Brooke, John: *King George III*, with a foreword by HRH The Prince of Wales (London: Constable, 1972)

Bryan III, J., and Murphy, Charles J.V.: *The Windsor Story* (London: Granada, 1979)

Cannadine, David and Price, Simon (ed.): *Rituals of Royalty: Power and Ceremonial in Traditional Societies* (Cambridge University Press, 1987)

Castle, Barbara: *The Castle Diaries 1964-70* (London: Weidenfeld and Nicolson, 1984)

Channon, Sir Henry: *'Chips': The Diaries of Sir Henry Channon,* edited by Robert Rhodes James (London: Weidenfeld and Nicolson, 1974)

Clarkson, Stephen and McCall, Christina: *Trudeau and Our Times: Vol I: The Magnificent Obsession* (Toronto: McClelland and Stewart, 1990)

Crawford, Marion: *The Little Princesses* (London: Cassell, 1950)

Crossman, Richard: *The Diaries of a Cabinet Minister, Vol III* (London: Hamish Hamilton and Jonathan Cape, 1977)

Dale, John: *The Prince and the Paranormal* (London: W.H. Allen, 1986)

Devere-Summers, Anthony: *Royal Survivors: The Ten Surviving Monarchies in Europe* (Rochester, Kent: Scribe Printing Ltd., 1984)

Donaldson, Frances: *Edward VIII* (London: Weidenfeld and Nicolson, 1974)

Duncan, Andrew: *The Reality of Monarchy* (London: Heinemann, 1970)

Edwards, Anne: *Matriarch: Queen Mary and The House of Windsor* (London: Hodder and Stoughton, 1984)
    Royal Sisters (London: Collins, 1990)

Flamini, Roland: *Sovereign: Elizabeth II and the Windsor Dynasty* (London: Bantam Press, 1991)

Gill, Crispin (ed.): *The Duchy of Cornwall,* with a foreword by HRH The Prince of Wales (Newton Abbot: David and Charles, 1987)

Gore, John: *King George V: A Personal Memoir* (London: John Murray, 1941)

Grigg, John: *The Monarchy Revisited* (London: W.H. Smith Contemporary Papers, 1992)

Hall, Philip: *Royal Fortune: Tax, Money and the Monarchy* (London: Bloomsbury, 1992)

Hamilton, Willie: *My Queen and I* (London: Quartet, 1975)

Heald, Tim: *The Duke: A Portrait of Prince Philip* (London: Hodder and Stoughton, 1991)

Hibbert, Christopher: *The Court of St James's* (London: Weidenfeld and Nicolson, 1979)

Higham, Charles and Moseley, Roy: *Elizabeth and Philip* (London: Sidgwick and Jackson, 1991)

Hitchens, Christopher: *The Monarchy* (Chatto *CounterBlasts* No 10) (London: Chatto and Windus, 1990)

Holden, Anthony: *Charles, Prince of Wales* (London: Weidenfeld and Nicolson, 1979)
> *Their Royal Highnesses* (London: Weidenfeld and Nicolson, 1981)
> *The Queen Mother* (London: Sphere, 1985, 1990)
> *Charles* (London: Weidenfeld and Nicolson, 1988)

Hough, Richard: *Mountbatten: Hero of Our Time* (London: Weidenfeld and Nicolson, 1980)
> *Born Royal: The Lives and Loves of the Young Windsors* (London: Andre Deutsch, 1988)
> *Edward and Alexandra* (London: Hodder and Stoughton, 1992)

Hughes, Ted: *Rain-Charm for the Duchy and other Laureate Poems* (London: Faber and Faber, 1992)

Hutchinson, Maxwell: *The Prince of Wales: Right or Wrong? An Architect Replies* (London: Faber and Faber, 1989)

Jay, Sir Antony: *Elizabeth R: The Role of the Monarchy Today* (London: BBC Books, 1992)

Jennings, W. Ivor: *The British Constitution* (Cambridge University Press, 1966)

Judd, Denis: *Prince Philip* (New York: Atheneum, 1981)

Junor, Penny: *Charles* (London: Sidgwick and Jackson, 1987)

Keay, Douglas: *Royal Pursuit* (London: Severn House, 1983
> *Elizabeth II: Portrait of a Monarch* (London: Ebury Press, 1991)

Lacey, Robert: *Majesty: Elizabeth II and the House of Windsor* (London: Hutchinson, 1977)
> *Princess* (London: Hutchinson, 1982)

Longford, Elizabeth: *Elizabeth R* (London: Weidenfeld and Nicolson, 1983)
> *The Royal House of Windsor* (London: Weidenfeld and Nicolson, 1974)
> *Royal Throne* (John Curtis/Hodder and Stoughton, 1993)

Lowry, Suzanne: *The Princess in the Mirror* (London: Chatto and Windus, 1985)

Maclean, Veronica: *Crowned Heads* (London: Hodder and Stoughton, 1993)

Magnus, Sir Philip: *King Edward VII* (London: John Murray, 1964)

Marigny, Alfred de: *A Conspiracy of Crowns* (London: Bantam Press, 1990)

Marples, Morris: *Princes in the Making: A Study of Royal Education* (London: Faber and Faber, 1965)

Martin, Kingsley: *The Crown and the Establishment* (London: Penguin, 1963)

Martin, Ralph: *The Woman He Loved* (London: W.H. Allen, 1974)
    Charles and Diana (London: Grafton Books, 1986)
Menkes, Suzy: *The Royal Jewels* (London: Grafton Books, 1985)
    Queen and Country (London: HarperCollins, 1992)
Morrah, Dermot: *To Be A King* (London: Hutchinson, 1968)
Morrow, Ann: *The Queen* (London: Granada, 1983)
Mortimer, Penelope: *Queen Elizabeth: A Life of the Queen Mother* (London: Viking, 1986)
Morton, Andrew: *Inside Kensington Palace* (London: Michael O'Mara, 1987)
    Theirs is the Kingdom: The Wealth of the Windsors (London: Michael O'Mara Books, 1990)
    Diana: Her True Story (London: Michael O'Mara Books, 1992)
Mount, Ferdinand: *The British Constitution Now* (London: Heinemann, 1992)
Nairn, Tom: *The Enchanted Glass* (London: Radius, 1988)
Nicolson, Harold: *King George V: His Life and Reign* (London: Constable, 1952)
Palmer, Alan: *Princes of Wales* (London: Weidenfeld and Nicolson, 1979)
Pearson, John: *The Ultimate Family* (London: Michael Joseph, 1986)
Pope-Hennessy, James: *Queen Mary* (London: Allen and Unwin, 1959)
Rose, Kenneth: *King George V* (London: Weidenfeld and Nicolson, 1983)
Sampson, Anthony: *The Essential Anatomy of Britain* (London: Hodder and Stoughton, 1992)
Townsend, Peter: *Time and Chance* (London: Collins, 1978)
Wales, HRH The Prince of: *A Vision of Britain* (London: Doubleday, 1989)
    Highgrove: Portrait of an Estate (London: Chapman, 1993)
Warwick, Christopher: *Princess Margaret* (London: Weidenfeld and Nicolson, 1983)
    Abdication (London: Sidgwick and Jackson, 1986)
Wheeler-Bennett, Sir John: *King George VI* (London: Macmillan, 1958)
Whitaker, James: *Settling Down* (London: Quartet, 1981)
Windsor, HRH The Duke of: *A King's Story: Memoirs of HRH The Duke of Windsor* (London: Cassell, 1951)
    The Crown and the People (London: Cassell, 1953)
    A Family Album (London: Cassell, 1960)
Young, Hugo: *One of Us* (London: Macmillan, 1989)
Ziegler, Philip: *Crown and People* (London: Collins, 1978)
    Mountbatten (London: Collins, 1985)
    Edward VIII (London: Collins, 1990)

SOURCE NOTES

CHAPTER 1: A HOUSE DIVIDED

3   **'to represent, express and affect'**: *Time*, New York, 5 January 1953, quoted in Lacey, *Majesty*, p. 186.

4   **'You can tell a lot about a country'**: Hitchens, *The Monarchy*.

5   **'another Joan of Arc'**: Martha Duffy, *Time*, 30 November 1992.

5   **an ever-changing feminine archetype**: The ideas in this paragraph are developed from a fascinating essay by Camille Paglia, discussed in more detail in Chapter 9.

7   **'The gap between myth and reality'**: 'The foundations wobble': *The Independent*, London, 28 November 1992.

9   **thirteen times the average national wage**: £14,066 p.a. gross. Based on figures in *Britain 1993: An Official Handbook* (Her Majesty's Stationery Office).

11   **'All are essential to the Queen's well-being'**: Richard Tomlinson, 'They Also Serve, Who Only Ush', *The Independent on Sunday*, London, 20 December 1992.

14   **'Never in a hundred years'**: Author's source requests anonymity.

15   **'Even in the let's-pretend world of Hollywood'**: 'A royal fudge', *The Economist*, London, 12 December 1992.

17   **'Why not have a Head of State'**: John Hines of St Leonards-on-Sea, East Sussex, letter to *The Sunday Times*, London, 6 December 1992.

18   **'guilty of high treason'**: Brian Porter, of Seasalter, Kent, letter to *The Sunday Times*, 6 December 1992.

18   **'I feel betrayed' . . . 'What cannot be achieved'**: Adrienne Nelson of Preston, Lancs, and John Atkins of Great Tarpot, Essex, letters to *The Sunday Times*, 20 December 1992.

18   **'Is not this the time'**: Robert Wythe, of Walberswick, Suffolk, letter to *The Sunday Times*, 6 December 1992.

19   **'Is it beyond our wit'**: Professor Stephen Haseler, Chairman, *Republic*, letter to *The Times*, London, 24 December 1992.

19   **'could rejuvenate itself as a republic'**: Ludovic Kennedy, Diary, *The Spectator*, London, 1 February 1992.

19   **'The trappings of monarchy'**: Ludovic Kennedy, 'Who should be president of Britain?', *The Times*, 18 December 1992.

19   **crimson velvet trimmed with ermine**: Allison and Riddell: *The Royal Encyclopedia*.

20   **'It is *our* soap opera'**: Janet Watts, *The Observer,* London, 22 March 1992.

21   **'Saint and sinner . . . why, after all'**: Mary Kenny, *The Sunday Telegraph,* London, 30 August 1992.

21   **'While a star might think'**: Hazel Davis, member of the Society of Analytical Psychology: *The Independent,* 16 December 1992.

22   **'The trouble is . . .'**: *The Sunday Times,* 3 September 1989.

22   **'It is the wholly unusual . . . lifestyle'**: *The Times,* 18 December 1992.

23   **'There is less confidence in the monarchy'**: Adrian Lithgow, 'The Queen: My Concern', *The Mail on Sunday,* London, 24 January 1993.

CHAPTER 2: 'ANNUS HORRIBILIS'

30   **'If this were an ordinary family'**: Bernard Levin, 'Long live the royals', *The Times,* 5 February 1993.

31   **A *Daily Express* poll**: Harris Research Centre poll for *The Daily Express,* London, 13 July 1992. (Harris interviewed 1,105 people throughout the UK between 6 and 9 July.)

35   **'The idea that the nation'**: Dr Robert Wilkins, *The Sunday Times,* 6 December 1992.

36   **'spectacularly out of touch'**: Hugo Young: 'You kneel, therefore I am', *The Guardian,* London, 26 November 1992.

37   **'While the castle stands'**: Janet Daley, 'Who owns Windsor Castle?', *The Times,* 24 November 1992.

41   **'If the Queen wants the sympathy'**: *The Evening Standard,* 26 November 1992.

46   **'the unacceptable face of monarchy'**: Anthony Holden, 'Ten tips towards a New Year of Majesty', *The Times,* 31 December 1992.

47   **'The monarchy is at a watershed'**: Alan Clark MP, *The Mail on Sunday,* 20 December 1992.

47   **'It has indeed been a terrible year'**: Sir John Junor, *The Mail on Sunday,* 20 December 1992.

48   **'a modest sermon'**: Alexander Chancellor, 'Heroes and Villains', *The Independent* magazine, 16 December 1992.

49   **'too old to change'**: Nigel Dempster, *The Daily Mail,* London, 18 November 1992.

CHAPTER 3: FOUR FAILED MARRIAGES

51   **'Learned scholars'**: HRH The Prince of Wales: foreword to Brooke, John: *King George III.*

52   **'In the Queen's eyes'**: Sanctioned as an 'official fault' to the author in the mid-1980s by a senior Buckingham Palace official, briefing him for a Central Office of Information 'profile' of the Queen to be used on overseas visits.

53   **'No feeling could seem more childish'**: Bagehot, *The English Constitution.*

53   **'Great weddings; shame about the marriages'**: Valerie Grove, 'And They All Lived Sadly Ever After', *The Times,* 20 March 1992.

54   **'like a lamb to the slaughter'**: Morton, *Diana: Her True Story.*

55   **strenuously denied**: The author's 1988 biography of Prince Charles, which ventured to suggest that all was not well with the Wales marriage, was described as 'fiction from beginning to end' by Tom Shebbeare, director of the Prince's Trust: *The Observer,* 13 November 1988.

56   **'Married, aren't you?'**: On this occasion, the author. Holden, 'Prince Charles and the Pursuit of Happiness', *The Observer,* 1 March 1981.

58   **'he would always love her'**: Morton, op.cit.

58   **'at the drop of a hat . . . irretrievably gone'**: Junor, *Charles.*

59   **'Diana became ill because'**: Mary Clarke interviewed by Geoffrey Levy, *Daily Mail,* 6 February 1993.

61   **'close friends of Prince Charles'**: Nigel Dempster, 'Cause for Concern', *Daily Mail,* 2 July 1991.

67   **'Won't it be nice'**: *Newsweek,* New York, 18 May 1981.

69   **'Our love, for such it was'**: Peter Townsend: *Time and Chance,* 1978.

71   **'It is high time'**: *The Sunday People,* London, 14 June 1953.

72   **'Could Princess Margaret and I'**: Townsend, op.cit.

86   **according to Player**: Lesley Player, *My Story,* Grafton Books, London, 1993, as serialized in *The News of the World,* 7 February 1993.

88   **'Victoria and I just wanted'**: Georgina Howell, *Tatler,* London, November 1992, and *The Sunday Times,* 22 March 1992.

89   **'the embodiment of the modern monarchy'**: *The Sunday Times,* 19 January 1992.

92   **'Nothing in her life as a royal'**: Janet Watts, *The Observer,* 22 March 1992.

CHAPTER 4: THE OVER-EXTENDED FAMILY

98 **'This country is at war'**: *The Sunday Times*, 10 February 1991.

100 **'the way to his heart'**: *The Guardian,* 12 February 1991.

101 **'a republican in his youth'**: *The Spectator*, 4 July 1992.

104 **'one editorial in one Sunday newspaper'**: Brian Mac-Arthur, 'A family at war', *The Sunday Times*, 17 February 1991.

105 **'an expensive luxury'**: MORI poll for the *Daily Mail*, 15 February 1992.

108 **'Offstage Laurence Olivier'**: *The Sunday Telegraph,* 7 July 1991.

108 **'a colossal mistake'**: *The Times*, 5 February 1993.

109 **'Such disproportionate importance'**: *The Sunday Telegraph*, 30 August 1992.

109 **'We have been encouraged'**: *The Sunday Telegraph*, 13 September 1992.

110 **'It's a big if'**: Hugh Massingberd, *The Daily Telegraph*, London, 29 August, 1992.

110 **'to make the vital separation'**: *Daily Mail*, 16 September 1992.

112 **Table**: Tim O'Donovan of Datchet, Berkshire, publishes an annual survey of royal engagements based on the Court Circular. This table is an expanded version of his 1992 statistics, announced in a letter to *The Times*, 2 January 1993.

114 **'Anyone know of a good accountant?'**: Marina Mowatt, 'Secret of the Queen's Shed', *The Sunday Express,* London, 29 November 1992.

114 **'photographs taken with a long lens'**: Quentin Crewe, letter to *The Times*, 14 January 1993.

118 **'some of the younger members of the royal family'**: Sir Kenneth Lewis, letter to *The Times*, 26 December 1992.

119 **'one ordinary, congenial family'**: Janet Daley, *The Times*, 25 August 1992.

119 **'It would be futile to expect'**: Valerie Grove, *The Times*, 20 March 1992.

119 **'Marital peace and sexual purity'**: Janet Daley, *The Times*, 25 August 1992.

CHAPTER 5: THE ROYAL FINANCES

122 **almost 80 per cent of the British people:** 79 per cent of respondents agreed with the proposition 'that the Queen should pay income tax on income generated by her wealth' in an NMR poll for *The Independent on Sunday*, 24 February 1991.

122 **When a Palace leak**: Michael Jones, 'Queen: Tax me and I'll have to sell Balmoral', *The Sunday Times*, 30 June 1991.

122 **a careless chance remark**: Author's source, who was present, wishes to remain anonymous.

125 **'There is a strong case'**: *Daily Mail*, 16 September 1992.

125 **'more in tune with the times'**: *The Observer*, 13 September 1992.

128 **a 1992 survey for *The Times***: Brian Moynahan, *The Times* Saturday Review, 1 February 1992.

129 **'As soon as the Queen'**: Suzy Menkes, *The Royal Jewels*, and in conversation with the author.

129 **'common law' husbands or wives**: *Despatches,* Channel 4, 2 June 1992.

130 **'may simply be the results'**: *The Daily Telegraph*, 15 September 1992.

130 **'The Queen is stinking rich'**: *The Sunday Times*, 19 January, 1992.

130 **a 1990 estimate of £600 million**: Morton, *Theirs is the Kingdom*.

130 **a 1992 assessment by Victor Levy**: *The Sunday Times, 30 August 1992.

132 **'small beer'**: Alan Hamilton, *The Times*, 18 July 1992.

133 **'cough up'**: *The Observer,* 13 September 1992.

133 **The term 'Civil List' dates from 1698**: This brief historical section owes a debt to Philip Hall's important book *Royal Fortune*. The author is indebted to Mr Hall for this and other help.

138 **'a suitable age for retirement'**: Heald, *The Duke*.

138 **vain attempts to have it edited out**: Duncan, *The Reality of Monarchy*.

138 **'one of the richest women in the world'**: Castle, *The Castle Diaries*.

138 **'It takes royalty to assume'**: Crossman, *The Diaries of a Cabinet Minister*.

140 **in favour of doing away with the Civil List**: Junor, *Charles*.

140 **'Parliament must not be manoeuvred'**: *The Evening Standard*, 14 September 1992.

141   'There is no indication': *The Times*, 14 September 1992.
141   'a serious issue': *The Times*, 27 November 1992.
143   'There are people in Britain': Hansard, Report of parliamentary proceedings, 11 February 1993.
147   'How about newspaper columnists?': Lynn Barber, 'The workaholic Queen and I', *The Independent on Sunday*, 14 February 1993.
148   'one of the great visitor attractions of Europe': Simon Jenkins, 'A palace fit for the public', *The Times*, 13 February 1993.
148   'There needs to be greater openness': 'Start of a royal revolution', *The Sunday Times*, 14 February 1993.
151   'It earns colossal sums overseas': *The News of the World*, London, 14 February 1993.
153   'lost touch with ordinary people': *The Daily Telegraph*, 9 February 1993.
153   'Not a penny, I suspect': Robyn Lewis of Nefyn, Gwynedd, letter to *The Sunday Times*, 21 February 1993.

CHAPTER 6: A 'FAMILY' MONARCHY: 1917–52

159   'might bring about its overthrow': 'Prinny and the Prince', Colin Matthew, *The Observer*, 14 June 1992.
160   'started and grew pale': Harold Nicolson, *King George V*.
161   'would not identify themselves': Gore, *King George V*.
161   'much occupied': Letter from Lord Stamfordham to Mr. George Barnes, 19 June, 1917.
161   'have down those hateful German banners': Pope-Hennessy, *Queen Mary*.
161   'my birth and parentage': Battenberg's letter of resignation to the First Lord of the Admiralty, Winston Churchill.
164   'We have never been nearer a revolution': Journals and Letters of Reginald, Viscount Esher (London: Nicholson and Watson, 1934, vol II).
165   'an old friend whom he could not bear': Longford, *The Royal House of Windsor*.
166   'When the Labour Party comes to power': ibid.
167   'no-one ever had employers': Crawford, *The Little Princesses*.
167   'the end of the period': *Daily Mail*, 21 November 1992.
168   'the comforts of central heating': Holden, *The Queen Mother*.
168   'Had this been true': Gloria Vanderbilt and Lady (Thelma)

Furness: *Double Exposure* (London: Frederick Muller, 1959).

169 **'The Warfields. . . have never had a divorce'**: The Duchess of Windsor: *The Heart has its Reasons*.

170 **a lethal injection**: Sarah Bradford, *George VI*, Weidenfeld & Nicolson, London, 1989.

170 **'even beyond the norm'**: Ziegler: *Edward VIII*.

171 **'whether it was a bad omen'**: HRH The Duke of Windsor, *A King's Story*.

172 **'It was a pleasant hour'**: Duchess of Windsor, op. cit.

172 **'the woman who killed my husband'**: Holden, op.cit. Private source.

173 **'really rather second-rate'**: Harold Nicolson, Diaries.

173 **'this obstinate little man'**: ibid.

173 **'When I was a little boy in Worcestershire'**: Keith Middlemas and John Barnes: *Baldwin* (Weidenfeld & Nicolson, 1969).

173 **'Didn't you find it terribly hot?'**: Pope-Hennessy, *Queen Mary*.

174 **'Your Majesty's personal affairs**: *The Times*, 29 November 1955.

174 **'Shocked and angered'**: Wheeler-Bennett, *King George VI*.

175 **'this is most grievous news**: ibid.

175 **'like the proverbial sheep being led to the slaughter'**: Wheeler-Bennett, ibid.

176 **'David said to Queen Mary'**: ibid.

178 **'Dickie, this is absolutely terrible'**: Lacey, *Majesty*.

180 **'a wrong and foolish thing'**: Wheeler-Bennett, op. cit.

180 **'a downgrading of expectations'**: Robert Lacey, 'Majesty and Magic,' *The Sunday Times*, 3 September 1989.

181 **'poor, bare, fork'd animal'**: Shakespeare, King Lear, III, iv, 113.

182 **'I am new to the job'**: Wheeler-Bennett, op. cit.

183 **'Once a person has become a Royal Highness'**: H. Montgomery Hyde: *Baldwin, The Unexpected Prime Minister* (London: Hart-Davis MacGibbon, 1973).

184 **'not by what they did'**: Donaldson, *Edward VIII*.

184 **'a grave constitutional impropriety'**: Grigg, *The Monarchy Revisited*.

186 **'I am a younger man than you'**: Holden, op. cit.

CHAPTER 7: QUEEN ELIZABETH II:
THE LAST BRITISH MONARCH?

189   **'To spend as long as possible'**: Holden, *Charles, Prince of Wales*.

189   **'For goodness sake'**: Crawford, *The Little Princesses*.

190   **'Philip couldn't help but be affected'**: Fiammetta Rocco, 'A Strange Life', *The Independent on Sunday*, London, 13 December 1992.

191   **penis gourd**: Judd, *Prince Philip*.

191   **Even in private**: Heald, *The Duke*.

191   **'I've never dared press the subject'**: Author's private conversation.

193   **'the whole world had dropped in on him'**: Boothroyd, *Philip*.

193   **'came to being the consort'**: Keay, *Elizabeth II*.

193   **'It was not my ambition'**: Rocco, op. cit.

194   **'I'm just a bloody amoeba'**: Pearson, *The Ultimate Family*

195   **'The Queen can be grateful'**: *The Times*, 3 January 1992.

197   **wanted to emigrate etc.**: 49 per cent of Britons say they 'would prefer to live abroad'. Gallup poll, *The Daily Telegraph*, 22 February 1993.

197   **'represents the people's aspirations'**: Longford, *Royal Throne*.

198   **'the worst first year'**: *The Sunday Telegraph*, 4 April 1993.

199   **'So much does the Queen'**: Hugh Massingberd, *The Daily Telegraph*, 29 August 1992.

200   **'The Queen's entourage'**: *National & English Review*, London, August 1957.

200   **'Japanese Shintoism'**: Grigg, *The Monarchy Revisited*.

201   **'It bores me, it depresses me'**: *Encounter*, London, October 1957.

201   **'a substitute or ersatz religion'**: *Saturday Evening Post*, New York, 19 October 1957.

202   **'tendency to regard as high treason'**: *The Sunday Times*, 2 January 1972.

202   **'It is more than time'**: *The Independent*, 6 June 1992.

203   **'a preoccuption with loyalty'**: *The Observer*, 26 January 1992.

203   **'Much of the blame'**: *The Mail on Sunday*, 23 August 1992.

203   **'The first is that the assumption'**: *The Times*, 27 November 1992.

203   **'The real damage has been inflicted'**: *Evening Standard*, 27 November 1992.

204   **'hanged at the yardarm'**: *The Times*, 5 February 1993.

204   **'The authority to commit our forces'**: *The Times*, 12 January 1991.

205   **'The crown does still remain'**: Blake, *The Office of the Prime Minister* (Lectures delivered as Provost of The Queen's College, Oxford), 1974.

205   **'There can be little doubt'**: John Grigg, *The Times*, 26 October 1992.

207   **'So it was settled'**: Harold Macmillan, *At the End of the Day* (London: Macmillan, 1973).

208   **'I suffered much at this time'**: Lord Butler, *The Art of the Possible* (London: Hamish Hamilton, 1971).

208   **'played the royal card'**: *Daily Mail*, 1 January 1993.

209   **'determined that Butler'**: Iain Macleod, *The Spectator*, London, 17 January 1964.

210   **'We handed Rab a loaded revolver'**: BBC2, *Reputations*, 13 July 1983.

211   **'played fast and loose'**: Keay, *Elizabeth II*.

211   **'open and above board'**: Lord Home, *The Way the Wind Blows* (London: Collins, 1976).

213   **The weekly meetings**: Sampson, *The Changing Anatomy of Britain*, 1982.

213   **'much of the human race'**: Young, *One of Us*.

215   **'She doesn't know about it'**: Tip O'Neill, *Man of the House* (London: Bodley Head, 1988).

216   **'to the point of outrage'**: 'The African Queen', *The Sunday Times*, 20 July 1986.

216   **'For one brief weekend'**: Young, *op. cit.*

216   **'even supposing that he or she knew'**: Letter to *The Times*, 28 July 1986.

217   **'some monstrous caged beast'**: *The Times*, 29 July 1986.

217   **'an indelible impression'**: *The Sunday Telegraph*, 27 July 1986.

218   **' very interested in the political side'**: Longford, *Elizabeth R.*

218   **'can't say good morning'**: Benn, *Conflicts of Interest, Diaries 1977-80* (London: Hutchinson, 1990).

218   **'As for departures from routine'**: *The Times*, 27 November 1992.

219   **'If you live this sort of life'**: *Elizabeth R*, BBC Television, 4 February 1992.

CHAPTER 8: CHARLES: THE HEIR APPARENT

223 **'If Prince Charles does believe'**: *Daily Mail*, 20 January 1992.

224 **'getting away with all sorts of things'**: Major Anthony Dryland, letter to *The Sunday Telegraph,* 24 January 1993.

224 **'You cannot have one rule'**: *The Sun*, 25 January 1993.

226 **'Looking back over history'**: BBC 1, *The Heart of the Matter*, 24 January 1993.

226 **'We expect our leaders'**: *The Times*, 1 February 1993.

226 **'a right old mess'**: BBC 1, Entertainment Express, 12 February 1993.

227 **'Talk dirty to us**: *The Sun*, 19 January 1993.

227 **'who has accepted for some time**: *Today*, 18 January 1993.

228 **more than a third of Britons**: The David Lewis Consultancy, poll for Sky TV's *The Royal Debate*, 16 February 1993.

229 **'silly, touching and filthy'**: *Evening Standard*, 14 January 1993.

229 **'We are entitled to be furious'**: *Evening Standard*, 14 May 1992.

229 **'One of the ablest medieval kings'**: Bruce Anderson, *Sunday Express*, 23 August 1992.

229 **'The prince is very unlikely'**: *Evening Standard*, 15 January 1993.

232 **'a model of environmental soundness'**: HRH The Prince of Wales & Charles Clother, *Highgrove: Portrait of an Estate,* and Annie Rankin, 'Raising royal eco-standards', The Times, 19 December 1992.

234 **'Sensitive to criticism'**: Harold Nicolson, *George V.*

235 **'phased out . . . for other initiatives'** *Building Design*, 14 October 1988.

235 **'to attend a meeting with the Trustees'**: Letter on Buckingham Palace notepaper leaked to the author by source requesting anonymity.

236 **'a characteristic contribution'**: Brian Appleyard, *The Times*, 9 December 1992.

237 **'Rushdie costs the taxpayer too much'**: *La Regle du Jeu*, Paris, January reported in *The Independent on Sunday*, 31 January 1993.

237 **'Dear God, how he screws things up'**: Brian Appleyard, 'The royal reign of terror that is ruining architecture', *The Sunday Times,* 18 August 1991.

240   **'For those committed Classicists'**: Kenneth Powell, *The Sunday Telegraph*, 4 October 1992.

242   **'moving from fiasco to fiasco'**: *The Sunday Correspondent*, 30 September 1990.

243   **'Slammed by his enemies'**: Kenneth Powell, *The Sunday Telegraph*, 4 October 1992.

244   **'more damaging than he can possibly realize'**: *The Times*, 9 December 1992.

244   **'The claim to be defending a democratic approach'**: Richard Rogers, 'Pulling down the Prince', *The Times*, 3 July 1989.

247   **'one of those unhappy fathers'**: *Daily Mail*, 17 November 1992.

248   **'Charles starts with great enthusiasm'**: Fiammetta Rocco, *The Independent on Sunday*, 13 December 1992.

251   **'Ah, the red rose man'**: Don Macintyre, 'The Man who would be King', *The Sunday Telegraph*, 10 February 1991.

252   **'If you don't define yourself'**: Peter Mandelson, *The Times*, 16 December 1992.

252   **'The general mood is familiar'**: Brian Appleyard, *The Times*, 9 December 1992.

253   **'A little girl lost'**: Rory Knight Bruce, *Evening Standard*, 26 January 1993.

255   **'bury himself in his work'**: Alan Hamilton, *The Times*, 19 February 1993.

CHAPTER 9: DIANA, PRINCESS OF WALES

259   **'a cynical disbelief'**: *The Times*, 15 February 1993.

259   **'Too many people have used AIDS'**: *Daily Mail*, 17 February 1993.

260   **'Hamlet without the prince'**: Private source, who was present at the occasion.

261   **'getting up smiling'**: *Daily Mail*, 3 March 1993.

262   **'precisely the kind of delicate royal duty'**: *Daily Mail*, 8 April 1993.

263   **'mixed up with her vanity'**: *News of the World*, 11 April 1993.

263   **'Those phone calls'**: *The Mail on Sunday*, 11 April 1993.

264   **'Diana. . . got the better of Charles'**: *Daily Mail*, 9 April 1993.

265   **'The Establishment is 100% against the princess'** . . . **'Leading members of the Establishment'** quotes from

St John, Casey, Westwood, Hailsham: *The Sunday Times*, 24 January 1993.

266   **'allowed to enjoy the spoils'**: *The Sunday Times*, 24 January 1993.

268   **'a familiar state of nervous excitement'**: Rory Knight Bruce, 'Now you see her. . . soon you won't', *Evening Standard*, 26 January 1993.

270   **'an international obsession'**: *The Guardian*, 30 July 1992. In a fascinating article reprinted from *The New Republic*, Paglia first presented the ideas summarized here. They were further discussed in a British television programme, 'Diana Unclothed', made by Rapido TV for *Without Walls*, Channel 4, 16 March 1993, in which the author took part.

272   **'Dogmeat'**: 'Diana Unclothed', Channel 4, 16 March 1993.

272   **'Cannot find much sympathy'**: Lesley White, *The Sunday Times*, 21 March 1993.

272   **'a sick woman'**: Penny Junor, *Today*, 6 July 1992.

273   **'I have always been very impressed'**: conversation with author.

273   **'not academically clever'**: *Daily Mail*, 17 November 1992.

275   **'Charles's parents!'**: Rocco, *The Independent on Sunday*, 13 December 1992.

278   **'the stress in the princess's marriage'**: Longford, *Royal Throne*.

278   **'the anger and hurt'**: Mary Clarke interviewed by Geoffrey Levy, *Daily Mail*, 6 February 1993.

280   **'done most to improve'**: *Daily Express,* 2 December 1993.

280   **'She could easily have been frightened off'** . . . **'drawn into adult relationships'** . . . **'Diana was not prepared'**: *The Sunday Times*, 21 March 1993.

CHAPTER 10: 'WE WILL GO QUIETLY'

285   **'We will go quietly'**: Lacey, *Majesty*.

285   **'if people don't want it'**: Sampson, *The Essential Anatomy of Britain*.

287   **'Heavily subsidized, monopolistic'**: Joanna Coles, *The Guardian*, 23 February 1991.

288   **'an officer appointed by parliament'**: *The Sunday Times*, 30 September 1990.

289   **'I am glad'**: *The Sunday Telegraph*, 7 June 1992.

289   **'Centralised, secretive regimes'**: *The Sunday Times,* 7 October 1990.

290   **'the same may soon be said'**: *The Spectator*, 1 February 1992.

290   **'a whiff of republicanism'**: *The Spectator*, 16 May 1992.

291   **'So what should British monarchists do?'**: *The Sunday Telegraph*, 29 November 1992.

291   **'I'm a republican'**: *The Observer*, 19 April 1992.

291   **'The damage has occurred'**: Eugene Robinson, *The Washington Post*, 13 September 1992.

291   **'The Queen is all right'**: *The Sunday Telegraph*, 2 August 1992.

292   **'Reposing the flame'**: Matthew Parris, *The Times*, 13 February 1993.

292   **'like their monarchs either old'**: Ziegler, *Crown and People*.

293   **'The great landed aristocracy**: Massingberd, *The Daily Telegraph*, 29 August, 1992.

293   **'it now seems unlikely'**: *The Independent on Sunday*, 4 October 1992.

294   **'As babies get older'**: *The Times*, 24 November 1992.

294   **Gallup poll for the League Against Cruel Sports**: *The Sunday Telegraph*, 1 November 1992.

295   **more than 30,000 birds**: John Bryant, Head of Research, The League Against Cruel Sports, *The Mail on Sunday*, 7 February 1993.

295   **'All that is required'**: Selina Hastings, *The Sunday Correspondent*, 7 October 1990.

295   **'a tax-evading bunch of adulterers'**: *The Guardian*, 22 February 1993.

296   **'cheap self-publicists'**: *The Guardian*, 9 June 1992.

296   **'an awful sight'**: Barbara Amiel, *The Sunday Times*, 13 September 1992.

296   **'a kind of Pied Piper'**: Longford, *Royal Throne*.

296   **'cancer in the soft underbelly'**: Shea, *The Times*, 1 December 1992.

297   **'Baloney'**: John le Carré, 'Don't trust Carruthers', *The Daily Telegraph*, 20 January 1993.

297   **'inextricably bound up'**: *The Daily Telegraph*, 6 June 1992.

298   **'Millions of our countrypeople'**: *The Times*, 16 January 1993.

299   **'Reason takes a holiday'**: *The Independent on Sunday*, 22 March 1992.

300   **'It is Rupert Murdoch'**: *The Times*, 15 February 1993.

301   **'I'm ambivalent about that'**: William Shawcross, *Rupert Murdoch: Ringmaster of the Information Circus* (London: Chatto & Windus, 1992).

302 **'Everyone likes flattery'** ... **'Last Tuesday'**: Hitchens: *Counterblasts* : 'The Monarchy'.

303 **'the emotions and instincts'**: Sir Antony Jay interviewed by Megan Tressider, *The Sunday Telegraph*, 26 January 1992

303 **'the apotheosis of the commonplace'**: *The Times*, 24 November 1992.

304 **a contradiction in terms**: *The Sunday Telegraph,* 7 July 1991.

305 **'a very precious part'**: John Major interviewed by Jonathon Holborow, editor, *The Mail on Sunday*, 21 Februrary 1993.

305 **'The Establishment always responds'**: *The Sunday Times*, 11 April 1993.

305 **'to take a job'** ... **'I think it of absolute importance... Misunderstanding of the situation'**: Prince Charles interviewed by Longford, *Royal Throne*.

306 **'the worst of all worlds'**: *The Daily Express*, 15 February 1993.

306 **'more worrying for the monarchy'**: *The Observer,* 14 June 1992.

307 **'we need to look at tax'**: *The Times*, 20 January 1993.

308 **24 per cent of Labour MPs**: *The Sunday Telegraph*, 24 January 1993.

308 **'The hereditary element'**: Interview with *The Times,* 9 February 1993.

308 **'better value for money'**: *The Times*, 8 February 1993.

309 **65 per cent of the public**: *The Daily Telegraph*, 8 February 1993.

309 **'disingenuous, to say the least'**: Grigg, *The Monarchy Revisited*.

309 **'deeply decadent'**: *Tribune*, London, 4 February 1993.

309 **'We have to ask the question'**: *The Sunday Times*, 14 February 1993.

309 **'a radical overhaul'** The Walden Interview, London Weekend Television, 7 February 1993.

310 **'What is needed is clear'**: *The Daily Telegraph*, 12 December 1992.

310 **a grand total of £25,000**: *The Sunday Times*, 25 April 1993.

312 **a tourist attraction**: *The Daily Express*, 13 July 1992.

312 **'a financial disaster'** ... **'the Queen does a great job'**: *News of the World*, 7 February 1993.

313 **a survey of American tourists**: *Condé Nast Traveler*, New York, July 1993. The author gratefully acknowledges the kind assistance of Ron Hall, London editor, and Clive Irving, senior consulting editor.

315   **'cheapen society'**: *The Times*, 31 December 1992.

316   **'a complete threat to the honours system'**: *Panorama*, BBC Television, 22 February 1993.

317   **'We don't change the constitution'**: *The Independent*, 8 June 1992.

317   **'It has to be asked'**: *The Mail on Sunday*, 31 January 1993.

317   **'The two go together'**: *The Times*, 5 September 1992

317   **'the official duties'**: *The Times*, 28 January 1993.

317   **'a compote of show business'**: *The Times*, 27 January 1993.

318   **'nothing in statute law'**: *The Independent*, 8 June 1992.

318   **'the greatest upheaval'**: *The Sunday Telegraph*, 7 March 1993.

319   **'difficult to envisage'**: *The Financial Times*, 1 February 1992.

322   **'corrupt dictatorships'**: Alan Watkins, *The Spectator*, 16 May 1992.

323   **'Monarchy is neither necessary'**: *The Times*, 8 June 1992.

325   **'a new and significant'**: *The Guardian*, 9 June 1992.

325   **'without the help of a single lawyer'**: conversation with author.

326   **'in the unfortunate situation'**: statement drafted for this book.

327   **'Many of the best political theorists'**: *Evening Standard*, 5 June 1992.

APPENDIX C: TONY BENN'S BILL
FOR A COMMONWEALTH OF BRITAIN

The full text of Tony Benn's Commonwealth of Britain Bill is available from Her Majesty's Stationery Office (Bill 103), and will be discussed in definitive detail in Mr Benn's forthcoming book *Common Sense* (London, Hutchinson, 1993). The author is very grateful to Mr Benn for permission to reproduce this summary.

THE ALLEGED 'HIGHGROVE TAPE'

CHARLES: To be honest, I've never really thought about it.
DIANA: Well, you wouldn't, would you?
CHARLES: Is there any reason why I should?
DIANA: Should what?
CHARLES: Think about it.
DIANA: Do I have to?
CHARLES: Is this really getting us anywhere?
DIANA: Not particularly, no.
CHARLES: Shall I just go?
DIANA: I don't think that would solve anything.
CHARLES: It may allow us to get some sleep tonight.
DIANA: I couldn't sleep on this!
CHARLES: Quiet, you'll wake the children.
DIANA: They know, anyway.
CHARLES: Look, three days is hardly a lifetime. Three days . . .
DIANA: My first reaction is: what do you mean by three days?
CHARLES: You know full well what I mean.
DIANA: Would you like to explain?
CHARLES: Circles, circles, round and round we go. I haven't seen anyone for days. God knows when I last picked up a newspaper or watched the TV. You make it sound as if all this is my fault. How can I explain something I don't even know?

DIANA: Well, there we are. Would you like to explain further?

CHARLES: Not now. Not here. Why?

DIANA: I want to know. I think it needs to be resolved.

CHARLES: But I keep saying – why here? Are you looking for a confrontation? Honestly, I don't want or need one. I just don't want or need one.

DIANA: Have you considered the implications of a custody battle?

CHARLES: For what?

DIANA: The children.

CHARLES: Oh, don't be so silly. No, no, I haven't.

DIANA: Well, that's what would happen. The children would suffer. You know that?

CHARLES: No, no, I don't. This is so silly, talking like crazy people, talking about custody. It won't come to that.

DIANA: No?

CHARLES: No.

DIANA: Well, as long as you are sure.

CHARLES: Please, let's not argue. Not now.

DIANA: But that's what we are getting to because we are re-solving nothing. Nothing is being decided. None of us will make a firm decision. A firm decision.

CHARLES: Is there really one needed now? We've spent all night going over the same thing without getting anywhere and now you're making demands for a decision? Please be sensible.

DIANA: No, no, no, no, no. Let's decide it now and then we can start afresh tomorrow morning. If nothing is decided now we'll be in the same position tomorrow, next week, next month, as we are tonight. If there's just one godforsaken thing we can do, let's decide tonight.

CHARLES: I am trying to see things your way. I just can't. It's too late.

DIANA: Well, for once could you put yourself out and think of me?

CHARLES: Don't you dare sit there and tell me to think of you. How the hell do you have the nerve to say that? I've done nothing but think of you and the children ever since this thing started. You . . .

DIANA: No, no. I don't believe that at all. For once stop being so self-centred. You still think of me as the person you married.

CHARLES: I stopped thinking like that years ago.

DIANA: Yes, I suppose that would be a good indication of why we drifted apart, my dear.

CHARLES: Can I say anything right? Tell me what it is you want me to say.

DIANA: Say something I want to hear.

CHARLES: I'm leaving.

DIANA: Oh, don't be so bloody childish.
CHARLES: Oh God.
DIANA: Must you always run when the pressure gets too much?
CHARLES: I'm not running. Unlike you, I want to deal with this like adults.
DIANA: I think I am. It's just that I want to get it done now rather than later. I don't want it to run on like a silly soap opera.
CHARLES: I'm going to bed.
DIANA: But why? You can sleep tomorrow. You can sleep anytime. But think of me for once, yes, think of me for once.
CHARLES: I'd rather think of the other parties involved. I don't know why, but right now I feel they are more important. You'll take care of yourself, you know that.
DIANA: How dare you be so presumptuous?
CHARLES: I'm tired. Good night.
DIANA: Look, you're doing it again. Come back. For Christ's sake, come back! How can you leave it like this?
CHARLES: I'll speak to you tomorrow.
DIANA: Oh no, you won't.
CHARLES: Good night.
DIANA: Can you come in here, please?

INDEX